The Collector's Encyclopedia of
MetalToys

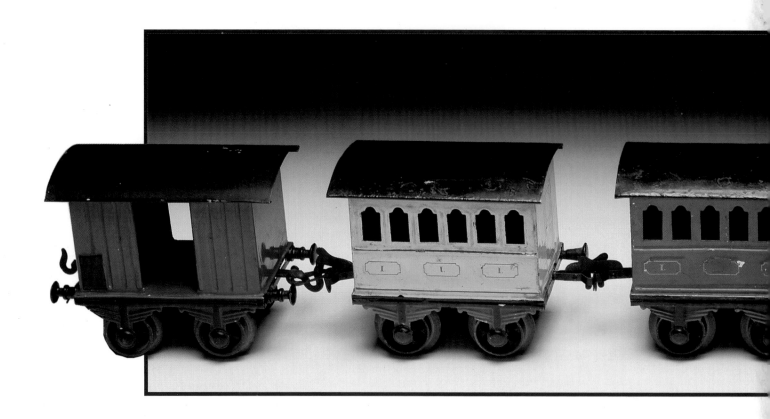

The Collector's Encyclopedia of MetalToys

A pictorial guide to over 2500 examples of tinplate and diecast toys dating from 1850 to the present day

Compiled by Richard O'Neill

CRESCENT BOOKS
New York

A Salamander Book

This 1988 edition published by
Crescent Books,
distributed by
Crown Publishers, Inc.,
225 Park Avenue South,
New York, New York 10003

Printed in Hong Kong

ISBN 0-517-66531-X

h g f e d c b a

Credits

Designers:
Barry Savage, Paul Johnson

Photography:
Terry Dilliway
© Salamander Books Ltd.

Filmset:
Instep Print & Design Ltd,
Modern Text Typesetting Ltd.

Colour Reproduction:
Melbourne Graphics Ltd,
Bantam Litho Ltd.

Gordon Gardiner is a consultant on toys, automobilia and militaria to a leading international auction house. He is the co-author of several authoritative works on these subjects.

Ron McCrindell is one of the best-known British toy collectors. His magnificent collection of railway toys, ships, clockwork automobiles, mechanical novelties, and aeronautical toys is internationally famous.

Alistair Morris holds a senior position with a famous international auction house. He is an acknowledged expert in the "fringe" categories generally called "Collectors' Items", on which he has written extensively.

Richard O'Neill is a freelance author and editor. He is the co-author of two books on toy collecting and has also written extensively on military subjects.

Andrew Rose is internationally known as both a collector and designer of toy soldiers. As author or contributor, he is responsible for a number of expert works in this field.

Acknowledgments

We wish to thank the individuals and organizations listed below, without whose most generous help this record of metal toys of the 19th and 20th centuries could not have been assembled;

R. V. Archard; Geoffrey Baker; Giles Brown, Dorset Soldiers; Jeanne Burley; Glen Butler; Pierce Carlson; David Chester; John Churchward; Jock Coutts; R. J. Dew/R. P. Dew; Dendy B. Easton/Dendy P. Easton; Peter Flataus; Louise Gardiner/ Gavin Gardiner; J. G. Garratt; David Griffiths/Roydon Griffiths; Michael Heydon; Hadley Hobbies; Allen Levy; The London Toy and Model Museum; Richard Lonsdale; Joe Lyndhurst; Warnham War Museum; Chris Littledale; The British Engineerium Museum; Shaun Magee Pedal Car Collection; Ken McCrae; Peter Moore; Vera Oliver/Tony Oliver; Danny O'Neill; Peter Pawson; David Pressland; J. T. Van Reimsdijk; Major E. Roche-Kelly; Andrew Rose; H. Taylor; Coralie Wearing; Alan Wickham; Clive Willoughby

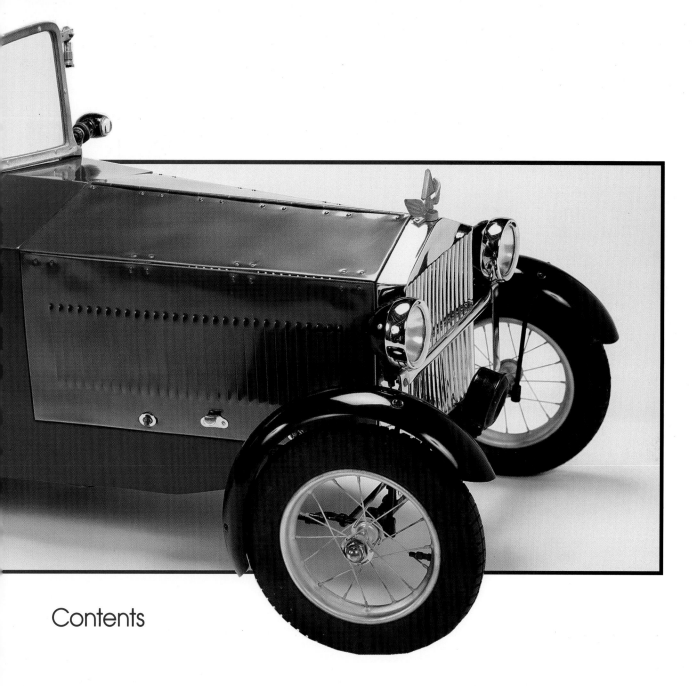

Contents

Introduction

Although this book is intended to give pleasure to all those who cherish memories of their childhoods, it is addressed primarily to those who are collectors – and most especially to those who would like to be collectors – of toys.

Collectors pursue their activities for many reasons: some, perhaps, simply to fulfil the deep-seated urge in man to gather and classify objects; some for purely aesthetic reasons, to gratify a desire to own objects that are perceived as interesting and beautiful; some, and especially so, perhaps, in the case of toy collectors, out of nostalgia, from a desire to re-create times past; and some, seeing "collectables" as a form of investment, for possible financial gain. This book has much to offer to collectors in all these categories – but it has not been planned to appeal to any one category alone.

SCOPE OF THE BOOK
In compiling this book, we have kept in mind always the needs of the average collector, who must perhaps operate on a limited budget, and of the novice or would-be collector. Thus, as well as showing a selection of fine and rare toys, we have attempted to show a wide range of the kind of material that may come the way of the ordinary collector. The period covered is roughly that of the last 130 years: an age of increasing production, and then of mass-production, leading to a number and variety of toys – and their consequent availability to the modern collector – that did not previously exist. In the period covered, markets expanded greatly – and the inventiveness and enterprise of toymakers expanded to match them.

Only *metal* toys are included; but these, of course, in any case constitute by far the largest category of toy and, for obvious reasons, the one that embraces the greatest number of surviving examples. Although some very rare and valuable toys are shown, simply because it was felt that such magnificent specimens of the toymaker's art could not be omitted, we have generally selected items for inclusion on the basis of their probable availability to the "average" collector in Europe and the United States.

We have excluded items in very poor condition and we have tried to show all the toys as nearly as possible in their original state: where restoration has been carried out, or where parts are missing, this is generally noted. It must be remembered, however, that since most toys will have once fulfilled their natural function – to be played with by children – their condition will often be what dealers politely describe as "play-worn". Further, enamelled or lithographed finishes on tinplate toys fade in time unless the item is most carefully preserved, while rust will invade tinplate toys kept in damp conditions: it is for these reasons that "classic" tinplate toys are now in short supply and, if in good condition, most valuable.

PRICE GUIDES
Although this book contains a great deal of historical information, it is not a history of toys. And although we have already had occasion to refer to the values of certain toys, neither is it a price guide. For this there are three major reasons. First, it is intended for an international readership, and prices will vary from country to country. Second, price

guides "date" fairly quickly, and it is hoped that this work may provide a useful reference for collectors for years to come. Thirdly, this book is intended as an introduction to the pleasure that can be derived from collecting toys, not as a guide to collecting for investment.

The collector, should, in any case, bear in mind that the information given in price guides must always be interpreted in terms of current market conditions. Remember that the prices quoted generally refer to toys in, at least, "very good" condition, and that they are usually based on auction records. Auction prices may vary widely in accordance with the venue, the presence or absence of major dealers and collectors, the "mood" of the bidding, and similar imponderables.

THE RARITY SCALE
We have attempted to give, wherever it is meaningful or possible to do so, an indication of the comparative rarity of the toys shown. Every item on every spread is individually captioned – and embodied in the caption, usually towards its end, the reader will find a classification of the toy's rarity in comparison with other toys of its kind. Note that a diecast car, for example, may be classified as "rare" in comparison with other diecast cars: it will not, of course, be of the same degree of rarity as a tinplate car by Carette or a tinplate battleship by Märklin.

The classification system we have used is as follows:

Rare: A toy seldom encountered, even by collectors who regularly patronise international auction houses and specialist dealers. This category includes toys made in

limited numbers (because of their original high selling price; because of limited sales; or because production was for some reason curtailed) and fragile toys with a low survival rate, such as early toy aircraft.

Scarce: A toy infrequently encountered, but likely to be found at major auctions, through specialist dealers, and sometimes at "swap meets". The fact that a toy is "scarce" does not necessarily imply a high value: it indicates that the toy is eagerly sought after by collectors and that demand exceeds supply.

Limited: A toy that, while still infrequently encountered, is more likely to be found by the average collector than one classified as "scarce". The fact that a toy is "limited" does not necessarily imply that it is of lower value than a "scarce" item.

Common: A toy that most dealers will have in stock or that will be readily available. Again, the fact that a toy is classified as "common" (sometimes with the modifiers "fairly" or "very") does not necessarily mean that it is of low value. Condition is of the greatest importance when considering toys in this category: there is little point in buying a "common" item in poor condition, since a further search may well be rewarded by the acquisition of a superior example.

Unclassified: A toy to which we have assigned no classification may generally be understood to rank on our scale somewhere between "limited" and "common". In the case of diecast vehicles, for example, supply roughly equals demand among collectors, and we have singled out as "limited" only those which we know to be in shorter supply. Some other items are unclassified because they fall into areas where collectors' interest

is, as yet, somewhat limited, and where there exist insufficient criteria to allow for a classification.

BEGINNING A COLLECTION

The novice collector must first decide which aspect of the world of toys most interests him (or her; the use of the male pronoun alone, for the sake of brevity, must not obscure the fact that there are very many female collectors). In taking this decision, he must also consider what kinds of toys he can *afford* to collect. He must consider the likely availability of the items that attract him, and what opportunities he will have to seek out and acquire specimens. And he must consider what space he has available for the display and storage of a growing collection.

The *theme* of the collection should always be borne in mind. It is all too easy to rush out in the first flush of enthusiasm and spend too much money on attractive but unrelated items. Again, the over-enthusiastic novice may buy items in such poor condition that they will never permit the attractive visual display that provides a great part of the satisfaction to be gained from a well-ordered collection. Or the collector may find that he has committed himself to a speciality in which, because of rarity or expense, new acquisitions are likely to be so rare that the pleasure of "capturing" a specimen is too infrequent to sustain his initial enthusiasm.

Advice on beginning a specialized collection in any one of the categories covered in this book — mechanical novelties, cars and transport toys, trains, ships, aeroplanes and toy soldiers — is given below, under individual headings. At this point, we will confine

ourselves to general advice to the novice collector, whatever his eventual speciality is to be.

SEEING AND BUYING

The novice collector should take every opportunity of increasing his understanding of the subject by examining toys of all kinds. As a result of the growth of general interest in the artifacts of the more recent past, most major museums in Europe and the USA now have on display toys of the past century, while in some cities there are excellent museums devoted to playthings alone. Visit such museums whenever possible, remembering that the items on display will sometimes be changed (since few museums have the space to display their entire collections at any one time) and that special loan exhibitions may be mounted from time to time.

Few specialist toy dealers will object to the novice — who may, after all, be tomorrow's big spender — browsing among their stock. Antique and junk shops, flea markets and garage sales are all worthwhile hunting grounds, but the toy collector may do best at "auto-jumbles", organized by motoring enthusiasts, where automotive toys (and "wheeled" toys of all kinds) are often to be found. Note, however, that at auto-jumbles, car-boot sales and other venues where amateur dealers predominate, there is a chance that, although bargains *may* be found, the prices asked may be higher than those of a professional dealer. Inexperienced vendors and buyers alike are sometimes inclined to believe that all "old" toys are not only collectable but also valuable.

Above: *In the mid-to-late 1930s, Bassett-Lowke of Great Britain produced Gauge "O" models in electric (as shown here) and clockwork of streamlined 4-6-2 locomotives of the London, Midland & Scottish Railway (LMS) and London and North Eastern Railway (LNER). These models with eight-wheeled corridor tenders are now very rare—only about 200 of the LNER versions were made—and the LNER locomotive seen here in the process of restoration by its present owner (Chris Littledale of the British Engineerium Museum, Hove, Sussex, a notable professional restorer of tinplate toys) is the rarest model of them all. The name-plates apparent at the front end are non-original and will be removed, and the locomotive will be restored to its original "Silver Link" shades of grey: the LNER versions also appeared in garter-blue livery as "Empire of India" and "Dominion of Canada". Since these models were almost entirely hand-made, with limited press-work, the price was very high for those days, at around £13 13s 0d (£13.65, $20.50).*

Above right: *The dire effects of "metal fatigue" on diecast models are clearly visible in the cracks seen in this view of the underside of Dinky Toys No 67a, the Junkers Ju 89 aircraft, produced in 1940-41. This problem may develop, especially in diecast models of the pre-World War II period, if toys are not kept at a fairly even temperature: widely varying temperatures may cause unstable alloys to "fight", leading first to slight expansion of the metal, then to cracks and blisters (as seen here), and finally to complete disintegration of the model.*

More expert judgement is likely to be met with at the "swap-meets" organized by collectors themselves for the sale or exchange of toys: whether or not he intends to buy, the novice can learn a great deal simply by attending. Membership of a collectors' society or a subscription to one of the journals catering to collectors in all fields will usually ensure knowledge of the venues of swap-meets.

AUCTIONS

As his experience grows, the collector will probably begin to think of buying or selling at auction. Toys are often included in the mixed lots offered at local auctions (often as part of house clearance sales) and the major international auction houses of Sotheby's, Christie's and Phillips now regularly mount special toy sales. The collector should not assume that these famous names always indicate high prices and should remember that auction houses are always ready to give advice on their buying and selling procedures. The collector who intends to buy at auction should be sure to attend the "view", the period before the sale when the forthcoming lots are available for examination. Even if he does not intend to buy, this may give him the chance to see and handle rare items.

Most major auction houses will accept for sale single toys or collections with a minimum value of around £50.00 ($75.00). A reserve price, below which the lot shall not be sold, is agreed between the vendor and the auctioneer: this price must be realistic, for if the item does not reach its reserve, a "not sold commission" may be payable by the vendor. A successful sale will entail payment to the auction house by the vendor of a commission of around 10-15 per cent. Many

auction houses now also levy a "buyer's premium" of some 10 per cent, to which, in the United Kingdom, Value Added Tax (VAT) must be added. Generally speaking, items are bought at auction "as seen" — but also "as catalogued"; thus, if an item purchased proves not to be as described in the catalogue, a refund may be obtained.

CONDITION OF TOYS

As a guide to potential buyers, the toys offered for sale by auction houses and reputable dealers are usually described, in terms of their condition, along the following lines:

Mint: As new, with the toy in its original packaging (if it was a packaged item) and with the packaging itself in good condition. If the original box or packaging is not in fine condition, the description "Factory Fresh" sometimes replaces "Mint".

Very Good: The toy shows slight wear, possibly with some damage to or fading of its finish, but with all its parts complete and undamaged. The toy may or may not be in the original box or packaging.

Good: A sound example of the toy, but with noticeable wear from handling and use and without box or packaging.

Play-Worn: A toy which has seen considerable use: it may have damaged or missing parts and may even have been repainted. Unless it is a rare or much-desired item, the collector should carefully consider the asking price of a toy in this condition, and should ask himself whether it will be possible for him to re-sell it, without loss, in the event of a better example being acquired at a later date.

RESTORATION

There will inevitably be occasions when a much-desired specimen is available only in

play-worn condition — and if the collector does decide to buy a rare toy in such a state, he may consider the possibility of restoring it as nearly as possible to its original condition. Indeed, there are collectors whose main interest lies in restoration and who will purchase play-worn toys simply for this purpose.

However, the average collector, unless he has great and well-founded confidence in his own skill, is best advised to entrust the work of restoration to a professional. The process will not be cheap but, properly carried out, it will enhance both the appearance and the value of the toy. Amateur restoration will usually add little to the appearance and will detract from the value. As a rough guide, it may be said that in the case of rare toys, restoration — depending always on the extent and the quality of the work — may reduce the value of a toy (in comparison with one in the same, but original, condition) by some 10-20 per cent. In the case of more common toys, restoration may reduce the value by 50 per cent or more.

If the collector envisages selling the toy at some time in the future, it may be better left unrestored, since many collectors will always prefer the unrestored item, however play-worn. The collector who is offered a toy that has already been restored must base his judgement on the fidelity of the restoration to the original.

VALUE JUDGEMENTS

What is a toy worth? The answer is the product of an equation involving four major factors — rarity, condition, desirability, availability — and every collector must work out the equation in terms of his own speciality.

It is partly true to say that a toy's value is no more and no less than the price the collector is prepared to pay for it. However, many "classic" toys by well known makers have a fairly well-established market value, and the novice collector should study the prices reached at auction and those asked by major dealers before buying "quality" items. But it is worth noting that certain kinds of toys may at certain times be "unfashionable", so that bargains may be obtained. The only way to establish these speculative areas is by watching the market.

Although "investment" is a word avoided by most true collectors, it would be foolish to deny that most of us derive pleasure from the thought that we have acquired an item that will maintain or increase its value and that may be turned into cash — perhaps to allow for the purchase of an even more desirable item — should the need arise. Generally speaking, most popular collectables have increased in value during recent years, some spectacularly, and even during recent periods of recession, when such items as postage stamps and coins suffered losses in value, toy prices held up very well.

Let us now turn to the consideration of the different categories of metal toys shown in this book.

MECHANICAL NOVELTY TOYS

A "novelty" toy is one that exerts its appeal not so much by its attractive appearance or by its fidelity to the "real" object that it represents, as by the ingenuity of its mechanism. The category is an extensive and rather loose one: novelties, as our illustrations show, range from the gravity-operated cast-iron money banks of 19th-century American makers to mechanical toys currently in production in the Far East.

The category is an especially interesting one for the historically-minded collector, for many novelties have undergone little change in basic design since the turn of the century, the German and French classics having been faithfully copied by later makers in other countries. Such simple novelties as clockwork mice and spinning tops may be found in examples made by makers of many nationalities at any time during the past eighty or more years.

Novelties, however, are not the easiest toys to collect, especially if the collector aims at an interesting balance between older and more modern examples. Early examples in good condition are likely to attract even higher prices than those of toys of equivalent quality in other categories.

As with other toys, the presence of the original packaging will enhance the value — but in the case of novelties, the packaging is not nearly so important as completeness and working order. Because they are comparatively fragile, but at the same time have a high "play value", novelties are often found in damaged condition and with parts missing. These parts may be very difficult to replace, sometimes calling for special manufacture — although clockwork motors may be simple enough for repair by the competent amateur. The toy may have to be disassembled for repair, and in the case of soldered tinplate toys, joints may have to be melted and the finish will inevitably suffer.

If a novelty is acquired in good, working condition, no renovation of the finish should be undertaken other than a light wash with mild soap, followed by thorough drying with a soft cloth. Mechanisms and moving parts may be very lightly lubricated if necessary. Like most other toys, novelties are best

Left: *Figures by Lucotte and Mignot, those by Lucotte being on the left of each pair. Of the two British Waterloo-period infantrymen, note the better modelling of the Lucotte figure. The arms are cast separately and located on lugs before soldering, while the Mignot arms are bent into position and the weapon soldered on. The Lucotte French 5th Hussar has movable reins and a detachable saddle with stirrups; the saddle of the Mignot Austrian Hussar figure is soldered on.*

Below left: *Snow White and the Seven Dwarfs, produced by Britains to commemorate the release of the Walt Disney film in the late 1930s. The figures are (from left to right): Doc, Sneezy, Grumpy, Happy, Snow White, Bashful, Sleepy and Dopey.*

Above right: *Toy soldier makers were quick to produce figures based on contemporary events. Like Britains, Johillco issued a number of interesting figures at the time of the Italian invasion of Abyssinia in 1935. In the foreground is the scarce Abyssinian mountain battery; behind it, an Abyssinian stretcher party is escorted by a squad of barefoot infantry. At the rear are tribesmen in assorted coloured robes, along with rather undersized figures of Italian infantrymen in tropical helmets.*

Below right: *Gauge "2" 4-4-0 "County of Devon" electric Locomotive and Six-Wheeled Tender, in Great Western Railway (GWR) livery. This model was marketed in the UK by Bassett-Lowke in 1912, but unlike many Bassett-Lowke items shown in this book it is neither German-made nor of tinplate, being made by one of several British firms that supplied models to Bassett-Lowke. It is fitted with Bassett-Lowke's early electric motor, the "Universal Lowko" with "Patent Automatic Reversing Switch", working on 8-12 volts. It is constructed of mild steel plate and sheet brass, with turned cast-iron wheels. Now fairly rare, it is a most pleasing model, with detail that includes a coal top on the tender. However, models like this are not as eagerly sought by collectors as their German-made counterparts.*

displayed in glazed cabinets, at an even temperature and out of direct sunlight.

CARS AND TRANSPORT TOYS

Toymakers were quick to take advantage of the fascination that motor vehicles exerted over so many of their potential customers, and by the beginning of the 20th century, metal toys representing cars and commercial vehicles of all kinds were appearing in sizes ranging from diminutive tinplate "penny toys", so called because this was their original selling price, to large tinplate toy cars and even child-carrying pedal cars. Diecast vehicles appeared at about the same time, but these did not become of much importance until the 1920s-1930s.

The collector who decides to specialize in automotive toys has, perhaps, the widest field of all in toy collecting open to him. Simply because the area of choice is so great, it is important that he should decide upon the theme of his collection before embarking on the purchase of specimens.

TINPLATE OR DIECAST?

There can be little doubt that the most attractive of all automotive toys are the fine tinplate cars and commercial vehicles produced in the first three decades of the 20th century by such makers as Bing, Carette, Günthermann and Märklin of Germany; CIJ, Citroën and Jep of France; and Kingsbury of the USA. However, unless his resources are near-limitless, the collector will not decide to specialize in classic tinplate vehicles for, depending upon condition, an early tinplate car by a well known maker may now be expected to fetch anything between £1,000 ($1,500) and £10,000 ($15,000) at auction. Even the prices asked for the tinplate vehicles made in the 1950s-1970s by Japanese makers are now putting these out of reach of many collectors, with good examples fetching three-figure sums. And a collector who lacks both deep pockets and several large rooms for storage should not choose to specialize in pedal cars, which will almost always be found only in condition that demands extensive

and comparatively expensive restoration.

Thus, although for the delight of all collectors we have included many fine examples of classic and modern tinplate vehicles, along with pedal cars, in our illustrations, our advice is that the new collector should, initially at any rate, decide upon the acquisition of diecast vehicles.

The advantages of collecting diecast vehicles are many. With the exception of some pre-World War II models by makers such as Manoil of the USA, they are fairly easily available; they are generally to be found in better condition than the more vulnerable tinplate toys; they are generally smaller than tinplate vehicles and are therefore much easier to store and display. And, of course, they are generally much cheaper to acquire than tinplate vehicles. Among the most sought-after diecast vehicles are those made by Dinky Toys of Great Britain between 1934 and 1940, and these currently fetch prices of between £25 ($40) and £300 ($450), with the majority tending

towards the bottom of this range. Post-1945 Dinky Toys range from around £20-£30 ($30-$45) for models of the late 1940s to as little as £3 ($5) and upwards for models of the 1960s-1970s. Many attractive and collectable diecast vehicles are currently in production.

THEMATIC COLLECTION: DIECAST VEHICLES

Just about every type of vehicle that has been produced in real life over the past eighty or so years has been represented by a diecast model from at least one maker. Thus, there is a wide choice of possible themes for the diecast vehicle collector. In arranging the diecast vehicles shown in this book, we have attempted a broadly thematic representation by showing saloon cars, sports cars, racing cars, lorries, buses, police cars and so on, on separate pages: this arrangement in itself may give the new collector some useful thematic hints.

He may decide to specialise in one kind of car or commercial vehicle – in open sports

cars, say, petrol tanker lorries or vans carrying advertising slogans. So far as cars are concerned, even to select a particular type may be too wide a field, and it may be better to narrow the choice to a single marque or to the products of a single maker. Even then, the collector must remember that for very popular marques, like Ford, Mercedes or Citroën, hundreds of different models have been produced. And as for single makers – more than 1,000 Dinky Toys (not counting colour and casting variations) have been issued, and such makers as Corgi, Lesney, Solido, Märklin and Mattel have been hardly less prolific.

Narrow the field down further. To take a single example: suppose the decision is to collect models of British saloon cars. Choose a specific maker, say Ford of Britain, and a specific period, say the 1960s. Now consult the increasing number of reference books which give check lists of the models produced by various makers to see if the choice is viable. In this case, the collector would have

a good choice of models made by Dinky, Corgi, Lesney (Matchbox), Tri-ang (Spot On) and Lone Star (Impy) of the UK, Solido of France, Politoys (Polistil) of Italy, and Gamda of Israel.

DISPLAYING TOY VEHICLES

How a collection is displayed will depend very much on its size and the amount of space available. Ideally, both tinplate and diecast vehicles should be displayed in glazed cabinets: on open shelves they will gather dust and become grubby in a surprisingly short time, and it is important that cleaning should be kept to a minimum to avoid undue wear.

Diecast vehicles can be dusted or cleaned with a soft brush to remove dirt from their crevices. If tinplate vehicles are particularly discoloured by dirt, the tinplate may be cleaned with mild soap and warm water and a final polish given with good-quality car wax and a soft, dry cloth. Clockwork mechanisms should be kept very slightly oiled. Vehicles

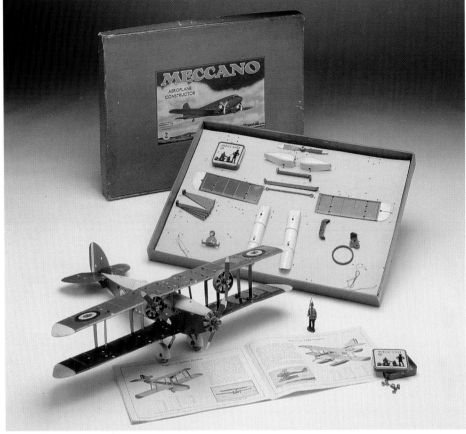

Above left: *Gauge "O" M Series "Silver Jubilee" Train Set by Hornby, Great Britain, dating from the late 1930s. The non-reversing clockwork locomotive came complete with tender, articulated coach set and track. In good condition and with the original box, sets are quite hard to find.*

Left: *Meccano's mid-1930s Aeroplane Constructor Set No 2 could be used to build a tri-motor biplane and other types.*

Above: *Medical and nursing figures by various makers form an attractive theme for a small collection of toy soldiers.*

Right: *This impressive battleship by Gebrüder Märklin dates from c1895 and is an extremely rare and valuable toy.*

Far right: *Tinplate Railway Station by Gebrüder Märklin, dating from c1900. Hand-enamelled, it is extremely rare.*

should not be exposed to direct sunlight, which will fade paint finishes. Diecast models especially should be kept at an even temperature, for extremes of temperature may "wake up" unstable alloys, especially in pre-World War II examples, and lead to metal fatigue.

TOY TRAINS

Toy trains of the unpowered push- or pull-along type, generally known to collectors as "floor trains" because they were not meant to run on tracks, appeared in the first half of the 19th century and were soon followed by simple live-steam models, called "piddlers" or "dribblers" from their habit of depositing a trail of moisture in their wake. Spring-driven and flywheel-driven locomotives followed in the 1860s-1870s, and by the 1880s toymakers were marketing both steam- and clockwork-powered locomotives that could be purchased

complete with simple rail layouts: the birth of the "train set" as we know it. Electric-powered toy trains were in production as early as the 1900s, but they did not achieve widespread popularity until the 1930s, when mains electricity became increasingly available in most areas.

The names of some of the leading makers of the early period, c1890-1910, will already be familiar to the reader, for Märklin, Bing and Carette of Germany were among the first in the field. Elsewhere, Ives and Lionel of the USA and Bassett-Lowke of Great Britain were prominent names. Bassett-Lowke, in fact, was mainly responsible for causing makers to specialize in locomotives built to standard gauges. These are (with the size of the gauge expressed as the distance between the inner edges of the track):
Gauge "4": 2.8125in (71.44mm) (commonly known as "3-inch Gauge")

Gauge "3": 2.5in (63.5mm)
Gauge "2": 2in (50.8mm)
Gauge "1": 1.75in (44.45mm)
Gauge "O": 1.25in (31.75mm)
Gauge "OO" or "HO": 0.625in (15.875mm)

THEMES IN TOY TRAINS

The collector of toy trains may decide to specialize in items of a single gauge; of a single type; of a single period; of a single maker; or in unpowered, steam, clockwork or electric propulsion. As in other areas, however, his choice will largely be dictated by his financial resources, for the products of the famous makers of the earlier periods now attract four- or even five-figure sums at auction. The choice will be limited, too, by the display space available — and, an important consideration, by whether the collector intends to "run" his trains.

The new collector might do well to

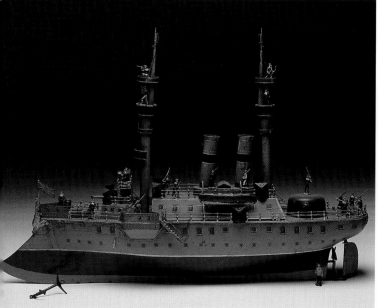

concentrate at first on Gauge "O" and "OO" material of the post-1945 period. Perhaps the most famous name in this field is that of Hornby of Great Britain, and, although prices have risen as Hornby material has become increasingly "fashionable", many most attractive Hornby items, in their original boxes, can still be acquired at swap-meets or from dealers at prices between £5-£10 ($8-$15). Hornby Gauge "O" pieces dating from before World War II will cost considerably more. Collectors who wish to run their trains as well as display them might do well to seek out electrically-driven items from the Hornby Dublo range. "Future collectables" may include the current Gauge "O" and "OO" products of the Italian maker Lima, the Gauge "OO" models of Rivarossi of Italy, and the Gauge "1", "OO" and "Z" (mini-gauge) trains now produced under the famous name of Märklin.

BUYING AND MAINTAINING TRAINS

Examine any item offered for sale for structural damage, missing parts, *originality* of parts and paintwork (for restored items are common), and for the cracks and blisters that herald metal fatigue (paying particular attention to the wheels of Hornby items). Make sure that a locomotive's tender is present — if it had one — and that it is the correct tender. If you intend to attempt restoration, check which parts are still available and which must be specially manufactured. If you intend to run the train, check that the mechanism is in order, or can be repaired, and that suitable track is available.

Ideally, toy trains should be displayed in running order on a permanent track layout. Failing this, models are best housed in shallow, glazed cabinets with strong shelves (toy locomotives can be heavy), and shown

on track lengths of the correct gauge. Conditions should be dry and at an even temperature; mechanisms and wheels should be kept lightly oiled. Tinplate items may be cleaned, if absolutely necessary, in the same way as tinplate vehicles (see page 11).

TOY SHIPS AND BOATS

Produced in types ranging from rowing boats to liners and battleships and in sizes ranging from a few inches to more than three feet (1m), tinplate ships and boats, as the reader may judge from our illustrations, are among the most beautiful and desirable of all toys. Sadly, they are also among the most scarce and costly of all toys: first, because of their fragility (especially of such fittings as masts, rigging, lifeboats etc); second, because of the likelihood of accidental loss of the "waterborne" examples; third, in the case of the finest specimens, because they were luxury toys that were produced only in limited numbers.

Among the most celebrated of the earlier makers were Radiguet of France and Schoenner of Germany, whose products are now very rare, and, in the earlier 20th century, Bing, Carette, Fleischmann, Hess, Lehmann, Märklin and Plank of Germany. The Arnold Company of West Germany deserves special mention: along with Fleischmann, it was about the last firm to maintain the German tradition of tinplate boats after World War II.

The collector who is lucky enough to locate affordable tinplate boats will find that such details as ships' boats, anchors, flags and rigging will often be missing or will prove to be replacements. Many boats will have been repaired or completely restored — but in this case, expert restoration will not significantly affect the boat's value. Ideally, boats should be displayed on purpose-made stands, in glazed cabinets, at an even temperature, away from damp and out of direct sunlight.

TOY AEROPLANES

Aeronautical toys based on balloons and dirigibles were made as early as the 1890s, and by around 1910 such famous German makers as Bing, Günthermann, Märklin and Plank were featuring toy aeroplanes in their catalogues. All these early aeronautical models are now scarce and valuable, and the average collector is more likely to encounter tinplate aeroplanes dating from after World War I, from such makers as Distler, Fleischmann, Günthermann and Tipp of Germany, Jep and Joustra of France, and Cardini of Italy.

After World War II, "space toys" began to flourish at the expense of conventional aircraft, although both German and, especially, Japanese makers continued to produce tinplate aeroplanes of fairly high quality. These are likely to become increasingly collectable. So, too, are diecast aircraft, which were until fairly recently "unfashionable" among toy collectors. Here, the attention of most collectors is likely to focus on the extensive range produced by Dinky Toys of Great Britain and France from the 1930s onwards.

In some diecast aeroplanes of the 1930s, tinplate was used for wings, but metal fatigue in the form of "wing droop" is all too common in diecast models. In the case of post-World War II issues, possession of the original box is particularly important for value — and in any case, diecast aeroplanes are best stored in their boxes, at an even temperature.

TOY SOLDIERS

Miniature figures of fighting men have been produced for more than 4,000 years, but the "toy soldier" as we know it today originated in the flat tin figures produced by German toymakers from the 1730s onwards. Semi-flat figures also originated in Germany, but the French maker Lucotte was the first identifiable maker of full-round solid lead figures, towards the end of the 18th century. The earlier German and French makers are well represented in our illustrations, but the name that the average collector is most likely to encounter is that of the British maker Britains, famous for the production of hollow-cast lead soldiers from the 1890s until the demise of the hollow-cast figure, in the face of

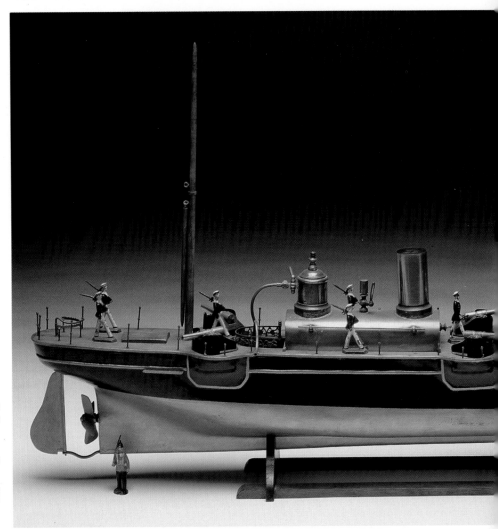

Above left: *Novelty Veteran Car by an unidentified Japanese maker, dating from the late 1960s — early 1970s. The car is tinplate, with plastic seats and other details, the plastic driver appears to operate the steering tiller as the battery-powered vehicle moves. Novelty toys of the "classic" tinplate period are becoming rare and expensive, but their Far Eastern-made equivalents are increasingly collectable.*

Above: *The small shunting set in the foreground is a Gauge "O" item by a Czechoslovakian maker, c1968. The "Mountain Express" and "Red Arrow" are friction-driven floor trains by Japanese makers, dating from c1962 and c1958-59.*

Left: *Steam-powered Gunboat by Radiguet of Paris, with a zinc hull, brass boiler, and the wooden deck and masts characteristic of its maker. Possibly dating from as early as 1880, and seen here on its original stand, but lacking rigging, this very rare boat has undergone some restoration.*

Below: *Some unusual French printed tin figures of unknown make: a flat tinplate French line infantry officer and drummer of the 1890s (right) and four conjoint tin figures, each formed of two curved sheets tabbed together: advancing Belgian and Turkish infantrymen, a kneeling Frenchman, and, in a smaller scale, a German cavalryman, all of 1914.*

Below: *From the Unity Toy series by O.H. & Co., c1920: a powerful gun responsible for many broken ranks, and a cheap range of target figures made for them by WTC.*

Right: *Two examples of boxed sets by Crescent, from the 1950s. That in the foreground contains small Scots Greys figures as shown. The large open box of "Medieval Knights" contains an assortment of figures covering a wide historical period. Note the modern Household Cavalry state trumpeter masquerading as a herald!*

Bottom left: *Possibly the nucleus of a "thematic" collection of diecast cars: three models of Volvo cars by Tekno, Denmark. The Amazon 122 S (left), maker's reference number (MRN) 810, was issued in 1957; the Amazon Estate Car (centre), MRN 830, was issued in 1961; the PV 544 (right), MRN 822, appeared in 1959. The two later models have jewelled headlights and detailed interiors. Lengths: (left) 3.937in (100mm); (centre) 4.016in (102mm); (right) 3.898in (99mm).*

Bottom right: *Two packets of "Assorted Cars" by Taiyo, Japan. Dating from the 1960s, when they were exported in great numbers (note the maker's consignment label on the three-pack) these brightly-printed cars in lightweight tinplate are the modern equivalent of "penny toys". Whether they will, in time, become as collectable and as highly valued as their diminutive forerunners remains to be seen.*

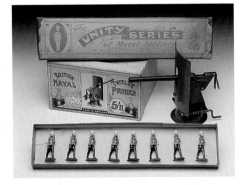

increasing production costs, safety regulations and the "plastic revolution", after World War II. Britains figures, mostly made to a scale of 1:32 — an infantryman thus being 2.12in (54mm) high from base to top of head (without head-dress) — therefore dominate our illustrations, although the firm's competitors are also well-represented.

In forming a collection of toy soldiers, the theme is again important. It may be the work of a particular maker, or soldiers in a particular material or from a specific country. Whatever the theme, remember that in the collection of toy soldiers in sets, as they were often issued, possession of the original box is of great importance: some collectors will not consider unboxed figures, and the presence of the original packaging can increase the value of a set by 50 per cent or more over the unboxed state.

IDENTIFICATION AND PRESERVATION

Where a soldier is marked with the maker's name, as are all Britains figures from the 1900s onwards, there is little problem of identification. An unmarked piece can often be identified by comparing the style with that of a soldier of known make, and to familiarize oneself with different makes is a matter of seeing and handling as many figures as possible. Makers' catalogues (originals are scarce, but some are now available in reprint from specialist dealers) are also a most useful aid to identification.

Although the collector will wish to acquire figures in near-perfect condition, it is inevitable that this will not always be possible, and the price of a scratched or damaged figure should always be less than that for a pristine example. The rarest figures are perhaps best left unrestored, but in other cases it is now possible to buy replacement parts — arms, heads, horses' legs, and so on — for figures by Britains and some other makers. With these, and with careful repainting if necessary, a satisfactory restoration may be effected — although if the items are later sold, it is only fair to indicate to the purchaser the amount of work that has been carried out.

The main problem with the preservation of lead toy figures is "lead disease" or "lead rot" — the formation of lead sulphide caused by the reaction of lead with sulphur in the atmosphere. In the early stages this shows as a grey powdery surface to exposed metal parts such as bases; in more advanced cases, the figure will feel rough and brittle and will ultimately disintegrate. The best cure is to avoid damp storage conditions. Do not use totally sealed display cabinets, and use absorbent materials such as tissue paper and cardboard when packing away.

PLAYING WITH TOYS

In concluding our necessarily brief introduction to the fascinating world of toy collecting, we believe we can give no better advice to the collector, expert or novice, than to quote the words of a famous British collector: "Never forget that toys were made for children — and toys are meant to be played with!" The collector who does not sometimes take his toys from their display cases for demonstration or "play", preferably in the company of children, is denying himself the full pleasure to be gained from his collection.

1

With their ingenious mechanisms and amusing actions, novelty toys are so attractive that a fascinating collection may be formed from only a few examples. This is just as well, for they are not the easiest toys to collect, earlier examples by such notable makers as Lehmann of Germany and Martin (later Bonnet et Cie) of France being both hard to find and expensive to purchase.

With the exception of the cast-iron novelties produced by some American makers of the 19th century, novelty toys are generally fragile. They will most often be found with "play-worn" finishes and with damaged or missing parts that may prove both difficult and expensive to replace. For some collectors of novelty toys, however, the restoration of damaged toys becomes as great a pleasure as the acquisition of perfect specimens.

Novelties of the post-World War II period, although often lacking the charm of earlier productions, are somewhat easier to find and are increasingly collectable. In recent years, Japanese and Far Eastern makers have established a near-monopoly in the production of tinplate novelties. Their products are well worth the collector's attention: with the exercise of a little discrimination, an attractive and worthwhile collection can be built up.

Mechanical Novelty Toys

1 Lehmann's "MAN DA RIN" was almost certainly one of the many "Chinese" toys inspired by the Boxer Rebellion of 1900. This toy has the early Lehmann trademark on the front and sides of the sedan chair, and bears the patent date "12 Mai 1903". It is powered by a clockwork mechanism in the lower half of the chair: hidden wheels propel the chair, and the coolies' legs are articulated to give them a realistic gait. The mandarin urges on the leading coolie by tugging on his pigtail. Length: 7·3in (185mm). Limited.

2 A water-driven Saw Mill by the German manufacturer Doll et Cie, dating from before 1920. This toy was intended to be powered by a steam engine, via a driving band on the wheel visible behind the chimney, but the mill wheel could also be hand-operated. Water is pumped into the mill's upper gallery, flowing thence onto the vanes of the water wheel, turning it anti-clockwise, and causing the saw to reciprocate via the crank-shaft. Note the hand-enamelled finish and the realistic pressed-tin roof and log. Width: 6·7in (17cm); height: 5·7 in (14·5cm). Limited.

3 "Adam" the Porter, by Lehmann; a popular toy with a long production life, this example dating from c1910. Clockwork concealed in the torso drives articulated legs. The detachable trunk bears the patent date "2 Jan 06" on the edge of the lid, with "E·P·L" (for Ernst Paul Lehmann) on the lid itself. The Lehmann trademark is litho-graphed on the porter's trousers;

his upper body is hand enamelled. Length: 8·27in (210mm). Limited.

4 "Naughty Nephew", another novelty from Lehmann's extensive range; this example dating from c1908. When the clockwork-driven vehicle is moving, the sailor-suited Nephew attempts to grab the steering tiller from Uncle—and receives an admonitory slap. The rear of the vehicle bears the Lehmann trademark and the patent date "May 12 1903". Length: 4·92in (125mm). Limited.

5 Dating from c1900, this Fireman is one of a number of popular climbing toys of the period. Clockwork in the hand-enamelled torso, wound by the non-removable cast key at the shoulder, operates a crankshaft that drives the legs in a climbing motion; the

fixed arms have hands pegged to fit the sides of a ladder. Height: 7·48in (190mm). Scarce.

6 Clockwork Swimming Seal, a realistic novelty animal by Lehmann, dating from c1920. It is mounted on a tricycle under-carriage: clockwork drives the front wheel, also activating the flippers, and the tail wheel steers a zig-zag course. A bell on the collar was standard. Length: 7in (178mm). Scarce.

7 Another popular Lehmann novelty, the "Bucking Broncho", re-mained in production for several years; this bears the patent date "19 June 1906". Clockwork in the wheeled base drives it forward and causes the broncho to buck realisti-ally in an attempt to unseat the cowboy, who has pivoted hands.

Note that Lehmann produced a similar toy without clockwork. Length: 6·1in (155mm). Limited.

8 This colourful clockwork-driven tinplate Tank (loosely modelled on the lozenge-shaped British Mark II tank of World War I) was made as the "Doughboy Tank" by the US maker Marx in c1935. As the tank moves along, the marksman slowly appears from his hatch, aims his rifle (as seen), and then quickly disappears. An almost identical toy was produced in Germany in the 1920s: examples bear the legend "Made in Germany", with no manu-

"Penny Toy" Van by G. Fischer, Germany, made before 1920. A cheap tinplate toy with attractive printed detail; note trademark on cab door. Length: 2·36in (60mm).

facturer's name, and are finished in different colours. Length: 9.5in (241mm). Limited.

9 "Paddy's Pride", an amusing novelty of a popular type; this example produced by Stock of Solingen, Germany, in c1920. Note Stock's trademark on the blue ribbon that encircles the prize porker. Clockwork within the "upturned bath" cart drives the rear wheels and causes "Paddy" to urge on the pig, which also has a wheel concealed beneath the blue ribbon. The toy can be set to move in circles. Other makers produced variations on this theme in the first decades of the century; notably Lehmann, whose "Paddy" had no cart, but rode precariously astride his fat pig. Length: 8in (203mm). Limited.

1 Pool Player by an unidentified German maker, *c*1910. This "classic" tinplate novelty was produced in various styles and sizes by several makers. A clockwork motor beneath the table powers the player's cue via a concealed rod, and also returns balls to play. Length: 11in (279mm). Limited.

2 Tightrope Walker by an unidentified maker, probably French, *c*1900. This ingenious tinplate balancing toy works by gravity. One end of the tightrope is fixed in a slightly higher position than the other, and the deeply-recessed front wheel of the wheelbarrow is placed on the rope at the upper end. The toy is kept upright by the lead weight —the "balance pole" is for effect only—and as it moves, the figure's legs "walk" via cranks from the front wheel. Length: 4·92in (125mm). Scarce.

3 Walking Dog by Blomer & Schüler, Nuremburg, West Germany, *c*1948-50. "Jumbo", the elephant trademark of this maker, is printed on the collar tag of this novelty. Length: 7·48in (190mm).

4 Walking Turkey by Blomer & Schüler, *c*1948-50. A most colourfully printed tinplate novelty, this clockwork-powered bird raises and spreads its tail as it walks. Length: 5·51in (140mm).

5 "Penny Toy" Car by an unidentified maker, probably German, *c*1910. This simple tinplate car is flywheel driven. The extended spindle of the rear-mounted flywheel rests on the rear wheels: when a cord wound around the spindle is pulled sharply, the power of the revolving flywheel is transmitted by friction. Length: 3·94in (100mm). Limited.

6 "Penny Toy" Sewing Machine by an unidentified German maker, *c*1910. In lightweight tinplate this is not a working model. Height: 3·54in (90mm).

7 "Penny Toy" Locomotive by an unidentified German maker, *c*1910. A pull-along toy with simple lithographed detail. Length: 3·35in (85mm).

8 Monorail Car by an unidentified German maker—it bears a trademark, "HR" within a shield— dating from the 1920s. The streamlined car of lightweight tinplate was probably intended to run on a circular monorail (the track shown is not original), on a radial arm connected to a clockwork driving mechanism. Length: 6·5in (165mm). Limited.

9 Santa Claus by Arnold, West Germany, 1950s. A clockwork-powered tinplate novelty for the Christmas season. The maker's trademark features prominently on the sack seen in the rear view. Height: 3·75in (95mm).

10 "Penny Toy" Platform Train by J. Ph. Meier, Nuremburg, Germany, *c*1900. This pull-along tinplate toy with pressed-tin detail and gilt wheels bears the "Dog Cart" trademark of a leading "penny toy" maker. Length: 3·94in (100mm).

11 Hydroplane by an unidentified maker, possibly Japanese, 1950s. This clockwork-powered tinplate "carpet toy" has brightly-printed detail. Length: 5·9in (150mm).

12 Speedboat by J. L. Hess, Nuremburg, Germany, 1920s. A tinplate "carpet toy" typical of a range from this maker in the 1920s; flywheel-powered. Length: 11·81in (300mm).

13 Rocket Ship by an unidentified maker, probably Japanese, 1930s. A fairly early "science fiction" toy; clockwork-powered. The on-off control lever can be seen at the tail, along with the remains of the original "sparking" device. Length: 7·09in (180mm).

14 "Beatrix" Tricycle car by Stock, Solingen, Germany, c1914. A simple clockwork mechanism drives the rear wheel of the tinplate car via a wire spring. The steering is non-variable, and the radially-spoked wheels, with printed tyres, are made of two dished tin

sections. Length: 4·53in (115mm).

15 Scissors Grinder by Arnold, West Germany, c1950. A tinplate novelty with an electric motor that drives the grinding-wheel via a connecting band (missing); a flint on the underside of the scissors produces a shower of sparks. Length: 5·71in (145mm).

16 Spinning Tops by an unidentified maker, possibly Japanese, post-1945. The arm on the rack-and-pinion plunger (left) engages with the projection at the upper side (right, in photograph) of the top to give a long-lasting "spin" when the plunger is "pumped" before removal. Common.

17 "Penny Toy" Pony and Trap by an unidentified Germany maker, c1910, with brightly gilt finish. Length: 4·13in (105mm).

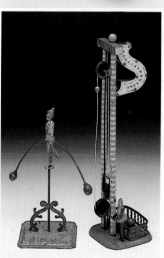

18 "Penny Toy" Horse and Cart by an unidentified German maker, c1910. A lithographed-tinplate horse pulls a pressed-tin cart. Length: 4·33in (110mm).

19 Soldier by an unidentified German maker, c1930. The detail of this clockwork-powered tinplate infantryman features the uniform of a British "Tommy", with equipment of German Army type. Length: 7·28in (185mm).

(Left) Balancing clown, probably by a French maker, c1900; a hand-enamelled tinplate toy. (Right) Rolling-Ball Game, probably French, c1900: the counter-weighted bucket takes a ball from the dispenser at the top, returns by gravity to the base, and tips the ball into a tray with numbered apertures.

All the toys shown on this spread were photographed at the London Toy & Model Museum.

1 Donald Duck Tricyclist by an unidentified maker, c1950. The composition figure, with cloth trousers, rides a tinplate tricycle. Clockwork drives the rear wheels, causing the figure's legs to move in a realistic pedalling motion. The creations of Walt Disney have long provided a rich area of inspiration for toy manufacturers: Mickey Mouse, Donald Duck, Goofy, and other characters are to be found in many forms. Height: 4in (102mm). Fairly common.

2 Clockwork Mouse by an unidentified maker (possibly Japanese). A modern item—similar toys remain in production—this has a pressed tinplate body and cloth tail. Length: 3·5in (89mm). Fairly common.

3 Hen and Chicken Cart by Hans Eberl, Nuremburg, Germany, c1918. This toy is driven forward by clockwork concealed within the cart (note winder) that also sets the chicken in motion. Length: 8·5in (216mm). Limited.

4 Aeroplane Novelty by Schuco, Germany, mid-1930s. The "New York-Paris" flyer—the design evidently influenced by the "record" solo flights of the period—is plush-covered and pilots a printed tin monoplane. Length: 4in (102mm).

5 Sulky Racer by an American maker, early 20th century. Racing in light two-wheeled carts known as sulkies was a popular sport in the USA and several US makers produced toys of the kind shown

here. It is cast iron, a traditional material of US toymakers until at last overtaken by tinplate. However, instead of being pull-/push-along, like most cast-iron toys, this incorporates a somewhat bulky clockwork mechanism. American cast-iron toys of this period have been reproduced, often with inferior finish by Continental makers. Length 8.875in (225mm). Scarce.

6 Clockwork Grasshopper by a European maker, dating from the 1940s. Insect novelties were produced both before and after World War II, and this is typical of post-war European production in bearing no maker's mark. Length: 7·125in (181mm). Common.

7 "Zikra" by Lehmann, Germany: a tinplate toy with a long production life beginning c1915. Clockwork in

the cart (note winder) causes the zebra to kick and buck, while the clown driver hauls at the reins. Lehmann produced more than one toy of this type, notably the "Balky Mule". Length: 7·125in (181mm).

8 Cyclist by Günthermann, Nuremburg, Germany, c1900. Clockwork powers the rear wheel in realistic manner by way of a chain drive; the tinplate cyclist pedals a wire bicycle with white rubber tyres. Length: 7·5in (190mm). Very scarce.

9 Native and Crocodile; a large, well-detailed version of a popular tinplate novelty which was produced (latterly in smaller sizes only) until the 1950s. Clockwork drives a pair of wheels linked to the crocodile's jaws, which open and close as it travels forward. Length: 15in (381mm). Common.

10 "Zig-Zag" by Lehmann, a tinplate
novelty, c1910. An ingenious
clockwork mechanism makes the
"car" sway and swing while following an erratic course. Length:
5·625in (143mm). Scarce.

11 Roller-Skating Bear by Bing,
Germany, c1910. Added charm is
given to this clockwork toy by its
covering of simulated fur. Note the
maker's mark as an ear-tag. Height:
8·5in (216mm). Scarce.

12-13 Travelling Circus by a European
maker, c1950. An ambitious
tinplate toy: the circus wagon
(13), with a detachable folding
cage, is drawn by an elephant
which "walks" when activated by
rods clockwork-driven via a
cranked axle beneath the wagon.
The simple tinplate animals and
clown, on connecting rods (12),

are drawn along behind. Length
(elephant and wagon together):
17·5in (445mm).

14 "Uncle Sam" Money Bank; an
American cast-iron novelty, c1890,
and typical of a very popular genre
of the period. A coin placed in
"Uncle Sam's" hand is dropped
into the "U.S." bag when the figure's
right arm is activated by pressure
on its beard. Height: 11·25in
(286mm). Scarce.

15 Clockwork Beetle by Egaway,
Japan, dating from before World
War II. Beetles which walked and
flapped their wings were popular
novelties, and this one is a
copy—complete with facsimile
trademark—of the famous tinplate
beetle made by Lehmann from
c1900 to the late 1920s. Length:
3·75in (95mm).

16 "Toonerville Trolley" by H. Fischer,
Nuremburg, c1925. This tinplate
toy was based on an American
strip cartoon (note copyright line
above winder); it moves forward,
rocking and swaying on its eccentric wheels, stops, and restarts,
when the driver cranks his handle.
Also to be found in a smaller
version, this toy is 5·25in (133mm)
long. Scarce.

17 Dancing Bear by a German maker,
pre-World War II. When its clockwork is wound, the articulated tinplate figure alternately bends and
stands upright. Note ring through
nose, and cloth apron. Height:
6·125in (156mm).

18 "Li-La" by Lehmann, c1910. A
classic clockwork tinplate toy: the
driver steers the horseless carriage
on an erratic course, while one

sister pushes open the cab hatch
with her parasol and the other
belabours the dog, which turns its
head. A number of colour and
wheel variants exist. Length: 5·25in
(133mm). Limited.

19 "Tut-Tut" by Lehmann, another
classic tinplate novelty, c1910.
Beneath the car, a bellows worked
by the clockwork motor causes the
amusingly oversized driver to
sound his trumpet as he careers
erratically along. Length: 6·75in
(171mm). Limited.

20 Pig Band by Schuco, c1936. When
wound, the three musicians of
cloth-covered tinplate mime the
playing of drum, flute and fiddle.
Schuco produced variations on
this theme: a military band is also to
be found. Height (single figure):
5·1in (130mm). Common.

25

The simple mechanical toy that operates on a track evolved only a little later than the train set. But although by no means new, the concept seems to have taken on a new lease of life after World War II. Comparatively unsophisticated and fairly robust "novelties", these toys are generally inexpensively-produced and are presumably aimed at children too young to appreciate a "real" train set. To an older child, the simple operation of these toys would soon become of little interest. From the collector's point of view, however, mechanical mediocrity is often outweighed by pleasing design and attractive printed detail.

1 Rack Railway by Chad Valley, Great Britain, dating from c1950. The clockwork-driven car climbs

the pivoted rack section under the power of its motor, a cog-wheel beneath it engaging with slots in the track. Upon reaching the summit, as the section tips forward, the motor cuts out and the car relies upon gravity to descend the second pivoted section, run up and back along the lower section, and return to the foot of the rack to make another clockwork-powered ascent. Overall length of track-base: 42·5in (108cm).

2 "Delhi Local Shuttle" by an Indian maker, dating from c1980. A brightly-coloured "tramcar" toy with a wealth of printed detail — and note the manufacturer's trademark and name, in an Asian script, on the side of the station to the left in the photograph. The clockwork-

powered tramcar pursues the "there and back again" course usual with these toys on its alternating (cross-over) tracks. Length: 25·6in (65cm). Common.

3 "Carpet Toy" Locomotive by INGAP, Padua, Italy, dating from c1950. The simple clockwork-powered locomotive, numbered "552", is something of an intruder on this spread, since it is a "floor toy" — of a kind popular since the 19th century — and is not intended to run on a track. Its tinplate side on which a 2-6-0 wheel configuration is printed conceals, in fact, four wheels only. Length: 6·5in (16·5cm).

4 "Condor" Signal Train by an unidentified German maker, dating from the 1950s. The clockwork-powered locomotive, numbered

"20 512" and with printed detail showing a 2-8-4 wheel configuration, operates the signals by tripping track-mounted levers. Length: 28·5in (72·5cm).

5 Liner and Lighthouse by Arnold, West Germany, dating from the 1950s — a variation on the land-based themes of the other novelties shown on this spread. The liner is mounted on a pivoted mechanism that causes it to "pitch" quite convincingly as it moves between the lighthouse and the harbour building, the latter concealing a clockwork motor. Note that here — as in the toys shown at (6), (8), (9), and (10) — it is the powered track that operates the non-powered vehicle. Length: 14·8in (37·5cm).

6 Turntable Train by Arnold, West

(Below) Airport; mechanical novelty by a German maker, c1950. As the tinplate airplanes circle the brightly-printed tinplate control tower, which conceals a clockwork motor, their large plastic propellers revolve. Height (assembled): 10·24in (26cm).

Germany, dating from c1948-50. The locomotive, turning on the turntables at either end of the track, pulls or pushes its coach between engine shed and station (the latter concealing the toy's clockwork motor). Note the attractively-printed detail of road transport beneath an embankment—as on the very similar French-made toy at (8)—along the side of the base. Length: 14·8in (37·5cm).

7 "Flèche d'Or" Rail Car by an unidentified French maker, dating from the 1950s. The removable key for the clockwork-powered rail car is shown here in place for winding. As in (4), the car trips the signals as it travels between the stations. Length: 30in (76cm).

8 Turntable Train by an unidentified French maker, dating from the

mid-1950s. Operation is similar to that described at (6) and, again, it is the clockwork-powered track, engaging on the underside of the locomotive, that drives the toy. Note the winding shaft in the station roof. Length: 14·8in (37·5cm).

9 Highway Toy by an unidentified Soviet Russian maker, dating from the 1970s; see the earlier, German-made version of this toy shown at (10). Two buses and a car are fixed on each of the two separate circular tracks, running beneath a raised central tunnel. The tracks are powered by a clockwork motor in the base of the brightly-printed toy; note the winding shaft on the right in the photograph. Length of base: 9·55in (24·25cm). Common.

10 Highway Toy by a West German maker (possibly "Technofix", Gebrüder Einfalt; a maker particularly noted for the production of toys of this kind in the post-World War II period), dating from c1950. In design and operation it closely resembles the later Soviet-made toy shown at (9), but in this example only two cars are moved by each of the two circular tracks. Length of base: 8·96in (22·75cm).

11 "Carpet Toy" Rail Car by an unidentified Japanese maker, probably dating from the 1930s. Like (3), this vehicle is not intended to run on a track. The clockwork-powered car, of futuristic shape, has wheels fixed at an angle so that it will run a circular course. Length: 3·54in (9cm).

2

Toy cars have been in production for almost as long as the real vehicles that they portray. Such famous makers as Bing and Carette featured tinplate toy cars in their ranges during the first decade of the 20th century, and although not scale models, these give a most realistic representation of the finest cars of the period: see, for example, the magnificent Limousine by Carette of Nuremburg, dating from c1910, shown at (4) on *pages 30-31*. Such toys are now generally most rare and valuable, even when in less than fine condition.

The tinplate cars of the 1920s and 1930s — from such notable makers as CIJ, Citroën and Jep of France; Bub, Günthermann and Tipp of Germany; and Kingsbury and Structo of the United States — have also been put beyond the reach of many collectors by a boom market. And even the values of tinplate cars produced by Japanese makers in the 1950s-1970s are now climbing steadily.

The new collector will do well to look carefully at the many diecast models shown on the following pages. With the exception of the rarer, pre-World War II examples, these attractive and well-detailed toys are still to be found at reasonable prices, allowing an excellent thematic collection to be built up for a moderate outlay. And while few collectors will have the resources — or the space — to acquire and display pedal cars like those shown on *pages 88-93*, these huge and handsome toys certainly demand both attention and admiration.

Toy Cars

These tinplate cars of the early 20th century have all the visual appeal of their full-size counterparts and, like them, are eagerly sought after by collectors and have become increasingly rare and expensive. Most are based on actual marques, although such parts as chassis, seats, and lamps were often designed to be interchangeable among the maker's various models. Many are of soldered construction with fine hand-enamelled finish, featuring such details as bevelled glass windows, working lamps and rubber tyres. They were, of course, toys for the well-to-do: the finer examples were sold before World War I at prices of up to £1 15s 0d (£1.75, $2.48) — perhaps a week's wages for a working man.

All the cars and accessories shown here were photographed at the London Toy & Model Museum.

1 Based on a Renault car of the pre-World War I period, this large and impressive Spanish-made car — the maker is possibly identified only by the initials "DL" — dates from around 1920. It has what was known in Europe as a "Berlin" body, in which the chauffeur — here a liveried figure with a bisque (porcelain) head — is exposed to the elements while the passengers travel in the luxury of an enclosed compartment. The toy is richly hand-enamelled and features such detail as opening doors, glass windows, bell-type headlamps, radially-spoked wire wheels with rubber tyres, and semi-

elliptic springing. Length: 22in (56cm). Rare.
2 Clockwork Car by Günthermann, Nuremburg, Germany, dating from around 1908. Loosely based on a landaulette type, with a rather unusual rectangular bonnet, it is of simple tinplate tab-and-slot construction, with pressed tin wheels and tyres. The body is lithographed and detail includes opening doors and glazed windows. It features an automatic brake mechanism: a small spring-loaded wheel fitted centrally at the rear stops the axle via a cog-wheel when the car is picked up or when the clockwork mechanism is wound while it is off the ground. Length: 9·75in (25cm). Limited.
3 Paris-Berlin Racing Car by Günthermann, with an early

Günthermann trademark on the hood and dating from before 1905. This clockwork car — note fixed key at rear — has a lithographed tinplate body, tinplate driver and spoked wheels and tyres of pressed tin. Length: 5·25in, (13cm). Limited.
4 Clockwork Limousine by Carette, Nuremburg, Germany, dating from c1910: a magnificent toy from a range which represents the zenith of tinplate car production before World War I. This example from the top of the range is hand-enamelled (it was available more cheaply with lithographed finish and lacking some of the refinements listed below); its detail includes a bolted-on top with baggage rack, opening doors, nickel-plated headlamps and side-lights, bevelled glass

windows, "button-backed" seats, an operating brake and reverse mechanism, and radially-spoked wheels with white rubber tyres. The liveried chauffeur is a composition figure. These Carette cars were made in three basic sizes— 8.5in (22cm), 12.5in (32cm), as seen here, and 16in (40cm), see (7)—with variations in finish and detail. Scarce.

5 Four-Seat Tourer (based on a Renault) by Bing, Germany, dating from c1905. Not so well proportioned as the Carette car at (4), this clockwork tinplate car is nevertheless very well constructed, with hand-enamelled finish, and features operating steering and brake. Detail includes a large detachable headlamp and two side lamps, and "button-backed" seats

of pressed tin. Note particularly the umbrella basket at the rear: this is usually missing from surviving examples. Length: 9.25in (23.5cm). Limited.

6 Clockwork Landaulette by Bing, Germany, dating from c1906. A tinplate car with a most attractive hand-enamelled finish (note the bright-work louvres on the bonnet), this has operating steering via a single crown wheel and bar. Detail includes a composition chauffeur, a single centrally-mounted headlamp, and white rubber tyres on diecast wheels. Length: 7.375in (18.5cm). Limited.

7 Clockwork Limousine by Carette, Germany, the largest from the range that included the car shown at (4), dating from c1910. This is one of the cheaper models from

that range, with lithographed coachwork, a tabbed and slotted roof, tinplate chauffeur, and pressed tin wheels and tyres; it has a bevelled windscreen but no side windows. However, the doors open, headlamps and sidelights are fitted, and the brake operates. Length: 16in (40cm). Scarce.

8 De Dion Two-Seater Runabout by Bing, Germany (with Bing trademark just visible on the trunk), dating from c1905. Tinplate with a hand-enamelled finish, the car is clockwork-driven and has adjustable steering. Detail includes a centrally-mounted headlamp, "button-backed" upholstery in pressed tin, and diecast wheels with rubber tyres. The model was made in four sizes, this example, 8.375in (21cm) long, being the

second-largest. Limited.

9 Rear-Entrance Tonneau by Carette, Germany, a clockwork-driven car of lithographed tinplate, dating from c1908. It carries a driver and passengers of hand-enamelled tinplate and includes in its detail lamps mounted on the windscreen pillars, a glass windscreen, operating brake, and diecast wheels with rubber tyres. Length: 12.5in (32cm). Scarce.

10 Street Lamp, an oil-burning diecast accessory, probably made by Bing, Germany, and featured in Britain in Bassett-Lowke's Catalogue issued in 1906.

11 Fuel Pumps, tinplate accessories by Charles Rossignol (the "CR" trademark is seen on the bases), Paris, c1920. Heights: (left) 3.25in (83mm); (right) 4.25in (108mm).

All the cars shown on this spread are from the collection of Ron McCrindell, Sidmouth, Devon.

1 Limousine by Tipp and Company, Nuremburg, Germany; dating from around 1928. This most attractively lithographed tinplate toy, with lithographed chauffeur and pressed-tin wheels and "Dunlop Cord" tyres, is clockwork-driven. This is one of Tipp's range of cheaper cars, with non-opening doors, sold in Great Britain in the late 1920s at 1s 9d (8½p, 10c). For an extra 9d (3½p, 4c), the identical car could be purchased with electric headlights: flat, white-backed bulbs in a tin holder were connected to a battery clipped beneath the car. The aperture intended to accommodate the on/off lever for

these lights is visible on the running-board, along with the slots on the side of the bonnet to take the light-holders. Tipp's cars have become increasingly popular—especially as cars by Bing and Carette move ever further beyond the financial reach of many collectors—and the one shown, in mint condition, is a scarce and desirable item. Length: 9·84in (24·99cm).

2 Rear-Entrance Tonneau Car by an unidentified European maker; dating from around 1907. It bears on the front, below the windscreen, the trademark "R & Co B", surmounted by a crown and followed by the number "205" (which also appears on the bonnet). This early litho-graphed car, with chauffeur, is of extremely fragile construction:

the tinplate is wafer-thin, and it is powered by the kind of simple coiled-spring mechanism then favoured by makers of cheap, mass-produced toys. The roof of this example is a replacement. Length: 7·87in (19·99cm).

3 Open Tourer by Brimtoy, Great Britain; dating from around 1919. The maker's familiar "Nelson's Column" trademark, with the words "Brimtoy Brand, British Made", is on the underside—but it is most instructive to compare this car with the Bing toy shown at (5), since there is a strong possibility that this example, also, was made by Bing in Nuremburg. Its clockwork mechanism is certainly by Bing, and the metal pressings are identical in both cars, although the finish and quality of (5) are superior.

Only the wheels are of a type not found on Bing cars. Limited. Length: 10·5in (26·67mm).

4 Saloon Car by Bing, Nuremburg, Germany; dating from 1932. This lithographed tinplate toy, clockwork-driven (note fixed key), is rather uninspired in comparison to Bing's earlier products: it is an example of Bing's very last production run of toy cars, and a rather sad reminder of the great company's decline. It is, nevertheless, a desirable collector's item. Length: 9in (22·86cm).

5 Open Tourer by Bing; dating from around 1913. The similarities between this car and (3) have already been noted: a single glance reveals that this is a much superior item, of heavier construction and with dark blue livery that contrasts

most pleasantly with the brightly-lithographed seats. Other refinements include a glass windscreen and an operating hand-brake. Note also the brackets for nickel-plated side-lights, unfortunately missing from this example, as is the tinplate chauffeur originally fitted. Rare. Length: 12·5in (31·7cm).

6 Taxi by H. Fischer & Co, Nuremburg, Germany; dating from c1910. This most attractively lithographed representation of a Paris taxi, with opening doors, pressed-tin driver and a taxi-meter, is one of a large range of cars only recently attributed to Fischer, a prolific producer of tinplate trains and cars from c1908 until the 1930s. It is clockwork-driven, with a fixed key. Limited. Length: 8·66in (21·99cm).

7 Open Tourer by Karl Bub, Nuremburg, Germany; dating from 1927. A pleasantly solid car of lithographed tinplate, complete with chauffeur (apparently dozing!), this is clockwork-driven, with a fixed key just in front of the rear wheel. This toy was catalogued by Bub in 1927 in no fewer than six sizes, ranging from 5·9in (150mm), to the largest, as shown here, at 13in (33·02cm).

8 Roadster by an unidentified US maker; dating from around 1915. Constructed of tinplate and painted yellow, this sporty little car is most pleasantly evocative of its era. It has a realistic drive: the starting-handle protruding from the front is cranked to wind a coiled-spring mechanism. This particular example lacks its driver

and the spare wheel that would originally have been mounted on the boot (note hole). Scarce. Length: 9·055in (22·99cm).

9 "Penny Toys" Limousine by J. Ph. Meier/Kohnstam, Germany; dating from c1927. This little car in lithographed tinplate is a good late example of a "penny toy"—so-called because toys of this type were sold for 1d (0.42p, 0.5c), or its equivalent, when they were first made in the 1890s. Most originated in and around Nuremburg, where one of the best-known makers was J. Ph. Meier. The firm was later take over by Moses Kohnstam, who continued to market its products throughout the 1920s. Limited. Length: 3·937in (9·99cm).

10 Taxi; c1928; lithographed tinplate with a coiled-spring mechanism.

The taxi-flag, "Libre", suggests that it was intended for the French market—but since it bears the rear number plate "M.3.423", while the "penny toy" at (9) has the number "M.3.523", we may assume that both are by the same maker, and that this taxi is probably one of the few larger toys by Meier/Kohnstam. Rare. Length: 5·51in (13·9cm).

11 Open Tourer by Bing; dating from c1928. A fairly late item—see also (4)—but nevertheless a very attractive tinplate car, lithographed in a lovely shade of green which is nicely complemented by the striped seats, orange wheels and blue-uniformed chauffeur. It is fitted with the fixed-key clockwork mechanism standard on Bing's smaller cars of the period. Scarce. Length: 8·66in (21·9cm).

All the cars and accessories shown on this spread were photographed at the London Toy & Model Museum.

1 Citroën B14 Sedan by André Citroën, France, dating from c1927. This impressive tinplate model, driven by a battery-operated electric motor, was one of the largest in the range produced by the famous automobile manufacturer from 1923 onward —an inspired way of promoting its "real life" output by fixing the name of Citroën firmly in the minds of the motorists of the future! It is, indeed, a close copy of the real thing, with opening doors, windows that wind up and down, working suspension and steering, electrically-operated headlights,

and a two-tone paint finish. This was the first model in the Citroën range—which extended from pedal cars to small diecast toys—to have rubber tyres. A taxi version of this most impressive car was also available.
Length: 21·5in (55cm). Scarce.
2 Clockwork Limousine by Karl Bub, Nuremburg, Germany, dating from the early 1930s; a rather more "toy-like" example than the Citroën shown at (1). Of lightweight tinplate construction, it has simulated balloon tyres (note the "Dunlop"

Robustly-constructed clockwork-powered car by Structo, USA, dating from the early 1930s. Note the famous slogan on the trademark transfer on the radiator: "Structo Toys Make Men Of Boys"!

legend) on "artillery-type" wheels of pressed tin, extremely simple headlights, and wide bumpers. Larger versions, with opening doors, a tin chauffeur, and other refinements were also produced. Length: 14in (36cm).

3 Avions Voisin Sedan by Jouets de Paris (J de P), France, dating from c1930. Note that in c1932 the maker's name was changed to Jouets en Paris (JEP), and it is as "Jep" that the company is generally known. This tinplate car is typical of the fairly wide range of Jep sedans and tourers: note the well-modelled radiator, pierced for the key to the clockwork mechanism. Other details include an electric spotlamp mounted on the windscreen pillar, operating steering, and single-sided wheels

and tyres of pressed tin. A klaxon mounted on the running-board and the licence plate "7392-JdeP", set well back beneath the radiator, cannot be seen in the photograph. Length: 13·25in (34cm). This item is limited.

4 Ford Model "T" by Bing, Germany, dating from c1922. This simple model in lightweight tinplate of one of the most famous automobiles of all time is clockwork-driven and, like the original on which it was based, is finished in black! Length: 6·375in (16cm).

5 Rolls Royce Phantom I by Jouets de Paris — see note at (3) — dating from c1928. This magnificent model was the masterpiece of the Jep range and is generally acknowledged to be one of the finest of all tinplate cars. Clock-

work-driven, with forward and reverse gears and a working brake, it has electric headlamps. Note the cantilever springs, just visible in front of the rear mudguard; other detail includes a sprung front bumper, front windscreen and auster screen, fully detailed radiator grille, and rubber tyres. It is shown here with its key, which incorporates a wrench in its handle, in place for winding. Length: 19·75in (50cm). Scarce.

6 "Roll-Top" Coupé by Günthermann, Nuremburg, Germany, dating from the 1930s. This tinplate car is clockwork-driven (note the permanently-fixed winder just in front of the rear wheel) and features a canvas "roll-back" top with a hinged rear quarter of tin, opening doors and

trunk, and a tinplate chauffeur. The tin wheels are typical of Günthermann's cars. Length: 18in (46cm). Limited.

7 Two-Door Coupé by Tipp and Company, Germany, dating from the 1930s and a fairly typical example of the maker's range of tinplate vehicles. It features opening doors, a spare wheel on the (opening) lid of the boot, and pressed tin wheels with simulated spokes and "Continental Record" tyres. Note the fixed winder just in front of the rear wheel. Length: 16in (41cm). Limited.

8 Traffic Policeman; a diecast accessory of French manufacture.

9 10 Street Lamps; simple tinplate accessories made by Charles Rossignol, Paris, to supplement the company's range of vehicles.

(Below) Fairlane "Ranch Wagon" by ATC (Asahi Toy Company Ltd), Tokyo, c1960. Friction-powered, plated brightwork front and rear, a celluloid windscreen and rubber tyres. Length: 15·75in (40cm).

Fine tinplate interpretations of American cars, like those shown here and on the following spreads, may well rank as Japanese makers' major contribution to the world of metal toys. The larger cars of this kind are already scarce, for they were made, for the US market, in limited numbers and styles that matched the many model changes among real cars in the 1950s and 1960s. Thus, for collectors, size as well as quality will be a criterion of desirability.

1 Coupé (probably based on a Mercury) by Haji (Mansei Toy Company Ltd), Tokyo, dating from the mid-1960s. This two-door, four-seater car is friction-powered and features opening doors, plastic windows, plated brightwork and a detailed interior. Length: 11in (28cm). Limited.

2 Coupé (probably based on a Dodge) bearing the trademark "ET" (Japanese maker), dating from the mid-1950s. This two-door car in a style typical of the 1950s is friction-powered. It has a tinted plastic windscreen, printed interior detail, and rubber tyres. Length: 11·8in (30cm). Limited.

3 Automobile by ATC (Asahi Toy Company Ltd), Tokyo, dating from c1960. An attractively-detailed model: note dual headlights, heavily-chromed bumper and radiator grille, applied two-tone trim, printed dashboard in interior, and printed hubcaps over rubber whitewall tyres; friction-powered. Length: 12·6in (32cm). Limited.

4 Ford Mustang (2+2 "Fastback") by an unidentified Japanese maker, dating from c1970. Friction-powered, it features plated radiator, bumpers and brightwork, pressed tin detail on the bonnet, and dished and perforated hubcaps over rubber tyres. Length: 10·8in (27·5cm). Limited.

5 Cadillac Fleetwood 60 Special by an unidentified Japanese maker (the trademark "Y" is just visible on the rear window), dating from the mid-1960s. This is an extremely impressive friction-powered model of a luxury car of 1962; well-detailed, with a tinted windscreen, printed interior detail. Length: 21·65in (55cm). Scarce.

6 Mercury Cougar by Bandai, Tokyo, c1970. This is a battery-operated model, with wheels for variable steering concealed beneath the chassis. Closely based on the real car, the two-door, four-seater model features sculptured wheels, printed interior detail, and rearlights mounted on the lid of the boot. Length: 10·2in (26cm). Limited.

7 Chevrolet Corvette by Taiyo, Japan, c1970. The realistic detail of this battery-powered model of a two-seater "fastback" sports car extends to simulation of detachable top sections of the real car. The lever just visible beneath the radiator controls variable-steering wheels. Length: 10·2in (26cm). Limited.

8 Chevrolet Camaro by an unidentified maker (probably Japanese), dating from the late 1960s. The body is tinplate and the top black plastic. A single variable-steering wheel is concealed beneath the chassis of this battery-powered model. Length: 10·6in (27cm). Limited.

9 Mercury Cougar Coupé by Asakusa, Tokyo, c1970. Compared to the smaller Bandai version at (6), this features more detail (although lacking the boot-mounted rearlights), including wing mirrors, a windscreen and quarterlights of tinted plastic; friction-powered. Length: 15·35in (39cm). Limited.

10 Rambler Station Wagon by Bandai, Tokyo, dating from the late 1950s. This unpowered push-along toy features a built-in roof-rack, plastic windscreen and windows, printed interior detail, plated brightwork, and rubber whitewall tyres. Length: 10·8in (27·5cm). Limited.

11 Pontiac Firebird (note name of model on licence plate) by Bandai, Tokyo, dating from the late 1960s. Its friction drive produces an "exhaust note" when in operation. This model of a two-door, four-seater coupé has a plastic windscreen and windows, printed interior detail, plated brightwork, and sculptured wheels. Length: 10·04in (25·5cm). Limited.

12 Lincoln Continental Convertible Coupé by Bandai, Tokyo, dating from the mid-1950s. Friction-powered, this car has additional detail in pressed tin and features most attractively printed seating. The steering-wheel is operational and the wheels have detailed hubcaps over rubber whitewall tyres. Length: 11·6in (29·5cm). Scarce.

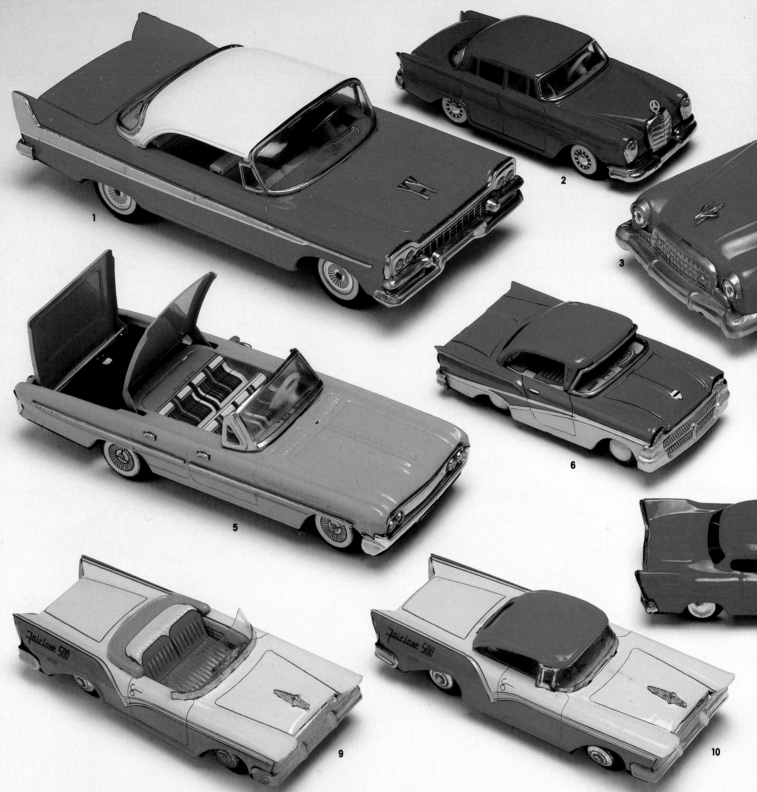

1 New Sedan by T.N. (Nomura Toys Limited), Tokyo, Japan, dating from c1958; it bears the maker's trademark and the words "Made in Japan" on the rear parcel shelf. This large and impressive toy is well-detailed, with a bright metal radiator and front and rear bumpers (incorporating pressed tind printed head- and rearlights), mascot, front and rear windscreen frames (with clear plastic screens), and side trim strips enclosing a yellow printed area. The pressed-tin interior is similarly well-detailed, including a steering column and wheel. A rear-mounted number plate reads: "M-1127". The wheels are rubber, with metal discs bearing printed details of spokes and whitewalls. The toy is friction-driven, on the rear wheels.

Length: 11·25in (28·575cm).

2 Mercedes-Benz 220S by SSS International, Japan, c1958; it bears the words "Made in Japan" on the rear parcel shelf. Bright metal details include the radiator (the Mercedes star above it is plastic), headlights, front and rear bumpers, and front and rear windscreen frames (with a clear plastic front screen). It has a pressed and printed interior, with front and rear seats and a plastic steering wheel. A number plate, "220S", is fitted at the rear. The rubber wheels, with friction drive on the front pair, have metal hubcaps and whitewalls. Length: 7·5in (19·05cm).

3 Station Wagon by an unidentified West German maker, c1956. The body pressing incorporates louvres in the front wings and an opening tailgate with a cast metal handle. The mascot is also cast metal, and as well as the usual brightwork details it has pressed-tin rear-lights applied by tab-and-slot. Rubber whitewall tyres are fitted to the metal wheels, the front pair friction-driven. Length: 11·125in (28·257cm).

4 Station Wagon by "KKK", Japan, 1950s; the name "Country Squire" is printed across the front doors on either side and the maker's trademark and "Made in Japan" appear on the rear parcel shelf. Printed details on the body include simulated wooden side-panels; bright metal details include a roof rack. The rubber wheels have metal discs with printed spokes and whitewalls. Friction powers the front wheels. Length: 8·75in (22·225cm).

5 Sedan-Convertible by an unidentified maker, c1960-61. The words "Made in China" are printed on the rear parcel shelf. This is an attractive and pleasingly-detailed toy, with bright metal details that include trim strips. Number plates at front and rear read "MF 748". When the green lever to the left of the rear seats is turned, the boot opens and a tinplate hardtop swings up and over, the boot closing again as it snaps into place. The plastic wheels, with printed spokes and whitewalls, are fitted with rubber tyres; friction drives the front pair. Length: 9in (22·86cm).

6 Saloon Car by an unidentified Japanese maker, c1958; "Made in Japan" is printed on the boot, below a number plate "FD 6941".

It has printed details on bright metal at front and rear and a simple printed interior. The rubber wheels (the rear pair friction-driven) are fitted with metal discs. Length: 5·75in (14·605cm).

7 Cadillac Sedan by an unidentified Japanese maker, c1958; a Red Indian Head trademark and "Made in Japan" are printed below the legend "Cadillac" on the left rear wing. This simple toy in lightweight tinplate has basic printed details inside and out and is fitted with rubber wheels and metal discs. Friction drives the rear wheels. Length: 4·75in (12·065cm).

8 "Gama 300" Saloon Car by Gama, West Germany, c1956-57; note the enamelled "Gama" badge above the bright metal radiator and the legend "Gama 300" in applied bright metal

letters along the front wings. This good-quality toy features much bright metal detail and a well-printed pressed-tin interior, with a plastic steering wheel (left-hand drive). The metal wheels have rubber tyres with inset plastic white-walls. Friction drives the rear wheels: the front wheels can be manually turned for varied courses. Length: 12·25in (31·115cm).

9-10 Convertible (9) and Hardtop (10) by an unidentified Japanese maker, c1958. These have the same basic body pressing. Both have "Fairlane 500" printed on both sides of the rear wings: on the Hardtop, "Japan" is printed below this on the right side. The bright metal details are fairly crude. Transmission and suspension details are printed on the bases.

Both cars have rubber wheels, the front pair friction-driven, with metal discs. Length: (each car): 6·25in (15·87cm).

11 Sedan by an unidentified Japanese maker, c1958; the word "Japan" is stamped on the base. With little detail other than the basic bright metal at front and rear, this car has rubber wheels, the rear pair friction-driven, fitted with metal discs. Length: 5in (12·7cm).

12 Limousine Car by Taguchi, Japan, c1958. It bears a transfer "Limousine" on both sides and tin plates printed with same legend are applied to the bright metal roof rack. A large applied plate at the rear is printed "Drive Carefully/Airport". The flywheel for the rear-wheel friction-drive is just

visible in the undetailed interior. The wheels are rubber with metal discs. Length: 5·375in (13·65cm).

13 New World Car by an unidentified Japanese maker, c1958; "Made in Japan" is stamped on the base. This simple tinplate toy lacks any interior detail; it has the usual bright metal exterior detail, including discs on the rubber wheels. Length: 5·25in (13·335cm).

14 Convertible by an unidentified Japanese maker, c1958; the rear number plate reads "Japan/M-372". A brightly-printed friction-drive (rear wheels) toy in lightweight tinplate, this has tabbed-and-slotted front and rear bumpers, printed details of radiator, mascot and interior, and rubber wheels fitted with metal discs. Length: 4in (10·16cm).

1 Cadillac Gear Shift Car by Bandai, Tokyo, Japan, made in c1965. This fine battery-driven toy has a tinplate body with a bright metal radiator grille and mascot and plated bumpers and door handles. The pressed-tin interior has printed upholstery detail; the windscreen, in a bright metal frame, is celluloid. Powered by two 1·5-volt batteries housed in a trap in the underside, it features operating steering (left-hand drive; like all the other representations of American cars on this spread), a working horn, and an "engine noise" mechanism. Its most notable features, however, are its working gear-levers, one giving high and low speeds and neutral gear, and the other giving forward, reverse and stop. It has well-modelled

plastic wheels fitted with rubber tyres. Length: 11·375in (28·89cm).
2 Chevrolet Convertible by Bandai, Japan; this is Number 710, dating from around 1960, in the maker's "Model Auto Series", which was marketed in boxes bearing the slogan "Over one hundred models. Start your collection now". See (5), (7), (8), (10) and (11) on this spread for other cars in the same series. Well-detailed, this friction-driven car has a bright metal radiator grille and front and rear bumpers, a tinted plastic windscreen framed in bright metal, and a pressed-tin interior with printed two-tone upholstery and a pressed-tin three-spoked steering wheel (left-hand drive). The pressed-tin wheels are painted with details of spokes, whitewalls and the

Chevrolet crest, and rubber tyres are fitted. The tinplate base bears printed details of transmission, exhaust system and suspension. Length: 6·25in (15·875cm).
3 New Ford Sedan by "H", Japan, c1957; the words "Made in Japan" are printed on the dashboard. This simple friction-drive car, with bright metal details and a printed interior, has rubber wheels fitted with bright metal discs. Length: 7·75in (19·685cm).
4 New Edsel by Haji (Mansei Toy Company), Japan, c1959. A well-detailed representation of Ford's ill-fated 1950's car (identified in bright metal letters on the rear wings), featuring the usual bright metal details and a printed interior with a pressed-tin steering wheel. A number plate at the rear

reads "84-A8259"; the maker's trademark is printed on the rear side of the front seats. The rubber wheels are fitted with metal whitewalls and hubcaps. Friction drives the front wheels. Length: 10·875in (27·62cm).
5 Chrysler Imperial Convertible; Number 748, dating from c1957-58, in Bandai's "Model Auto Series". All details of construction are as (2). On this toy note particularly the pressing for the boot-mounted spare wheel, with its bright metal disc, and the maker's applied paper label—"Model Auto Series/ Imperial Group"—on the rear parcel shelf. Length: 8·5in (21·59cm).
6 Plymouth Sedan by Ichiko, Japan, c1958. An attractive toy, with the usual brightwork details, including side trim strips and gilt

metal sidelights, this has a nicely-printed interior. It has pressed-tin wheels with rubber tyres and is friction-driven, with a mechanism producing a "siren" sound. Length: 6·375in (16·19cm).

7 Chevrolet Station Wagon; Number 716 in Bandai's "Model Auto Series". All details of construction are as (2). The maker's applied paper label on the bonnet reads: "Model Auto Series/Chevrolet Group". Note that the tinted plastic windscreen is not matched by a rear window. Length: 8·375in (21·27cm).

8 Buick Convertible; Number 723, dating from c1959, in Bandai's "Model Auto Series". All details of construction are as (2). Length: 6·125in (15·56cm).

9 New Desoto by Taiyo (Taiyo Kogyo Company), Tokyo, Japan,

c1957; it is marked "Made in Japan" on the rear parcel shelf. An applied tin trim strip in blue supplements the usual brightwork detail on this friction-drive car, which has lightly-tinted plastic front and rear screens. The wheels and tyres are rubber, with pressed-tin discs. Length: 7·875in (20cm).

10 Ford Thunderbird; Number 716, dating from c1957, in Bandai's "Model Auto Series", and heralded on the box as "America's Most Individual Car". All details of construction are as (2). Length: 8·5in (21·5cm).

11 Pontiac Convertible; Number 711, dating from c1957, in Bandai's "Model Auto Series". All details of construction are as (2). The maker's applied paper label on the automobile's boot reads: "Model

Auto Series/Pontiac Group". Length: 6·125in (15·56cm).

12 "Fairlane 500" Sedan by an unidentified Japanese maker, dating from c1957: the legend "Made in Japan" is stamped below the words "Fairlane 500" on the side of the model facing away from the camera in this photograph. For such a small toy, it is well-detailed, with a nicely-printed interior. It has rubber wheels (the front pair friction-driven) with metal discs. Length: 4·25in (10·795cm).

13-15 "Three-Style Car" by "MT" (Modern Toys; K.K. Masutoku Toy Factory), Tokyo, Japan, dating from c1958. Produced by one of the more senior Japanese makers, in operation since 1924, this set features the same body pressing in three different finishes: a Yellow

Taxi, printed "Yellow Cab" on boot top (13), a Desoto Sedan (14), and a Checker Taxi (15). Note the bright metal bumpers on these fairly basic tinplate, friction-drive cars, and the figures of drivers and passengers printed on the upper bodies. Applied metal plates at the rear — just visible on (13) and (15) in this photograph — bear road safety slogans. The rubber wheels are fitted with bright metal discs. These little cars are typical of the cheaper toys of the period: they were made of very light tinplate, permitting the kind of lithography that would not be possible on the heavier-gauge metal required under modern safety regulations. Length (each car): 5·875in (14·92cm).

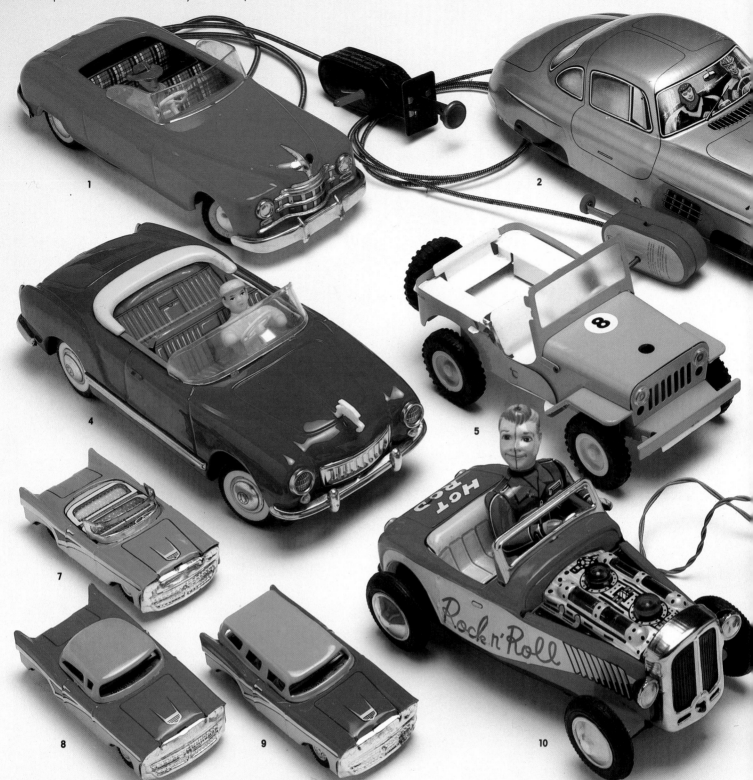

1Remote-Control Convertible by
Arnold, West Germany, made in
c1954. This is a fairly simple
tinplate toy, with pressed-tin
seats printed in a tartan pattern
and bright metal detail, including
front and rear bumpers, radiator
and mascot. The steering wheel
(right-hand drive) and wraparound
windscreen are plastic; the driver
is a composition figure. It has
plastic wheels with metal discs
and rubber whitewall tyres; the
name "Arnold" is stamped on the
whitewalls, and the Arnold trademark and the words "Made in
Western Germany" are also stamped
on the bright metal base. The line
transmitting power from the
handset consists of an outer and
an inner cable: the handle on the
handset turns the outer cable,

which joins a sprocket in the car
and acts through a crown-wheel and
piston to give forward or reverse
motion; the inner cable, activated
by the plunger on the handset,
steers the car right (pushed in)
or left (pulled out). Length:
10in (25·4cm).
2Mercedes-Benz Remote-Control
Sedan by Arnold, West Germany,
c1957. A simple but attractive
toy: the body is a single pressing,
tabbed-and-slotted to the base
plate, and all the detail—the
Mercedes star, the colourful driver
(left-hand drive) and passenger,
and the simulation of the "gull-
wing" doors that featured on the
real car—is printed. The wheels
are rubber. It is remote-controlled
by the same system as (1), and has
the same maker's marks on the

base. Length: 11·75in (29·845cm).
3Streamline Electric Sedan by
an unidentified maker, c1961; a
paper sticker on the base reads
"Made in the People's Republic of
China" in both English and Chinese.
This American-styled car (left-hand
drive), with pressed-tin fins
rather clumsily tabbed on, has
the usual bright metal detail—
radiator, bumpers, windscreen
frames, body trim, door handles
and mascot—and has a pressed-tin
interior with a plastic steering
wheel. The head- and rear-lights
are of coloured plastic and a
rear-mounted number plate of gilt
metal bears the number "10100".
The wheels, whitewalls and hubcaps
are metal, with rubber tyres.
Battery-powered, with an on/off
switch on the base, the car runs

a variable course determined by a
single pivoted wheel mounted
between its front wheels. Length:
9·5in (24.13cm).
4Convertible by "KY", People's
Republic of China, c1966: note
maker's mark on hubcaps. It has
bright metal front and rear trim,
coloured plastic side- and rearlights, and a plastic mascot above
the radiator. The pressed-tin
interior has simple printed
upholstery detail and the driver,
a rubber half-figure in Mao-style
dress, sits behind a plastic
steering wheel (left-hand drive).
The wheels and whitewalls are
plastic, with metal hubcaps and
rubber tyres. A rear-mounted
number plate reads: "ME-612".
Batteries power the near-side wheel
and the front wheels are spring-

loaded to steer in a circle.
Length: 9·75in (24·765cm).
5 Jeep by Ites (Koh-I-Noor Hardtmuth), Czechoslovakia, 1950s. This is a robust tinplate toy of simple tab-and-slot construction, featuring a perspex windscreen that folds forward and a rear-mounted spare wheel. The wheels are plastic with rubber tyres. Clockwork (note the winding shaft in the bonnet) powers the front wheels of this left-hand drive car. Length: 7in (17·78cm).
6 M101 Aston-Martin Secret Ejector Car by an unidentified Japanese maker, 1960s. Inspired by the "James Bond" films (but not described as a "James Bond" car on its box), this ingenious toy features a remotely-operated "bullet-proof" shield at the rear,

realistically-sparking machine guns at the front, crash bumpers that extend and retract, and push-button ejection of the plastic passenger through a roof trap. Power is supplied by three 1·5-volt batteries in the handset, and a two-wheel swivel in the base gives a variable course. The radiator, bumpers, lights and tinted wind-screens are plastic; the rubber wheels have plastic discs printed with details of spokes and hubcaps. The words "Made in Japan" .re stamped on the rear parcel shelf. Length: 11in (27·94cm).
7-9 Three Assorted Cars, marketed together as a boxed set with this title, by "K", Japan, 1950s-60s. These simple tinplate cars—a Convertible (7), Sedan (8) and Station Wagon (9)—are all of the

same basic construction, with rubber wheels fitted with metal discs, and are friction-powered (rear wheels). All bear the trade-mark "K" and the words "Made in Japan" on the left rear wing. A fairly scarce set. Length: (each car): 4·19in (10·64cm).
10 Hot Rod by T.N. (Nomura Toys), Japan, c1957. This colourful battery-powered toy is fully decribed at (4), pages 34-35, where it is shown with its original box. Length: 7·375in (18·73cm).
11 MGA Sports Roadster by Lincoln International, Hong Kong, 1960s. Note that the body pressing is the same as that of the MGA Hardtop at (12). It has the usual brightwork detail. The figure of the driver (right-hand drive) is rubber and the wheels, also rubber, have

metal discs. Two 1·5-volt batteries in the handset allow the car to be driven forward or in reverse, but it cannot be steered. Length: 7in (17·78cm).
12 MGA Hardtop Sports Saloon by Motorway Models; this utilizes the same body pressing as (11), with the addition of a black hardtop and pressed-tin door- and boot-handles, and is presumably a Hong Kong-made toy of the same period; its base is stamped "Empire Made". It is friction-powered (rear wheels). Length: 7in (17·78cm).
13 Jaguar XK150 by an unidentified maker—the base is stamped "Empire Made"—dating from the 1960s. With brightwork details, it has a basic pressed-tin interior and is friction-powered (rear wheels). Length: 6in (15·24cm).

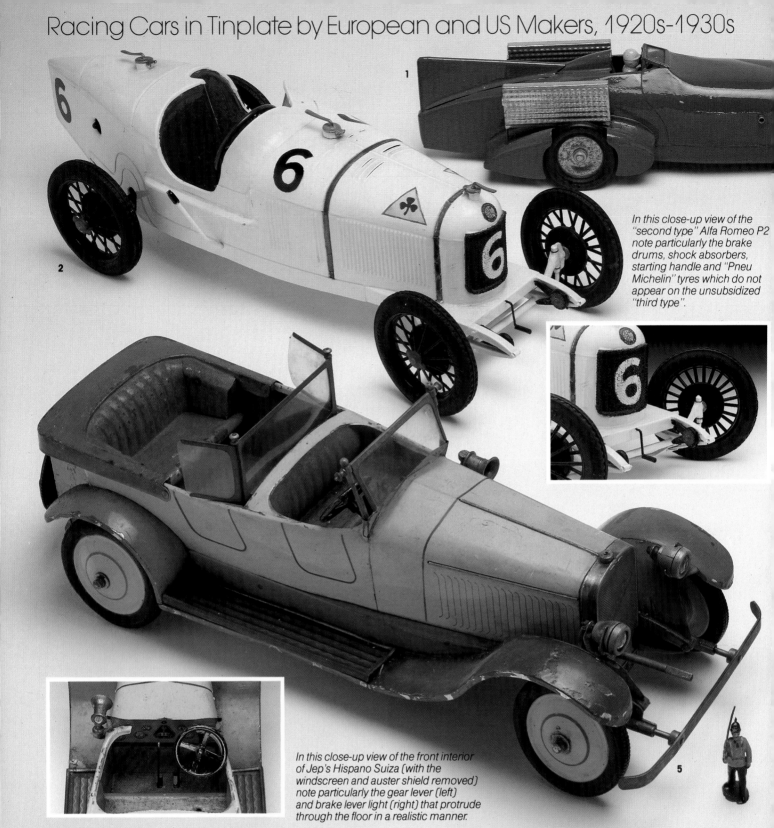

In this close-up view of the "second type" Alfa Romeo P2 note particularly the brake drums, shock absorbers, starting handle and "Pneu Michelin" tyres which do not appear on the unsubsidized "third type".

In this close-up view of the front interior of Jep's Hispano Suiza (with the windscreen and auster shield removed) note particularly the gear lever (left) and brake lever light (right) that protrude through the floor in a realistic manner.

1 "Napier Campbell" "Bluebird II" World Land Speed Record Car, by Kingsbury, New Hampshire, USA, dating from the late 1920s-early 1930s. Models of the "Bluebird" cars in which Sir Malcolm Campbell captured world land speed records for Great Britain in the 1920s and 1930s were produced by a number of makers, notably Günthermann of Germany and Kingsbury of the USA, both firms being noted for their specialization in "record cars" at this period. Shown here is Kingsbury's model of "Bluebird II" in which Campbell set a record of 206·96mph (332·99km/h) at Daytona Beach, Florida, USA, on 19 February 1928. (Günthermann produced a model of "Bluebird III" in which Campbell set new

records in 1931 and 1932.) The car is constructed of heavy-gauge tinplate—note the side-mounted radiators—and has disk wheels fitted with "Dunlop Cord" rubber tyres. The figure of the driver is cast-iron. It is fitted with a powerful clockwork motor which is wound from the underside of the car with a large, non-removable, disk-shaped key. Note that the example shown in the illustration above has been repainted. Length: 18·1in (46cm). Limited.

2 Alfa Romeo P2 Racing Car by Compagnie Industrielle du Jouet (CIJ), Paris, France. Introduced in the mid-1920s and in production for some years, this model was available until the mid-1930s, and is generally acknowledged to be one of the finest of all tinplate toys.

The example shown is of the "second type": it has treaded "Michelin" tyres, whereas the "first type" had smooth, large-section balloon tyres. Note that this specimen has been repainted and now bears the number "6": examples in original finish are (it is believed) always numbered "2" —and see further remarks on colour finishes at (3) and (4). The superb detail includes leather straps and accurately-modelled louvres on the bonnet, a fine-mesh radiator grille with a replica Alfa Romeo badge above and a starting-handle below, opening filler caps, detailed suspension, operating handbrake, and front-wheel steering. Note the shock absorbers and brake drums on the wire-spoked wheels. The aperture

for the key to wind the powerful clockwork motor is visible near the tail. The model was originally priced at £1 5s 0d (£1.25, $1.77). Length: 20·9in (53cm). Limited.

3 Alfa Romeo P2 Racing Car by CIJ: a further example of the "second type"; this view showing the exhaust pipe. Like (2), this specimen has been repainted: it bears the number "4" instead of the original "2". The Alfa Romeo was originally issued in a choice of three colour finishes, corresponding to the national colours of France (blue), Italy (red), and Germany (white, or silver). By the time of the "second type" in c1929, however, this very popular model was also available in green, lilac, and a number of other colours. Limited.

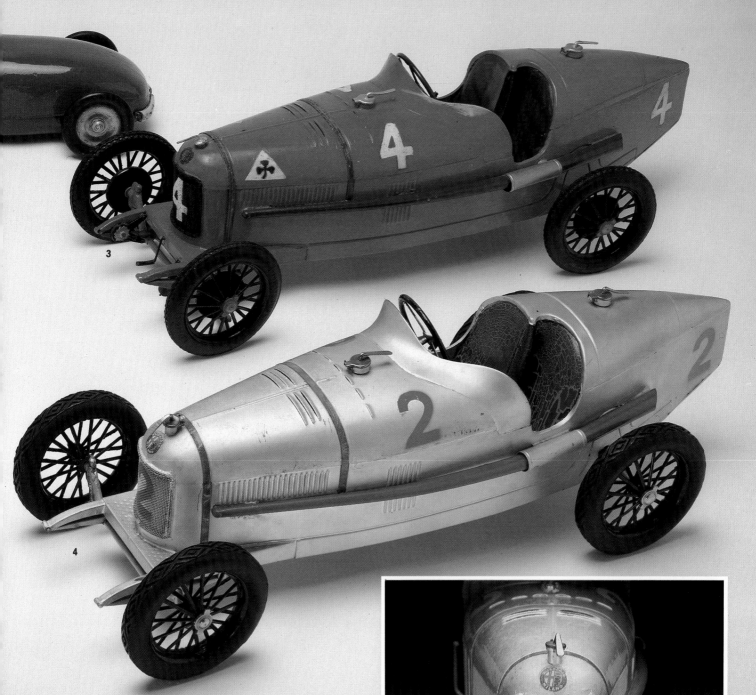

Left: Comparison of the "second type" (left) and "third type" Alfa Romeo P2 wheels. Note the eared "knock-off" wheel nuts. The front view of the "third type" (right) shows detail of the rack-and-pinion steering, operating from the steering wheel.

4 Alfa Romeo P2 Racing Car by CIJ: a "third type" model dating from the mid-1930s and, in comparison with (2) and (3), lacking such detail as the starting-handle, brake drums, and shock absorbers. However, this example is in its original finish, numbered "2" and, in this case, in the silver racing livery of Germany. Note that it has large-section rubber tyres bearing no maker's name: (2) and (3) have "Michelin" tyres. By the time this

version appeared, the tyre and shock-absorber manufacturers who had formerly subsidised the toy as an advertisement for their products had withdrawn their support and, in consequence, the price of the toy had risen to £1 15s 0d (£1.75, $2.48). However, it would appear that, since the toy was comparatively expensive, it was better-preserved than most: although the Alfa Romeo is now eagerly sought by collectors, and may change hands at prices in excess of £750 ($1,065), examples in reasonable condition still appear regularly at auctions, swap-meets, and auto-jumbles. Limited.

5 Hispano Suiza Touring Car by Jep (Jouets en Paris), Paris, France, dating from c1929 — when, in fact, the maker was still known

as Jouets de Paris (J de P), the change to "Jep" being made in 1932. Jep's famous Rolls Royce Phantom I model of c1928 is shown at (5) on *pages 34-35*, and the almost equally fine car shown here is another "classic" automotive toy (and much scarcer) than the Alfa Romeo P2). Constructed of tinplate, with soldered joints, it features such detail as a sprung front bumper, a fine-mesh radiator with the marque

name applied, working electric lamps, steering from the steering-wheel via a worm mechanism, an opening windscreen and an auster (rear seat) shield, and disk wheels with brake drums, fitted with treaded rubber tyres. Its powerful clockwork motor (note the long winding-shaft beneath the radiator) is fitted with operating levers for the brake and forward and reverse gears. Length: 20·47in (52cm). Rare.

Because racing and record-breaking cars appealed strongly to adult buyers as well as to children, toy manufacturers took some trouble to keep pace with developments in the world of speed. "Record" cars were particularly popular in the late 1920s and 1930s, when the world land speed record changed hands fairly frequently; after World War II, emphasis shifted towards motor racing.

All the cars shown on this spread were photographed at the London Toy and Model Museum.

1 "Super Racer" by a Japanese maker; a large scale tinplate racing car based on the type driven on the motor speedways of the USA, such as Indianapolis, dating from the

late 1950s. This car is of fairly good quality: note such detail as the tin windscreen, exterior exhaust for a four-cylinder engine, and large section rubber tyres (with larger diameter tyres at the rear). Printed detail includes advertising for "Shell" and "BP" and for the Montlhéry (France) racing circuit. Length: 18·5in (47cm).
2 "Super Racer" by Wo Co, German Federal Republic; very similar to the Japanese-made car at (1) and again dating from the 1950s. Note, however, that the wheels, with simulated "knock-off" hubcaps, and the rubber tyres, marked "Dunlop", differ considerably from those of (1). Again, "Shell" is advertised, also Monza (Italy) racing circuit. Length: 18·75in (48cm).
3 "Railton" Record Car by a British

maker, c1950, a tinplate, clockwork-driven model of a car used in record-breaking attempts by John Cobb before and after World War II. Note the facsimile autograph of the driver across the body. In this car, known post-War as the "Mobil Special", Cobb raised the world land speed record to 394mph (634km/h) in 1947: the crossed flags on the nose indicate that this British car made its record run at an American venue. Length: 10·125in (26cm).
4 Racing Car by Mettoy Co Limited, Britain, c1950. Mettoy produced a large range of cheap, lightweight tinplate vehicles like this car, with its simple clockwork mechanism (note fixed winder). The driver is barely three-dimensional; basic detail includes a cutaway

windscreen and pressed-tin wheels and tyres with a rather unusual printed tread pattern. Length: 12in (30·5cm). Common.
5 "Sunbeam Silver Bullet" Record Car by Günthermann, Nuremburg, Germany, c1930; a fine, tinplate, clockwork-driven model. Note the brake lever beside the cockpit. Günthermann made at least three versions of this car: variations from the example shown include one with British and American flags on the nose cowling and the "Silver Bullet" legend on the bonnet sides, and a chromium-plated version (the latter is now scarce). Note that this car does not bear a Günthermann trademark: it is simply marked "Foreign". Length: 22in (56cm). Limited.
6 M.G. Record Car by a British

maker, c1950; a friction-drive tinplate model of the car in which Goldie Gardner (note facsimile autograph) set endurance records in Belgium. The model is fairly well detailed, with off-set cockpit and crossed British and Belgian flags on the nose, but is finished in red: the real car was in "M.G. green". Length: 9·875in (25cm).

7 "Bluebird" Record Car; a British maker's version, late 1930s, of the 1935 model (there were several "Bluebird" marques) of Sir Malcolm Campbell's land speed record car. Models of the various Bluebirds were produced by British, American (Kingsbury), and German (Günthermann)—see (10)—makers. The dual rear wheels and streamlined body of this tinplate, clockwork-drive car

are reasonably faithful to the original, but the cockpit, in reality slightly off-set, is in a central position. Note facsimile autograph on body. Length: 16in (41cm).

8 Racing Car by Jouets en Paris (Jep), France, c1950; a simple clockwork-driven model in light-weight tinplate from a company famed for its large and impressive toy cars of the pre-World War II period. The wheels are diecast; the tyres (and also the driver's helmeted head) are rubber. Length: 12·25in (31cm).

9 "Golden Arrow" Record Car by Günthermann, Germany, c1929; another of this maker's range of record cars—see also (5) and (10). This fine tinplate model of the car in which Sir Henry Segrave broke the land speed record in March 1929

has a separately-applied tinplate Union Jack on its tailfin, a strikingly faired bonnet, a brake for its clock-work mechanism (visible on far side of cockpit), and pressed tin wheels and tyres. The tinplate driver is missing from this example. Length: 21in (53cm).

10 "Bluebird" by Günthermann, Germany (note "Foreign" marking beneath "Bluebird" legend), c1930; a smaller edition of the maker's standard 20in (51cm) version of one of Campbell's record cars, and showing an earlier "Bluebird" marque than the British-made example at (7). In tinplate, it is clockwork-powered (note the permanent winder forward of the rear wheel) and has lithographed British and US flags on its tailfin and radiator cowling.

Length: 12·375in (31·5cm). Limited.

11 Mercedes Grand Prix Car by Schuco, Germany, later 1930s. This ingenious little clockwork car has exposed working differential and rack-and-pinion steering, and rubber-tyred wheels with printed spokes: the sides of the wheels have different-coloured spokes for timed wheel-changes! It is key-wound, but with a keyless winding facility, and was supplied with a tool kit. Available in various colours —here in the silver racing colours of Germany—and with different numbers, it was also produced after World War II; later models have unspoked wheels. Because of its long production life, this near-classic toy is still relatively common. Length: 5·5in (14cm).

Diecast Cars by Dinky Toys, Britain and France, 1934-1950

1 Ambulance by Dinky Toys, Great Britain; Dinky Toys Reference Number (DT No) 30f. Shown here is the fourth version, dating from 1947-48, of a model first issued in August 1935. The identification points of the various versions are: (1935-38) red-and-grey body, moulded chassis, plain radiator and open side windows; (1938-40) black-and-grey body, moulded chassis, radiator with badge, open side windows; (1947-48), as seen, with cream body, black moulded chassis, no side windows. All versions have red crosses on the sides. Both the pre-World War II versions are rare; both post-War versions are quite common. Length: 3·898in (99mm).

2 Ambulance; DT No 24a. This is the original version of the model first issued in April 1934 and available in this form until 1938. It appeared in cream-and-red or grey-and-red and had a criss-cross chassis and a plain radiator. The second version, issued in 1938-40, was made in green-and-red or grey-and-red and had a radiator with a badge. Both versions are rare. Length: 4·016in (102mm).

3-5 Daimler; DT No 30c. This model was first issued in August 1935 and was made until 1940 in green, fawn, brown and light blue body finishes. It was reissued in 1946, remaining available until 1950, in green-and-black (3), cream-and-black (4), and brown-and-black (5), and possibly in other colours. The pre-War version has an open chassis; the post-War version may be found with an open chassis or a plain chassis. The pre-War version is rare; the post-War version is limited. Length: 3·858in (98mm).

6-8 Vauxhall; DT No 30d. Shown here are three examples, displaying colour variations, of the final version, dating from 1946-48, of a long-lived model. The first version, issued in 1935 and available until 1938, is identifiable by its brown open chassis and its wing-mounted spare wheel. The second version, made in 1937-38, has no spare wheel. The third version, made in 1938-40, has a radiator with a badge, and may be found with or without a spare wheel. The fourth version, as shown, is the only one made with a black (open or plain) chassis; it has no spare wheel. The three pre-War versions are rare; the post-War version is of limited availability Length: 3·858in (98mm).

9 Chrysler "Airflow" Saloon by Dinky Toys, Great Britain. This model was announced as DT No 32 in January 1935, but by June 1935 it had appeared as DT No 30a. A one-piece casting with no chassis, it appeared in two versions. The first version, 1935-40, was made in blue or green. The second version, reissued in 1946 and available until 1948, was made in blue, cream or green. The pre-War version is rare; the post-War version is scarce. Length: 4·055in (103mm).

10-11 Austin 7 Saloon; DT No 35a. This model was first issued in 1936 and was available in grey only until 1940; these pre-War examples have white solid rubber wheels. It was reissued in 1946

and remained available until 1948; post-War versions, like the two shown here, have black solid rubber wheels. Both versions are fairly scarce. Length: 2·008in (51mm).

12-13 Austin 7 Tourer; DT No 35d. First issued in 1938, this appeared up to 1940 in several colours, with a wire windscreen and white solid rubber wheels. It was reissued in 1946-48, as shown, lacking the windscreen and with black solid rubber wheels. Both versions are limited. Length: 1·969in (50mm).

14 Grand Sport (4-Seater) by Dinky Toys, France; French Dinky Toys Reference Number (FDT No) 24g, dating from 1935-48. This is the French-made version of the Sports Tourer (4-Seater), second version, issued by Dinky Toys, Great Britain, in 1938-40. Note that the French

models shown at (14-17) have solid wheels and tyres of post-1940 type. Length: 3·858in (98mm).

15 Grand Sport Coupé; FDT No 24f: the French-made version of the Sportsman's Coupé (second version) made in Britain in 1938-40. Length: 3·937in (100mm).

16 Grand Sport (2-Seater); FDT No 24h: the French-made version of the Sports Tourer (2-Seater), second version, made in Britain in 1938-40. Length: 3·858in (98mm).

17 Limousine; FDT No 24b: the French-made version of the model made with same name and number in Britain in 1938-40 (second version). Length: 3·858in (98mm).

18-20 Rolls Royce by Dinky Toys, Great Britain; DT No 30b. This model was first issued in August

1935 and was made in various colours, with an open chassis, until 1940. It was reissued, as shown, in various colours, with black open or plain chassis, in 1946-50. The pre-War version is rare; the post-War version is limited. Length: 3·976in (101mm).

21 Fiat (2-Seater) Saloon by Dinky Toys, France; FDT No 35a. This model, first issued in July 1939, was marketed in France as the Simca 5 (since the Fiat 500 "Topolino" was known by that designation in France, where it was manufactured under licence by Simca) and in Britain as a Fiat, DT No 35az. It has rubber wheels and is a simple one-piece casting with no base plate. Length: 2·323in (59mm).

22 Vogue Saloon; FDT No 24d: the

French version of the model made in Britain under the same name and number in 1938-40 (second version). Note that this and (23) are fitted with wheels and tyres of pre-1940 type. Length: 4·016in (102mm).

23 Super Streamline Saloon; FDT No 24e: the French version of the model made in Britain under the same name and reference number in 1938-40 (second version). Length: 3·819in (97mm).

24 Peugeot Car; FDT No 24k. First issued in July 1939 and available only until 1940, this model was marketed in France as the Peugeot 402 and in Great Britain as the Peugeot Car, DT No 24kz; see also (21). Appearing only in red finish, as shown, it has a tinplate front bumper. Length: 3·74in (95mm).

Inset: *(Right) A modern copy of the Limousine, DT No 24b; a "24 Series" model first issued in 1934 (although the absence of a wing-mounted spare wheel marks this example as a copy of the later version, issued in 1938). (Left) The "criss-cross" chassis, as seen in this modern copy of the "24 Series" Sportsman's Coupé, DT No 24f, was used only from 1934 to 1938.*

1

2

3

4

16

17

18

All the toy cars of the Dinky Toys "36 Series" are shown here. The range was announced in July 1938, when all six models of British "quality" cars of the time became available either separately or as a complete set, priced then at 5s 6d (27½p, 33c). Dinky based these models on the body castings of the "24 Series", first issued in 1934, but without the wing-mounted spare wheels that featured in the earlier series, and with the notable addition of "make" radiators in place of a universal type. As noted below, in the pre-War examples provision was made for fitting figures (tinplate in the closed cars; cast metal in the open models) of drivers and passengers. Not all pre-War versions of the series

were fitted with such figures, and examples in which they are present are now very highly valued by collectors of Dinky Toys.

1-2 Rover Saloon, Dinky Toys Reference Number (DT No) 36d. The cars shown here are post-World War II versions of the model made from 1938 to 1940 as the Rover Streamlined Saloon, under the same reference number. The post-War version, made from 1946 to 1948, was produced, as seen here, with a blue (1) or green (2) body on a black moulded chassis. The pre-War version was produced with a green or black body on a green chassis, or in two-tone red. Its moulded chassis was pierced to accommodate the tinplate figures of a driver and passenger (although

these figures were not always fitted); this feature was absent from the post-War version. Both versions were fitted with "make" radiators; note the Rover badge visible at (1). The pre-War version complete with figures is very rare—and neither the pre-War version without figures nor the post-War version shown here is common. Note that the lengths given for this car and others here are taken from post-War examples. Because of metal fatigue, pre-War cars may now prove to be as much as 0·275in (7mm) long than post-War examples. Length: 3·7in (94mm).

3-5 Bentley Two-Seater Sports Coupé, DT No 36b. This model first appeared in July 1938, when it was priced at 11d (4½p, 5c), and remained in production until 1940.

The examples shown here, however, are post-War versions, produced between 1946 and 1948. The pre-War version was made with a green and black or cream and black body (other colours may also have been used) and had a base plate pierced with slots to accommodate the tinplate figures of driver and passenger (not always fitted). This feature did not appear in the post-War models, which were made with green (5), grey, cream (3) or blue (4) bodies (again, other colours may have been used). Both versions had a moulded chassis. The rarest examples are those complete with driver and passenger; the pre-War version without figures may prove hard to find, but post-War versions are not uncommon. Length: 3·661in (93mm).

6-10 Armstrong-Siddeley Limousine, DT No 36a. This model was first issued in July 1938, at the then standard price for "36 Series" models of 11d (4½p, 5c), and remained in production until 1940. Like the other models in the series, it was reissued under the same reference number in 1946-48. The pre-War version was produced with a blue or brown and black body; the post-War version, as seen here, in green (6), maroon (7), blue (8-9) or grey (10). Both versions had a moulded chassis, but in the pre-War model the base plate was pierced with slots to accommodate the tinplate figure of driver and passenger (or footman, since these were "quality" cars!). As usual, models complete with figures are the most valuable.

Length: 3·819in (97mm).

11-12 British Salmson (Four-Seater Sports), DT No 36f. The pre-War version, issued from July 1938 to 1940, was produced with a red and brown or a two-tone green body; the post-War version, as seen here, produced in 1946-48, had a green (11) or grey (12) body on a black chassis. Both versions had a moulded chassis and a solid windscreen; in the pre-War model, the front seat was pierced with a hole to accommodate the peg-in diecast figure of a driver. The post-War version has no such hole and has a cast-in steering wheel. Again, the pre-War version with driver is very rare, and all versions of the four-seater Salmson may prove hard to find. Length: 3·779in (96mm).

13-15 British Salmson (Two-Seater Sports), DT No 36e. The pre-War version, made in 1938-40, appeared in red and black, blue and black, or with a grey body on a red moulded chassis (other colours may also be found); the post-War model, as seen here, was made only in red (13) or blue (14-15), on a black moulded chassis, in 1946-48. Some, but not all, pre-War versions were made with a rubber spare wheel on the right hand side; the spare wheel was never fitted on post-War models. The seat of the pre-War model was pierced with a hole for a peg-in diecast driver and, as usual, the pre-War model with driver is now rare and valuable; even without the driver it is hard to find. The solid windscreen is common to all versions, but only the post-War model has a cast-in steering wheel. Length: 3·661in (93mm).

16-18 Humber Vogue, DT No 36c. The pre-War version, produced in 1938-40, was made in grey and black, two-tone green, and probably in other colours; the post-War model, as shown, was made in 1946-48 in green and black, blue and black (16), brown and black (17) and grey and black (18). In the pre-War version the moulded chassis was slotted for the tinplate figures of a driver and passenger; as usual, this feature was absent in the moulded chassis of the post-War model. The model complete with tinplate figures is rare and valuable and no pre-War version of this car is at all common. Length: 3·819in (97mm).

Above: *A modern copy of the Triumph Dolomite Sports Coupé announced in 1939 as No 38e of Dinky's "38 Series". War halted production and this model was never issued: it was replaced in 1946 by the Armstrong-Siddeley shown at (1-2).*

1-2 Armstrong-Siddeley Coupé, Dinky Toys Reference Number (DT No) 38e. This model was introduced in December 1946, replacing the planned Triumph Dolomite (see *Inset*) in the "38 Series". It was Dinky's first model of a car of post-World War II manufacture, and remained in production until late 1949 or early 1950. It has a plastic windscreen and detachable rubber tyres; the black-painted tinplate base bears the maker's name and "Armstrong-Siddeley". This model may prove hard to find. Length: 3·78in (96mm).

3-4 Lagonda Sports Coupé, DT No 38c. This model was introduced in April 1946 and was deleted from the catalogue in 1950. It was made in grey with grey seats (3), in green with matt black seats (4),

and in maroon with black seats. The black-painted base plate bears the maker's name and "Lagonda". Again it has a plastic windscreen and detachable rubber tyres; the separately-cast steering wheel may be found in both solid and open forms. This is quite a scarce model. Length: 4·016in (102mm).

5-7 Sunbeam-Talbot Sports, DT No 38b. This model was announced in June 1939, along with five other "38 Series" sports cars: the Frazer-Nash B.M.W., No 38a, see (10-12); Lagonda, 38c (3-4); Alvis, 38d (8-9); Triumph Dolomite, 38e, (Inset); and Jaguar, 38f (13-15). Of these, only the Frazer-Nash B.M.W., Sunbeam-Talbot and Alvis were in production, probably only in small numbers, before World War II halted production in 1940. The

model shown here was reissued in 1946 and deleted in 1949. Both pre- and post-War versions were made in various colous, of which three variations are shown here, with matt-painted tonneau covers. The only major difference between pre- and post-War versions is that the former have unpainted tinplate base plates and the latter black-painted base plates; in both cases they bear the maker's name and "Sunbeam-Talbot". In post-War versions the steering wheel may be solid or open; both versions have a plastic windscreen, slotted into the base, and rubber tyres. Neither is common. Length: 3·622in (92mm).

8-9 Alvis Sports Tourer, DT No 38d. The production history of this "38 Series" sports car is the same as that of the Sunbeam-Talbot

Sports (5-7). Again, it was made in a number of colour schemes and had a plastic windscreen and detachable rubber tyres. Pre-War versions have a bare metal base plate, post-War versions a black-painted one, in both cases bearing the maker's name and "Alvis". In post-War models the steering wheel may be solid or open. As in the Lagonda (3-4), Sunbeam-Talbot (5-7) and Jaguar (13-15), the head-lights are separately cast and are set into the front wings, while the steering wheels are also separate castings: both features are liable to be lost or damaged. All versions of the Alvis are fairly scarce. Length: 3·74in (95mm).

10-12 Frazer-Nash B.M.W. Sports Car, DT No 38a; production history as (5-7) and (8-9). Neither pre-

nor post-War versions are easy to find. Length: 3·228in (82mm).

13-15 Jaguar Sports Car, DT No 38f. This model of the famous "SS 100" was announced, as noted above, in June 1939, but it is probable that none was made before its "re-issue" in November 1946. It was deleted in 1949. Made in at least three colours, with the contrasting seats typical of the series, it had a black-painted base plate bearing the maker's name and "Jaguar". Note particularly the two small plastic windscreens. Like most models in the "38 Series", this is fairly scarce. Length: 3·15in (80mm).

16 Austin A90 Atlantic, DT No 106. This was originally issued in April 1951 as the Austin Atlantic Convertible, No 140a; it was re-numbered in 1954 and remained in production until 1958. It was made in blue, as seen, black or pink, and is comparatively scarce. Length: 3·74in (95mm).

17 Sunbeam Alpine (Competition Finish), DT No 107. This was first issued in November 1955 and was deleted in 1959. It was made with a blue body with the racing number "26", as seen, and in pink with the number "34". Like (18-21), it was later issued in "touring finish" —see (22). It is quite scarce. Length: 3·70in (94mm).

18 M.G. Midget (Competition Finish), DT No 108. First issued in April 1955, this model of an M.G. TF was deleted in 1959. It was made with a white body numbered "28", as shown, or in red numbered "24"; see also (22). Again, quite a scarce item. Length: 3·268in (83mm).

19 Austin Healey 100 (Competition Finish), DT No 109. First issued in June 1955 and deleted in 1959, this was produced in yellow numbered "21", as shown, or in cream numbered "23". It is quite scarce. Length: 3·346in (85mm).

20 Aston Martin DB3S (Competition Finish), DT No 110. Issued in March 1956, and made in green with the number "22", as shown, this model differed from the others in the series in having no plastic windscreen. It was deleted in 1959. It is more easily found than the other sports cars shown on this spread. Length: 3·425in (87mm).

21 Triumph T.R.2 (Competition Finish), DT No 111. Introduced in February 1956, this model was made in pink with the number "29", as shown, or in turquoise with the number "25". It was deleted in 1959. Again, it may prove hard to find. Length: 3·307in (84mm).

22 M.G. Midget (Touring Finish), DT No 102. First issued in August 1957, and made in green, as shown, or yellow, this was the touring version, with a driver in civilian clothes rather than racing overalls, and bearing no racing number, of the M.G Midget, No 108, see (18). The Sunbeam Alpine (17), Austin Healey 100 (19), Aston Martin DB3S (20), and Triumph T.R.2 (21) were issued in similar "touring versions" in 1957, numbered DT No 101, 103, 104 and 105 respectively. All were deleted in 1960. Like the version in competition finish, this MG in touring finish is fairly scarce. Length: 3·268in (83mm).

1-2 Packard Super 8 Touring Sedan Car, Dinky Toys Reference Number (DT No) 39a. This model was first announced in June-July 1939 as part of the "39 Series" set, along with the Oldsmobile Six Sedan Car (see 3-4); the Lincoln Zephyr Coupé (5-6); the Buick Viceroy Saloon Car (7-8); the Chrysler Royal Sedan (9-10); and the Studebaker State Commander Saloon Car (11-12). It is probable that these models were not, in fact, issued until 1940, and by 1941 all production had been ended by World War II. However, the set was re-issued, with the changes detailed below, in 1946 and remained available until 1949-50. All the cars in the set could, of course, be purchased as separate items. When first issued, priced at 10d

(4p, 5c) each pre-War, these constituted Dinky's first set of American cars and, another innovation, each had its name stamped on the base plate. The two versions of the Packard Super 8 shown here date from 1946-50, when the model was issued in brown (1) or green (2), with silver trim, with a black-painted tinplate base plate. The pre-War version, issued in brown or grey, with silver trim, had an unpainted tinplate base plate. Both versions had an open chassis and detachable rubber tyres (these two features being common to all the models in the series), a moulded spare wheel on the left wing, and separately-cast headlights. Neither version is particularly easy to find, the pre-War car being

considerably the rarer. Length: 4·21in (107mm).
3-4 Oldsmobile Six Sedan Car, DT No 39b; production history as (1-2). The post-War version was made in blue (3), grey (4), green or brown finish, with silver trim, and had a black-painted tinplate base plate. The pre-War version was issued in blue or green with silver trim and had an unpainted base plate. The pre-War version is scarce; post-War examples are quite scarce. Length: 3·937in (100mm).
5-6 Lincoln Zephyr Coupé, DT No 39c; production history as (1-2). The post-War version was available in brown (5) or grey (6) and had a black-painted tinplate base plate; the pre-War version was available in grey, brown or cream and had an unpainted base plate. Again, the

pre-War version is quite rare, and even the post-War version is hard to find. Length: 4·17in (106mm).
7-8 Buick Viceroy Saloon Car, DT No 39d; production history as (1-2), but note that production of this model may have ended in 1949. The pre-War version was issued in maroon (7) or grey (8) finish, with an unpainted base plate; the post-War version appeared in brown, green or maroon, with black-painted base plate. As in (1-2), both versions had a moulded spare wheel and separately-cast headlights. Current availability of this car is as (5-6). Length: 4·055in (103mm).
9-10 Chrysler Royal Sedan, DT No 39e; production history as (1-2), but again production may have ended in 1949. The pre-War version was made in blue, green (9), grey

Inset: *The unpainted, bare metal base plate distinguishes this model as a pre-War version of the Chrysler Royal Sedan; Number 39e of Dinky Toys' "39 Series".*

(10), or yellow finish, with an unpainted base plate; the post-War version appeared in blue, cream or grey, with a black-painted base plate. Current availability as (5-6). Length: 4·17in (106mm).

11-12 Studebaker State Commander Saloon Car, DT No 39f; production history as (1-2), but production may have ended in 1949. The pre-War version was made in green (11), dark grey or yellow, with unpainted base plate; the post-War version in green, blue (12), brown or grey, with black-painted base plate. Current availability as (5-6). Length: 4·055in (103mm).

13 Estate Car, DT No 27f. This model was first issued in February 1950, when it was priced at 2s 10d (14p, 17c) and was classified as one of Dinky's series of farm

vehicles; it was renumbered 344 in 1954 and remained in production until 1956. It was issued only as shown here, with a fawn body and brown simulated-wood side panels. This car should not be too hard to find. Length: 4·134in (105mm).

14-15 Ford Fordor Sedan, DT No 139a. This model was first issued in August 1949, priced at 2s 6d (12½p, 15c), when it may have been intended as the first of a new series—the "139 Series" of US cars to follow the "39 Series" that was then beginning to go out of production; see also (16-17). It was renumbered 170 in 1954 and remained in production until 1959. The same casting was used for the Ford Fordor US Army Staff Car, in matt green finish with a white star on the bonnet, which was made

in 1957-58 for the US market (some examples appear to have been sold in the UK). It appeared in 1949-54 with a red or brown body; in 1954-56 with a red, green (14) or yellow (15) body; and in 1956-59 in two-tone finish, either cream-and-red or pink-and-blue. The US Army Staff Car version is rare in the UK; the brown-finished 1949-54 version may be a little harder to find than the others, while the two-tone versions are the most common. Length: 4·016in (102mm).

16-17 Hudson Commodore Sedan, DT No 139b. This model was first issued in July 1950, was renumbered 171 in 1954 and was deleted in 1958. It was issued in 1950-56 in two-tone finish, either maroon-and-fawn (16) or fawn-and-blue (17), and in 1956-58 in either red-and-

blue or blue-and-grey. The later versions may prove harder to find. Length: 4·37 (111mm).

18-19 Studebaker Land Cruiser, DT No 172. This model was issued in April 1954, just one month after Dinky Toys abandoned its former practice of giving each model a letter as well as a number. Priced initially at 2s 8d (13p, 16c), it was issued until July 1956 in green or blue (18) finish, and from then until 1958, when it went out of production, in two-tone finish, either maroon-and-cream or fawn-and-brown (19). On the earlier versions, the tinplate base is stamped with the maker's name and "Studebaker"; later versions also bear the number "172". In neither case should it be too hard to find. Length: 4·21in (107mm).

Inset (above): *Variations in the chassis of the Standard Vanguard Saloon, DT No 40e (renumbered 153 in 1955); see also notes at (11-14) below. In both cases the chassis of the first version (1948-50) is shown, with open rear wheel arches and the information on the tinplate base plate stamped in small letters – but note the variation in the method used to secure the rear axle of the model.*

1-4 Riley Saloon, Dinky Toys Reference Number (DT No) 40a. This was the first model in the "40 Series" of British cars (the "39 Series" consisted of models of American cars; see *pages 54-55)* and was issued in July 1947. It was renumbered 158 in 1955 and remained in production until 1960.

Between 1947 and 1955 the model was issued in grey (1), blue (2), cream (3) or green (4) finish, with a tinplate base plate stamped with the maker's name and model designation in small capital letters. Between March 1954 and 1960 (there was some overlap between the versions, as is the case with other models described here) it appeared in blue or cream, with the letters on the base plate in large letters. See also *Inset* (top right). Neither version should be too hard to find. Length: 3·66in (93mm).

5-6 Triumph 1800 Saloon, DT No 40b. The second model in the "40 Series", this was first issued in July 1948. The first version, made only in 1948-49 and in fawn, blue or grey finish, had its rear axle

held in place by pillars on either side and had a tinplate base plate stamped with the maker's name and the number "40B". The second version, made between 1949 and 1955, appeared in the same colours but had its rear axle held in place by the base plate, which was stamped only with the maker's name. In 1955 the model was renumbered 151, and thereafter appeared in blue (5) or brown (6) until 1960, with a base plate stamped with the maker's name and "Triumph". The first and second versions are more highly valued. Length: 3·583in (91mm).

7-10 Austin Devon Saloon, DT No 40d. The third car in the "40 Series" (the number 40c was not used), this appeared in January 1949. It was made in blue (7),

green (8) or maroon (9) finish, with a base plate stamped with the maker's name and "40D", until 1955, when it was renumbered 152. In 1954-56 it appeared in maroon or blue, with the base plate stamped with the maker's name and "Austin Devon". From August 1956 until production ended in 1960, it was made in two-tone finishes, either blue-and-yellow (10) or grey-and-cerise, the base plate being the same. No version is particularly rare. Length: 3·346in (85mm).

11-14 Standard Vanguard Saloon, DT No 40e. The fourth car in the "40 Series", this was first issued in November 1948. The first version –as seen at (11) and (12)– had open rear wheel arches; a plain boot, as seen at (12); and the maker's name, "Vanguard", and

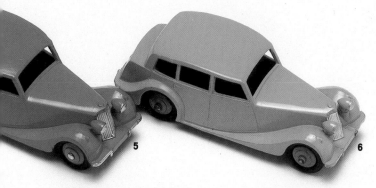

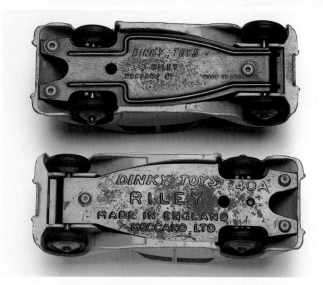

Inset (right): *A view of the differing base plates of the Riley Saloon, DT No 40a (renumbered 158 in 1955); see also notes at (1-4) below. (Top) The tinplate base plate of the first version, issued from July 1947 until 1955, has the maker's and model's names stamped in small letters. (Bottom) On the second version, issued from March 1954 until 1960, the information is stamped in large letters.*

sometimes "40E", stamped on the base in small letters. This version appeared in brown or maroon until April 1950. The second version, finished in fawn or blue, was made between April 1950 and 1955. As seen at (13), it had covered rear wheel housings. The model was renumbered 153 in 1955, and the third version, made from 1954 until 1960, appeared in blue, cream or fawn (14). This had a ridge running horizontally across the boot, base plate information in large letters, and covered rear wheel housings. The first and second versions are not easy to find. Length: 3·583in (91mm).

15 Jaguar XK 120, DT No 157. This was first issued in March 1954 and appeared in green, white or yellow until March 1956. From that date

it was issued in two-tone finish, either cerise-and-turquoise or grey-and-yellow, until production ended in 1962. The two-tone versions are easier to find. Length: 3·819in (97mm).

16 Austin Somerset, DT No 40j. This "40 Series" model first appeared in June 1949 and was made in red or blue, with a base plate stamped with the maker's name, "Austin Somerset" and "40J", until 1955, when it was renumbered 161. It appeared from 1954 until August 1956 in blue only, the base plate carrying the new number. Both versions are of average availability. Length: 3·504in (89mm).

17-18 Rover 75 Saloon, DT No 140b. This model was first issued in April 1951 and was made in maroon (18) only until 1954, when it

was renumbered 156. From May 1954 until January 1956 it was issued in cream (17) only, and from January 1956 until production ended in 1960 in two-tone finish, blue-and-cream or two-tone green. Base plates of the first and second versions are stamped with the maker's name and "Rover 75"; on the third version, the number "156" sometimes appears. Length: 3·976in (101mm).

19-20 Hillman Minx Saloon, DT No 40f. This "40 Series" model was first issued in February 1951 and appeared in light green, dark green, light brown and dark brown until 1955, when it was renumbered 154. From May 1954 until September 1956 it was made in green (19) or brown (20), and from September 1956 until production

ended in 1958 in two-tone finish, either green-and-yellow or cerise-and-blue. Base plate details as (17-18). Length: 3·465in (88mm).

21-22 Morris Oxford Saloon, DT No 40g. First issued in June 1950, this "40 Series" model appeared in green or grey-and-fawn until 1955, when it was renumbered 159. The base plate of the first version is stamped only with the maker's name. From March 1954 until January 1956 it appeared in fawn (21) or green (22), and thereafter, until production ended in 1960, in two-tone finish, either green-and-cream or white-and-red. The base plates of the second and third versions are stamped with the maker's name and "Morris Oxford". The two-tone versions are scarcest. Length: 3·66in (93mm).

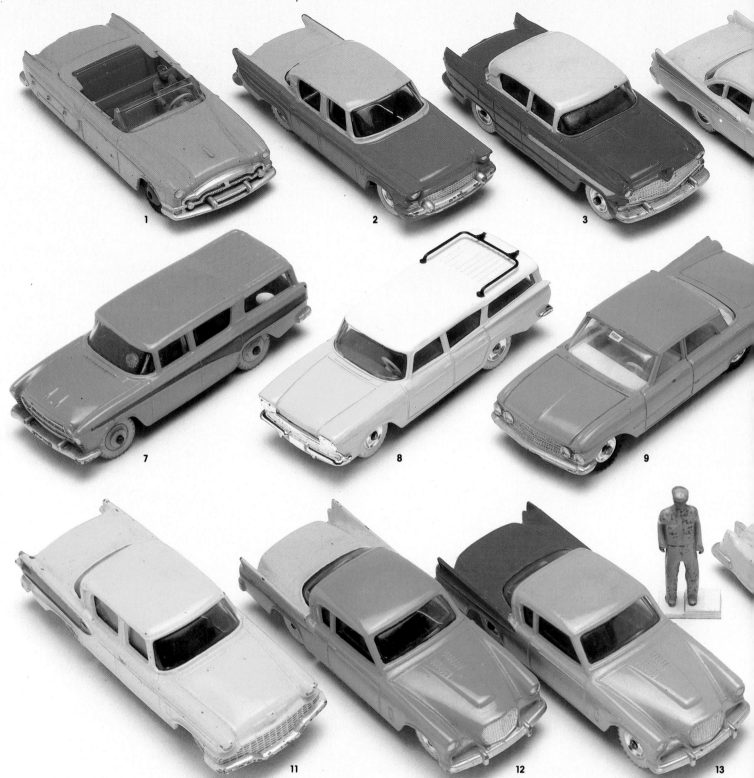

1 Packard Convertible by Dinky Toys, Great Britain; Dinky Toys Reference Number (DT No) 132. This model was first issued in November 1955 and remained available until 1961. It was made in fawn, cream or light green body finish and featured a detailed interior, with separately-cast steering wheel and the figure of a driver (left-hand drive),and a plastic windscreen. Its tinplate base is stamped with the maker's name, "132", and "Packard". This is now an item of limited availability. Length: 4·488in (114mm).

2 Packard Clipper, DT No 180; first issued in September 1958 and available until 1963. Made in grey-and-orange, fawn-and-pink, and possibly in other colours, it is fitted with windows (which Dinky

then stressed as a special feature, Corgi Toys with windows having been marketed since 1956). The tinplate base bears the maker's name, "180" and "Packard Clipper". Limited. Length: 4·409in (112mm).

3 Hudson Hornet, DT No 174; note that the same number was later given to the Ford Mercury Cougar of 1969-72, shown at (10). First issued in August 1958 and available until 1963, this was produced in red-and-cream or yellow-and-grey. It is fitted with windows and its tinplate base is stamped with the maker's name, "174" and "Hudson Hornet". This is a limited item. Length: 4·37in (111mm).

4 Dodge Royal Sedan, DT No 191; issued in March 1959 and available until 1964. Made in cream with a brown trim strip or in green with

a black strip, it is fitted with windows. Its tinplate base plate bears the maker's name, "191" and "Dodge Royal Sedan". It may be hard to find. Length: 4·37in (111mm).

5 Lincoln Continental, DT No 170; issued in October 1964 and available until 1969. Made in blue-and-white or metallic orange-and-white, it features windows, opening bonnet and boot, jewelled headlights in a chromed radiator and bumper assembly, and a detailed interior. Its diecast base bears the maker's name and "Lincoln Continental". A suspension system is fitted. A limited item. Length: 5in (127mm).

6 Ford Thunderbird by Solido, France, dating from 1959. It is interesting to compare this model, featuring a wrap-around windscreen and fitted with a

suspension system, with the Dinky models of US cars shown on this spread. Length: 4·3125in (110mm).

7 Nash Rambler, DT No 173; issued in April 1958 and available until 1962. Made in green with a cerise trim strip, or pink with a blue strip, it is fitted with windows. The tinplate base is stamped with the maker's name, "173" and "Nash Rambler". This is a limited item. Length: 3·976in (101mm).

8 Rambler Cross-Country Station Wagon, DT No 193; first issued in July 1961 and available until 1968. Produced in yellow-and-white only, this model features a roof-rack, chromed radiator and bumpers, and a detailed interior. It is fitted with a suspension system and the tinplate base plate is stamped with the maker's name, "193"

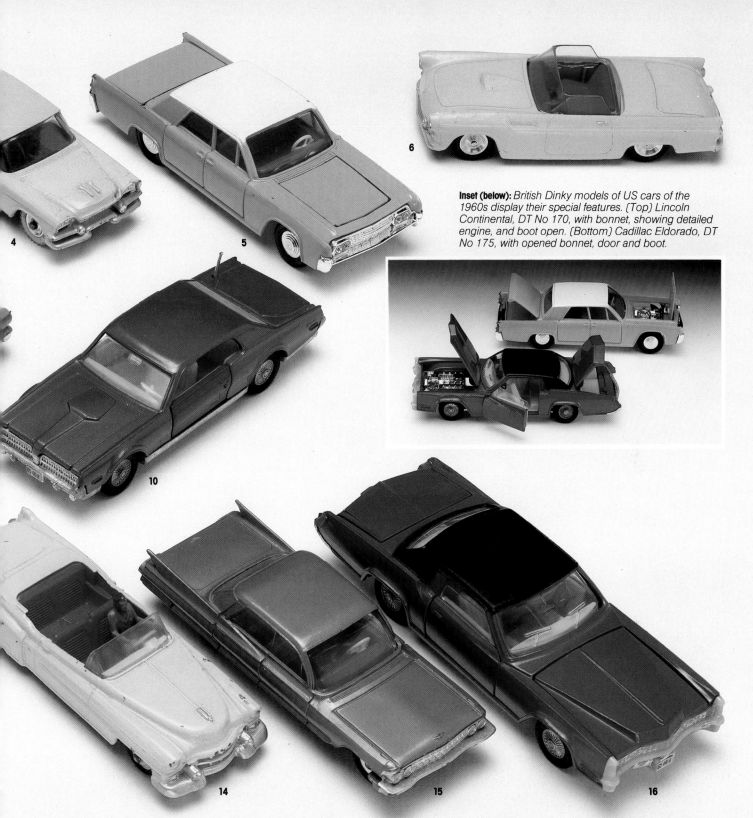

Inset (below): *British Dinky models of US cars of the 1960s display their special features. (Top) Lincoln Continental, DT No 170, with bonnet, showing detailed engine, and boot open. (Bottom) Cadillac Eldorado, DT No 175, with opened bonnet, door and boot.*

and "Rambler Cross-Country". Like most of these models of US cars, it is of limited availability. Length: 4·016in (102mm).

9 Ford Fairlane, DT No 148; first issued in January 1962 and available until 1965. Produced in green body finish only, this model is fitted with windows and has a detailed interior. A suspension system is fitted; the tinplate base plate is stamped with the maker's name, "148" and "Ford Fairlane". Another limited item. Length: 4·37in (111mm).

10 Ford Mercury Cougar, DT No 174; first issued in 1969 and available until 1972. This model was made only in blue finish and features opening doors, a radio aerial, and seats. It is fitted with suspension and speedwheels and has a diecast

base. The model is fairly common. Length: 4·803in (122mm).

11 Studebaker President, DT No 179; first issued in October 1958 and available until 1963. This model was produced in yellow with a blue trim strip, or in blue with a dark blue trim strip. Windows are fitted, but there is no interior detail. The tinplate base is stamped with the maker's name, "179" and "Studebaker President". This is one of the less common models of its period. Length: 4·252in (108mm).

12-13 Studebaker Golden Hawk, DT No. 169; first issued in November 1958, this model remained available until 1963. It was produced only in the colour schemes shown here: green-and-fawn (12) or fawn-and-red (13). The

model is fitted with windows but has no interior detail. The tinplate base plate is stamped with the maker's name, "169" and "Studebaker Golden Hawk". Limited. Length: 4·17in (106mm).

14 Cadillac Eldorado, DT No 131. This model — for a later version of the same car, see (16) — was first issued in June 1956, and remained available until 1963. It appeared in yellow, pink or fawn body finish. It has a plastic windscreen, a detailed interior with a separately-cast steering wheel and the figure of a driver (left-hand drive), an opening boot and spoked wheels. The tinplate base is stamped with the maker's name, "131" and "Cadillac Eldorado". Its availability is limited. Length: 4·646in (118mm).

15 Cadillac 62, DT No 147; first issued in October 1962, when it was priced at 4s 11d (24½p, 29c), and available until 1968. It was made in metallic green finish only, and has windows, a detailed interior and a suspension system. The tinplate base is stamped with the maker's name, "147" and "Cadillac". Another limited item. Length: 4·449in (113mm).

16 Cadillac Eldorado, DT No 175; first issued in 1969 and available until 1972. This large and impressive model was produced in purple-and-black (as shown) and possibly in other colours. It features opening doors, boot and bonnet and a detailed interior, and is fitted with a suspension system and speedwheels. It is fairly common. Length: 5·236in (133mm).

1 Hillman Minx by Dinky Toys, Great Britain; Dinky Toys Reference Number (DT No) 175. This model was first issued in August 1958 and remained available until 1961. Appearing in grey-and-blue (as shown) or pink-and-green finish, it is fitted with windows. Its tinplate base is stamped with the maker's name and "Hillman Minx". It is now of limited availability. Length: 3·465in (88mm).

2 Hillman Imp; DT No 138, issued in November 1963 and available until 1972. Made in metallic green or blue, it features windows, a detailed interior, an opening bonnet (with engine detail) and an opening boot (with luggage). A suspension system is fitted. Its diecast base bears the maker's name, "138" and "Hillman Imp".

This is a fairly common item. Length: 3·386in (86mm).

3 Ford Capri; DT No 143, issued in August 1962 and available until 1966. Made in green-and-white only, it features windows, interior detail, suspension and fingertip steering. Its tinplate base is stamped with the maker's name, "143" and "Ford Capri". Fairly common. Length: 3·5625in (90mm).

4 Ford Consul Corsair; DT No 130, issued in June 1964 and available until 1968. Made in blue, red, and possibly other colours, it has sliding windows, interior detail, opening bonnet (with engine) and jewelled headlights. Suspension is fitted and the diecast base bears the maker's name, "130" and "Ford Corsair". Its availability is now limited. Length: 4·17in (106mm).

5 Ford Cortina; DT No 139, issued in June 1963 and available until 1964. Made in metallic blue only, it features windows, interior detail, opening doors, suspension and fingertip steering. Its tinplate base bears the maker's name, "139" and "Ford Cortina". Limited. Length: 4·016in (102mm).

6-7 Austin A105; DT No 176, issued in August 1958 and available until 1963. It is known to have appeared in cream with a blue strip, as at (6), or grey with red strip; a two-tone variant is shown at (7). This was the first Dinky car to be fitted with windows, but it has no interior detail. Its tinplate base bears the maker's name, "176" and "Austin A105". Limited. Length: 4·016in (102mm).

8 Triumph 2000; DT No 135, issued in November 1963 and available until 1968. Made in blue-and-white, as seen, and possibly in other colours, it features windows, interior detail, opening doors, bonnet (with engine) and boot (with luggage), suspension and fingertip steering. Its diecast base bears the maker's name, "135" and "Triumph 2000". Limited. Length: 4·134in (105mm).

9 Triumph Vitesse; DT No 134, issued in November 1963 and available until 1968. Made in metallic green or blue, it features windows, interior detail and suspension. Its tinplate base bears the maker's name, "134" and "Triumph Vitesse". Limited. Length: 3·425in (87mm).

10 Triumph 1300; DT No 162, issued in 1966 and available until 1969.

It features windows, interior
detail, jewelled headlights,
opening bonnet (with engine) and
boot, and suspension with fingertip
steering. Its base is diecast.
Limited. Length: 3·622in (92mm).

11 Vauxhall Viva; DT No 136, issued
in May 1964 and available until
1972. Made in blue or white, it
features windows, interior detail,
opening bonnet (with engine) and
boot, and suspension with fingertip
steering. Its diecast base bears
the maker's name, "136" and
"Vauxhall Viva". Fairly common.
Length: 3·66in (93mm).

12 Vauxhall Cresta; DT No 164,
issued in March 1957 and available
until 1960. Made in green-and-grey
or maroon-and-cream, it has neither
windows nor interior detail. Its tinplate base bears the maker's name,

"164" and "Vauxhall Cresta". Fairly
scarce. Length: 3·78in (96mm).

13 Vauxhall Victor Estate Car;
DT No 141, issued in April 1963
and available until 1967. Made in
yellow only, it features windows,
interior detail, an opening tailgate, and suspension with fingertip steering. Its tinplate base
bears the maker's name, "141" and
"Victor Estate". Fairly common.
Length: 3·622in (92mm).

14 Volkswagen 1500; DT No 144,
issued in March 1963 and available
until 1966. Made in white only, it
features windows, interior detail
(left-hand drive), opening bonnet
(with plastic luggage), and
suspension with fingertip steering.
Its tinplate base bears the maker's
name, "144" and "VW 1500". Fairly
common. Length: 3·66in (93mm).

15 Volkswagen; DT No 181, issued
in February 1956 and available until
1969. Made in blue, grey or
green, it has neither windows
nor interior detail. Its tinplate
base bears the maker's name,
"Volkswagen" and, sometimes, the
number "181". A limited item.
Length: 3·5625in (90mm).

16 Volkswagen Karmann Ghia Coupé;
DT No 187, issued in November
1959 and available until 1963. Made
in green-and-cream or red-and-
black, it features windows and
suspension. Its tinplate base bears
the maker's name and "Volkswagen
Karmann Ghia". Fairly common.
Length: 3·78in (96mm).

17 Volvo 122S; DT No 184, issued
in December 1961 and available
until 1964. Made in red only, it has
windows, interior detail and

suspension. Its tinplate base bears
the maker's name, "184" and "Volvo
122S". Fairly common. Length:
3·858in (98mm).

18 Opel Kapitan; DT No 177, issued
in August 1961 and available until
1967. Made in blue only, it has
windows, interior detail, and
suspension with fingertip steering.
Its tinplate base bears the maker's
name and "Opel Kapitan". Limited.
Length: 3·937in (100mm).

19 Daimler V.8 2½ Litre; DT No
146, issued in January 1963 and
available until 1966. Made in
metallic green only, it features
windows, interior detail, and
suspension with fingertip steering.
Its tinplate base bears the maker's
name and "Daimler 2.5 litre". This
is now a fairly scarce item.
Length: 3·74in (95mm).

1 Ford Vedette (1953 Model) by
Dinky Toys, France; French Dinky
Toys Reference Number (FDT No)
24x. This model was first issued
in 1954 and remained available
until 1956. Finished in grey, it
has neither windows nor interior
detail. It was also available in
a taxi version (FDT No 24xt).
Length: 4·134in (105mm).
2 Ford Vedette (1949 Model); FDT
No 24q, first issued in 1950 and
available until 1955. The first
model of a Ford car to be issued
by Dinky Toys, France, this may
be found with a number of
variations to its tinplate base.
Length: 3·937in (100mm).
3 Panhard PL17 Saloon; FDT No
547, first issued in 1960 and
available until 1968. Three
versions of this model were made:

in the first two types, the door
handles are so positioned as to
suggest that the doors (non-opening
on the model) open from front to
back; in the third version, as
seen here, the door handles are
correctly placed. Finished in red,
this model features windows and
a detailed interior, including
steering wheel (left-hand drive).
A suspension system is fitted.
Length: 4·17in (106mm).
4-5 Peugeot 203 Sedan; FDT No 24r.
This model first appeared in 1954;
it was renumbered 533 in 1959 and
was deleted from the range in the
same year. Shown here in green
(4) and blue (5) finish, this model
appeared in three versions, the
major variations being in the size
of the rear window. The model at
(4) is an early version, with a

small rear window; that at (5) is
a later type, with a large rear
window (the difference is just
apparent in the photograph). Note
also that (4) has painted wheels,
whereas (5) has plated wheels.
Length: 3·858in (98mm).
6 Peugeot 403 UF Estate Car; FDT
No 24f. This model was first issued
in 1958 and remained available until
1962. Finished in pale blue, it
has neither windows nor interior
detail. Length: 4·17in (106mm).
7 Peugeot 403 Saloon; FDT No 521,
dating from 1960. Note that
this model, finished in grey, is
fitted with windows and that the
casting incorporates a sun-roof. See
also (8). Length: 4·09in (104mm).
8 Peugeot 403 Saloon; FDT No 24b,
dating from 1956. This model
is almost identical with (7), but

is not fitted with windows.
Length: 4·09in (104mm).
9 Simca Aronde; FDT No 544,
dating from 1959. In two-tone,
finish, maroon with a white roof
and with a silver body trim strip,
this model is fitted with windows.
Length: 3·8125in (97mm).
10-12 Simca 9 Aronde; FDT No
24u. This model was first issued
in 1953; it was renumbered 536
in 1959 and was deleted from the
range in the same year. It
appeared in three versions, of which two
are shown here. The models at (10)
and (12), finished in green and
grey respectively, are of the
first type, issued in 1953-55: in
comparison with (11), note the
different radiator grille and the
painted wheels of (10) and (12).
The model at (11) is of the third

type, issued in 1958-59; it is in two-tone finish, grey with a green roof, and has chromed wheels. Length: 3·66in (93mm).

13 Simca Chambord; FDT No 24k. This model was first issued in 1959 and was renumbered 528 in the same year. It remained available until 1961. Seen here in a two-tone finish—dark green lower body and roof and pale green upper body—it is fitted with plastic windows but has no interior detail. Length: 4·252in (108mm).

14 Simca Versailles; FDT No 24z. This model was first issued in 1956; it was renumbered 541 in 1969 and remained available until 1960. In two-tone finish, blue with a white roof, this model has neither windows nor interior detail. Length: 4·055in (103mm).

15 Renault Dauphine; FDT No 24e, dating from 1957. Finished in green, this is another simple model, without windows or interior detail. Length: 3·5625in (90mm).

16 Renault Floride Coupé, FDT No 543, first issued in 1960 and available until 1963. Finished in gold, this model features plastic windows and a suspension system. Length: 3·819in (97mm).

17-18 Citroën DS19, FDT No 24c. This model was first issued in 1956; it was renumbered 522 in 1959 and remained available until 1968—obviously a most popular model of a famous car of innovatory design. As seen in the two versions in two-tone finish—white-and-black and cream-and-black—shown here, it was originally issued, from 1956 to 1957, without windows.

It appeared with plastic windows from 1958-59 onward, and subsequently underwent other improvements. On the two examples shown, note that (17) has concave wheels and that (18) has ridged wheels. Length: 4·375in (111mm).

19-20 Citroën 11BL; FDT No 24n. This model was first issued in 1949 and remained available until 1955. Two versions are shown: the car in grey finish at (19) is of the later type, issued in 1953-55; the casting incorporates a boot and it has a plain radiator. The car in black finish at (20) is of the earlier type, issued in 1949-51, without a boot, but with a cast-on spare wheel (the edge just visible at the rear of the car in this photograph), a tinplate front bumper and a detailed radiator.

Lengths (19): 4·17in (106mm); (20): 3·75in (95mm).

21-22 Citroën 2CV (1950 Model); FDT No 24t. This model was first issued in 1952, renumbered 535 in 1959, and remained available until 1963—another long-lived model of a French car that has inspired worldwide affection. The two examples shown, in different two-tone finishes, are early versions, lacking windows and interior detail. Note that (21) has ridged wheels and that (22) has concave wheels. A later, improved version (FDT No 535), appearing in 1962 and fitted with windows and a suspension system, was issued under the same reference number in Great Britain in 1962, remaining available until 1965. Length: 3·465in (88mm).

1 Chevrolet Corvair by Dinky Toys, France; French Dinky Toys Reference Number (FDT No) 552, dating from 1961. Finished in red, this model features windows and a detailed moulded interior with steering wheel (left-hand drive). It is fitted with a suspension system and has "fingertip steering". Length: 4·125in (105mm).

2 Studebaker Commander Coupé; FDT No 24y, first issued in 1955. This model was renumbered 540 in 1959 and remained available until 1961. The example shown is of the earlier type. It is finished in pale grey with a maroon roof and has no windows or interior detail. In the later type, the lower parts of the front wings and doors were finished in the same colour as the roof. Length: 4·25in (108mm).

3 Ford Thunderbird Convertible; FDT No 555, dating from 1961. The identical model, under the same reference number and in the original French packaging, was marketed in Great Britain from July 1962—when eleven other models of French origin, including the Chrysler Saratoga shown at (19), also appeared in Britain—until 1965. It was priced in Britain at 7s 8d (38½p, 46c). The model was made only with a white body. It features a detailed moulded plastic interior, with a separately-cast steering wheel and the figure of a driver (left-hand drive), and a plastic windscreen. With a suspension system and "fingertip steering", it has a tinplate base plate stamped with the maker's name, "Ford Thunderbird", "1/43" (scale),

"61" (year of French issue), and "555". This is a model with limited availability in Britain. Length: 4·764in (121mm).

4-5 Ford Galaxie 500; FDT No 1402, dating from 1968. This model, shown here in two finishes—fawn with maroon interior (4); black with cream interior (5)—features opening doors, bonnet and boot, windows (incorporating detail of rear-view mirror), and a detailed interior. The base is diecast. Length: 4·875in (124mm).

6-7 Ford Thunderbird Coupé; FDT No 1419, dating from 1969. Shown here in two finishes—metallic green (6) and metallic green with a black roof (7), in both cases with cream interior—this model features windows and a detailed interior. The base is made of plastic.

Length: 4·6875in (119mm).

8-9 De Soto 59 Diplomat; FDT No 545, dating from 1960. This model, shown in two finishes—green with cream roof (8) and orange with black roof (9), in both cases with a silver body trim strip—is fitted with windows, but it features no interior detail: Length: 4·4375in (113mm).

10-11 Lincoln Premier; FDT No 532, first issued in 1959 and available until 1965. This model, again shown in two finishes—blue with a silver roof (10) and pale green with a dark green roof (11)—is fitted with windows but has no interior detail. Length: 4·6875in (119mm).

12-13 Buick Roadmaster; FDT No 24v. This model was first issued in 1954; it was renumbered 538 in 1959, but was deleted from the

6

7

11

12

13

17

18

19

range in the same year. Shown here in two finishes—cream with a green roof (12) and light blue with a dark blue roof (13)—it has neither windows nor interior detail, but the casting incorporates a red-enamelled mascot on the bonnet. Length: 4·375in (111mm).

14-15 Plymouth Belvedere Coupé; FDT No 24d. This model was first issued in 1957; it was renumbered 523 in 1959 and was deleted from the range in 1961. Again, it is, shown in two different finishes— grey, with a red trim area on the lower body and a red roof (14); green, with a black trim area on the lower body and a black roof (15). The model has neither windows nor interior detail, but the casting incorporates a plated mascot on the bonnet.

Length: 4·3125in (110mm).
16-18 Chrysler New Yorker Convertible (1955 Model); FDT No 24a. This model was first issued in 1956; it was renumbered 520 in 1959 and was deleted from the range in 1961. Three examples are shown here, marking both variations in finish—yellow with green interior (16); red with cream interior (17-18)—and, particularly, the variation in the radiator grille between (16-17) and (18). The model features a plastic windscreen and a detailed interior complete with steering wheel (left-hand drive). The casting incorporates a silver-finished mascot on the bonnet. Length: 4·3125in (110mm).
19 Chrysler Saratoga; FDT No 550, first issued in France in 1960

and remaining available in that country until 1966. The identical model, under the same reference number and in its original French packaging, was marketed in Great Britain, where it was initially priced at 7s 8d (38½p, 46c), from 1962 until 1965. As noted at (3), besides this model and the Ford Thunderbird Convertible shown at (3), ten other models from the French Dinky factory were released in Great Britain at this time. They were (with FDT No in each case): Renault 4L (518); 2CV Citroën (535); Peugeot 404 (553); Citroën Delivery Van "Cibié" (561; a later version, "Glaces Gervais", was marketed only in France); Estafette Renault (Renault Pick-Up) (563); Panhard Armoured Car (815); A.M.X. 13-Ton Tank (817); M3 Half-

Track (822); Brockway Military Truck with Pontoon Bridge (884); and Unic Tractor and Boilot Car Transporter Trailer (894). This model of the Chrysler Saratoga was produced only in pink-and-white finish, as shown here; it features windows and a detailed interior with a separately-cast steering wheel (left-hand drive). With a suspension system and "fingertip steering" (called "Prestomatic" in Great Britain), it has a tinplate base plate stamped with the maker's name, "Chrysler Saratoga", "1/43", "61", and "550". This model is perhaps a little easier to find in Britain than the Ford Thunderbird Convertible, with similar production history, shown at (3). Length: 5·079in (129mm).

1 **Renault 4L "P&T"** by Dinky Toys, France; French Dinky Toys Reference Number (FDT No) 561, dating from 1972. With a body finished in yellow, this model features windows and a detailed moulded interior complete with steering column (left-hand drive, like all the other models with interior detail shown on this spread). It has a plastic base and suspension is fitted. Note the provision of number plates on this and some of the other French Dinky Toys shown on this spread. Length: 3·346in (85mm).

2 **Renault 4L "Depannage Autoroutes"**; FDT No 518, dating from 1970. The identical model, still in its French packaging, was issued under the same reference number by Dinky Toys, Great Britain,

in July 1962; it remained available in Britain until 1965. The model was boxed with a road sign (not shown here). Finished in orange, this model features a plastic whip-aerial, plastic windows, a detailed moulded interior, and "fingertip steering" (Called "Prestomatic" by the British factory) with a suspension system. It has a tinplate base on which is stamped the maker's name, "Renault 4L", and "518". Length: 3·346in (85mm).

3 **Renault 6**; FDT No 1416, dating from 1969. Finished in red, this model features opening front doors, windows, and a detailed moulded interior. It has a plastic base and suspension is fitted. Length: 3·5in (89mm).

4 **Renault 12 Gordini**; FDT No

1424g, dating from 1971. Finished in blue with white side stripes, this model features windows—note the detail of the rear-view mirror, as on some other models shown on this spread—opening doors and a detailed moulded interior. It has a plastic base and suspension is fitted. Length: 4·8125in (122mm).

5 **Renault R8**; FDT No 103 (Junior), dating from 1964. Finished in red, this is a simple model, without interior detail or windows, using the same body casting as the more detailed car shown at (6). Length: 3·474in (88mm).

6 **Renault R8 Gordini**; FDT No 1414, dating from 1969. In blue-and-white rally finish with the race number "36", this model features a detailed moulded interior that

includes the figure of a driver, windows, and jewelled headlights. A suspension system is fitted. Length: 3·474in (88mm).

7 **Simca 1500 GLS Shooting Brake**; FDT No 507, dating from 1967. Finished in dark grey, this features opening front doors and tailgate, windows (including sliding side windows), and a detailed moulded interior that includes a removable picnic table (as shown here). Length: 3·75in (95mm).

8 **Peugeot 404**; FDT No 101 (Junior), dating from 1963. Finished in orange, this lacks windows and interior detail. Note that the same body casting, with sun-roof, is used for the more detailed car at (12). Length: 4in (102mm).

9 **Peugeot 404 Pininfarina**; DT No 528, introduced in 1966 and

4   5   6   7

11   12   13   14

18   19   20   21

deleted in 1971. Finished in blue, this well-detailed model features jewelled headlights, a plastic windshield, and a detailed moulded interior that includes the plastic figure of a lady driver. It has a diecast base and suspension is fitted. Length: 4in (102mm).

10 Peugeot 204 Cabriolet; DT No 511, dating from 1968. Finished in pale blue, this model features opening doors and bonnet, a well-modelled plastic windscreen, and a detailed moulded interior with tilting seats. It has a diecast base. Length: 3·3125in (84mm).

11 Peugeot 404 Shooting Brake; FDT No 525, dating from 1964. Finished in cream, this model features windows, jewelled head-lights, an opening tailgate, and a detailed moulded interior that

includes a fold-down rear seat. A suspension system is fitted. Length: 4·125in (105mm).

12 Peugeot 404; FDT No 536, dating from 1965. Finished in red, this model—shown here with the plastic Monoroute (Trailer), FDT No 812—features windows, a detailed moulded interior, and a body casting that incorporates a sun-roof. A suspension system is fitted. Length: 4in (102mm).

13 Simca 1000; FDT No 519, dating from 1963. Finished in blue, this model features windows and a detailed moulded interior. A suspension system is fitted. Length: 3·375in (86mm).

14 Simca 1000; FDT No 104 (Junior), dating from 1964. Finished in light green, this is the simpler version of the model at (13),

without windows or interior detail. Length: 3·375in (86mm).

15 Fiat 600; FDT No 520, dating from 1963. Finished in red, this diminutive model features windows, a detailed moulded interior, and suspension. Length: 3in (76mm).

16 Fiat 1800 Estate Car; FDT No 548, dating from 1960. In two-tone finish of cream-and-gold, this model features windows, a detailed moulded interior, and suspension. Length: 4in (102mm).

17 Fiat 1200 Grande Vue; FDT No 531, dating from 1959. In two-tone gold-and-white, this car has windows but lacks any interior detail. Length: 3·5in (89mm).

18 Panhard 24; FDT No 524, dating from 1964. Finished in dark grey, this has slide-down side windows and a detailed moulded

interior. Suspension is fitted. Length: 3·8125in (97mm).

19 Opel Admiral; FDT No 513, dating from 1966. Finished in red, this has an opening bonnet and boot and a detailed moulded interior. It has a diecast base and suspension is fitted. Length: 4·48in (114mm).

20 Opel Rekord; FDT No 554, dating from 1961. In two-tone fawn-and-white, this has windows and a detailed moulded interior. Note "Rekord" incorporated into the body casting on the right rear wing. A suspension system is fitted. Length: 4·06in (103mm).

21 Opel Kadett Saloon; FDT No 540, dating from 1963. Finished in red, it has slide-down side windows and a detailed moulded interior. A suspension system is fitted. Length: 3·5in (89mm).

1
2
3
4

9
10
11

16
17
18

1 Iso Rivolta by Politoys, Italy; maker's reference number (MRN) 515, dating from the 1960s. Finished in metallic grey, this has an opening bonnet, doors and boot, and a detailed moulded interior (left-hand drive) with folding seats. Note the model's round, plated headlights. Length: 4·3125in (110mm).

2 Lancia Flavia Coupé by Mercury, Italy; MRN 32, dating from the 1960s. Finished in metallic greenish-gold, this model features an opening bonnet, doors and boot; jewelled dual headlights and fog-lamps; plated front and rear bumpers; and a detailed moulded plastic interior (left-hand drive). Length: 4·134in (105mm).

3 Ferrari 250 GT 2+2 by Solido, France, dating from the 1960s-70s. Finished in red, it has opening

doors, a detailed interior and rather crudely-rendered headlights. Length: 4·134in (105mm).

4 Ferrari 250 GT Berlinetta by Politoys, Italy; MRN 504, dating from the 1960s. Finished in metallic blue, this model features an opening bonnet, doors and boot, and a detailed interior. A suspension system is fitted, and its diecast base incorporates details of transmission and exhaust. Length: 4·016in (102mm).

5 Ferrari 330 GTC by Politoys, Italy; MRN N652, dating from the 1960s. Finished in silver, this model features opening doors and a detailed interior (left-hand drive). The body casting incorporates side vents and a marque badge on the bonnet. It has a diecast base which incorporates details

of transmission and exhaust. Length: 4·016in (102mm).

6 Ferrari 275 GTB by Dinky Toys, Spain; MRN 506, dating from the 1960s. Finished in yellow, this model features opening bonnet, doors and boot; plated front and rear bumpers; clear plastic windows with a windscreen incorporating wipers; headlights with clear plastic lenses; and a detailed interior. Length: 3·898in (99mm).

7 Ferrari 250 GT by Dinky Toys, Spain; MRN 515, dating from the 1960s. Finished in metallic blue, this model features an opening bonnet and boot and a detailed interior (right-hand drive). A suspension system is fitted. Length: 4·252in (108mm).

8 Ferrari 250 LM by Mercury, Italy; dating from the 1960s.

Finished in red, with applied badges and a white trim strip, this model has opening doors, a detailed moulded interior (right-hand drive) and a lift-off cover over the rear engine compartment. Length: 3·74in (95mm).

9 Alfa Romeo 2600 by Solido, France; MRN 125, dated (on base) March 1963. Finished in metallic gold, this has opening doors and a detailed interior (left-hand drive). Length: 4·134in (105mm).

10 Alfa Romeo Giulia TZ by Politoys, Italy; MRN 516, dating from the 1960s. Finished in red, this model features plated wing mirrors, opening doors, and a detailed interior (left-hand drive) which includes folding seats. Length: 3·74in (95mm).

11 Alfa Romeo Giulia SS by

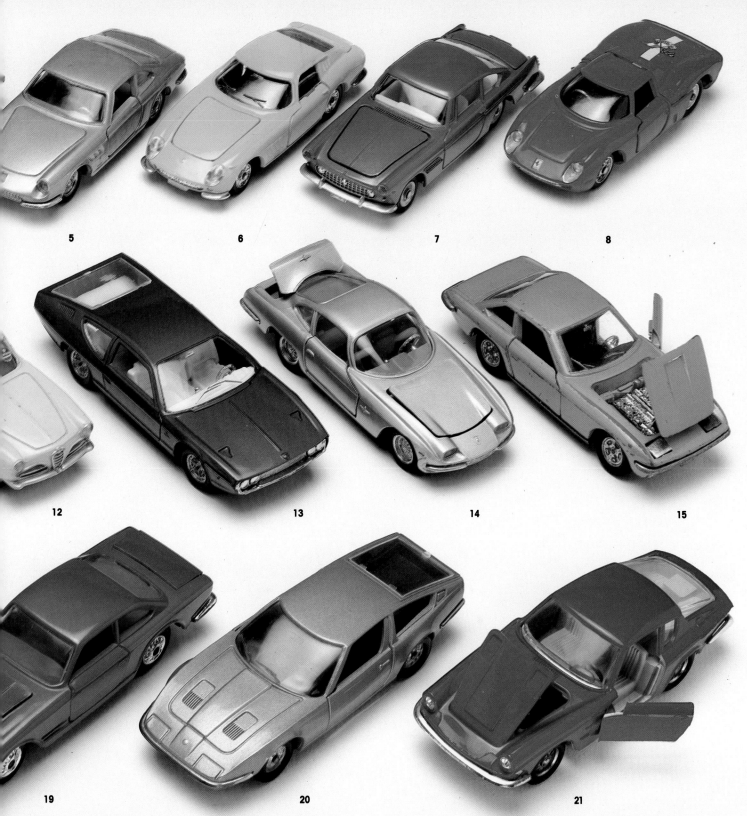

5   6   7   8

12   13   14   15

19   20   21

Politoys, Italy; MRN 506, dating from the 1960s. Finished in gold, this model has opening doors and boot and a detailed interior (left-hand drive) with folding seats. Length: 3·898in (99mm).

12 Alfa Romeo 1900 Super Sprint by Dinky Toys, Great Britain; Dinky Toys Reference Number (DT No) 185, first issued in January 1961 and available until 1963. Appearing only in yellow or red finish, this model features a moulded plastic interior (left-hand drive) and a suspension system incorporating "fingertip steering". It is now an item of limited availability. Length: 4·016in (102mm).

13 Lamborghini Bertone Espada by Politoys, Italy; MRN 587, dating from the 1960s. Finished in green, this model features opening bonnet,

doors and boot and a detailed interior (left-hand drive). It is fitted with plastic speedwheels. Length: 4·252in (108mm).

14 Lamborghini 350 GT by Politoys, Italy; MRN 539, dating from the 1960s. Finished in silver, this has opening bonnet, doors and boot, and a detailed interior (left-hand drive) with folding seats. Length: 4·016in (102mm).

15 Lamborghini Islero by Politoys, Italy; MRN 558, dating from the 1960s. Finished in gold, this model features a bonnet that opens to show a detailed engine; flip-up headlights; opening doors and a detailed interior (left-hand drive). Length: 4·134in (105mm).

16 Porsche 356A Coupé by Dinky Toys, Great Britain; DT No 182, first issued in September 1958

and available until 1966. Appearing in blue or cream finish only, it has clear plastic windows but no interior detail. It is fitted with metal wheels with detachable rubber tyres; its tinplate base is stamped with the maker's name, the number "182" and "Porsche 356A". Length: 3·504in (89mm).

17 Porsche 912 by Politoys, Italy; MRN 527, dating from the 1960s. Finished in silver, this has an opening bonnet, doors and boot, a detailed interior (left-hand drive), and a diecast base with suspension. Length: 3·74in (95mm).

18 Ghibli Maserati Ghia by Politoys, Italy; MRN 591, dating from the 1960s. Finished in yellow with a blue-and-white trim strip, it has opening doors and a detailed interior (left-hand drive). It is

fitted with plastic speedwheels. Length: 3·898in (99mm).

19 Maserati 3500 GT by Politoys, Italy; MRN 50, dating from the 1960s. Finished in blue, it has an opening bonnet, doors and boot, and a detailed interior (left-hand drive) with folding seats. Length: 4·252in (108mm).

20 Maserati Indy by Solido, France; MRN 185, dated (on base) February 1971. Finished in gold, it has opening doors and boot, a detailed interior (left-hand drive) and a plastic base. Length: 4·252in (108mm).

21 Maserati Coupé by Politoys, Italy; MRN 119, dating from the 1960s. Finished in red, it has an opening bonnet and doors, a detailed interior (left-hand drive), and a boot with a clear plastic cover. Length: 4·134in (105mm).

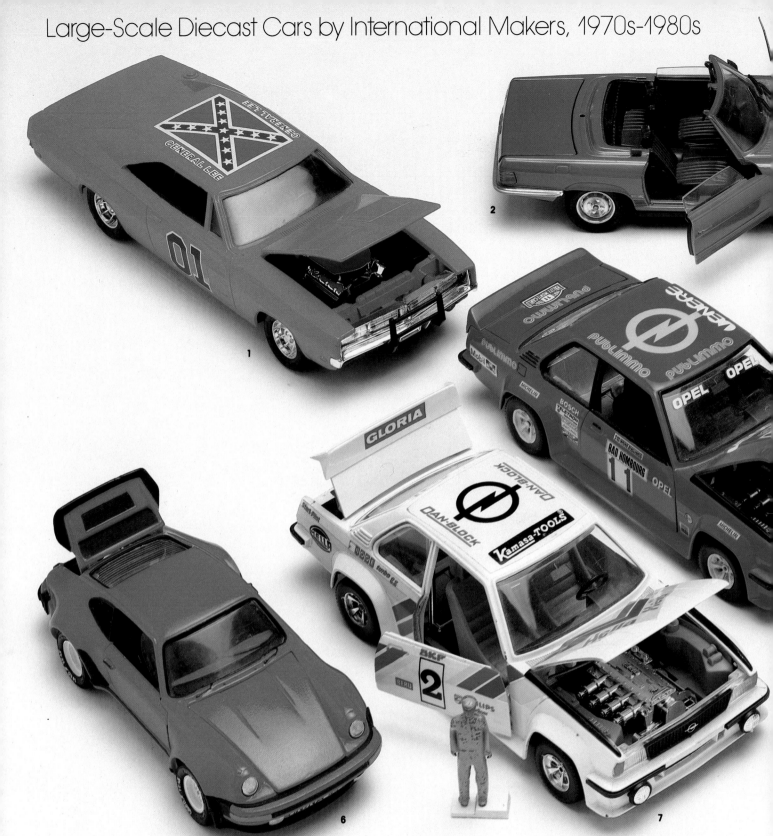

1 "General Lee" Car by Ertl, USA; dating from c1978 and made to a scale of approximately 1:24. Finished in orange, with the flag of the Confederate States applied on the roof, and the number "01" on the side, this model features a bonnet that opens to show a basically-detailed engine of plated plastic. The doors and boot do not open. It has a tinted plastic windscreen, front quarterlights and rear window, a bright-plated plastic radiator and bumpers, and red plastic rearlights. The detailed interior of moulded plastic includes a roll-cage over the front seats. It is fitted with sculptured plastic wheels with fat, treaded "Good Year" rubber tyres. Its plastic base has moulded details of transmission, suspension and

exhaust. Length: 8·3125in (211mm).

2 Mercedes Benz 450SL by Polistil, Italy; dating from c1977 and made to a scale of 1:25. Finished in metallic blue, with a removable canopy (shown here in front of the model) of black plastic and a detailed black plastic interior (left-hand drive), this model has a bonnet that opens to show a fully-detailed engine of moulded plastic, opening doors and an opening boot. It has a plated plastic radiator, whip aerial and front and rear bumpers. A number plate, "SLM-P300", is fitted front and rear. It has a clear plastic windscreen and side windows, the latter shown in the half-down position. The plated plastic wheels are fitted with plastic tyres and the black plastic base bears

moulded details, including a bright-plated sump pan and exhaust system. Length: 7in (178mm).

3 Ford Capri by Dinky Toys, Great Britain; Dinky Toys Reference Number (DT No) 2162, first issued in 1974 and available until 1976. Two other versions of this large-scale model were issued at the same time: Ford Capri Rally Car, "Shell", DT No 2214; Ford Capri Police Car, DT No 2253. Finished in metallic blue with a black roof, this model has a bonnet (bearing the cast word "Ford") that opens to show a chromed plastic engine. It has opening front doors and an opening boot that bears the cast words "Ford" and "GXL". The front and rear bumpers and headlights are of chromed plastic; the rear lights are coloured plastic. It is fitted

with clear plastic windows (note the black plastic windscreen wipers) and has a detailed interior (right-hand drive) that includes folding seats. A number plate, "BTN 76", is fitted at the rear. The sculptured metal wheels are fitted with treaded plastic tyres, and the metal base plate has applied plastic details of transmission and exhaust. All three versions of this model are fairly common. Length: 6·89in (175mm).

4 B.M.W. 525 Berlina by Polistil, Italy; dating from c1975 and made to a scale of 1:25. Finished in metallic blue, this has an opening bonnet, showing an engine of plated plastic; opening front doors with plated plastic handles; and an opening boot. It has plated plastic front and rear bumpers and

headlights and red plastic rear-lights. The detailed interior includes a plated plastic steering wheel (left-hand drive) and gear lever. A number plate, "M1 W52107", is fitted front and rear. It has sculptured metal wheels with treaded plastic tyres and a plastic base with full moulded details. Length: 7·0625in (179mm).

5 Volkswagen by Polistil, Itay; dating from c1975 and made to a scale of 1:25. Finished in metallic blue, the model features a removable black plastic canopy and an opening bonnet. The front and rear bumpers, hood trim strip, whip aerial and windscreen wipers are black plastic; it has clear plastic headlights and red plastic rear-lights. The moulded plastic interior includes folding seats

and a plated plastic steering wheel and gear lever. A number plate, "M1-V3 4824", is fitted at the rear. It has sculptured plastic wheels with treaded plastic tyres and a well-detailed plated plastic base. Length: 6·625in (168mm).

6 Porsche 930 Turbo by "G", Japan; dating from c1975 and made to a scale of 1:28. Finished in red with black trim, it has opening doors and a rear engine compartment, with spoiler, that opens to show a moulded plastic engine. The detailed interior (left-hand drive) is diecast and has tipping seats. The number plate, "IN-NA 44", is fitted front and rear. The sculptured metal wheels are fitted with fat, treaded rubber "Good Year" tyres. The metal base carries plated plastic details of the

suspension, sump and exhaust. Length: 6·125in (156mm).

7-9 Opel Ascona 400 Rally Car by Durago, Italy; dating from c1980 and made to a scale of 1:24. Three versions are shown. At (7), the model is finished in white, with a wealth of applied badges and trim strips and the number "2". The bonnet, edged with raised trim strips of black plastic, opens to show a plated plastic engine. The doors open on a moulded plastic interior (left-hand drive) with a plated plastic roll-cage at the rear. The boot, with spoiler, opens to show reserve petrol tanks of moulded plastic. It has a black plastic radiator with clear plastic headlights and orange plastic flashers, plated plastic foglights, and a rearlight assembly of

coloured plastic. A number plate, "M1-14292M", is fitted at the rear. The sculptured plastic wheels are fitted with fat plastic tyres; the front wheels are steerable. The plastic base has plated plastic details of transmission and exhaust, with twin pipes protruding at the rear. The car at (8), finished in metallic blue with a similar wealth of applied detail, differs from (7) in having no roll-cage, a different number plate ("CG-CJ 649"), and a base with moulded details that include a plated petrol tank. The car at (9), finished in red, has a base like that of (8), but features a roll-cage and has plastic spotlights fitted to the radiator. It bears the same rear number plate, "M1-14292M" as the car shown at (7). Length: 7·125in (181mm).

1 Rolls Royce Camargue by Durago, Italy; maker's reference number (MRN) 3001, dating from c1978 and made to a scale of 1:22. Finished in metallic grey, this large model features an opening bonnet, showing a detailed engine (complete with hoses of black plastic) of bright-plated moulded plastic, opening doors and an opening boot. The detailed interior (right-hand drive) includes folding seats and a simulated walnut dashboard with bright-plated instruments. A number plate, "PXC 162R", is fitted front and rear. It has clear plastic windows (the windscreen incorporating raised details of mirror and wind-screen wipers), plated plastic headlights and coloured plastic sidelights and flashers. The plated

radiator incorporates the famous Rolls Royce mascot. The metal wheels are fitted with plastic "Avon" tyres and it has a plastic base with moulded details of transmission and exhaust systems Length: 9·375in (238mm).

2 1912 Rolls Royce Silver Ghost by Corgi Toys, Great Britain; "Corgi Classics" Series Number 9041, issued in 1966 and available until 1970. Appearing in silver and black finish only, this model has a gilt metal roof rack (with spare tyre), tool box and spoked wheels (with treaded plastic tyres), metal radiator (with mascot), jewelled headlights, plated plastic carriage lamps, clear plastic windows and a detailed interior (right-hand drive) of moulded plastic. It has a cast chassis

incorporating full transmission details and a plastic exhaust system. Like all models in this series, it is increasingly hard to find. Length: 4·646in (118mm).

3-4 Rolls Royce Silver Shadow II by Durago, Italy; MRN 0134, dating from c1975 and made to a scale of 1:24. Two versions are shown, differing only in colour finish, (3) being in metallic blue and (4) in metallic grey, and in number plates: "SAR 841T" on (3) and "HFM 600N" on (4). The model has an opening bonnet, showing a detailed moulded plastic engine; front doors that open on to a detailed interior (left-hand drive) with folding front seats; and an opening boot. The radiator and dual headlight surrounds are plated plastic; the inset bumpers are

black plastic. It is fitted with sculptured plastic wheels and has a plastic base with details that include a plated exhaust system. Length: 7in (178mm).

5 Rolls Royce Phantom V by Dinky Toys, Great Britain; DT No 152, first issued in 1967 and available until 1975. Made only in dark blue or metallic blue (later examples), this model has doors that open on to a detailed plastic interior that includes the plastic half-figure of a chauffeur (right-hand drive). The radiator and front and rear bumpers are plated; it has jewelled dual headlights but rather crudely-painted red rearlights. The metal wheels are fitted with removable rubber tyres and the black metal base has basic details of exhaust and transmission. Suspension is

fitted. This model is quite common. Length: 5·55in (141mm).

6 Bentley T Series by Corgi Toys, Great Britain; MRN 274, available 1970-72. Made only in pinkish-red finish, it has an opening bonnet, showing a plated plastic engine; front doors opening on to a detailed interior with folding seats and applied dashboard detail; and an opening boot. It has jewelled dual headlights and a plated metal radiator and bumpers. Fitted with sculptured plastic "whizzwheels", it has a plain grey metal base. This is one of the less common models in the series. Length: 4·724in (120mm).

7 Rolls Royce Corniche by Corgi Toys, Great Britain; issued in 1979 and currently available. Appearing also in metallic maroon finish, it

features opening doors, bonnet and boot and a well-detailed interior. Common. Length: 5·67in (144mm).

8 Rolls Royce Silver Cloud III by Polistil, Italy; dating from c1975 and made to a scale of 1:30. Finished in metallic grey, this model features such refinements as plated plastic wing mirrors and radio aerial; a two-piece bonnet that opens in gull-wing fashion to show a moulded plastic engine; black plastic windscreen wipers; and front doors with exterior and interior cast handles and interior cast detail of map pockets. A number plate, "FKV 899M", is fitted front and rear. The plastic wheels, with bright metal discs, are fitted with treaded plastic tyres and the plastic base is fully detailed. Length: 7·1875in (183mm).

9 Rolls Royce Silver Wraith by Dinky Toys, Great Britain; DT No 150, issued in 1959 and available until 1966. Made only in grey-and-dark-grey, it has chromed metal bumpers, radiator and headlights, and clear plastic windows. The aluminium wheels are fitted with detachable rubber tyres. The base plate is tinplate and a suspension system is fitted. Its availability is limited. Length: 4·606in (117mm).

10, 12 and **13** Rolls Royce Phantom III (1939 Model) by Solido, France; dated (on base) November 1976 and made to a scale of 1:43. Three versions of this model are shown. At (10) is an open car, finished in cream-and-black, with a simulated folded soft-top. At (12) is a "Berlin", with a cast metal top extending over the rear seats

and a rear-mounted boot. At (13) is a model with a black plastic soft-top fitted with plated plastic bracers. All are well-detailed with plated plastic parts and having wing-mounted spare wheels (plated plastic with treaded plastic tyres) and black cast metal bases with plastic details. Length: 5·0625in (129mm).

11 Rolls Royce Camargue by Asahi, Japan; dating from c1980 and made to a scale of 1:43. Finished in metallic dark grey, it has a bonnet that opens to show a plated plastic engine; opening front doors and a detailed interior that includes folding seats; and an opening boot. It has metal wheels fitted with treaded rubber "Avon" tyres and a detailed cast metal chassis. Length: 4·875in (124mm).

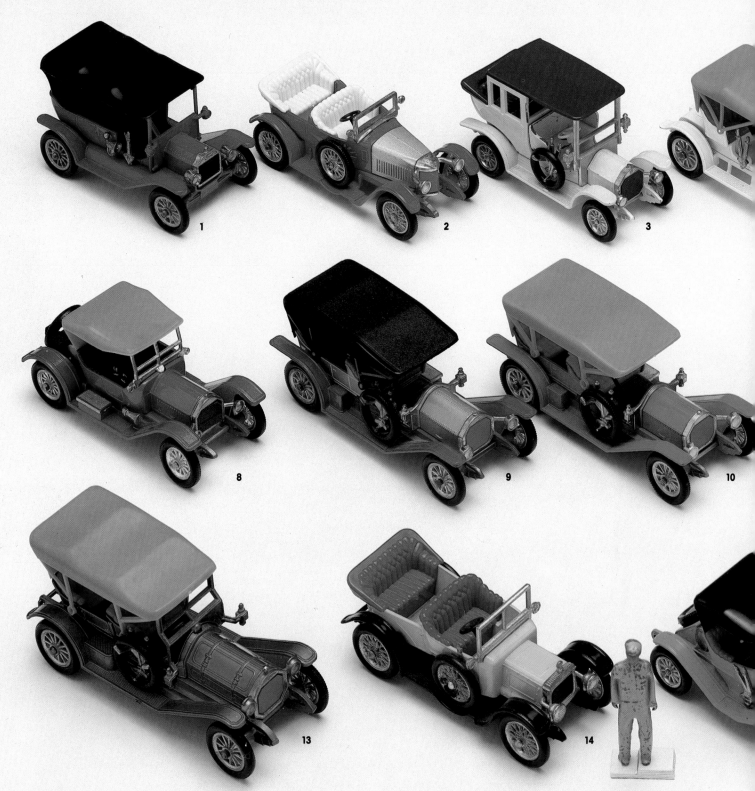

1

2

3

8

9

10

13

14

1 1911 Model "T" Ford by Lesney, Great Britain; Models of Yesteryear Number (MoY) Y-1 (2nd Issue), first issued, as shown, in 1964. A version with a white body and red roof was issued in 1974. In 1976, a limited edition of 1,000, with black body and black roof, was produced for the US market. This is rare and forgeries are known to exist; the other two versions are fairly common. Length: 2·992in (76mm).

2 1914 Prince Henry Vauxhall; MoY Y-2 (3rd Issue), first issued, as shown, in 1970; a variant with red seats is rare. A version with blue chassis and body and a silver bonnet was issued in 1974; a version with black chassis, red body and silver bonnet in 1979. All are common. Length: 3·5625in (90mm).

3 1910 Benz Limousine; MoY Y-3 (2nd Issue), first issued, as shown, in 1966. A version with pale green body and lemon roof was issued in 1968, and one with either pale green or dark metallic green body and black roof in 1970. The 1970 version is fairly common; others are limited. Length: 3·268in (83mm).

4 1909 Opel Coupé; MoY Y-4 (3rd Issue), first issued, as shown, with gold metal spoked wheels, in 1966. A version with orange body, black roof and silver plastic spoked wheels was issued in 1974. The later version is the harder to find. Length: 3·189in (81mm).

5 1907 Peugeot; MoY Y-5 (3rd Issue), first issued, as shown, with gold metal spoked wheels, in 1969. A version with bronze-orange body and roof, black seats

and plastic spoked wheels was issued in 1974. Common. Length: 3·5625in (90mm).

6 1913 Cadillac; MoY Y-6 (3rd Issue), first issued, as shown, with gold metal spoked wheels, in 1967. A version with green body, black roof and silver plastic spoked wheels was issued in 1974. Both versions are fairly common. Length: 3·386in (86mm).

7 1912 Rolls Royce; MoY Y-7 (3rd Issue), first issued, as shown, with a red smooth roof and gold metal spoked wheels, in 1968. The subsequent versions were: (1969) silver body and grey smooth roof; (1970) silver body and grey ribbed roof; (1970, second change) silver body and red ribbed roof; (1974) gold body, red ribbed roof; silver plastic spoked wheels; (1979) yellow

body, black ribbed roof, red plastic spoked wheels. The second 1970 version is rare; the 1968 and 1969 versions are limited; all others are fairly common. Length: 3·858in (98mm).

8 1914 Stutz; MoY Y-8 (3rd Issue), first issued, as shown, with gold metal spoked wheels, in 1969. A version with blue body, black roof and silver plastic spoked wheels was issued in 1974. Both are quite common. Length: 3·504in (89mm).

9-10 1912 Simplex; MoY Y-9 (2nd Issue), first issued in 1968. The versions shown here are: (9) 1971 version, with plastic spoked wheels; (10) 1969 version, with metal spoked wheels. Other versions are: (1968) yellow-green body, tan roof, red seats and gold metal spoked

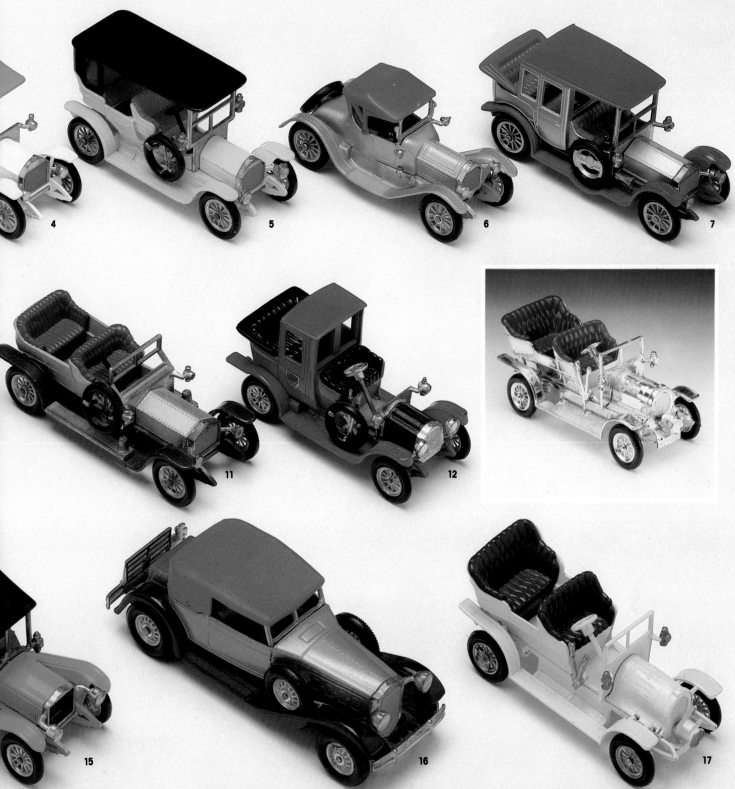

4

5

6

7

11

12

15

16

17

wheels; (1974) red body, black roof, yellow seats, red plastic spoked wheels; (1979) black chassis, red body, yellow roof and seats, red plastic spoked wheels. The 1968 and 1969 versions are limited; the others are fairly common. Length: 3·78in (96mm).

11 1906 Rolls Royce "Silver Ghost"; MoY Y-10 (3rd Issue), first issued, as shown, with gold metal spoked wheels, in 1969. Further versions were: (1974) white body, black seats (also found with red seats), silver plastic spoked wheels; (1979) silver body, dark red seats, red plastic spoked wheels; (1979, second change) silver body, yellow seats, red plastic spoked wheels. The version shown is limited; the rest should not be too hard to find. Length: 3·622in (92mm).

12 1912 Packard Landaulet; MoY Y-11 (2nd Issue), issued in 1964. It is found with either gold or silver metal spoked wheels and a metal or plastic steering wheel. Common. Length: 3·15in (80mm).

13 1909 Thomas Flyabout; MoY Y-12 (2nd Issue), first issued, with blue body, tan roof, yellow seats and gold or silver metal spoked wheels, in 1967. The second version of 1967, shown here, differed in having dark red seats. The 1974 version had a red body, black roof, white seats and silver metal spoked wheels. Both the version shown and the 1974 version are common. Length: 3·898in (99mm).

14 1911 Daimler; MoY Y-13 (2nd Issue), first issued, with yellow body, black chassis, black seats

and gold metal spoked wheels, in 1966. The 1967 version, shown here, differs in having red seats. Common. Length: 3·307in (84mm).

15 1911 Maxwell Roadster; MoY Y-14 (2nd Issue), issued in 1965. This model may be found with a black or tan roof and with gold or silver metal spoked wheels. It is fairly common. Length: 3·228in (82mm).

16 1930 Packard Victoria; MoY Y-15 (2nd Issue), first issued, as shown, in 1969. This version may be found with gold or silver metal spoked wheels. Other versions are: (1974) greenish-gold body, black roof and silver plastic spoked wheels (1979) black and red body, white roof, silver plastic bolt head wheels and whitewall tyres. The 1969 version is limited;

the other versions are common. Length: 4·291in (109mm).

17 1904 Spyker; MoY Y-16 (1st Issue), first issued, as shown, in 1961. The version issued in 1968 has a darker yellow body. Both versions are limited. Length: 3·268in (83mm).

Inset (above centre): *The 1904 Spyker, Model of Yesteryear Number Y-16 (1st Issue), is shown here in chrome-plated form. Models found in this finish (and also in gold) were originally sold mounted on ashtrays, cigarette boxes and the like. They will be found to have mounting holes for this purpose in their base plates; similar holes may also be found on some other models which have otherwise conventional finishes.*

1-3 Racing Car by Dinky Toys, Great Britain; Dinky Toys Reference Number (DT No) 23a. Three examples are shown of a very simple yet long-lived model that first appeared in April 1934. (Note that the colour finishes on the models shown appear to be non-original). The various versions of this model, with their major identification points, are: (1934-35) orange-and-green body, four exhaust stubs and no driver—as (3); (1935-38) blue-and-white body, with driver and cast detail of six-branched exhaust system—as (1) and (2)—with raised ridge around racing number; (1938-40) red body with cream flash, no ridge around racing number; (1946-48) blue body with silver flash, cast-in driver, no race

number; (1949-52) red body with silver flash, race number "4" in black circle; (1953-54) silver body with red flash, number "4" in red circle. The 1934-35 version is rare; the versions issued between 1935 and 1948 are scarce; 1949-54 versions are of limited availability: a desirable item in any version. Length (all versions): 3·7in (94mm).

4 Mercedes Benz Racing Car ("Large Open Racing Car"); DT No 23c. This model was first issued in May 1936 and was available in red or blue, with the race number "2" in a yellow circle, until 1940. It was reissued, renamed "Large Open Racing Car", in 1947-50, appearing in silver or blue finish, as shown. The pre-War version is scarce;

the post-War version is limited. Length: 3·622in (92mm).

5 Auto Union Racing Car; DT No 23d. This was first issued in May 1936 and was available in red or blue, with various race numbers in white or yellow circles and with the diecast figure of a driver slotted in, until 1940. It was reissued in 1947-50, as shown, without a driver. The pre-War version is scarce; the post-War version is extremely limited. Length: 3·937mm (100mm).

6 Alpine F111 Racing Car by Solido, France; maker's reference number (MRN) 142, issued in July 1965. It is fitted with suspension and has an overalled plastic driver. Length: 3·307in (84mm).

7 Lola Climax V8 F1 (ie, Formula One) Racing Car by Solido,

France; MRN 135, issued in July 1964. It is fitted with suspension and has engine and exhaust detail; the figure of the driver is plastic. Length: 3·504in (89mm).

8 Ferrari V12 F1 by Solido, France; MRN 167, issued in June 1968. This model has no driver and is not fitted with suspension, but it has a detailed engine and exhaust system. See also (15). Length: 3·74in (95mm).

9 Matra Sports F2 (ie, Formula Two) Racing Car by Norev, France; MRN 601, dating from c1966. This model is fitted with suspension and has a detailed exhaust; the figure of the driver is plastic. Length: 3·7in (94mm).

10 Cooper Maserati Racing Car by Corgi Toys, Great Britain; MRN 156. First issued in 1967 and

available until 1969, it has a detailed engine and exhaust, a plastic driver and plated mirrors. Length: 3·5625in (90mm).

11 Matra V112 F1 by Dinky Toys, France; French Dinky Toys Reference Number (FDT No) 1417, dating from 1969. A fully-detailed model, fitted with suspension system. Length: 3·74in (95mm).

12 Lotus Climax Racing Car by Corgi Toys, Great Britain; MRN 155, issued in 1965-68. A well-detailed model, with plated rear-view mirror and exhaust system, fitted with suspension. Like the other Corgi models shown on this spread, it is fairly easy to find. Length: 3·5625in (90mm).

13 Surtees TS5 by Dinky Toys, France; FDT No 1433, dating from 1971. A well-detailed model with

suspension. Length: 3·7in (94mm).

14 Matra V8 F1 by Solido, France; MRN 173, issued in June 1969. The wealth of detail on this model includes a cast aerofoil at the rear. Length: 4·055in (103mm).

15 Ferrari V12 F1 by Solido, France; MRN 167, issued in June 1968. This is basically the same model as (8), but with the addition of an aero-foil and the figure of a driver. Length: 3·74in (95mm).

16 Lotus Climax Racing Car by Corgi Toys, Great Britain; MRN 158, issued in 1969-72. It differs from the earlier version shown at (12), most obviously in having an aerofoil. It is fitted with a suspension system and features driver-controlled steering; the driver is a plastic figure. Length: 3·504in (89mm).

17 Ferrari V12 F1 by Dinky Toys, France; FDT No 1422, dating from 1969. It features rather more detail that the model of the same car by Solido, shown at (15). Length: 3·7in (94mm).

18 Cooper Maserati by Corgi Toys, Great Britain; MRN 159, issued in 1969-72. Like (16), this model features driver-controlled steering; the driver is plastic and it is fitted with suspension. An earlier version (MRN 156, dating from 1967-69) was finished in blue with the race number "7"; see (10). Length: 3·5625in (90mm).

19-24 Cooper Norton Racing Car by Tekno, Denmark; MRN 812, dating from around 1958. This most attractive little model, with a plastic driver and detail of engine and exhaust, with suspension

fitted, is shown in the racing colours of France (19), Great Britain (20), Switzerland (21), Netherlands (22), the German Federal Republic (23), and Belgium (24). Length: 2·9375in (75mm).

25 Indianapolis S.T.P. Turbine Car by Faracars, France (made under licence from USA); MRN 101, dating from c1970. A solid and well-detailed model of good quality, this represents the first turbine-engined car (Pratt & Whitney STGB-62 550bhp turbine) to run at the famous "Indy" track in the USA, in 1967. Length: 3·504in (89mm).

26 Harvey Aluminium Indianapolis Special by Solido, France; MRN 138, issued in February 1965. This model is fitted with a suspension system and has a plastic driver. Length: 3·15in (80mm).

1 Alta Racing Car by Scamold, Great Britain; maker's reference number (MRN) 105, dating from around 1950. Finished in silver, with a green cockpit, this model features a detailed cockpit and exhaust system and is fitted with treaded rubber tyres. Length: 4·37in (111mm).

2-3 Maserati Racing Car by Scamold, Great Britain; MRN 103, dating from c1950. Two versions are shown: (2) is finished in dark blue, with a lighter blue cockpit; (3) is finished in dark blue, with a silver radiator and brown cockpit. The major difference is that (3) is fitted with a spring motor; note the winding-shaft that protrudes at the base of the radiator. Note also that (2), like the other unpowered Scamold models shown here, has a clearly-visible aperture in the

body casting to accommodate a winding-shaft Both racing cars are fitted with treaded rubber tyres. Length: 4·252in (108mm).

4-6 E.R.A. Racing Car by Scamold, Great Britain; MRN 101, dating from around 1950. Three versions are shown: (4) is finished in light green, with a grey radiator and cockpit, and is not fitted with a motor; (5) is finished in dark green, with a blue radiator and cockpit, and is fitted with a spring motor; (6) is finished in yellow, with a black radiator bearing the race number "34", bonnet straps in black and blue cockpit, and, like the car at (4), is unpowered. All are fitted with treaded rubber tyres. Length: 4·37in (111mm).

7 Maserati Racing Car by Mercury, Italy; MRN 31, dating from 1960. Finished in red, with white treaded

rubber tyres, this simple model bears on its tail the race number "2". Length: 3·504in (89mm).

8 Cisitalia 1100 Racing Car by Mercury, Italy; MRN 37, dating from 1955, and finished in blue, with a silver radiator and brown cockpit. This model bears the race number "6" and has cast wheels fitted with detachable grey rubber treaded tyres. Length: 3·74in (95mm).

9 Maserati Grand Prix Racing Car by Mercury, Italy; MRN 34, dating from 1957. Finished in red, with a silver radiator and the race number "7", this model is fitted with detachable white treaded rubber tyres. Length: 4·252in (108mm).

10 S.V.A. Racing Car by Mercury, Italy; MRN 39, dating from 1955. Finished in green, with a silver radiator and the race number "6",

this racing car is fitted with detachable black treaded rubber tyres. Length: 3·504in (89mm).

11 Alfa Romeo Alfette 158 Racing Car by Mercury, Italy; MRN 35, dating from 1957. Finished in red, with a silver radiator but no race number, this model has detachable brown treaded rubber tyres. Length: 4·252in (108mm).

12 Mercedes Benz 1500 Racing Car by Mercury, Italy; MRN 40, dating from 1955. Finished in white, with a black-barred radiator, brown cockpit and the race number "3", this simple but nicely finished model is fitted with detachable grey rubber treaded tyres. Length: 4·17in (106mm).

13 Ferrari 1500 Racing Car by Mercury, Italy; MRN 36, dating from 1955. Finished in red, with a silver

radiator and the race number "5" in white, this model is fitted with detachable treaded rubber tyres. Length: 4·252in (108mm).

14 Cisitalia 1500 Grand Prix Racing Car by Mercury, Italy; MRN 38, dating from 1955. Finished in silver, with a black-barred radiator, black cockpit and black-outlined door panels, and without a race number, this racing car is fitted with detachable grey rubber treaded tyres. Length: 4·3125in (110mm).

15 Vanwall Formula One Racing Car by Solido, France; dating from the 1960s. Finished in dark green, with the applied name "Vanwall" and race number "9", this model features a clear plastic wraparound windscreen; a cockpit with the plastic figure of an overalled, helmeted driver; and, like the other Solido

models shown here, wheels that incorporate details of brake drums. Length: 4·016 (102mm).

16 Maserati 250 Racing Car by Solido, France; dating from the 1960s. Finished in yellow, with the race number "3", this model features a clear plastic windscreen, a cockpit with plastic driver, and a cast metal exhaust system at the side. Length: 3·74in (95mm).

17 Lola Climax V8 Formula One Racing Car by Solido, France; dating from the 1960s. Finished in dark blue, with a red-banded nose and the race number "2", this model features a cockpit with driver, bright-plated details of engine and exhaust pipes, and a detailed cast metal suspension system. Length: 3·504in (89mm).

18-19 Porsche F.11 Racing Car by

Solido, France; dating from the 1960s. Two versions are shown: (18) is finished in light green and bears the race number "10"; (19) is finished in silver, with a tri-colour trim strip, and bears the race number "3". The model has a body casting that incorporates the outline of an engine cover, and it features a clear plastic wraparound windscreen, a cockpit with the plastic figure of a driver, and rear exhaust details. Length: 3·268in (83mm).

20 Lotus Formula One Racing Car by Solido, France; MRN 118, dating from 1961. Made to a scale of 1:43, like all the Solido racing cars of the late 1950s-early 1960s shown on this spread, it is finished in dark green and bears the race number "3" on its nose. The cockpit, with an overalled and helmeted driver,

is protected by a full wraparound screen of clear plastic, and it has cast metal details of an exhaust system. Length: 3·071in (78mm).

21 Cooper 1·5-Litre Racing Car by Solido, France; MRN 116, dating from 1959. Finished in dark green, with the race number "3", this model features a cockpit with a driver protected by a wraparound screen, and a cast metal exhaust system. Length: 3·071in (78mm).

22 B.R.M. V8 Racing Car by Solido, France; MRN 131, dated (on base) February 1964. Finished in dark green, with the race number "3", this model has a clear plastic wraparound windscreen, a cockpit with driver, cast details of a roll-over bar behind the cockpit, and a cast metal exhaust system. Length: 3·386in (86mm).

Diecast Racing Cars by British and French Makers, 1936-1964

1 **B.R.M. Mark II Grand Prix Car** by Crescent Toys, Great Britain; Crescent Toys Reference Number (CTN) 1285, issued in 1957. Crescent's series of eight racing cars and two sports racing cars—shown on this spread at (1-7) and (9-11)—probably includes this maker's most sought-after models. As in all Diecast racing cars, the figure of the overalled driver is cast as part of the base plate. Length: 3·858in (98mm).

2 **Maserati 2·5-litre Grand Prix Car**: CTN 1290, issued in 1957. Note that the example shown here has been repainted, with added detail on such features as the driver's helmet and the filler cap on the car's tail. Length: 3·898in (99mm).

3 **"D" Type, Jaguar 3·5-litre Sports Racing Car**; CTN 1292, issued in 1957. The example shown has been carefully repainted, with certain details highlighted, as at (2). Length: 3·74in (95mm).

4 **Aston Martin D.B.3S 2·9-litre Sports Racing Car**; CTN 1291, issued in 1957. This attractive model is finished in American racing colours. Length: 3·74in (95mm).

5 **Mercedes-Benz 2·5-litre Grand Prix Car**; CTN 1284, issued in 1957. Length: 4·17in (106mm).

6 **Connaught 2-litre Grand Prix Car**; CTN 1287, issued in 1957. Length: 3·858in (98mm).

7 **Gordini 2·5-litre Grand Prix Car**; CTN 1289, issued in 1957. This example has been repainted. Note that it has also been refitted with tyres of the kind used on the racing cars issued by Corgi Toys, Great Britain; compare with the

other Crescent cars shown here. Length: 3·346in (85mm).

8 **Ferrari Racing Car** by Dinky Toys, France; French Dinky Toys Reference Number 23j, issued in 1957. It is finished in red, the racing colours of Italy; note the similarity otherwise with the British-made version in the racing colours of Argentina, shown at (15). Length: 3·937in (100mm).

9 **Ferrari 2·5-litre Grand Prix Car**; CTN 1286, issued in 1957. Note that the example shown here has been repainted and that new transfer detail has been applied. Length: 3·937in (100mm).

10 **Cooper Bristol 2-litre Grand Prix Car**; CTN 1288, issued in 1957. Length: 3·307in 984mm).

11 **Vanwall 2·5-litre Grand Prix Car**; CTN 1293, issued in 1957.

This is the hardest model to find of the set of Crescent racing cars. Length: 4·055in (103mm).

12 **H.W.M. Racing Car** by Dinky Toys, Great Britain; Dinky Toys Reference Number (DT No) 23j, first issued in May 1953, renumbered 235 in 1954, and available until 1960. It appeared only in green with the race number "7" in yellow. As in the other Dinky racing cars shown on this spread, the figure of the driver and also the steering wheel are cast in. The model's tinplate base plate is stamped with the maker's name, "23J" ("235" on later examples) and "H.W.M." It is of limited availability, examples numbered "23J" being more highly valued by collectors. Length: 3·989in (99mm).

13 Maserati Racing Car; DT No 23n, first issued in June 1953, renumbered 231 in 1954, and available until 1964. Appearing only in red with a white flash (Swiss racing colours), with the number "9" in white, it has a tinplate base that bears the maker's name, "23N" ("231" later) and "Maserati". Its availability is as noted for the item at (12). Length: 3·7in (94mm).

14 Talbot-Lago Racing Car; DT No 23k, first issued in September 1953, renumbered 230 in 1954, and available until 1964. Appearing only in blue with the number "4" in yellow, it has a tinplate base that bears the maker's name, "23K" ("230" later) and "Talbot Lago". As with (13), (15), (16) and (17), earlier versions have

ridged diecast wheels, while later examples (like the ones shown on this spread), dating from about the last two years of manufacture, may have plastic wheels; rubber tyres being fitted in all cases. Availability of this model is as (12). Length: 4·055in (103mm).

15 Ferrari Racing Car; DT No 23h, issued in April 1953, renumbered 234 in 1954, and available until 1964. It appeared only in blue, but earlier versions have an all-yellow nose whereas later examples, like that shown here, have a yellow triangle. All bear the race number "5" in yellow. Its tinplate base bears the maker's name, "23H" ("234" later) and "Ferrari". Availability as (12). Length: 3·976in (101mm).

16 Alfa-Romeo Racing Car; DT No 23f, issued in August 1952, renum-

bered 232 in 1954, and available until 1964. It appeared only in red with the white number "8". Its tinplate base bears the maker's name, "23F" ("232" later) and "Alfa-Romeo". Availability as (12). Length: 3·937in (100mm).

17 Cooper-Bristol Racing Car; DT No 23g, first issued in March 1953, renumbered 233 in 1954, and available until 1964. It appeared only in green with the race number "6" in white. Its tinplate base bears the maker's name, "23G" ("233" later) and "Cooper-Bristol". Availability as (12). It is worth noting that the six Dinky racing cars shown here at (12-17) were issued as Gift Set Number 4, available from 1953 until 1955 and now scarce and eagerly sought. Length: 3·504in (89mm).

Inset (top right): *Racer by Dinky Toys, Great Britain; Dinky Toys Reference Number 35b. Three versions of this long-lived, if diminutive, model are shown. (Left) As issued in 1939-40, with silver body, brown driver, red grille, and solid black rubber wheels: length: 2·323in (59mm). (Centre) As first issued in 1936-39, with red body, silver grille, no driver, and solid black (also found with white) rubber wheels; length: 2·402in (61mm). (Right) As issued in 1954-57, when the model was renamed Midget Racer and renumbered 200. Red or silver versions are recorded: this example finished in green appears to be a variant. Length: 2·244in (57mm). All versions are of fairly limited availability.*

1 Aston Martin DB3 (thus catalogued; in fact, an Aston Martin DB 2-4 Mk III) by Spot On (Tri-ang); Lines Bros Ltd), Great Britain; maker's reference number (MRN) 113, issued in 1960. Finished in metallic green, and appearing also in other colours, this has clear plastic windows and a detailed interior. Like all the Spot On cars shown here, it is made to a scale of 1:42, and, like all save (9), it has a metal chassis and is fitted with treaded rubber tyres. Like most Spot On models, it is now of scarce availability. Length: 4·094in (104mm).

2 Jaguar XKSS by Spot On; MRN 107, issued in 1960. Appearing only in red or green, this is fitted with front and rear number plates and has a clear plastic windscreen, interior detail, and a body casting that

incorporates a folded hood. It is one of the less common Spot On cars. Length: 3·583in (91mm).

3 Daimler SP250 Dart by Spot On; MRN 215, issued in 1962. Finished in yellow, and appearing also in other colours, this has a bright-plated radiator. Like (2), it may be hard to find. Length: 3·819in (97mm).

4 Sunbeam Alpine Convertible by Spot On; MRN 191, issued in 1963: a hard-top version was issued under the same number in the same year. Finished in blue, and appearing also in other colours, this has plated bumpers, radiator and headlight surrounds. The convertible may be slightly easier to find than the hardtop. Length: 3·74in (95mm).

5 M.G.A. Sports Car by Spot On; MRN 104, issued in 1959. Finished in red, and appearing also in white

or blue, this has a particularly well-detailed interior. It is one of the scarcer items in the Spot On range. Length: 3·74in (95mm).

6 M.G. Midget Mk II by Spot On; MRN 281, issued in 1966. Finished in white, this features plated parts and a detailed interior with a cast driver. Length: 3·268in (83mm).

7-8 M.G. Sports Car by Dinky Toys, Great Britain; Dinky Toys Reference Number (DT No) 35c. This model was first issued in 1936, remaining available until 1940: pre-War versions, in red, green or blue finish, have solid white rubber wheels. It was reissued, in red (7) or green (8), with solid black rubber wheels, in 1946-48. Both pre- and post-War versions are now hard to find. Length: 2·047in (52mm).

9 M.G. PB Midget (1935 Model) by

Spot On; MRN 729, issued in 1965. Appearing only in red-and-black finish, this model has a plastic chassis. It features plated parts and a detailed interior, and has cast-in spoked wheels. Another scarce item. Length: 3·11in (79mm).

10 M.G. TD Midget by Tekno, Denmark; dating from the early 1950s. Finished in red, with cream and pink trim, this model has a detailed interior with a bright-plated steering wheel (left-hand drive), and like the MG at (9), a rear-mounted spare wheel. Length: 3·465in (88mm).

11 M.G.C. GT by Corgi Toys, Great Britain; MRN 378, issued in 1970 and available until 1972. Appearing only in red-and-black finish, this model features jewelled headlights, opening doors and hatchback (with tool kit, as shown) tinted plastic

windows and a detailed interior. It is fitted with plastic "whizz-wheels". Length: 3·5625in (90mm).

12 M.G.B. GT by Corgi Toys; MRN 327, issued in 1967 and available until 1968. Appearing only in red, this model has jewelled headlights, an opening bonnet, doors and hatchback (including tool kit), and a detailed interior. Like (11), it will not be particularly easy to find. Length: 3·5625in (90mm).

13 Jaguar XK120 by Tekno, Denmark; dating from the early 1950s. This quite elegant little model has twin aero-screens of clear plastic and a detailed interior (left-hand drive). Length: 3·386in (86mm).

14 Austin Healey 100 (Touring Finish) by Dinky Toys, Great Britain; DT No 103, first issued in 1957 and available until 1960. Appearing only

in red and cream finish, this has a cast driver, a tinplate base and detachable rubber tyres. Limited. Length: 3·425in (87mm).

15 Austin Healey 100-4 by Corgi Toys; MRN 300, issued in 1956 and available until 1963. Compare this car with the Dinky Toys model at (14). This has a cast-in steering wheel, but no driver. It is of limited availability. Length: 3·386in (86mm).

16 Austin Healey Sprite Mark II by Dinky Toys, Great Britain; DT No 112, issued in November 1961 and available until 1966. Appearing only in red, this model is fitted with suspension and a "fingertip steering" system. Its availability is limited. Length: 3·071in (78mm).

17 M.G.A. Coupé by Tekno, Denmark; dating from the late 1950s. Finished in light blue, it has a detailed

moulded interior (left-hand drive). Length: 3·5625in (90mm).

18 Jaguar "E" Type by Corgi Toys; MRN 374, issued in 1970 and available until 1976. Finished in dark blue, this has plated parts, a detailed interior and "whizz-wheels". Length: 4·252in (108mm).

19-20 Vanwall Racing Car by Corgi Toys; MRN 150/150S. No 150, without driver or suspension, was available 1957-61; No 150S, with driver and suspension, was available 1961-65. It is now a limited item. Length: 3·583in (91mm).

21 B.R.M. Racing Car by Corgi Toys; MRN 152/152S. No 152, without suspension, was available 1958-61; No 152S, with suspension, was available 1961-65. Neither is common. Length: 3·583in (91mm).

22 Mercedes Benz 196 Grand Prix

Racing Car by Mercury, Italy; MRN 55, dating from 1960. Finished in silver, with the number "66", this is a fairly simple model. Scarce. Length: 4·016in (102mm).

23 Ferrari Supersqualo by Mercury, Italy; MRN 53, dating from 1960. Finished in red, this is another fairly basic model in 1:43 scale. Scarce. Length: 3·583in (91mm).

24 Mercedes Benz 196 Grand Prix Racing Car (Streamlined) by Mercury, Italy; MRN 56, dating from 1960. It is finished in silver, with the race number "48". Another scarce model. Length: 3·74in (95mm).

25 Lancia D.50 Grand Prix Racing Car by Mercury, Italy; MRN 54, dating from 1960. It is finished in red and bears the race number "92". Again, a scarce item from an early series. Length: 3·425in (87mm).

1 Ferrari Dino by Intercars, Spain; dating from around 1970. Finished in metallic blue, with a Ferrari badge and the race number "27", this model features opening doors and basic moulded interior. Length: 4·6875in (119mm).

2 Porsche GT Le Mans by Dalia Solido; Spain; makers' reference number (MRN) 134, dated (on base) March 1964. Finished in silver, with a black, red and gold trim strip (West German national colours) and the race number "30", this model has opening doors and a detailed interior (left-hand drive). Length: 3·622in (92mm).

3 Ferrari 330 P2 by Mercury, Italy; dating from around 1968-70. Finished in yellow, with a red, white and green strip (Italian national colours) and the race

number "24", this is a very well-detailed model, with plated wing-mirrors and windscreen wiper; opening doors and a moulded interior (right-hand drive); and a rear cover that lifts off, as seen here, to show a fully-detailed engine and a rear-mounted spare wheel. Length: 3·819in (97mm).

4 Fiat Abarth 1000 by Dalia Solido, Spain; MRN 124, dated (on base) September 1962. Finished in silver, with a red-and-white strip, and the race number "5", this model has opening doors and a detailed interior (left-hand drive). Length: 3·189in (81mm).

5 Aston Martin DB4 by Corgi Toys, Great Britain; MRN 309, first issued in 1962 and available until 1965. Appearing only in green-and-white, with the race numbers "3"

or "1", this model features a bonnet that opens to show a detailed engine, a moulded interior (right-hand drive), jewelled headlights, and a suspension system. It is one of the less common items in Corgi's range of racing and rally cars. Length: 3·74in (95mm).

6 Alfa Romeo Giulia T2 by Dalia Solido, Spain; MRN 148, dated (on base) June 1966. Finished in red with white trim, with the race number "82", this model features headlights with coloured plastic lenses, opening doors, and a detailed interior (left-hand drive). Length: 3·504in (89mm).

7 Fiat Abarth 1000 Bialbero by Mercury, Italy; dating from 1966. Finished in silver, with a badge and the race number "182", this model has opening doors, a

detailed moulded interior (left-hand drive), and an opening boot. Length: 4·3125in (110mm).

8 Ferrari Racing Sports Car by Tekno, Denmark; MRN 813, dating from 1958. In red-and-cream finish that incorporates the Danish emblem, with the race number "5", this simple but attractive model has an open cockpit with a clear plastic windscreen and a driver wearing racing overalls. Length: 3·74in (95mm).

9 DB Panhard Le Mans by Dalia Solido, Spain; dating from the 1960s. Finished in blue, with a tricolour strip (French national colours) and the race number "46", this model has an open cockpit with a wraparound plastic wind-screen and a driver (right-hand drive) in racing overalls and red

helmet. Length: 3·307in (84mm).
10 Ferrari 2·5-Litre by Dalia Solido, Spain; MRN 129, dated January 1964. Finished in red, with badges and the race number "152", this has a body casting incorporating front air vents and a rear spoiler; the detailed cockpit, with wraparound plastic windscreen, holds an overalled, helmeted driver (right-hand drive). Length: 3·622in (92mm).
11-12 Ferrari Racing Sports Car by Mercury, Italy; dating from around 1970. Two versions are shown. The car at (11) is finished in British racing green (note the Union flag on the rear compartment cover, shown here removed), with badges and the race number "18". The car at (12) is finished in metallic silver and red, with the

race number "4". The model has a detailed open cockpit with driver (right-hand drive), opening doors, and a rear cover (with cast air intake) that is removable, showing a fully-detailed engine and a spare wheel. Length: 3·74in (95mm).
13 Lancia D24 by Mercury, Italy; MRN N26, dating from 1960. Finished in red with the race number "84", this is a plain and simple model with a fairly basically-detailed body casting. Length: 3·622in (92mm).
14 Aston Martin 3L DBRI 300 by Solido, France; dating from the 1960s. Finished in green with the race number "2", this model has details of vents and fairings incorporated into its body casting. It has an open cockpit with an overalled driver (right-hand drive)

behind a wraparound windscreen. Length: 3·622in (92mm).
15 Aston Martin 3L by Dalia Solido, Spain; dating from the 1960s. It is interesting to compare this model, finished in yellow, with that of the same car issued by Solido, France; shown at (14). The same body casting is used for the model issued by the Spanish company: only the wheels are different. Length: 3·622in (92mm).
16 Jaguar Le Mans "D" Type by Solido, France; dating from the 1960s. Finished in dark green with the race number "8", this has a body casting that incorporates a tail-fin. The overalled, helmeted driver is protected by a clear plastic wraparound windscreen. Length: 3·622in (92mm).
17 Dino Sport by Mercury, Italy;

dating from the 1960s. Finished in red with the race number "186", this is fitted with opening doors and boot; the cast cockpit, with the rather crude figure of a driver, also houses a moulded plastic engine. Length: 3·622in (92mm).
18 Porsche Spyder by Dalia Solido, Spain; dating from the 1960s. Finished in silver with the race number "5", this features a plastic canopy over the right side only of the left-hand-drive cockpit. Length: 3·386in (86mm).
19 Ferrari Type 500 TRC by Dalia Solido, Spain; dating from the 1960s. Finished in red, with badges and the race number "4", this has a detailed cockpit with driver (right-hand drive) and a clear plastic wraparound windscreen. Length: 3·74in (95mm).

Diecast Rally Cars by Solido, France, 1974-1981

1 B.M.W. 2002 Turbo by Solido, France; maker's reference number (MRN) 28, dated October 1975. (Note that all the cars in this series have a date—in the example shown, "10-75"—stamped on the base.) Like all the models on this spread, it represents a left-hand drive car and is made to a scale of 1:43. Finished in metallic grey, with red-and-blue "Turbo" side trim strip, this model has a number plate, "M-KM 1843", applied front and rear. It has bright metal headlights, red plastic rearlights and sculptured plastic wheels and tyres. The metal base has cast details of transmission, exhaust and suspension. Length: 3·858in (98mm).

2 B.M.W. 530; MRN 89, dated July 1979. Finished in metallic grey, with applied make and rally badges and blue-and-red trim strips, this model has plastic windows (the driver's part-open); a detailed plastic interior, including a roll-cage at the rear; sculptured plastic wheels, and a plastic base with basic transmission details moulded in. Length: 4·055in (103mm).

3 Alfa Romeo Alfetta GTV; MRN 82, dated March 1979. Finished in white with a black bonnet, with applied badges and the number "31", this model features plastic windows and steering wheel; it has jewelled dual headlights and red-painted cast rearlights. Fitted with sculptured plastic wheels, it has a plastic base with transmission details. Length: 3·7in (94mm).

4 Opel Kadett Coupé GTE; MRN 70, dated November 1978. Finished in orange, with applied badges and the number "31", this model has plastic windows and a detailed interior. Its front and rear bumpers and lights are of plated plastic. It has sculptured plastic wheels and a plastic base with basic details of suspension and exhaust moulded in. Length: 3·858in (98mm).

5 Toyota Celica; MRN 1094, dated March 1980. Finished in cream, with applied badges and the number "29", this car has an applied number plate, "E.1388", front and rear. It has plastic windows and a detailed interior with a roll-cage at the rear. The radiator and front and rear bumpers are inset plastic; the headlights and spots are bright metal. It has sculptured plastic wheels and tyres and a metal base with details of transmission and exhaust. Length: 3·858in (98mm).

6 Lancia Stratos; MRN 73, dated January 1979. Finished in white, with applied badges and the number "19", this features a plastic spoiler and louvred rear window. Note also the array of cast headlights. It has plastic wheels and a plain metal base. Length: 3·386in (86mm).

7 B.M.W. M1; MRN 1031, dated April 1981. Finished in dark blue, with applied badges and the number "41", this model has a diecast spoiler and a louvred plastic rear window. It has non-opening doors and inset plastic head- and rearlights. The wheels and the base, with basic suspension details, are plastic. Length: 4·17in (106mm).

8 Ford Capri 2600 RV; MRN 26, dated September 1974. Finished in metallic blue with white stripes, with applied badges and the number

"55", this features jewelled dual headlights and plastic rally lamps with covers on the front bumper. With opening doors, it is equipped with sculptured plastic wheels and is fitted with a plain plastic base. Length: 3·858in (98mm).

9 Peugeot 504 Coupé V6; MRN 1055, dated February 1980. Finished in white, with applied badges and the number "02", it has spotlights, front splash-guards and rear bumper of bright metal; the inset radiator, headlights and mud flaps on rear wheels are plastic. Its detailed plastic interior includes a rear roll-cage. It has sculptured plastic wheels and a plastic base with moulded details of transmission. Length: 3·937in (100mm).

10 B.M.W. 3.0 CLS; MRN 25, dated May 1974. Finished in white with

blue-and-red trim, the number "31" and applied badges, this model has bright metal headlights, red plastic rearlights and an inset plastic radiator. It has opening doors and a detailed interior with tip-up front seats. Its sculptured plastic wheels are fitted with fat, smooth plastic tyres. Its metal base is fully detailed. Length: 4·17mm (106mm).

11 Fiat Abarth 131 Rallye; MRN 54, dated November 1977. Finished in blue and yellow, with applied badges and the number "5", this model features a plastic rear spoiler, red plastic rearlights, and bright metal headlights and spots. Plastic windows are fitted all round and it has a detailed interior with a rear roll-cage. It has sculptured plastic wheels and a yellow metal base with cast detail of transmission and

black metal axle boxes and exhaust system. Length: 3·937in (100mm).

12 B.M.W. 3.0 CSL; MRN 75, dated June 1978. Finished in orange, with applied badges and the number "21", it has jewelled dual headlights and inset red plastic rearlights. It has opening doors and a detailed interior. With sculptured plastic wheels, it has a plastic base with details of transmission and exhaust. Length: 4·016in (102mm).

13 Ford Escort L; MRN 45, dated June 1976. Finished in white and black, with applied badges and the number "15", this has bright metal headlights and plated plastic spotlights and front and rear bumpers. It has a detailed interior, sculptured plastic wheels and is fitted with a plain plastic base. Length: 3·7in (94mm).

14 Renault 5 Turbo; MRN 1023, dated July 1981. Finished in metallic blue, with applied badges and the number "18", and applied number plates, "6891 VK 38", front and rear, this model has a blue plastic base that sweeps upward to incorporate details of sills and front and rear bumpers. Its detailed interior includes a plastic roll-cage. Length: 3·386in (86mm).

Inset (top right): *The bases of three of the Solido rally cars. (Left to right): the basically-detailed black plastic base of the Opel Kadett Coupé GTE (4); the yellow metal base of the Fiat Abarth 131 Rallye (11), bearing cast metal details of transmission, axle boxes and exhaust; and the plain black plastic base of the Ford Escort L (13).*

Pedal and Powered Cars by British and French Makers, 1930s

Right: *Atco Trainer Two-Seater Car by Atco (Austin Motor Company), Great Britain; dating from the 1930s.* This most interesting vehicle falls into a category somewhere between that of a toy and an educational aid, since it was marketed as a training aid for young drivers. One may conclude, however, that its true function will have been that of a fascinating and expensive plaything, since even in the more spacious 1930s it is hardly likely to have been used on the road by a juvenile driver. The car is powered by a single-cylinder petrol engine mounted at the rear (the lid of the engine compartment is shown open), which is started by a lever (clearly seen in the photograph) set in the centre of the PVC-upholstered bench seat. Note the gear lever set to the driver's right and the exterior-mounted handbrake. Ackerman steering is fitted. The body is of pressed steel, with bright steel bumpers at front and rear and a bright radiator grille. Bicycle-type

mudguards are fitted over the split-rim wheels with their pneumatic treaded tyres. This example has undergone some restoration and is now finished in dark green, with a modified Austin "Flying A" bonnet mascot and the maker's name and a Royal Warrant badge on the bonnet side. Length: 72in (183cm).

Above: *"Bugatti" Pedal Racing Car by Eureka, France; dating from the early 1930s:* the front axle is stamped "12/32", probably signifying that the car was made, or its design registered, in December 1932. The example shown was the cheapest and simplest in the French maker's "Bugatti" series. It has a well-modelled radiator, a pressed-steel body incorporating two sets of horizontal louvres on either side of the bonnet, and pressed-steel wheels with solid rubber tyres that bear a moulded tread pattern. This example has been restored, but only the bulb-horn is non-original. Eureka produced its "Bugatti" in a larger "touring" version, with the addition of bumpers, lights and a side-mounted spare wheel; and in a still larger version, with an opening bonnet, perforated disc wheels fitted with pneumatic tyres, and a freewheel mechanism incorporated into its pedal drive. Length: 33in (84cm).

Above: *"Argyle" Pedal Car by Tansad, Great Britain; dating from the early 1930s.* Seen here in partially restored condition, but in its original red finish with printed yellow louvres and bonnet trim, this single-seat car has an all-pressed-steel body and a radiator with a printed grille. It is fitted with an opening door, a windscreen that folds down, and a padded seat-back. The dashboard bears a fine array of printed instrument dials. The metal disc wheels are fitted with solid rubber tyres that retain traces of a moulded tread pattern. The rear of the car bears a contemporary "National Road Safety Campaign" transfer. Although of the correct period type, the "Red-X" petrol can mounted on the running-board is not the one originally fitted: Tansad cars with this feature usually had "Pratts" petrol cans (and, it may be noted, Tri-ang cars of the same period usually had "Shell" cans). Length: 33·5in (85cm).

Left: "Buick Regal" Pedal Car by Tri-ang (Lines Brothers Ltd), Great Britain; dating from around 1931. This is a toy of extremely good quality and it is shown here in excellent original condition, having undergone no restoration. (It is worth noting here that the general opinion among collectors seems to be that the value of a toy that has been professionally restored to near-original condition may be around 70-75 per cent of the value of an unrestored item in very good condition.) This car has a pressed-steel, single-seat body, incorporating bonnet fairings and louvres, tubular steel front bumpers, and a well-modelled radiator with a chromed frame, surmounted by a cast metal mascot. It is fitted with working, battery-powered headlights and sidelights (with an on/off switch mounted on the dashboard) and has an opening door with a cast handle. Other details visible in the photograph include a front number plate, an imitation "road tax disc" in a holder mounted just below the near-side sidelight, a fold-down windshield with a chromed frame and a clear perspex screen, a rear-view mirror, and a simulated folded hood. The dashboard bears a well-printed array of instrument panels. Its wire-spoked wheels are fitted with treaded tyres of solid rubber, and it has a suspension system with half-elliptic springing. A detachable boot with a luggage rack was originally bolted on at the rear, but is now missing. Length: 43in (109cm).

Left: *"Bullnose Morris" Pedal Car by Tri-ang (Lines Brothers Ltd), Great Britain;* dating from the 1920s. With a metal frame and wooden panels, this most attractive representation of a famous British-built touring car has a bicycle-type chain drive. It is fitted with a sprung front bumper, front and rear number plates and a rear luggage rack. Other features include a well-modelled radiator (with Lines Brothers' punning trademark impressed on its crown) surmounted by a realistic filler cap and temperature gauge, an opening door with a chromed handle, a wood-rimmed steering wheel and an adjustable seat. It is fitted with a battery-powered buzzer that simulates a starter-motor. The fold-down windscreen that was originally provided is missing from this otherwise excellent example. The detachable disc wheels are fitted with solid rubber tyres. This high-quality toy was advertised in 1927 at a price of £5 5s 0d (£5.25, $6.30), which was then more than the weekly wage of the average British worker; one of the more expensive items in Tri-ang's range. Length: 49in (124·5cm).

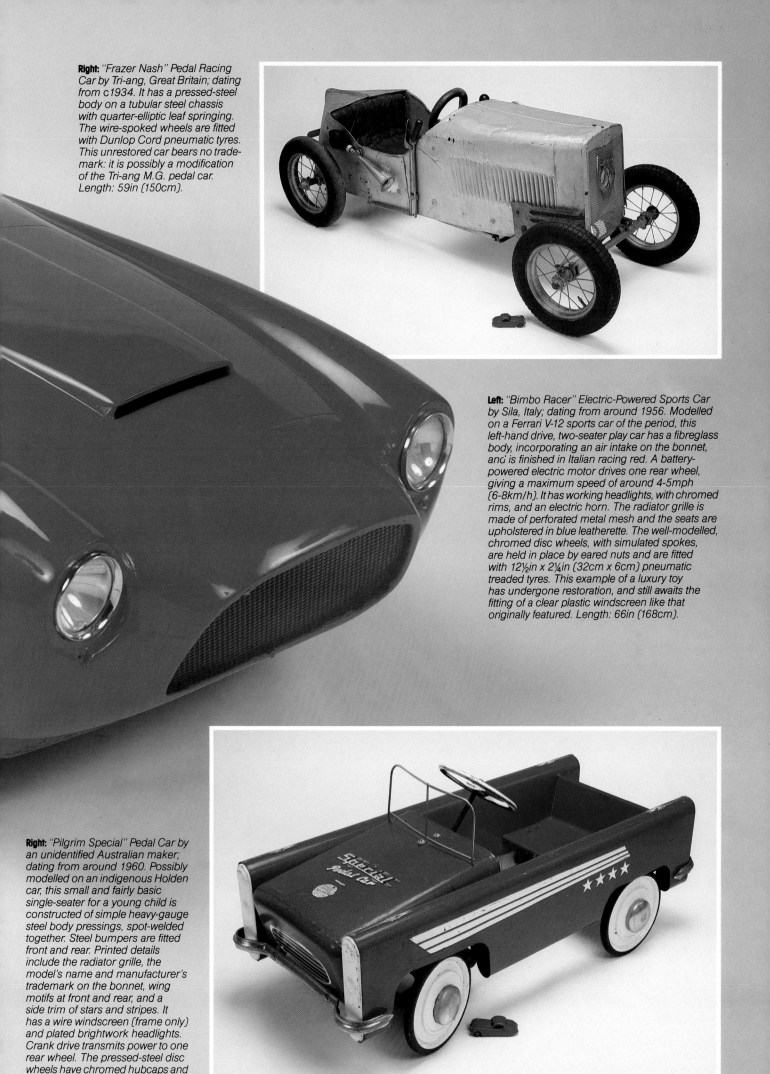

Right: "Frazer Nash" Pedal Racing Car by Tri-ang, Great Britain; dating from c1934. It has a pressed-steel body on a tubular steel chassis with quarter-elliptic leaf springing. The wire-spoked wheels are fitted with Dunlop Cord pneumatic tyres. This unrestored car bears no trademark: it is possibly a modification of the Tri-ang M.G. pedal car. Length: 59in (150cm).

Left: "Bimbo Racer" Electric-Powered Sports Car by Sila, Italy; dating from around 1956. Modelled on a Ferrari V-12 sports car of the period, this left-hand drive, two-seater play car has a fibreglass body, incorporating an air intake on the bonnet, and is finished in Italian racing red. A battery-powered electric motor drives one rear wheel, giving a maximum speed of around 4-5mph (6-8km/h). It has working headlights, with chromed rims, and an electric horn. The radiator grille is made of perforated metal mesh and the seats are upholstered in blue leatherette. The well-modelled, chromed disc wheels, with simulated spokes, are held in place by eared nuts and are fitted with 12½in x 2¼in (32cm x 6cm) pneumatic treaded tyres. This example of a luxury toy has undergone restoration, and still awaits the fitting of a clear plastic windscreen like that originally featured. Length: 66in (168cm).

Right: "Pilgrim Special" Pedal Car by an unidentified Australian maker; dating from around 1960. Possibly modelled on an indigenous Holden car, this small and fairly basic single-seater for a young child is constructed of simple heavy-gauge steel body pressings, spot-welded together. Steel bumpers are fitted front and rear. Printed details include the radiator grille, the model's name and manufacturer's trademark on the bonnet, wing motifs at front and rear, and a side trim of stars and stripes. It has a wire windscreen (frame only) and plated brightwork headlights. Crank drive transmits power to one rear wheel. The pressed-steel disc wheels have chromed hubcaps and are fitted with solid tyres of smooth rubber. Length: 38in (97cm).

Pedal Cars by British and US Makers, 1950s-1970s

1

2

3

1 "Ford Zephyr" Pedal Car by Triang (Lines Brothers Limited), Great Britain, early 1950s. This has an all-metal body, with plated brightwork bumper bars, radiator grille, and hubcaps, and rubber tyres. It features battery-powered headlights, an exterior-mounted handbrake, and a simulated column-mounted gear lever. Length: 48in (122cm).

2 "Marx-Mobile" Electric-Powered Automobile by Marx, USA, c1960. Battery-powered, the all-metal car, with brightly-printed finish and featuring the tail fins typical of the period, is controlled by the forward-reverse lever to the driver's right; the lever also has a "neutral", free-wheel, position. The foot-rests, (note driving position in maker's brochure) may be pushed

into the body. Also in the maker's brochure, note the dashboard detail, including a "real" ignition key. Length: 27in (68·5cm).

3 "De Dion" Pedal Car by Triang, Great Britain, 1960s. This "Vintage" car has a tubular metal chassis with a sprung rear axle; a pressed-steel body; plastic mudguards, steering-wheel, and side-lamps; and a plastic-upholstered, wooden-backed seat. The starting-handle mounted in the front of the body incorporates a "clicker" device, and the wheels are fitted with moulded rubber tyres. Length: 36in (91·5cm).

4 "Austin J (Junior) Forty" Pedal Car, often called the "Austin Joycar", by the Austin Motor Company Limited, Birmingham, Great Britain, built between 1950

and 1971. The red finish dates this as a later model—the same colours were used as on Austin's real cars of the period: light green and fawn on earlier models, and red, white or darker green on later ones. However, the "Flying A" mascot on the hood shows that it is not a very late example: in line with British laws prohibiting such projections on real cars, mascots were not fitted to late-production "Joycars". It is possible roughly to date examples from the chassis number

(Top) A publicity brochure of the 1950s for the Austin "J Forty" Pedal Car; see (4) above. (Bottom) "The Magic Motor Car", a British children's book of the 1920s, featuring Triang's Rolls Royce electric-powered car.

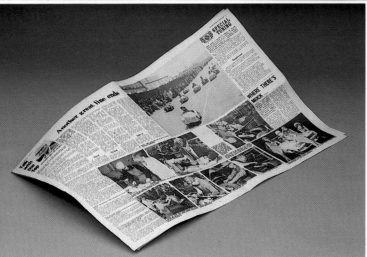

stamped on the floor of the boot. This pedal car is of unusually robust construction, since it is made of sheet steel of the same gauge as that used on Austin's real cars. Surplus material from Austin's production line was transported to a specially-constructed factory at Bargoed, Wales, where "Joycars" were built by disabled miners as part of a rehabilitation programme. The "Joycar" features chromed bumpers, radiator grille and hubcaps; battery-operated headlights and horn; a bonnet that

The end of production of the Austin "Joycar" is announced on the centre-spread of the manufacturer's house journal, issued in May 1971.

opens to reveal an "engine" complete with sparking plugs and leads; a felt-padded, leather-cloth-upholstered seat; a two-position interior handbrake; and pressed-steel wheels with Dunlop pneumatic tyres. Total production over 21 years amounted to 32,100 "Joycars", and they are still fairly common. Length: 63in (160cm).

5 Pedal Car by Leeway, Great Britain, early 1950s. The chrome-plated brightwork radiator is of "Triumph Dolomite" type, but Leeway's designation for this toy was "Model 16/11". Its all-steel body has an opening door, and features include simulated head- and side-lights, pressed-steel "balloon-type" wheels with moulded rubber tyres, and a two-speed gear lever. Length: 45in (114cm).

3

Since the turn of the century toymakers have produced, at first in cast-iron and tinplate and later in diecast metal, representations of almost every kind of commercial vehicle that has entered service on the world's highways: lorries and vans, buses and trams, fire engines and bulldozers, ambulances and police cars, cranes and diggers. Vehicles of all these kinds feature on the following pages.

For many collectors, transport toys have even more appeal than toy cars, for the variation of models is so much greater: the modern car is still a recognisable descendant of the "horseless carriage", but a Horse-Drawn Fire Engine in cast iron, like the example by an American maker shown at (3) on *pages 112-113*, has little in common with its modern equivalents, like the modern fire vehicles shown on *pages 114-115*.

Thus, in the case of transport toys, a thematic collection, perhaps combining both the rarer tinplate and the more easily acquired diecast items, can result in the assembly of an impressive display consisting of relatively few specimens.

Transport Toys

Although most makers of toy cars also produced a range of commercial vehicles, such toys are generally felt to be of smaller interest to the collector of tinplate vehicles than cars are, since the commercial vehicle ranges were generally less extensive and incorporated fewer changes in style. An exception must be made, however, for commercial vehicles that bear well-marked advertising motifs. It should be noted also that toy commercial vehicles are more likely to be found in "play-worn" condition: many were designed for "active play" during which they were loaded with sand, etc. All the vehicles shown on this spread were photographed at the London Toy & Model Museum.

1 Pick-Up Truck, based on a Model "T" Ford, by "Buddy L" (The Moline Pressed Steel Company, East Moline, Illinois), USA, dating from the 1930s. This maker is chiefly known for the production of vehicles in heavy gauge sheet steel, like the example shown here; see also the Bus shown at (3) on *pages 110-111* and the Pumping Engine shown at (2) on *pages 112-113*. This vehicle has diecast "artillery type" spoked wheels and, like the original Model "T", is finished in black. Of extremely robust construction and obviously intended for "active play", it has little in the way of detail. Length: 12in (30·5cm).

2 "Sentinel Rigid Six Wheeler" Steam Lorry by Tipp and Company, Germany, c1930. This clockwork-driven tinplate vehicle was

produced in Germany as a promotional toy for the British company Sentinel, a manufacturer of steam wagons and other heavy plant. (It is worth noting that most of the real Sentinel wagons were four-wheeled; only a few six-wheelers were built). It has a tipping body with a hinged tailgate, and pressed tin wheels and tyres with lithographed detail of tread and spokes. Length: 20in (51cm). This truck is scarce.

3 Army Truck by Mettoy Co. Limited, Britain, c1940. Very much a wartime "utility" toy, this simple and cheaply-priced clockwork truck (note permanent winder) has a canvas canopy and is finished in camouflage of a kind more commonly associated with German than British military vehicles.

Length: 9in (23cm). A fairly common toy.

4 Motor Coach by Tipp and Company, Germany, c1928. This large tinplate vehicle, clockwork-driven, is attractively finished in red, lined with yellow and black, and has pressed tin wheels with lithographed spokes and "Dunlop Cord" tyres; note also the lithographed spare tyre at the rear. Other detail includes interior seating and battery-operated electric headlights. The same chassis was used by Tipp for other vehicles. Length: 17·5in (44·5cm). A limited item.

5 Mack "Coal" Truck by Arcade Models, an American maker, dating from c1930. Massively made in the cast iron long favoured by American makers, this push-/pull-along toy

features a crank-operated tipping mechanism and has rubber tyres (note dual tyres at rear). A virtually indestructible toy, it has some cast detail—springs, radiator, "Mack" on cab door—but generally lacks the sophistication of its European tinplate contemporaries. Length: 10·125in (26cm).

6 Tipping Truck by Gebrüder Bing, Nuremburg, Germany, c1908. In excellent condition, this fine early example of a tinplate commercial vehicle has a hand-enamelled finish, cast "artillery type" wheels with rubber tyres, and a canvas canopy above the cab. It is clockwork-powered, with steering operating from the wheel and manually-operated tipping action. Length: 11·5in (29cm). A very scarce specimen.

7 Tipping Truck by Paya, Alicante, Spain, c1930. This clockwork-driven tinplate truck is attractively finished and derives a certain charm from the fact that the same simple tinplate silhouette of the driver appears on both doors. The spoked wheels are of pressed tin and the maker's trademark is visible on the near door. Length: 10in (25·4cm).

8 Pickup Truck by André Citroën, France, c1929. A fine model from this justly celebrated range—see note at (1), *pages 34-35*—this truck is based on the Citroën C6 chassis. It features opening doors, operating steering, and electric headlights, and has rubber tyres. Note the detail of the radiator, with the Citroën chevrons and swan badge. As shown, it was sold complete

with a load of sacks, also bearing the Citroën chevrons. Length: 17in (43cm). Scarce. (A Road Sweeping Vehicle was produced on the same chassis; this is now very scarce.)

9 Trailer Truck by Wyn-Toy, Australia, c1950; note the maker's trademark on the cab door. This simple but effective toy is of pressed tin construction, with pressed tin wheels and a plated radiator. Length overall: 18·25in (46cm).

10 Petrol Pump and Oil Cabinet Set by Tipp and Company, Germany, dating from c1920; a most attractive accessory—with considerable period charm for the present-day motorist! In those days, it was common for filling stations to offer for sale several brands of petrol—and here

we see the familiar names of "Shell" and "BP" alongside the now-forgotten "Pratts". The glass globes of the fuel pumps are electrically lit by means of a battery concealed within the attractively-lithographed tinplate "Double Shell Motor Oil" cabinet, and the curved island on which the pumps and cabinet are mounted also incorporates "In" and "Out" signs. Length: 9·5in (24cm). Limited. (The water can shown in front of the set is a diecast garage accessory and was not made by Tipp and Company.)

11-12 Unlike Citroën—see (8)—most makers did not supply loads for their commercial vehicles. There must be few children who have not used composition blocks like these to load their vehicles.

1 Diesel Road Roller by an unidentified British maker; dating from around 1950. The only marks of origin on this toy are the words "Made in England" printed across its upper front. It is of pressed tinplate construction with printed details, the canopy being provided with wire supports, and is complete with the two-piece tinplate figure of a driver. An exposed clockwork motor at the rear (the large spring is just visible in the photograph), with a permanently-fixed winder, drives the rear wheels in alternate forward and reverse motion, a common feature in toy rollers; the model is steered via its swivel-mounted front roller. Fairly common. Length: 7·75in (19·685cm).
2 Diesel Road Roller by Mettoy Company Limited, Great Britain;

dating from around 1950. Made of pressed and printed tinplate, this model features an open cab with a pressed-tin seat and a cast metal steering wheel. A rear-mounted clockwork motor with a permanently-fixed winder (just visible in the photograph) drives the rear wheels in alternate forward and reverse motion; a steerable front roller is fitted. Fairly common. Length: 7·625in (19·3675cm).
3 Fire Service Car by an unidentified French maker, dating from around 1935-40. This was originally made as a novelty confectionary tin, its hinged roof forming a lid, and was intended to function as a toy when emptied; see also (11). Its tinplate body is pleasingly printed with such details as radiator grille, bonnet ventilators, a crest on the

door and a crew of firemen. The pressing incorporates a front bumper and close-fitting mud-guards and running-boards. A clockwork motor with a wire spring drives the rear wheels; note the permanently-fixed winder. It is fitted with pressed-tin wheels with printed details of "Dunlop" tyres. This is of limited availability, and in the case of such items toy collectors are likely to face stiff competition from collectors of tinplate containers — a rivalry that may well be reflected in the prices that are demanded! Length: 6·625in (16·8275cm).
4 "Ubilda" Fire Engine by Chad Valley, Great Britain; dating from around 1950. Chad Valley produced a number of vehicle construction kits in its "Ubilda" series both before and after World War II,

among them the tinplate fire engine which is shown here fully assembled. Nuts, bolts, axles, a clockwork motor and a spanner were supplied with the kit, and assembly of the sectional body and detachable fire escape on the pressed-tin chassis was quite simple. A separate key was provided for the clockwork motor, which drives the rear wheels. The radiator bears the printed number-plate "C.V. 10033". Limited. Length: 10·5in (26·67cm).
5 Fire Engine by C. Rossignol, Paris, France; dating from around 1940. Bearing the maker's "C.R." mark on the lower edge of its bonnet, this simple push-along toy is of lightweight tinplate, with a pressed chassis and printed cab and bonnet. It is fitted with a simple

5

6

7

10

11

revolving turntable ladder and has single-sided tinplate wheels. Limited. Length: 7·5in (19·05cm).

6 Turntable Fire Engine by an unidentified maker, probably of British or German manufacture; dating from around 1954. This forward-control vehicle is of lightweight tinplate construction; it has printed details and is equipped with two pressed-tin figures of seated firemen. A clockwork motor with a separate key (note the winding-shank towards the rear of the vehicle) drives the rear wheels. The nearside rear mudguard is missing. It is a limited item. Length: 10·00in (25·4cm).

7 Fire Engine by Jep (Jouets en Paris), France; dating from the 1930s. This two-seater fire engine with its pressed-tin firemen is a

rather pleasingly proportioned toy from a notable maker. It has printed details and is fitted with an elevating ladder. It has single-sided pressed-tin wheels, the rear pair driven by a clockwork motor with diecast cogs; note the rather over-sized permanently-fixed winder towards the rear of the chassis. Limited. Length: 7·625in (19·367cm).

8 "Breakdown Service" Lorry by an unidentified British maker; dating from around 1940. Note particularly the "Automobile Association" emblem on the cab doors; other printed details include radiator grille, bonnet ventilators, and spokes and "5 x 19 Balloon Tyres" on the two-piece pressed-tin wheels. The tinplate figure of the driver is just visible. A clockwork motor drives the rear wheels. The

manually-operated crane on the example shown is a replacement item. It is possible that this toy is the work of Wells Brimtoy. Limited. Length: 8·25in (20·955cm).

9 Ambulance by Gama, West Germany; dating from around 1955. This good-quality toy of heavy-gauge tinplate construction has a pressed body with an opening rear door and a bright-plated radiator grille and headlights. It is fitted with perforated-disc wheels with treaded black rubber tyres marked "10 x 35". The ambulance is fitted with a "push-and-go" mechanism that also produces a "siren" sound. A limited item. Length: 8·625in (21·9075cm).

10 Ambulance by Burnett Limited, Great Britain; dating from around 1940. This simple toy of lightweight

tinplate has a most attractive colour-printed finish; note that the mudguards and running-boards are edged with white, a common condition of real vehicles in the "blackout" conditions prevailing in Britain during the war years. This model is fitted with two-piece pressed-tin wheels, the rear pair driven by a clockwork motor with a permanently-fixed winder on the near side. This is a limited item. Length: 5·875in (14·9225cm).

11 Ambulance by an unidentified French maker; dating from around 1935-40. This is the same pressing as the Fire Service Car shown at (3); only the finish is different. Like (3), this ambulance has a hinged roof and was originally made as a novelty confectionery tin. Limited. Length: 6·625in (16·827cm).

1 Renault-Type Tipping Lorry by C. Rossignol, Paris, France; dating from 1937-39. This toy bears no maker's mark but is fairly confidently attributed to Rossignol on stylistic grounds. With a painted finish in mottled red-and-fawn, it is fitted with a simple tipping rear body with a hinged tailboard. The chassis has pressed side-members. The two-piece wheels are of pressed tin and a clockwork motor drives the rear pair. A limited item. Length: 7·125in (18·0975cm).

2 Articulated Lorry by an unidentified British maker—it has "Made in England" printed along the tops of the mudguards—dating from c1946-50. This simple lorry of tabbed-and-slotted tinplate construction, with pressed and printed details, is possibly the work of the Mettoy Company Limited. A clockwork motor concealed within the cab, with a permanently-fixed winder protruding from the left central chassis, drives the rear pair of two-piece printed-tin wheels on the cab unit. Fairly common. Length: 9·06in (23·012cm).

3 Tipping Lorry by an unidentified British maker—note that it has "Made in England" printed on the side of the cab—dating from c1935-40. This model of a forward-control lorry (the term is used of a cab without a bonnet) has a simple tipping rear body with pressed detail simulating planked sides. The tailboard is fixed. A clockwork motor with a permanently-fixed winder drives the rear wheels. Note the printed "Dunlop Fort" tyres. This is a fairly common item.

Length: 7·68in (19·507cm).

4 "Games" Delivery Van by Chad Valley, Great Britain; this example dating from c1946. The Chad Valley "Games Van" so called because of the many games by the maker illustrated on its roof and upper sides, was one of the most attractive tinplate vans produced in Britain in the 1930s-40s. It is fitted with a "Dennis" radiator and has the numberplate "CV 10032" above its nicely-printed bonnet. The sides bear the company's name and its Royal Warrant, with crest and "By Appointment . . ." legend. The van is fitted with an opening rear door and a flat-spring clockwork motor drives its rear wheels. This very popular model is scarce, but easier to find than the very similar toy shown at (5).

Length: 9·75in (24·765cm).

5 "Crumpsall Cream Crackers" Delivery Van by Chad Valley, Great Britain; dating from c1938. The same pressing as (4), but with an appropriate finish, this was produced as a novelty biscuit tin (to function as a toy when emptied) for the Co-Operative Wholesale Society; note the "CWS" monograms among the wealth of printed detail. Its rear wheels are driven by a clockwork motor that has a wire spring; this was to allow the biscuit compartment to have a flat base. A fairly scarce item. Length: 9·75in (24·765cm).

6 Tipping Lorry by an unidentified British maker; dating from c1948-52. In lightweight tinplate, with a tin driver, this has a lever-operated tipping rear body that is held in

place by twisted tabs (one is visible in the photograph). It has a pressed chassis with running-boards and is fitted with two-piece printed wheels, the rear pair clockwork-driven. It is fairly typical of the low-priced tinplate toys made in Britain in the 1930s-50s. Fairly common. Length: 9·875in (25·0825cm).

7 Tipping Lorry by Camtoy, Great Britain; dating from c1948. This model of a forward-control lorry has fully-printed details, including windows, with the numberplate "PT 668". Its tipping rear body is held in place by turned-over tabs and it has two-piece printed wheels. This is a fairly common item. Length: 6·75in (17·145cm).

8 Push-Along Lorry by an unidentified maker; dating from the 1940s. It bears what appears to be an "S/F"

trademark on the cab doors. Constructed of lightweight tinplate, it has printed details that include bonnet ventilators, and it is fitted with two-piece pressed-tin wheels. Limited. Length: 7·25in (18·415cm).

9 Light Truck by Paya, Spain; dating from c1940. This cheaply-made toy of lightweight tinplate has a clockwork motor that drives the rear wheels. Note the maker's trademark printed to the rear of the cab door; the cab incorporates the tinplate silhouette figure of a driver. This is a fairly limited item. Length: 7·58in (19·253cm).

10 "Colis Express" Delivery Van by Memo, France; dating from c1945-50. Note the maker's trademark on the door of this lightweight tinplate toy with its rather pleasing printed details. The

pressed-tin radiator was probably used by the maker on several other models. A clockwork motor, with an over-length permanently-fixed winder protruding from the base on the left side, drives the rear wheels. It is fairly common. Length: 5·75in (14·605cm).

11 "Express Delivery" Van by Wells, Great Britain; note that "British Made" is printed along the bottom of the radiator. This tinplate toy dates from c1935, although it has a considerably earlier appearance. The maker produced the same model in the finish of the "Carter Paterson" haulage company. A limited item. Length: 4·75in (12·065cm).

12 "Express Transport" Van by Wells, Great Britain — with "Made in England" printed on the front doors

— dating from c1947. Of tabbed-and-slotted tinplate, this toy is fitted with printed perforated-disc wheels, the rear pair driven by a clockwork motor with a permanently-fixed winder. This is a limited item. Length: 7·25in (18·415cm).

13 "Express Road Transport" Van by Burnett, Great Britain; dating from c1950. Established in Birmingham before World War I, Burnett Limited moved to London around 1914 and later became part of the Chad Valley company. This example of a Burnett toy is an extremely simple pressing in lightweight tinplate, with basic printed detail. A clockwork motor with a permanently-fixed winder drives the rear wheels, which are of two-piece pressed tin. This is an item of limited availability. Length: 5·875in (14·923cm).

1 "Shell" and "BP" Articulated Petrol Tanker by an unidentified British maker, dating from the 1940s. In view of the similarities in pressing and dimensions between this model — see also (2) — and that shown at (3), which is certainly by Mettoy, we may safely say that this is probably the work of Mettoy. It is of tabbed-and-slotted tinplate construction, with "Shell" printed on the left side of the tank, "BP" on the right, and the legend "Shell-Mex B.P. Ltd" on the cab doors, with crest, and over the radiator. The number "7756", probably the maker's reference number, is also printed on the cab door. Among the other well-printed details are filler caps, a ladder on the left rear side of the tank, and tyre-tread and hub details on the six pressed-tin wheels. The

rear wheels of the tractor unit are driven by a simple clockwork motor with a permanently-fixed winder that protrudes at the left centre of its chassis. A fairly common item. Length: 7·87in (19·989cm).

2 "Esso" Articulated Petrol Tanker by an unidentified British maker — it has "Made in England" printed along the tops of both front mudguards — dating from the 1940s. This is of the same tabbed-and-slotted tinplate construction as (1), and the rear wheels of the cab unit are driven by a simple clockwork motor with a permanently-fixed winder that protrudes at the centre left of the chassis. Its printed detail includes "Esso" on both sides of the tank, filler caps, radiator and headlights (pressed out a little), and tyre treads and hubs on its six pressed-

tin wheels. Again, as at (1), with regard to the similarities in pressing and dimensions between this and the model at (3), it is possible that this toy also is the work of Mettoy, perhaps made specially for marketing by another wholesaler or for sale through special retail outlets. It is a fairly common item. Length: 7·87in (19·989cm).

3 "International Oil" Articulated Petrol Tanker by Mettoy Company Limited, Great Britain; dating from the 1940s. This toymaking company was established in 1934 by a refugee from Germany, the dispossessed owner of the well-known German maker Tipp and Company, Nuremburg. Mettoy established a reputation for its relatively cheap tinplate clockwork toys in the immediate pre-War

period — and was eventually to become the "parent" company of the famous Corgi Toys range of diecast models, shown elsewhere in this book. On this model, Mettoy's trademark appears above the printed radiator, while the legend "Made in England" is printed along the tops of the front mudguards. The pressing and dimensions closely resemble those of the models shown at (1) and (2), which we have thus tentatively ascribed to Mettoy. The printed details include "International Oil" and logo on the tank sides, the legends "Capacity 800 Gallons" and "Highly Inflammable" on the lower part of the tank, filler caps and cab doors. The wheels are printed tinplate with plain tyres; a clockwork motor with a permanently-fixed

winder drives the rear wheels of the tractor unit. This is a limited item. Length: 7·87in (19·989cm).

4 "Pool" Articulated Petrol Tanker by Mettoy, Great Britain; dating from the 1940s. Again with the maker's trade-mark above the radiator and "Made in England" printed on the tops of the mudguards, this tabbed-and-slotted, clockwork-driven tinplate model has a suitably austere wartime finish, in drab grey with white details. "Pool" petrol represented the output in the 1940s of the major petroleum companies, which, in Britain, "pooled" their resources in wartime. Note also that the mudguards of this vehicle are finished in white: it was a common practice in wartime Britain to have the extremities of vehicles painted white, in an

attempt to lessen the hazards of driving on dimmed and shielded lights in the anti-air raid "blackouts" of the period. A fairly limited item. Length: 7·87in (19·989cm).

5 Renault-Type Petrol Tanker by C. Rossignol, Paris, France; dating from the years immediately before World War II. Although it lacks such details as mudguards and head-lamps, this model, of lightweight tinplate construction, has a pressed-tin chassis with simulated springing and a pressed filler cap that is fixed to the top of the tank by tab-and-slot. Its printed details include the legend "Essence Pour Automobiles/Shell" on the sides of the tank, a petrol can on the cab door, and a bonnet securing-catch. Overall, it has a most pleasing "toy-like" quality and is most

attractively coloured. The two-piece tinplate wheels are single-sided; the rear pair are driven by a clockwork motor with a permanently-fixed winder (note its folding top) protruding at the right rear of the chassis. The Rossignol company, founded by Charles Rossignol in the 1860s, had established a reputation with its "carpet toy" trains by the turn of the century. Between World Wars I and II, the maker produced cheap ranges of clockwork and electric trains in Gauge "0" and, in the 1920s, began to make road vehicles, including a range of Paris buses, continuing in production until the early 1960s. This is an item of fairly limited availability. Length: 8·17in (20·752cm).

6-7 "Campsa" Petrol Tanker by Rico, Alicante, Spain; dating from the

1940s. Note the maker's "R.S.A." trademark and wagon motif printed on the cab door of this simple model in lightweight tinplate, and, at (6), the repetition of the "R.S.A." mark in large letters at the rear of the tank. It is fitted with perforated disc wheels of pressed tin. Printed details include "Campsa" on the sides of the tank, filler caps, hoses on the lower sides of the tank, and mudguards. The rear wheels are driven by a clockwork motor with a permanently-fixed winder which, as can be seen at (7), protrudes from the lower rear of the chassis. The Rico company was in production with tinplate vehicles, aeroplanes and novelty toys both before and after World War II. This is a limited item. Length: 7·09in (18·009cm).

103

The small clockwork models made by Tri-ang (Lines Brothers Limited), Great Britain, under the "Minic" name formed a very successful alternative to the diecast models of Dinky Toys. They were in production from the mid-1930s until World War II, and again post-War into the 1950s: of more than one hundred different models produced, most were commercial vehicles, as seen here and on *pages 106-107*. All are of tabbed-and-slotted tinplate.

1 "London Transport" Double-Deck Bus; a pre-World War II Minic model, dating from around 1938. It has a detailed interior, with wooden seats and a metal steering column and wheel. It bears decals advertising "Ovaltine" on the left upper side and "Bisto" on the right

upper side and at the rear, where the number plate "AYV 604" is fitted. Its destination board is for route number "177", with a full list of staging points from Kingsway to Mitcham. The clockwork motor drives the front pair of wheels, which are of tinplate and are fitted with white rubber tyres. This is a scarce item. Length: 7·1875in (183mm).

2 "London Transport" Double-Deck Bus; the same model as (1), but finished in more familiar London Transport red, with the grey roof normally seen on pre-World War II London double-deckers. A scarce item. Length: 7·1875in (183mm).

3 "London Transport" Double-Deck Bus; a post-World War II example, dating from around 1948. Construction is as (1), but interior detail is less and the advertising

decals have changed: "Ovaltine" is on the right side and "Bovril" on the left. The destination board is unchanged. It is finished in London Transport's post-War red-and-cream livery and is fitted with black rubber tyres. A limited item. Length: 7·1875in (183mm).

4 "London Transport" Double-Deck Bus; a later example than (3), dating from around 1950. Construction is still as (1-3), but both details and wheels have changed. The cream finish is restricted to the upper deck; the advertising decals are for "Penguin" models on the left "Minic" on the right and "Tri-ang Toys" at the rear; the numberplate "LBL 174" is fitted (these letters were used by *Lines Brothers Limited* on many models!); and the destination board is for route number "14",

from King's Cross to Putney. It has cast metal wheels fitted with black rubber balloon tyres. Limited. Length: 7·1875in (183mm).

5 "London Transport" Double-Deck Bus; dating from around 1953. Most details are as (4), but the cream finish is now reduced to a narrow strip around the bottom of the upper deck and the overall red finish extends to the mudguards, black on all earlier models. The decals advertise "Tri-ang Pedal Motors" (left), "Pedigree Dolls" (right), and "Frog" and "Penguin" models at the rear — all Lines Brothers ranges. A limited item. Length: 7·1875in (183mm).

6 "Green Line" Single-Deck Bus; dating from around 1950. For this model, Tri-ang used the chassis and lower deck of the double-decker

(1-5), with a pressed-tin roof. The destination board is for "Dorking", and decals at the rear, where the numberplate "LBL 174"—the same as (4)—is fitted, advertise "Frog" and "Penguin" models. A limited item. Length: 7·1875in (183mm).

7 "L.C.C." Ambulance; dating from around 1954. This model of a forward control vehicle was produced only in the post-World-War-II period. It has plastic wheels fitted with black rubber balloon tyres; a clockwork motor concealed within the cab drives the front pair of wheels. Note the raised "Ambulance" sign on the roof; it also bears Red Cross and "L.C.C." (London County Council) decals. This is of limited availability. Length: 4·875in (124mm).

8 Fire Engine; dating from around 1939. This pre-War model features battery-powered headlights (the bulbs only can be seen here: the tin cowls originally fitted are missing); it reappeared without working lights in the post-War period. It is provided with a bell and a detachable two-stage ladder and has opening side-hatches for the hose- and battery-storage compartments. Note also the well-modelled radiator. This is a scarce item. Length: 6·375in (162mm).

9 Traction Engine and Trailer; dating from around 1952. The engine has a tinplate body and is fitted with a brass front cover, chimney and valve cover. The simple trailer also has a tinplate body, and both vehicles are fitted with large and rather unconvincing black plastic wheels. This model is limited.

Length overall: 8·875in (225mm).
10 Steam Roller; dating from around 1950. This model has a tinplate body with a brass filler cap (in fact, the securing nut for the steerable front roller), chimney and valve cover. The roller and wheels are of grey plastic and, as at (9), tend to detract from the otherwise pleasing appearance of the model. The clockwork mechanism is geared to give alternate forward and reverse movement. This is a limited item. Length: 5·125in (130mm).

11 London Taxi Cab; dating from around 1950. This very well-detailed model, complete with tinplate bumpers, a "For Hire" sign and taxi-meter, a "Taxi" sign on the roof, plastic-lensed headlights, and a spare-wheel cover at the rear, has a clockwork motor that drives the

rear wheels. It is a limited item. Length: 4·125in (105mm).

12-13 London Taxi Cab; dating from around 1938. The two examples shown, (12) finished in dark blue and (13) in red, with a black roof and rear canopy in both cases, are of the same construction as (11). These pre-War models have grey floors and spare "Shell Petrol" cans. They are limited items. Length: 4·134in (105mm).

14 Traffic Control Car; dating from around 1948. This model of a Vauxhall police vehicle was the only Minic model reissued after World War II to retain a diecast driver and passenger. It is fitted with a single roof-mounted loudspeaker and has headlights that are soldered to their supports. A limited item. Length: 5·125in (130mm).

1 Breakdown Lorry; dating from *c*1938. This was the only model in the "Minic" range of clockwork-powered vehicles of tabbed tinplate to be fitted with two clockwork motors: one to drive the front wheels in the usual way, the other to raise and lower the hook on the tinplate jib, an operation controlled by a lever engaging on a cog. The angle of the jib can be altered by use of the crank-handle on the nearside rear — just visible in the model shown at (3). A positive stop/start control for the vehicle is also fitted. The pre-World-War-II example shown here is distinguished by its tinplate wheels with white rubber tyres, by the spare petrol can (not visible in the photograph) mounted on the nearside running-board, and by its early-type "Minic" and

"Tri-ang" decals on the sides. Scarce. Length: 6·25in (159mm).
2 Breakdown Lorry; dating from *c*1954. The details of construction and mechanism are as (1), but this post-War model has later-type decals, front mudguards that are painted rather than plated, and plastic wheels with black rubber balloon tyres. It is a limited item. Length: 6·25in (159mm).
3 Breakdown Lorry; dating from *c*1950 (when one of the authors was given the example shown here as a birthday present!). Construction and mechanism are as (1-2), but this is the intermediate-type model, with large decals of pre-War size, plated front mudguards and cast metal wheels. A limited item. Length: 6·25in (159mm).
4 "L.N.E.R." Van; dating from *c*1946-

48. In the immediate post-War period, using van pressings of pre-War type, Tri-ang produced delivery vans in the colours of the four regional railway companies of the pre-nationalisation period. The L.N.E.R. (London and North-Eastern Railway) version shown here carries "Express Parcels Service" decals and "Tri-ang Pedal Motors" stickers. It is fitted with opening rear doors with a locking-bar and has tinplate wheels of pre-War type. A limited item. Length: 5·625in (143mm).
5 "L.M.S." Van; dating from *c*1946-48. The same model as (4), but in L.M.S. (London, Midland and Scottish Railway) colours and with a sticker advertising "Tri-ang Dolls' Houses". Limited. Length: 5·625in (143mm).
6 "Southern Railway" Van; dating

from *c*1946-48. As (4) and (5), but in S.R. green and with a sticker advertising "Penguin" aircraft. Limited. Length: 5·625in (143mm).
7 Carter Paterson Delivery Van; dating from *c*1938. The body and chassis are as (4-6), but this pre-War model has plated mudguards, a petrol can on the nearside running-board and white rubber tyres. Scarce. Length: 5·625in (143mm).
8 Mechanical Horse and Pantechnicon; dating from *c*1938. This uses the same pre-War-type cab pressing as (1). On this pre-War example, the model is steered via an adjustable rear axle on the Horse and an adjustable front axle on the Pantechnicon. In post-War models, the Pantechnicon had no front wheels and was mounted directly on to the Horse,

as seen at (17). A scarce item. Length: 7·75in (197mm).

9 Delivery Van; dating from c1938. Details are as (1-7), but this model, although of pre-War production (with its spare petrol can just visible on the nearside running-board) is fitted with black tyres. It bears "Minic Transport" decals. Limited. Length: 5·625in (143mm).

10 Shutter Van; dating from c1954. This Minic model of a forward-control van was produced only during the post-War period; note, however, that the plated radiator is the same as that used on the earlier models. A clockwork motor within the cab drives the front wheels, which are of the late type, made of plastic and fitted with black rubber balloon tyres. It bears "Minic Transport" decals. This is a limited

item. Length: 4·875in (124mm).

11 Ford Light Delivery Van; dating from c1938. The clockwork motor drives the rear wheels, which are of pressed-steel-disc-type with white rubber tyres. The chassis and bumper are a single pressing, but the radiator, without headlights, is separate. A "Shell Petrol" can is mounted on the nearside running-board and the van bears small "Minic Transport" decals. Limited. Length: 5·5in (140mm).

12 Articulated Milk Tanker; dating from c1950. This model uses the same Mechanical Horse as shown at (8), but the example shown here is of post-War type, with cast metal wheels and no spare petrol can. In fact, this Tanker appeared only during the post-War period. The tank, fitted with three filler domes

and with a hose box at the rear, bears "Minic Dairies" decals. Limited. Length: 7·00in (178mm).

13 Mechanical Horse and Watney's Barrel Trailer; dating from c1954. For this purpose of this model, a tinplate "Watney" sign was mounted at the front of the roof of the Horse and a red plastic barrel on the roof top. The Trailer is of turned wood. Length: 5·5in (140mm).

14 Dustcart; dating from c1948. The chassis and cab are as (1-7), post-War type, and the special dustcart body is fitted with six bright-plated sliding covers. It bears "Minic" and "Tri-ang" decals. Limited. Length: 5·5in (140mm).

15 Tipping Lorry; dating from c1938. The chassis and cab are as (1-7), pre-War type. The rear body, with a hinged tailboard, is manually

tipped. A limited model. Length: 5·625in (143mm).

16 Searchlight Lorry; dating from c1938. This has the standard chassis and cab of pre-War type, but with a platform body to accommodate a battery-powered searchlight and a battery-box with a hinged lid. The searchlight has an on/off screw and can be fully traversed and elevated. Limited. Length: 5·1875in (132mm).

17 Mechanical Horse and Cable-Drum Trailer; dating from c1954. The forward-control Horse is a late model, with characteristic radiator and headlights; it is fitted with a steerable rear axle. The double rear wheels of the Trailer, with plastic Cable Drums, are cast metal with balloon tyres. Limited. Length: 8·5in (216mm).

1 Wrecker Truck by an unidentified West German maker; dating from around 1957. The words "Made in Western Germany" are printed along the bottom of the bright metal radiator. This is a large and robust toy of heavy-gauge tinplate: a simple push-along model. The turntable-mounted crane turns through 360° and its hook is raised and lowered by means of the manually-operated crank handle at the left of its base. The headlights are plastic and the single-sided wheels are of heavy moulded plastic. Length: 15·125in (38·42cm).

2 Cement Mixer on Heavy Duty Diesel Truck by SSS International, Japan; dating from 1960-61. This large and solid toy is tinplate throughout, with the exception of grey plastic sleeves around the

bonnet-mounted exhaust pipes. Note the pressed details of the radiator and cab roof, the yellow-and-black printed bumper, and the bright metal headlights and steps to the cab. The wheels (the two rear pairs double) are of rubber and are fitted with metal discs. Friction drives the rear-most pair of wheels and works from them through a worm gear to rotate the drum of the cement mixer. When a small lever set into the truck chassis just to the rear of the cab (on the side of the truck away from the camera) is depressed, a hydraulic-type ram raises the drum of the cement mixer through an angle of about 45°, as is shown in this photograph, as if to empty it of its contents. Length: 13·75in (34·925cm).

3 Remote-Control Mechanical Shovel by Gama, West Germany; dating from around 1959. The words "Made in Western Germany" are printed on the white metal arm that controls the jib; note also the maker's trademark applied to the cab door. Except for its well-modelled plastic wheels, which are fitted with heavy-treaded rubber tyres, this ingenious toy is of good-quality tinplate throughout. Batteries housed in the remote-control handset shown in the background transmit power to the rear pair of wheels of the six-wheeled truck for forward and reverse movement (controlled by the buttons on the handset) and for operation of the shovel. The plastic-housed spotlight on the roof of the truck cab lights up when

the toy is in operation. The movements of the shovel are controlled by levers on either side of the cab: a manually-operated lever to the left is used to raise or lower the jib; a remote-controlled lever to the right controls the pulley mechanism that raises, lowers, opens or closes the bucket. Length: 12in (30·48cm).

4 Remote-Control Wreck Truck by Asahi, Japan; dating from around 1961. Of tinplate throughout, save for its treaded rubber wheels with metal discs, this truck has a yellow-and-black printed bumper, bright metal radiator, gold metal head-lights, and basic pressed details. The pressed-tin handset shown beside it houses batteries that power the double rear wheels: the buttons on the handset control

forward and reverse motion; the wheel on the handset steers the truck's front wheels. The crane is traversed manually and a lever at the lower rear of the truck controls the raising and lowering of the jib. The truck bears the rear number-plate: "7343—Made in Japan". Length: 10·375in (26·35cm).

5 Remote-Control Dump Truck by Asahi, Japan; dating from around 1961. The toy is tinplate throughout and is fitted with heavy-treaded rubber wheels with metal discs. Note that its printed, pressed and bright metal details exactly resemble those of (4), by the same maker—and see also (7): all three toys appear to make use of the same cab. The remote-control system is the same as that described for (4). A red light in the exhaust column

flashes when the vehicle is moving; when it is stationary, the tipping mechanism is activated by pushing up the blue lever (just visible in the photograph) at the rear of the chassis. This truck bears the same rear numberplate as (4) and (7). Length:10·375in (26·35cm).

6 Dump Truck by Tada, Japan; dating from around 1958. This simple tinplate truck has basic bright metal details—bumper and radiator, bonnet ornament, windscreen frame—and a tabbed-in "Dump" badge on the cab doors. The word "Japan" is stamped on the base. The wheels are rubber with metal discs; the front pair are friction-driven. The tipping body is activated by a lever set on the left side of the chassis, just behind the cab. Length: 8·5in (21·59cm).

7 Remote-Control Lift Dump Truck by Asahi, Japan; dating from around 1961. All the details of the cab of this good-quality tinplate toy are identical with those of the Asahi trucks described at (4) and (5), but in this case the truck itself is six-wheeled and its remote-control system is more complex. When the blue lever situated at the rear of the chassis is pushed to the right, the buttons on the handset control forward and reverse motion, with a siren sound and a flashing light in the bonnet-mounted exhaust stack, while the wheel on the handset steers the truck's front wheels; when the blue lever is pushed to the left, the buttons are used to raise the truck body on its cleverly-jointed platform and to tip it. This quite complex mechanism

is clearly visible in the photograph. The truck has heavy-treaded rubber wheels with metal discs and, like (4) and (5), bears a rear numberplate printed with the legend "7343—Made in Japan". Length: 10·75in (27·3cm).

8 Dump Truck by T.N. (Nomura Toys), Japan; dating from around 1958. This is a simple and strongly-made toy of good-quality tinplate, with bright metal bumper and radiator, pressed details on the bonnet, and a clear plastic wind-screen. It is fitted with heavy-treaded rubber wheels with metal discs; the front wheels are friction-driven. The dumper body of the truck, with pressed-tin ribbing, is activated by a lever (visible in photograph) on the left side of the chassis. Length: 8in (20·32cm).

All the vehicles shown on this spread were photographed at the London Toy & Model Museum.

1 "General" Double-Deck Bus, tinplate, by Günthermann, Nuremburg, Germany, c1930. This British-style clockwork-driven bus, with an open cab (note pressed tin driver) and staircase, and a covered upper deck, has pressed tin wheels with lithographed spokes. It carries lithographed advertisements. Length: 9·25in (23·5cm). Scarce.

2 "General" Six-Wheeled Double-Deck Bus, tinplate, possibly British-made, c1929, for the wellknown British confectionery maker Huntley & Palmers, whose lithographed advertisement appears on the side. The top may

be removed to reveal (originally) a cargo of biscuits—a popular marketing idea during the Christmas period. It is clockwork, the motor driving the rear pair of wheels, with a winder concealed beneath the body. The lithographed advertisements immediately above the side windows are "reversed": this was a feature of the real buses, where these messages were intended to be read from the inside. Note particularly the very attractive lithographed detail of individual passengers. Length: 9·5in (24cm). Very scarce.

3 Single-Deck Bus by Buddy "L" (The Moline Pressed Steel Company, East Moline, Illinois), USA, dating from the early 1930s. This company is noted for the manufacture of some of the largest

and toughest toy vehicles ever made—and this "Buddy "L" Transportation Co" (legend on the destination board, above the cab) bus, of heavy gauge sheet steel, is a fine example. A pull/push-along toy, it features working steering, opening doors (note maker's transfer on the inner side), and interior seating. The cast metal wheels (dual at the rear) are detachable and two spares are carried, one on either side of the bonnet. Length: 29in (74cm). Scarce: especially as seen here with the original paint finish.

4 "Inter-State" Bus, numbered "109", by Strauss, USA, dating from the 1920s (before the purchase of the company by Louis Marx, as a step towards his toy-making empire). Made for the domestic market, this

open-topped double-decker in tinplate has clockwork driving the rear pair of pressed tin wheels. The finish, with lithographed detail of slatted seats, is rather unusual. Length: 10·125in (26cm). Scarce.

5 Six-Wheeled "Greyhound Scenicruiser" by a Japanese maker, 1960s. Made for the US market, this is a good example of latter-day tinplate toy production. Length: 14·5in (37cm). Fairly common, especially in the USA.

6 Four-Wheeled "Greyhound Scenicruiser", again by a Japanese maker (it bears a "Globe" trademark) for the US market, late 1960s. This is finished to a generally lower standard than the larger example at (5). Length: 8·75in (22cm). Fairly common.

7 Paris Bus (note lithographed

"Bastille Etoile" destination board) by a French maker, c1930. This cheaply-made push-along toy, with lithographed detail and printed passengers, is really a later equivalent of the "Penny Toys" of the pre-World War I period. Length: 3·5in (9cm).

8"General" Six-Wheeled Double-Deck Bus, made in Germany for the British market, c1930. Although on a slightly smaller scale than the French bus shown at (7), this tinplate toy with lithographed detail is clockwork-driven. Length: 2·875in (7·3cm).

9"General" Double-Deck Bus by Johann Distler, Nuremburg, Germany, c1929. This is a fine example of the work of a noted maker of cheaper tinplate toys. The British-style open-topped bus

—with the whimsical destination board "Route 29 To Toyland", large "Virol" advertisement, and small "reversed" advertisements above the windows—is clockwork-driven (note permanent winder) and has a staircase, wheels, and tyres of pressed tin. Marketed as the "Fares Please" model, it incorporates a novelty feature: as the bus travels, the conductor moves backwards and forwards on the top deck as if collecting fares. Length: 8·625in (22cm). Scarce.

10"General" Double-Deck Bus, numbered "K 200", by Gebrüder Bing, Nuremburg, Germany, mid-1920s; one of the more simple, but still very desirable, products of a famous maker. Clockwork-driven, it has artillery-type wheels with lithographed tyre tread detail:

the "Wright's Coal Tar Soap" advertisement combines with other lithographed detail to give an accurate "feeling" of a London bus of the period. Length: 7·125in (18cm). Limited.

11"Lehmann's Autobus", numbered "590", by Lehmann, Brandenburg, Germany, c1920. This tinplate double-decker was produced both before and after World War I and was a very popular model in both Europe and the USA. Clockwork-driven, it features spoked wheels (the rear pair larger than the front, with simple steering by turning the latter) and a pressed tin driver. Length: 8in (20cm). Scarce.

12Double-Deck Bus by a German maker (without trademark), mid-1930s. This is a well-made tinplate model with pressed tin

wheels and tyres, the rear pair driven by clockwork (note permanent winder). Length: 10·5in (27cm). Scarce.

13"London Transport" Double-Deck Bus (based on a contemporary AEC bus) by Chad Valley, Great Britain, c1950. This tinplate model continues the tradition of novelty biscuit tins into the 1950s: the detachable top gave access to a cargo of "Carr's Biscuits", and it was sold in both clockwork-driven (as shown, note winding shaft forward of rear wheels) and push-along forms. Length: 10in (25·4cm). Limited.

14Double-Deck Bus, numbered "6", by Rico, Spain, probably 1950s; a very simple clockwork-driven toy in lightweight tinplate. Length: 6in (15cm). Fairly common.

Fire Engines by European, Japanese, and US Makers, 1890-1950s

Fire engines and other fire-fighting equipment are almost invariably finished in red. A collection of them may therefore seem to lack variety, but toys of this kind have always been popular with children—no doubt the clanging bells on many add considerably to their appeal! All the vehicles shown on this spread were photographed at the London Toy & Model Museum.

1 Fire Pump by Union, USA, dating from c1900. This fine toy of basically cast-iron construction features live-steam operation of a pump with twin cylinders of oscillating type. The spirit-fired brass boiler drives twin flywheels which operate the pump via con-rods. The smaller brass container visible beneath the cylinders is the water reservoir and the nozzle that arches over the driver's head would originally have been fitted with a hose. The cast-iron driver should, of course, be urging on a team of horses. Length: 10·25in (26cm). Scarce.

2 Water Tower by Buddy "L" (Moline Pressed Steel Company, East Moline, Illinois), USA, dating from c1930. Made in the heavy gauge sheet steel favoured by this manufacturer, this is an extremely tough pull/push-along toy, with an operating steering wheel and such detail as a bell above the radiator, headlamps and swiveling spotlamp, and a manually-operated tower with a pump worked by a lever (visible here in the "up" position) immediately behind the driver's seat. The pump, fed by the large water tank (with the cap missing in this example) in the body of the vehicle, forces water up a channel in the tower, which is turned to direct the jet. The wheels and tyres of the vehicle are diecast and it is finished (inevitably) in red enamel, with the maker's transfer below the pump base and a "CFD" (City Fire Department) transfer below the driver's seat. Length: 41in (104cm). Fairly scarce, especially outside the USA.

3 Horse-Drawn Fire Engine by R.W.S., USA, dating from c1890-1900. This large and impressive pull-along toy in cast iron, with a two-piece chassis, has detachable ladders and two detachable drivers. It is drawn by three galloping horses and the rear-most driver holds a wheel (non-operating on the model) that, on the real engine, was used to steer the rear wheels to negotiate tight bends. Length: 28·5in (72cm). Scarce, especially outside the USA—and collectors are advised to beware of later copies of such classic American cast-iron toys.

4 Fire Chief's Car by Günthermann, Nuremburg, Germany, c1930; note the maker's trademark on the boot. A bell again features prominently on this clockwork-driven tinplate car, with pressed tin firemen, artillery-type spoked wheels of pressed tin, and attractive lithographed detail and finish. Length: 7·125in (18cm).

5 Fire Pump, probably by Distler, Germany, late 1920s. The tinplate vehicle with its bright-finish boiler carries a crew of three pressed tin

112

figures; the wheels and tyres are also of pressed tin. Clockwork-driven, it has an operating brake. Length: 8·125in (20·5cm).

6 Fire Pump by an American maker, c1920. This cast-iron pull-along toy is of two-piece construction and has attractive cast detail. Length: 8·25in (21cm).

7 Fire Pump by a Japanese maker, dating from after World War II. This simple tinplate vehicle, with a pressed tin driver and pressed tin wheels and tyres, features a bell and a detachable ladder. Length: 5·5in (14cm). Common.

8 Fire Pump by an American maker, c1935 — a late date for a cast-iron toy. The cast detail is somewhat crude; note that the rubber tyres are badly perished. Length: 4·875in (12cm). Fairly common.

9 Horse-Drawn Fire Pump by an American maker (possibly Kenton), c1900. This is a cheap and simple cast-iron pull-along toy of two-piece construction: the line of the joint can be clearly seen. Length: 9·5in (24cm). Limited.

10-12 Firemen and Fireguards: para-military figures in tin — including riflemen (10) and a bugler (12) — by a French maker, probably Faivre, dating from around 1900. Height of individual figure: 3·375in (8·5cm). Limited.

Hook-and-Ladder Fire Truck by Marx, USA, c1960. The trailer vehicle is tinplate with printed detail and has several plastic features, including windscreen, spotlight, control panel, and driver. Length: 36·5in (91cm).

1 Fire Engine by "K", Japan; dating from 1958-59. This toy is fully described at (7), *pages 306-307*, where it is shown with its packaging. Length: 13in (33·02cm).

2 Fire Engine by Arnold, West Germany; dating from around 1956. This is a simple and strongly-made push-along toy of tabbed-and-slotted tinplate construction. It has a white metal ladder with a gilt bell on either side, but all other details are printed. The metal wheels are fitted with heavy-treaded rubber tyres; the maker's name is printed on the metal whitewalls. The crank-handle at the left rear of the two-section ladder is used to extend it via a simple cord-and-pulley system. Length: 11in (27·94cm).

3 Fire Engine by Lincoln International, "Empire Made" (Hong Kong);

dating from around 1968. This small tinplate toy has bright metal front bumpers, radiator, bonnet ornament, cab steps and wind-screen frame. A yellow plastic spotlight is mounted on the left side of the bonnet and a yellow plastic hose-drum, complete with clear plastic hose, in the centre of the body. It was sold complete with plastic figure of a fireman (shown at rear). The rubber wheels, the front pair friction-driven, are fitted with metal discs. The two-section ladder swivels freely on a turntable mounting and can easily be extended and elevated manually. Length: 7·125in (18·097cm).

4 Fire Chief Car by Ichiro, Japan; dating from around 1959. Modelled on a Ford saloon, with "Ford" numberplates at front and rear,

this tinplate car has bright metal details that include the frames of the tinted plastic windows at front and rear. Like most vehicles shown on this spread, it bears appropriate printed badges, and in this case the legend "Fire Chief". It has a pressed-tin interior with printed details. A yellow plastic spotlight is mounted in a swivelling socket on the roof. The rubber wheels are fitted with metal discs; the rear pair are friction-driven, motion producing a siren sound. Length: 9·5in (24·13cm).

5 Fire Escape Truck by an unidentified West German maker; dating from around 1957. This large and robust push-along toy is made of heavy-gauge tinplate. It is a simple pressing, with a bright metal radiator and plastic headlights, but

little other detail. The six wheels are made of moulded plastic and are single-sided. The escape swivels freely on its turntable; when the catch visible at the front of the turntable is released, a simple spring-loaded mechanism elevates and extends the escape ladder. Length: 15in (38·1cm).

6 Super Fire King Ladder Trailer by SSS International, Japan; dating from 1960-61. This is an attractive and well-detailed tinplate toy. The cab has the usual bright metal details, including a divided frame for the clear plastic windscreen, and has a pressed and printed interior complete with steering wheel. Note the pressed-tin fuel tanks and, on the articulated trailer, the raised gilt "S.F.D." lettering and gilt platforms. The trailer also

features retractable pressed-tin stabilisers, a seat and wheel for simulated rear steering, and bright pressed-tin wheels that are used manually to raise and extend the ladder (via worm-gear) on its revolving turntable. The wheels of the vehicle are metal with heavy-treaded rubber tyres; friction drives the front wheels of the cab. Length: 17·75in (45·085cm).

7 Fire Command Car by "T.N." (Nomura Toys), Japan; dating from 1958-59. This large and impressive tinplate toy has a bright metal front bumper and metal mesh radiator; an inset metal "FD" emblem on the bonnet and an applied "Fire Dept. No.1" badge below its clear plastic windscreen; well-modelled, articulated tinplate figures of driver and passenger;

and a pressed-tin radio and jerrican at the rear. The wheels are rubber with metal discs; note the rear-mounted spare. Batteries housed in a base trap drive a two-wheeled turntable mounted towards the front of the base. The vehicle pursues an erratic course as the driver appears to steer; when it stops, intermittently, a buzzer sounds, the passenger raises his radio-telephone to his ear, and green plastic lights flash on either side of the radio set. Length: 11in (27·94cm).

8 Fire Engine by "K", Japan, dating from around 1958. This closely resembles the toy by the same maker at (1): some details of the colour printing vary, the ladder is of different construction and has no fireman at its upper end, but the

same pressing appears to have been used for the bodies of the two vehicles. Note that the lever operating the pop-up ladder is clearly seen in this photograph. Length: 13in (33·02cm).

9 Fire Department Car by unidentified Japanese maker; dating from around 1960. A fairly typical cheap tinplate toy, with most details printed and a pressed-out printed spotlight on the roof. The wheels are rubber with metal discs; the rear pair are friction-driven. The words "Made in Japan" are printed below the "F.D." badge on the boot. Length: 6·375in (16·19cm).

10 Fire Engine by "T.N." (Nomura Toys), Japan; dating from around 1961. This toy is of good-quality tinplate, with a wealth of printed detail and bumpers, radiator,

headlights and rear platform of bright metal. The tinplate firemen are attractively modelled, and the whole has a most pleasant "toy-like" quality. The rubber wheels are fitted with metal discs; the rear pair are friction-driven. As the vehicle moves, a siren noise is produced and the fireman mounted on the left of the cab (nearest camera) raises and lowers his articulated arm with its red flag. Length: 10·5in (26·67cm).

11 Fire Chief Car by an unidentified Japanese maker; dating from around 1960. This simple saloon car with brightly-printed details has bright metal bumpers, radiator and headlights. Its rubber wheels are fitted with metal discs and the rear pair are friction-driven. Length: 5·375in (13·6525cm).

1 T.V. Control Highway Patrol Car by an unidentified Japanese maker; dating from around 1959. Based on a Chevrolet Impala (note the applied "Chevrolet" lettering on the bonnet), with the "Highway Patrol" and "Police Department" lettering and colourfully-printed badges that are common to most of the toys on this spread, this tinplate car has a well-modelled radiator of bright metal, into which are set plastic-lensed headlights. It has tinted plastic windows at front and rear and a printed interior with a plastic steering wheel (left-hand drive). The red plastic warning light on the roof lights up when the car is in motion. The wheels are rubber, with well-modelled metal discs and printed hubcaps. It is powered by a battery housed in a base trap,

driving a bump-and-go turntable mounted towards the front of the base. The metal remote-control handset incorporates an on/off switch and a button that controls a siren sound. The "TV screen" on the handset lights up and, when not used for remote-control, may be clipped to the bracket on the car's boot. See also car at (2). Length: 14in (35·56cm).

2 Highway Patrol Car by an unidentified Japanese maker; dating from around 1959. This is in all respects save one — it has no remote-control facility — the same model as (1), and is again battery-powered with bump-and-go action. An on/off switch is situated towards the front of the base. Length: 14in (35·56cm).

3 Ford Highway Patrol Car by Ichiko,

Japan; dating from around 1958. This tinplate friction-driven car is fully described at (1), pages 306-307, where its packaging is shown. Length: 9·37in (23·81cm).

4 Highway Patrol Car by an unidentified Japanese maker; dating from around 1959. Bearing the usual printed lettering and badges, and with bright metal radiator, bumpers, trim strips and windscreen frames, this car has "Lincoln" numberplates at front and rear, windows of tinted plastic and has a printed interior with a plastic steering wheel (left-hand drive). A coloured plastic spotlight is mounted on the bonnet and the bright metal warning light on the roof has a red plastic lens. The wheels are rubber, with metal discs with printed whitewalls and

hubcaps. Friction drives the rear wheels: as the car moves, the warning light revolves and a siren noise is also produced. Length: 11·125in (28·257cm).

5 Remote-Control Police Car by Arnold, West Germany; dating from 1952-53. Only the plastic "Police" sign in a raised metal housing on its roof indicates that this solid toy of good-quality tinplate is a police vehicle. It has rather crude bright metal bumpers and other details; its plastic wheels, with bright metal hubcaps, are fitted with rubber whitewall tyres. The toy is powered by Arnold's usual hand-cranked remote-control system; fully described at (5), pages 306-307. Length: 10in (25·4cm).

6 Police Car by an unidentified Japanese maker; dating from

Above: *Rear detail of (4). When the screw is released with the special key and the catch set to "Open", the door opens and an alarm bell rings.*

around 1958. This simple Ford-type saloon, with bright metal and printed details, bears the rear numberplate "102507". Note the coiled-wire aerial with a red plastic knob. The wheels—the rear pair friction-driven, with siren sound—are rubber with metal discs. Length: 5·375in (13·65cm).

7 Police Car by an unidentified maker (it is stamped "Empire Made"; presumably Hong Kong); dating from c1958. This rather crudely-pressed tinplate toy has a plastic "Police Car" plaque in a raised metal frame on the roof and has quite extensive bright metal details, including windscreen frames. The wing-mounted siren and radio aerial are plastic. The rubber wheels, the rear pair friction-driven with siren sound,

are fitted with bright metal discs. Length: 6in (15·24cm).

8 Patrol Auto-Tricycle by T.N. (Nomura Toys); dating from 1958-59. This well-made tinplate toy has an ingenious action: batteries housed in the base drive a rear wheel to give a figure-eight course, while the driver appears to steer. The action is stop-start: when it stops, the driver's whistle sounds; when it moves the headlight operates. It has treaded rubber wheels with printed metal discs. Length: 9·75in (24·765cm).

9 Armoured Car Savings Bank by "H", Japan; dating from c1958. This attractively-printed novelty toy has bright metal front and rear bumpers and headlights. It has a divided windscreen of clear plastic and a printed cab with a plastic

steering wheel (left-hand drive). The rubber wheels, the front pair friction-driven, are fitted with metal discs. Note the money slot at top rear; and see *Inset* for more detail. Length: 10in (25·4cm).

10 Mystery Police Car by T.N. (Nomura Toys), Japan; dating from c1960. This is an attractive tinplate toy with bright metal details that include applied "Police" lettering and a siren, with a pressed-tin radio set mounted at the rear. It has rubber wheels with metal discs. Batteries power a two-wheeled bump-and-go turntable mounted between the front wheels. The articulated driver is linked to the wheels so that he appears to steer the car. As it moves, a siren sound is made and the blue light flashes. Length: 10in (25·4cm).

11 Bump-'n-Go F.B.I. Car by "K.O.", Japan; dating from c1959. Its wheels are printed pressed-tin. A friction flywheel, activated by a crank-handle on the base, drives the screw of a front-mounted bump-and-go turntable. As the car moves, the pressed-tin driver traverses his plastic machine gun and a "firing" noise is made. Length: 6·5in (16·51cm).

12 Police Car by "K.O.", Japan; dating from c1960. It has a pair of pressed-tin wheels at the rear: at the front are two rubber wheels of a bump-and-go turntable, powered by batteries. As the car moves, the warning light on the bonnet flashes and the articulated pressed-tin driver cranks his siren, with an appropriate sound. Length: 7·75in (19·685cm).

1 Power Shovel by SSS Quality Toys, Japan (presumably an offshoot of SSS International); dating from 1959-60. This robust tinplate toy is made in two parts: a circular turret-mount on the base of the mechanical shovel's cab slots into a half-moon recess on the body of the six-wheeled push-along truck, permitting the shovel to swivel freely. Note the steps to the cab on the truck, and the effective pressed details of the cab roof and exhaust stacks. The truck has yellow-and-black printed bumpers. Its steerable front wheels are rubber with metal discs; the rear wheels (both pairs double) are metal, fitted with treaded rubber tyres and featuring simple suspension brackets. To operate the power shovel, the long lever on the side of the cab is pulled back to

"cock" a clockwork mechanism: when the control button on the top of the cab is depressed, the shovel performs repeated scooping, raising and dumping actions. Lengths: (truck chassis) 12·75in (32·385cm); (with shovel extended) 16in (40·64cm).

2 Automatic Dock Crane by Biller, West Germany; dating from c1958. This well-made and colourful tinplate toy, with railway lines and a turntable printed on top of its base and transport scenes around the sides, is clockwork-powered; note permanent winder at end of base. The wooden-handled lever to the right of the winder is the on/off control; the lever to the left controls the rotation of the crane and the raising and lowering of its jib. The plunger below the left-hand lever

activates a wire that runs through a spring-loaded suspension arm to open or close the crane's bucket. Length of base: 8·5in (21·59cm); height of crane: 7in (17·78cm).

3 Mechanical Digger by Gama, West Germany; serial number 282, dating from c1956. This fine mechanical toy is of heavy-gauge tinplate, with a plastic spotlight, clear plastic windows, and white rubber crawler tracks on metal wheels. Its clockwork mechanism is wound via the long yellow crank on its side. The on/off lever and the levers controlling the powered raising and lowering of the bucket, via pulleys and chains, are at the rear of the cab. The knurled knob (on the left in photograph) is for manual traverse of the jib; the lever on the right manually adjusts the

jib's elevation. Length (including jib): 16·75in (42·545cm).

4 Mechanical Digger by Gama, West Germany; serial number 2808, dating from c1957. This toy has a tough plastic cab but is otherwise of good-quality tinplate. Batteries housed in a recess in the base power the wheels, with white rubber crawler tracks, and light up the roof-mounted, plastic-housed spots when the digger is in motion. Otherwise, all operations are manual: a lever on the right (in photograph) controls the jib's elevation; a crank handle on the left raises, lowers, opens or closes the bucket. Length (jib included): 16in (40·64cm).

5 Electric Motor Crane by MFZ, West Germany; dating from c 1955. The rims of the roof-mounted spotlights

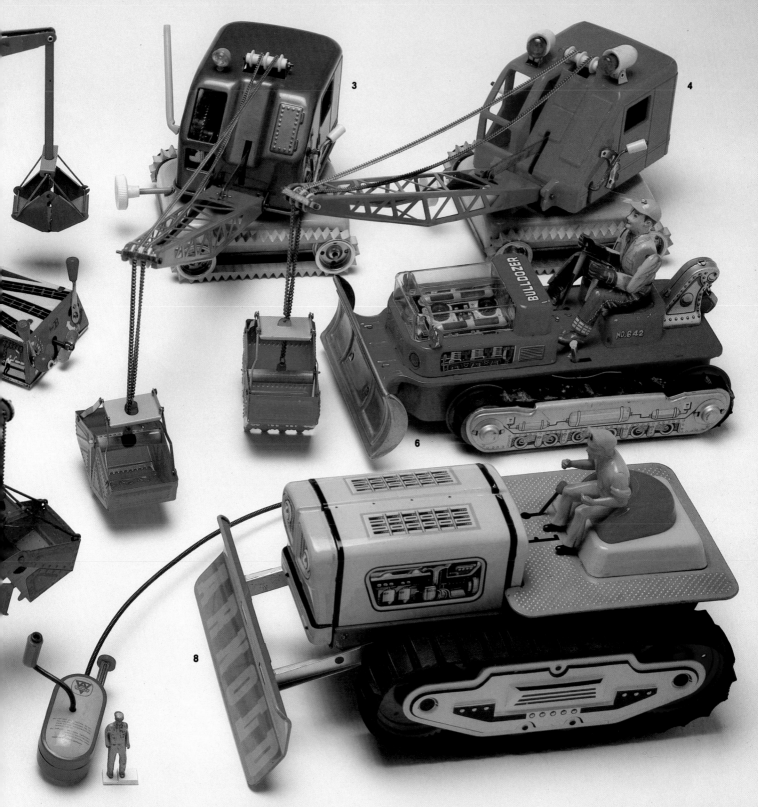

are plastic and the crawler tracks are white rubber, otherwise this fairly simply-made toy is tinplate throughout. Batteries housed in the base power the wheels, spotlights and, via a lever mounted at the back of the cab, the pulley-and-chain mechanism of the bucket. The larger lever at the rear of the cab is for manual elevation or depression of the jib. Length (including jib): 14in (35·56cm).

6 Magic Action Bulldozer by T.N. (Nomura Toys), Japan; dating from c1958. In this fine toy, note the wealth of printed detail and, in particular, the truly remarkable press-work that has gone into the well-articulated, detachable figure of the driver. Batteries housed in a trap on the base drive a bump-and-go action turntable mounted

towards the front of the base. The on/off switch is visible near the driver's foot. When the vehicle moves, the black rubber crawler tracks revolve; the coloured plastic lights on the printed tin engine flash beneath the clear plastic bonnet; and cranks from the turntable move the levers "held" by the driver so that he appears to steer the vehicle. An engine noise is also produced. Length: 9·625in (24·45cm).

7 Mechanical Shovel and Trailer by Gescha, West Germany; dating from c1953. The maker's name and the number "B-720" are printed along the bottom of the shovel unit's white metal radiator. The shovel unit has a plastic exhaust stack and steering wheel and is fitted with white rubber crawler tracks; the figure of the driver

is composition, otherwise the toy is of fairly good-quality tinplate throughout. It is unpowered: a crank mounted on the side away from the camera is used to lower the shovel and to raise it through an angle of more than 90°, so that sand or gravel may be picked up from in front and dumped to the rear — perhaps into the waiting trailer, which engages with a hook on the shovel's rear; the trailer has a tipping mechanism operated by a lever mounted on the side away from the camera, and a hinged tailgate. The trailer's wheels are metal, with treaded rubber tyres. Lengths: (shovel unit, with shovel lowered) 8·375in (21·27cm); (trailer, with draw-bar) 11in (27·94cm).

8 Remote-Controlled Bulldozer by Arnold, West Germany; dating

from 1956-57. This high-quality toy was marketed both assembled (as shown) and in construction kit form. The major parts are tinplate with printed details. The drive wheels are plastic, with wooden idler wheels for the black rubber crawler tracks; the figure of the driver is plastic, as is his seat. The lever to the driver's right is for the manual raising or lowering of the blade (which has the maker's name printed across it), which is locked into place by small protrusions that fit into grooves on the sides of the radiator. The toy is powered by Arnold's own ingenious mechanism — described at length at (5), *pages 306-307* — via a cored cable from the hand-cranked control set, with a plunger that steers the vehicle. Length overall: 11·375in (28·89).

1-4 Mechanical Horse and Open Wagon by Dinky Toys, Great Britain; Dinky Toys Reference Number (DT No) 33w. This model, issued in October 1947, used the castings for two pre-World War II models: the three-wheeled Mechanical Horse (DT No 33a, in production 1935-40) and the two-wheeled Open Truck Trailer (DT No 33c, in production 1935-40). The original version, appearing in brown, as at (1) and (4), olive green (3) and other colours, had a tinplate base plate stamped with the maker's name. In 1953 it was reissued, now all diecast and again with the maker's name: the commonest colour finish for the later version is a blue horse and cream trailer, as shown at (2). The model was renumbered 415 in 1954 and

remained in production until 1959. It is fairly common; the earlier version may be harder to find. Lengths: (horse) 2·48in (63mm); (trailer) 2·441in (62mm); (overall length of model when assembled) 4·016in (102mm).

5 Austin Wagon; DT No 412, first issued in June 1950, when it was numbered 30j, renumbered 412 in 1954, and in production until 1960. It appeared in blue, as shown, brown and maroon (and possibly other colours). It is fitted with a towing-hook and has a tinplate base plate stamped with the maker's name, "30J" (missing from later examples) and "Austin". It is still a fairly common model. Length: 4.094 (104mm).

6 Austin Covered Wagon; DT No 413. Issued in September 1950, when it

was numbered 30s, this model used the same casting as (5), with the addition of a tinplate canopy. It was renumbered 413 in 1954 and remained in production until 1960. Appearing in maroon-and-fawn, as shown, and other colour combinations, it is fitted with a towing-hook and has a tinplate base plate stamped with the maker's name, "30S" and "Austin". It is fairly common. The model was also issued for sale in the USA, in US Army olive-green finish, at first numbered 30sm and then 625. Length: 4.094in (104mm).

7 Bedford Articulated Flat Truck; Dinky Dublo No 072, issued in June 1959 and in production until 1964. Dinky Dublo models, in "00" scale for use with Hornby Dublo toy train layouts, were introduced in

December 1957. The series was not very successful, perhaps because Lesney's "Matchbox" range dominated the British market for small diecast toys, and only 20 models (including railway staff and other figures, cars and commercial vehicles) were issued in 1957-70. All Dinky Dublo vehicles have solid wheels of grey or black plastic; some, like this example, have clear plastic windows. All were made in only one finish; in this case, yellow/orange-and-red. This is a fairly common item. Length: 4·567in (116mm).

8 Bedford Flat Truck; Dinky Dublo No 066, issued in December 1957 and in production until 1960. It has no windows; see note at (7). This will be quite easy to find. Length: 4·567in (116mm).

9-10 Fordson Thames Flat Truck; DT No 30r, issued in February 1951, renumbered 422 in March 1954, and in production until 1960. Appearing only in red or green, it is fitted with a towing-hook. The earlier version has a tinplate base plate stamped with the maker's name and "Fordson"; on the post-renumbering version, which was marketed as "Thames Flat Truck", the number "422" also appears. Some later versions may have clear plastic windows: these are harder to find than other versions, which are fairly common. The example at (9) is towing the Four-Wheeled Trailer (DT No 25g), which first appeared in 1935. Length: 4·409in (112mm).

11 Rear Tipping Wagon; DT No 30m, issued in August 1950, renumbered

414 in 1954, and in production until 1964. Before renumbering, this was made in orange; after renumbering, when it was marketed as "Dodge Rear Tipping Wagon", in grey-and-blue, as shown, and green-and-orange. A crank-handle on the left side raises the tipping mechanism; it has a hinged tailboard and a tinplate base plate. It is a fairly common item. Length: 3·898in (99mm).

12-13 Farm Produce Wagon; DT No 30n, issued in May 1950, renumbered 343 in 1954, and in production until 1964. Using the same Dodge casting as (11), this model appeared in green-and-yellow (12) or, less commonly, red-and-blue (13). It is fitted with a towing-hook but, according to authoritative sources, should *not*

feature the tipping action shown at (12). It is a fairly common item. Length: 4·21in (107mm).

14-15 Forward Control Lorry; DT No 25r, issued in May 1948, renumbered 420 in October 1954, and in production, latterly as "Leyland Forward Control Lorry", until 1961. This model appeared in green (14), cream (15), red or grey; it is fitted with a towing-hook. Fairly common. Length: 4·21in (107mm).

16-18 Bedford Breakdown Van; DT No 30e, issued in August 1935 and in production until 1940, and reissued in 1946-48. All versions are one-piece castings fitted with a solid cast searchlight and crane, the latter with a wire hook. Pre-War versions have a rear window in the cab; on post-War versions, this is filled in. Of the examples shown

here, (16) and (17) are post-War versions; (18) is a pre-War model, distinguished not only by the rear window (which cannot be seen in the photograph), but also by its black-painted front and rear wings and white rubber tyres. The pre-War model is limited, verging on scarce; post-War versions are fairly common. Length: 3·622in (92mm).

19-20 Motor Truck; DT No 22c, first issued in May 1935. This was in production until 1940 and was reissued in 1946-50. As at (16-18), pre-War models have a rear window in the cab and post-War models have not. Of the examples shown here, (19) is pre-War – note the white rubber tyres; (20) is post-War. The pre-War version is limited; the post-War version is fairly common. Length: 3·307in (84mm).

1-2 Renault Covered Wagon (*Camion 7-T Renault*) by L.E., France; dating from the 1950s. It is interesting to compare this model by a lesser-known maker with the similar models made by Dinky Toys, France, around the same time. In a smaller scale than the Dinky models shown here, but quite well detailed, this lorry is fitted with a tinplate canopy. The example at (1) has a wire towing-hook; the lorry at (2) possibly a later production version, has a tinplate towing-hook. Limited. Lengths: (1) 4·134in (105mm); (2) 4·3125in (110mm).

3 Renault Tipping Truck by CIJ, France; dating from the 1950s. The cab and chassis are very solidly cast; the tipping rear body (activated by a lever on the side

away from the camera) is of tinplate. Limited. Length: 4·134in (105mm).

4 Two-Wheeled Covered Trailer (*Remorque à deux roues bâchée*) by Dinky Toys, France; French Dinky Toys Reference Number (FDT No) 25T, issued in June 1949 and in production until March 1955. This was based on the Two-Wheeled Trailer, FDT No 25S, produced in 1948-52, with the addition of a tinplate canopy. The tow-bar is soldered to the front and a towing-hook is fitted at the rear. The model appeared in a number of colour combinations, at first (1949 only) with metal wheels, and then, as shown, with cast wheels fitted with smooth black rubber tyres. Like most French Dinky Toys, its availability in Great Britain is limited. Length: 2·9375in (75mm).

5 Four-Wheeled Covered Trailer by L.E., France; dating from the 1950s. It has a bright tinplate tow-bar, a swivelling front axle and a tinplate canopy. A limited item. Length: 3·346in (85mm).

6 Ford Tipping Wagon (*Ford Benne basculante*); FDT No 25M, issued in 1950 and in production until 1955. The tipping action of the rear body is activated by a crank-handle on the left side of the chassis. A hinged tailboard is fitted. Earlier versions have black wheels, as shown; later ones (1954-55) have green wheels. See (15) for a similar model, with the same reference number, with a Studebaker cab. Limited. Length: 3·70in (94mm).

7 Ford Tanker Wagon "Esso" (*Ford Camion Citerne "Esso"*); FDT No 25U, issued in 1950 and in

production until 1952. This model was originally intended to have a towing-hook and a spare wheel, and early versions will be found with the tinplate base cut away to accommodate a moulded support for these features, which were never fitted. The red finish was standard, but later versions (1952) have smaller "Esso" decals on the sides and rear. A limited item. Length: 4·134in (105mm).

8 Ford Cattle Wagon (*Ford Bétaillère*); FDT No 25A, issued in 1950 and in production until 1952. It is fitted with a spare wheel and a tinplate towing-hook. As well as the finish shown, it appeared in metallic-light-blue with yellow wheels; a version with a yellow cab and red rear body and wheels is rare. Limited. Length: 3·70in (94mm).

9 Ford Milk Wagon (*Ford laitier*); FDT No 250, issued in 1950 and in production until 1954. This model has ten moulded milk churns on the lower sides and ten removable churns that are housed in the upper body. It is fitted with a spare wheel and a towing-hook. The "Nestle" legend may be found as either a stamp or a decal. Limited. Length: 3·70in (94mm).

10 Ford Covered Wagon "Grands Moulins De Paris" (*Ford Camion Bache "Grands Moulins De Paris"*); FDT No 25JV, issued in 1951 and in production until 1953. The example shown is of the second type (1953), finished in grey with a black canopy (note that part of the decal is missing from this example) and red wheels; an early version with the body finished

in green is much rarer. Limited. Length: 4·016in (102mm).

11 Ford Recovery Wagon with Crane (*Ford Dépannage avec Grue*); FDT No 25R, issued in April 1954 and in production until March 1955. Fitted wth a tinplate crane and towing-hook, this model has "Dinky Service" stamped on its tailboard. A late production version, without the advertisement and with chromed wheels fitted with white tyres, is rare. A limited model. Length: 4·606in (117mm).

12 Ford Refuse Wagon (*Ford benne a ordures*); FDT No 25V, issued in October 1950 and in production until 1955. The rear body, tipping by means of rack mechanism, is of pressed tinplate, with two sliding covers and a hinged rear flap. Limited. Length: 3·74in (95mm).

13 Ford Beverage Truck (*Ford Plateau Brasseur*); FDT No 25H, issued in 1949 and in production until 1960. This model appeared in a wide variety of colour finishes; early versions have metal wheels, but later ones have rubber tyres. Limited. Length: 4·016in (102mm).

14 Studebaker Market Gardener's Van (*Studebaker Maraicher*); FDT No 25K, issued in 1949 and in production until 1952. This model, which appeared in various two-tone finishes, is fitted with a spare wheel. Limited. Length: 4·134in (105mm).

15 Studebaker Tipping Wagon (*Studebaker Benne basculante*); FDT No 25M, issued in May 1949 and in production until April 1954. As (6), with Studebaker cab. Limited Length: 4·134in (105mm).

16 Studebaker Covered Van

(*Studebaker Camionnette bâchée*); FDT No 25Q, issued in June 1949 and in production until 1952. Fitted with a tinplate canopy, this model appeared always in two-tone finish. Length: 4·134in (105mm).

17 Studebaker Milk Wagon (*Studebaker Laitier*); FDT No 250, issued in April 1949 and in production until April 1954. As (9), with Studebaker cab. Limited. Length: 4·134in (105mm).

18 Studebaker Breakdown Van with Crane (*Studebaker Camionnette de dépannage avec grue*); FDT No 25R, issued in May 1949 and in production until April 1954. Examples made in 1949 only are to be found with metal wheels and without the "Dinky Service" stamp along the sides of the vehicle. Limited. Length: 4·724in (120mm).

1 Foden 14-Ton Tanker, "Regent", by Dinky Toys, Great Britain; Dinky Toys Reference Number (DT No) 942, issued in June 1955 and in production until 1957. This most attractive model in the Dinky Supertoys range appeared only in the red-white-and-blue finish seen here, with "Regent" in gold. It has an eight-wheeled chassis and is fitted with the second-type Foden radiator; see (10) for an example of the first-type radiator. It has detachable treaded rubber tyres, with a spare wheel fitted beneath the body. The tinplate base plate is stamped with the maker's name and "Foden". Limited; becoming scarce. Length: 7·402in (188mm).

2 Foden Flat Truck with Chains; DT No 505. This Supertoys model was issued in September 1955, and remained in production until 1964. It appeared throughout its life in green, as shown, and was also made in maroon in 1952-54. The eight-wheeled chassis is the same as that of (1); again, it has a second-type Foden radiator, a spare wheel beneath its body, and a tinplate base plate stamped with the maker's name and "Foden". It is a limited item. Length: 7·402in (188mm).

3 Racehorse Transport; DT No 979. This Supertoys model was issued in October 1961 and was in production until 1964. It appeared only in pale-grey-and-yellow finish, with "Racehorse Transport" and a horse's-head logo above the cab and "Newmarket Racehorse Transport Service Ltd" and the same logo on the sides. It is fitted with opening side and rear doors

that hinge down to form ramps. Its diecast base bears the maker's name and "Horsebox". It was sold complete with two plastic horses (not shown). A limited item. Length: 6·889in (175mm).

4 Horse Box; DT No 581, issued in April 1953, renumbered 981 in January 1955, and in production until 1960. Appearing only in maroon, this model bears "British Railways" decals above the cab and on the sides towards the rear, and (not visible in the photograph because the ramp is lowered) the decals "Express/Horse Box/Hire Service" on the sides towards the front. It was issued in the USA without "British Railways" decals. The side and rear ramps are hinged and it has a diecast base bearing the maker's name and

"Horse box". A limited item. Length: 6·889in (175mm).

5 4000-Gallon Tanker, "Shell BP"; DT No 944, issued in July 1963 and in production until 1970. This Supertoys model on the eight-wheeled Leyland Octopus chassis has "Shell" and "BP" on the sides of its plastic tank. It appeared only in yellow-and-white. Clear plastic windows are fitted and there is a towing-hook at the rear. Its tinplate base bears the maker's name and "Leyland Octopus". A limited item. Length: 7·559in (192mm).

6 Leyland Octopus Tanker, "Esso"; DT No 943, issued in March 1958 and in production until 1964. This Supertoys model appeared only in red, with "Esso Petroleum Company Ltd" decals on sides and back. Note that the diecast tank incorporates

a ladder and catwalk. Its tinplate base plate bears the maker's name and "Leyland Octopus". Limited. Length: 7·559in (192mm).

7 Leyland Octopus Wagon; DT No 934, issued in April 1956 and in production until 1964. This Supertoys model appeared in various two-tone finishes; see also (9). Using the same chassis as (5) and (6), it is fitted with spare wheel and hook. Limited. Length: 7·638in (194mm).

8 Leyland Octopus Flat Truck with Chains; DT No 935, issued in 1964 and in production until 1966. Using the same chassis as (5-7), this appeared in various two-tone finishes. It is a limited item. Length: 7·559in (192mm).

9 Leyland Octopus Wagon; a colour variation of the model shown at (7).

10 Foden Diesel Eight-Wheel Wagon; DT No 501, issued in 1947 and in production until 1952. This was one of the first Dinky Supertoys— see also (11) and (12); it is a one-piece casting with the first-type Foden radiator. It appeared in various two-tone finishes. On the earliest models, no towing-hook is fitted at the rear of the eight-wheeled chassis (with spare wheel fitted beneath). It has a tinplate base plate stamped with the maker's name and "Foden". The model was reissued with the second-type Foden radiator in 1952, was renumbered 901 in 1954, and remained in production until 1957. All versions are of limited availability. Length: 7·402in (188mm).

11 Foden Flat Truck; DT No 502, issued in October 1947 and in production

until 1952, when it was reissued as DT No 902 with the second-type Foden radiator, remaining in production until 1960. It is always found with a towing-hook. A limited item; but more easily found than (10). Length: 7·402in (188mm).

12 Foden Flat Truck with Tailboard; DT No 503, issued in October 1947, reissued with the second-type radiator in 1952, renumbered 903 in 1954, and remaining in production until 1960. Limited; as (10). Length: 7·402in (188mm).

13 Foden Flat Truck with Chains; DT No 505, issued in January 1952 and in production in its original form in 1952 only. In September 1952 it was reissued with the second-type radiator; it was renumbered 905 in 1954 and remained in production until 1964.

It is limited; the later versions may prove to be harder to find. Length: 7·402in (188mm).

14 Foden 14-Ton Tanker; DT No 504. As seen here, with the first-type radiator, this Supertoys model was first issued in December 1948, in two-tone blue or red-and-fawn finish, remaining available until 1952. It was made with the second-type radiator, in two-tone blue finish only, in 1953-54; in 1953 there appeared also a version with second-type radiator, in red finish, with "Mobilgas" decals on its tinplate tank. The "Mobilgas" version was renumbered 941 in 1954 and remained in production until 1957. The first two versions of this model are of limited availability; the "Mobilgas" version is scarce. Length: 7·402in (188mm).

Diecast Vehicles by Dinky Toys, Great Britain, 1940s-1960s

1 B.B.C. TV Mobile Control Room by Dinky Toys, Great Britain; Dinky Toys Reference Number (DT No) 967, issued in July 1959 and in production until 1964. This Dinky Supertoys model is fitted with clear plastic windows and bears "B.B.C. Television Service" and coats-of-arms decals. It has a tinplate base plate stamped with the maker's name, "967" and "TV mobile control room". A limited item. Length: 5·866in (149mm).

2 B.B.C. TV Extending Mast Vehicle; DT No 969, issued in October 1959 and in production until 1964. The metal mast is extended and elevated by a crank-handle; it has a rotating dish aerial at its top. The vehicle has clear plastic windows and bears B.B.C. coats-of-arms decals. Limited. Length: 6·496in (165mm).

3 B.B.C. TV Roving Eye Vehicle; DT No 968, issued in May 1959 and in production until 1964. This model was the first of the three "B.B.C. TV" Supertoys to be issued, and was the first large commercial vehicle by Dinky Toys to feature plastic windows. Both the mast and the figure of the cameraman are rotatable. A limited item. Length: 4·3125in(110mm).

4 A.B.C. TV Transmitter Van; DT No 988, issued in May 1962 and in production until 1968. This Supertoys models, with an "A.B.C.-TV" decal above the cab and a logo on the sides, has a revolving dish aerial on its roof. Its tinplate base plate is stamped with the maker's name and "Transmitter van". A limited item. Length: 4·449in (113mm).

5 A.B.C. TV Control Room; DT No 987, issued in July 1962 and in production until 1969. Completing the Supertoys "A.B.C.-TV" set, this bears the same decals as (4), plus "A.B.C. Television Service" along the upper sides. It was sold complete with the separate figures of a cameraman and camera (not shown), with plastic cables running from the camera to a "power panel" in the van's lower left side. It has a tinplate base plate stamped with the maker's name and "TV Mobile control room". A limited item. Length: 5·945in (151mm).

6-7 A.E.C. Tanker; DT No 591, issued in September 1952, renumbered 991 in January 1955, and in production until 1958. It appeared only in red-and-yellow finish. The earlier version shown at (6) has a "Shell Chemicals Limited" transfer; the version at (7) dates from post-1955, when this became "Shell Chemicals". A transfer at the rear, indicating a 20mph speed restriction, was dropped in 1957. Both versions of the model are limited. Length: 5·945in (151mm).

8 Guy Van, "Ever Ready/Batteries for life!"; DT No 918, issued in December 1955 and in production until 1958. Like (9) and (10), this Supertoys model is fitted with the second-type Guy front and has opening rear doors, a spare wheel fitted beneath it, and a tinplate base plate stamped with the maker's name and "Guy". It is a limited item: verging on scarce. Length: 5·276 (134mm).

9 Guy Van, "Spratts/Spratt's Bonio, Ovals & Dog Cakes"; DT No 514, issued in July 1953, renumbered

917 in 1954, and in production until 1956. A scarce model. Length: 5·276in (134mm).

10 Guy Van, "Slumberland/Spring Interior/Mattresses" (with crest); DT No 514, issued in December 1949 and in production until 1952. Note that the number is the same as that used for (9). A limited item. Length: 5·276in (134mm).

11 Guy 4-Ton Lorry; DT No 911. This Supertoys model, with a Warrior-type Guy front, was issued in January 1954 as a renumbered version of DT No 511; see (20-21). It was renumbered 431 in 1956 and remained in production until 1964. Limited. Length: 5·197in (132mm).

12-13 Bedford Articulated Lorry; DT No 521, issued in April 1948, renumbered 921 in 1954, again renumbered 409 in 1956, and in

production until 1963. The colour finishes of the examples shown here are those most commonly found on this Supertoys model. It has a spare wheel fitted behind the cab and is equipped with a towing-hook. A common item. Length: (overall): 6·535in (166mm).

14/16-17 Bedford End Tipper; DT No 25m, issued in March 1948, renumbered 410 in 1954, and in production until 1963. A crank-handle on the left side of the body works via a worm-gear to tip the rear of the lorry, which has a hinged tailboard. The model originally appeared in orange (14), green (16), red-and-cream (17) and other colours. After renumbering, it appeared in brown-and-yellow and blue-and-yellow in 1955-63, and in red-and-cream, with the

addition of clear plastic windows, in 1962-63. Fairly common. Length: 3·858in (98mm).

15 Bedford Truck; DT No 25w, issued in February 1949, renumbered 411 in 1954, and in production until 1960. It appeared only in green finish, as seen here, and is fitted with a towing-hook. Its tinplate base plate is stamped with the maker's name and "Bedford". This is a fairly common item. Length:4·094in (104mm).

16-17 Bedford End Tipper; see (14).

18 Guy Flat Truck with Tailboard; DT No 513, issued in October 1947, renumbered 913 in 1954, again renumbered 433 in 1956, and in production until 1958. This Super-toys model was originally made with first-type front and was fitted with the second-type front after

1954. All versions are limited. Length: 5·197in (132mm).

19 Guy Flat Truck; DT No 512, issued in October 1947, renumbered 912 in 1954, again renumbered 432 in 1956, and in production until 1958. All other details are as (18). Limited. Length: 5·197in (132mm).

20-21 Guy 4-Ton Lorry; DT No 511, issued in October 1947, re-numbered 911 — see (11) — in 1954, again renumbered 431 in 1956, and in production until 1964. These examples have the first-type front. A limited item. Length: 5·197in (132mm).

22-23 Big Bedford Lorry; DT No 522, issued in October 1952, re-numbered 922 in 1954, again renumbered 408 in 1956, and in production until 1963. Limited. Length: 5·748in (146mm).

1 Petrol Tanker, "Petrol", by Dinky Toys, Great Britain; Dinky Toys Reference Number (DT No) 30p. This model was first issued in 1952, appearing also with a green body, and remained in production until 1954. For some reason known only to the maker, this set of petrol tankers—of which further examples are shown at (2-5)—was modelled on an American Studebaker. The availability of this model is limited. Length: 4·409in (112mm).

2 Petrol Tanker, "Castrol"; DT No 441, first issued in 1954 and in production until 1960. This model was originally issued as DT No 30pa in 1952, remaining available under this number until 1954. In both cases, the model appeared only with a green body. The availabilty of both versions is

limited; however, the later version shown here may be a little harder to find. Length: 4·409in (112mm).

3 Petrol Tanker, "Mobilgas"; DT No 440, first issued in 1956 and in production until 1961. This model was originally issued as DT No 30p—the same number as the "Petrol" version shown at (1)—in 1952, remaining available under this number until 1954. In both cases the model appeared with a red body, but examples of DT No 440 produced after 1957 may have the "Mobilgas" decal with a white background. All versions are presently of limited availability. Length: 4·409in (112mm).

4 Petrol Tanker, "National Benzole Mixture"; DT No 443, first issued in 1957 and in production until 1958. This is the hardest to find of the

Studebaker-type tankers: it was produced only for a short period and only in the finish shown, with a yellow body and wheel hubs, silver trim, and lettering in black. Fairly scarce. Length: 4·409in (112mm).

5 Petrol Tanker, "Esso Motor Oil Petrol"; DT No 442, first issued in 1954 and available until 1960. This model was originally issued as DT No 30pb, appearing in 1952 and remaining available under this number until 1954. Both versions appeared with red body finish only, and both are of limited availability. Length: 4·409in (112mm).

6 Morris 10cwt Van, "Have a Capstan"; DT No 465, first issued in 1957 and in production until 1959. This model appeared only in the finish shown, with a body in two shades of blue, a silver radiator

and a cigarette motif. It is now quite scarce. Length: 3·071in (78mm).

7 Trojan 15cwt Van, "Chivers Jellies/Always turn out well"; DT No 31c, first issued in 1953 and in production until 1954, when it was renumbered DT No 452, remaining available under this number until 1957. Both versions appeared only in green body finish. The Trojans were the first "advertising vans" to be produced by Dinky Toys after World War II: the model appeared in six different logos, all of which are shown on this spread (7-12). All have one-piece diecast bodies and are fitted with tinplate baseplates. This model is of limited availability under both numbers. Length: 3·346in (85mm).

8 Trojan 15cwt Van, "Brooke Bond Tea"; DT No 455, first issued in

4

5

6

11

12

19

16

17

18

1957 and in production until 1961. See also note at (9). Limited. Length: 3·346in (85mm).

9 Trojan 15cwt Van, "Beefy Oxo"; DT No 31d, first issued in 1953 and in production until 1954. In the latter year this model was renumbered DT No 453, but was withdrawn within a few weeks to be replaced by the "Brooke Bond Tea" models shown at (8); possibly because of the real-life takeover of the Oxo company by Brooke Bond at that time. It is by far the hardest to find of the Trojan vans and must be described as very scarce. Length: 3·346in (85mm).

10 Trojan 15cwt Van, "Dunlop/The World's Master Tyre"; DT No 451, first issued in 1955 and in production until 1957. This model was originally issued as DT No

31b, appearing in 1952 and remaining available under this number until 1954. Both versions are of limited availability, but the earlier one may be harder to find. Length: 3·346in (85mm).

11 Trojan 15cwt Van, "Drink/Cydrax/ Sweet/Sparkling"; DT No 454, first issued in 1957 and in production until 1959. It is of limited availability. Length: 3·346in (85mm).

12 Trojan 15cwt Van, "Esso"; DT No 450, first issued in 1955 and in production until 1957. This model was originally issued as DT No 31a in 1951, remaining available under this number until 1954. Both versions are of limited availability. Length: 3·346in (85mm).

13 Austin Van, "Shell-BP"; DT No 470, first issued in 1954 and in production until 1956. This model

based on an Austin A40 10cwt van was produced by Dinky Toys with three advertising logos, all of which are shown on this spread (13-15). All appeared only in the finishes shown. Note that on this model the "Shell" decal is on the side nearest the camera; a "BP" decal appears on the other side, and both decals feature on the rear doors. Its availability is certainly limited. Length: 3·504in (89mm).

14 Austin Van, "Raleigh Cycles"; DT No 472, first issued in 1957 and in production until 1960. Limited. Length: 3·504in (89mm).

15 Austin Van, "Nestlé's"; DT No 471, first issued in 1955 and in production until 1960. Limited. Length: 3·504in (89mm).

16 Bedford Van, "Kodak/Cameras & Films"; DT No 480, first issued in

1954 and in production until 1956. This model based on a Bedford CA 10cwt van was made with three logos, all of which are shown on this spread (16-18). Limited availability. Length: 3·268in (83mm).

17 Bedford Van, "Ovaltine/& Ovaltine Biscuits"; DT No 481, first issued in 1955 and in production until 1960. Limited. Length: 3·268in (83mm).

18 Bedford Van, "Dinky Toys"; DT No 482, first issued in 1956 and in production until 1960. Limited. Length: 3·268in (83mm).

19 Bedford 12cwt Van, "Evening Standard", by Corgi Toys, Great Britain; maker's reference number 421. This model was first issued in 1960 and remained in production until 1962. It appeared only in the black, silver and red finish shown. Length: 3·268in (83mm).

1 Camping Caravan Caravelair 420 by Dinky Toys, France; French Dinky Toys Reference Number (FDT No) 564, in production 1969-71. The model has a detailed interior, clear plastic windows and a plastic tow-bar. Length: 5·315in (135mm).

2 Camping Caravan; FDT No 811, in production 1959-62. This model is fitted with a metal tow-bar. Length: 5·315in (135mm).

3-4 Caravan by Dinky Toys, Great Britain; Dinky Toys Reference Number (DT No) 190, issued in May 1956 and in production until 1960. It appeared in various two-tone finishes and is fitted with a metal tow-bar. Its tinplate base plate bears the maker's name, "190" and "Caravan". A common item. Length: 4·646in (118mm).

5-8 Four-Berth Caravan; DT No 188. This model was issued in April 1961 and remained in production in the form seen at (5) and (8), with a small sky-light and windows of clear plastic, a basically detailed interior and an opening plastic door, until 1963. In August 1963, the same casting was used for the version shown at (6) and (7), which had a transparent roof and larger end windows. This had the DT No 117, but was sold in the same box as DT No 188, with a "117" sticker. It was available thus until 1969. Both versions are fairly common; the earlier one may be harder to find. Length: 5·197in (132mm).

9 Caravan Trailer; DT No 30g, issued in April 1936 and in production until 1940 — the only "30 Series" vehicle not to be reissued post-War. It is a one-piece casting and is fitted with a wire tow-bar. It appeared in various two-tone finishes and may be found with the roof-lights voided, as seen, or filled in. Note the grey rubber tyres. This is now a fairly scarce item. Length: 3·189in (81mm).

10-11 Four-Wheeled Hand Truck; DT No 105c, issued in June 1949, renumbered 383 in 1954, and in production until 1958. This model in Dinky Toys Farm and Garden range appeared in green (11) in 1949-54, and blue (10) in 1954-58. It has swivelling front wheels and is fitted with a towing-hook. It has metal wheels. Common. Length (with handle): 4·961in (126mm).

12 Healey Sports Boat on Trailer; DT No 796, issued in September 1960

and in production until 1967. The boat is plastic, with windscreen and steering wheel; the trailer is diecast, with plastic wheels. Fairly common. Lengths (boat): 3·70in (94mm); (trailer) 3·858in (98mm).

13 Renault Estafette Camping by Dinky Toys, France; FDT No 565, in production 1965-71. It has a detailed interior and a sliding side door. Length: 3·66in (93mm).

14-15 Loudspeaker Van; DT No 34c, issued in February 1948, re-numbered 492 in 1954, and in production until 1957. This is a one-piece third-type "28 Series" van casting with un-voided rear windows; it has a diecast speaker unit mounted on the roof. It appeared in various colours, two of which are shown. Fairly common. Length: 3·189in (81mm).

16 Delivery Van; DT No 280, issued in 1948 and in production until 1954. The same casting as (14-15), this appeared in red or blue. Note that DT No 280 was later used for an Observation Coach (1954-60). Fairly common. Length: 3·189in (81mm).

17-22 Electric Dairy Van; DT No 30v. This model was first issued in 1949 in the form shown at (21) and (22), with "NCB" decal. The version with "Express Dairy" decal, shown at (18) and (20), first appeared in 1951, and the promotional model with "Job's Dairy" decal (17) in 1953. In 1954, the "Express Dairy" version was renumbered 490 and the "NCB" and "Job's Dairy" versions became No 491. It is believed that the later "NCB" version was intended for sale

overseas. The "Express Dairy" version is fairly common; "NCB" will be harder to find; "Job's Dairy" is limited, verging on scarce. Length: 3·346in (85mm).

23 "Pathe News" Camera Car; DT No 281, issued in 1968 and in production until 1970. The Fiat 2300 Station Wagon on which the cameraman and camera are mounted has clear plastic windows, a detailed interior and opening bonnet, doors and tailgate. It appeared only in black. Common. Length: 4·252in (108mm).

24 "Radio Telé/Luxembourg" Camera Car, Citroën ID 19 Shooting Brake, by Dinky Toys, France; FDT No 1404, dating from the early 1970s. Length: 4·528in (115mm).

25-27 B.E.V. Electric Truck; DT No 14a, issued in July 1948,

renumbered 400 in 1954, and in production until 1960. Fitted with a diecast driver and a towing-hook, this model will be easy to find. Length: 3·346in (85mm).

28 Bedford Dormobile by Corgi Toys, Great Britain; maker's reference number 404, issued in 1956 and in production until 1962. Appearing in various colours, this model is fairly common, but a version with friction drive, made in 1956-59, is scarce. Length: 3·268in (83mm).

29-30 Atlas Kenebrake Bus; DT No 295, issued in May 1960 and in production until 1964. Normally appearing in light-blue-and-grey (30), it is shown here with a colour variant (29). This was the first Dinky Toys vehicle to feature a detailed interior and the first Dinky bus with clear plastic windows. It also features

suspension. Fairly common. Length: 3·386in (86mm).

31 Three-Wheeled Delivery Van (*Triporteur*) by Dinky Toys, France; FDT No 14z, in production 1937-40. The box has an opening lid. It was available in Britain from 1938 onward. A limited item. Length: 2·756in (70mm).

32 Mersey Tunnel Police Van; DT No 255, issued in September 1955 and in production until 1961. Appearing only in red, it has a towing-hook. A common item. Length: 3·031in (77mm).

33 "Prisoner" Mini-Moke; DT No 106, issued in 1967 (as a tie-in with the popular TV series, "The Prisoner") and in production until 1970. It appeared only in the finish shown. It is a fairly common model. Length: 2·874in (73mm).

1 1930 Ford Model "A" Van, "Maggi Soups", by Lesney, Great Britain; Models of Yesteryear (MoY) Y-22 (1st Issue; second type). First appearing in 1983, this model is currently available. A variation in finish on (2), this van bears the Maggi company's advertising in the German language; a version in the same yellow and red finish, but with English-language advertising, is harder to find. A common item. Length: 4·016in (102mm).

2 1930 Ford Model "A" Van, "Oxo/It's Meat & Drink To You"; MoY Y-22 (1st Issue; first type). First appearing in 1982 and currently available, this model may be found with its black roof in either rough or smooth finish. Like (1), it has silver plastic spoked wheels with whitewall tyres. A common

item. Length: 4·016in (102mm).
3 1930 Ford Model "A" Van, "Walters' Delicious Creemy (*sic*)/Palm Toffee"; MoY Y-22 (1st Issue; third type).First appearing in 1984 and currently available, this model is a further variation on (1) and (2); it is fitted with gold plastic spoked wheels without whitewalls. Common. Length: 4·016in (102mm).
4 1930 Ford Model "A" Van, "Ever Ready/Batteries/for longer life!"; first appearing in 1984 and still available. A further variation on (1), (2) and (3), again with silver plastic spoked wheels and whitewall tyres. For a similarly-finished "Ever Ready" van—but a quite different model—see (7). A common item. Length: 4·016in (102mm).
5 1930 Ford Model "A" Van, "Toblerone"; MoY Y-22 (1st Issue;

fifth type), first appearing in 1985 and currently available. At the time of writing (Spring 1985), this was the most recent variation in finish in the Model "A" range. Common. Length: 4·016in (102mm).
6 Ford Model "A" Woody Wagon, "A & J Box/General Stores"; MoY Y-21 (1st Issue; third type). This variation first appeared in 1983 and is currently available. The first type of Woody Wagon (so called from its wood-panelled body) appeared in 1981, with a yellow body, dark brown chassis and black roof; the second type, appearing in 1982, has a yellow body, black chassis and black roof. All three types are common; the earlier ones may be a little harder to find. Length: 3·937in (100mm).
7 1927 Talbot Van, "Ever Ready/

Batteries for life!"; MoY Y-5 (4th Issue; tenth type). This variation in finish in the large Talbot Van range first appeared in 1983 and is currently available. The tan seats of this example mark it as the first issue of its type; a second issue, with black seats, appeared in the same year. Both are common. Length: 3·74in (95mm).
8 1927 Talbot Van, "Talbot"; MoY Y-5 (4th Issue; unidentified type). This version, which carries advertising for the maker of the prototype vehicle, has artillery-type wheels of the early pattern: of large diameter and fitted with smooth plastic tyres. It is thought to be of limited availability. Length: 3·74in (95mm).
9 1927 Talbot Van, "Taystee/Old Fashioned/Enriched Bread"; MoY

Y-5 (4th Issue; fourth type). The type first appeared in 1980; however, the black chassis of this example marks it as the colour-change version that appeared in 1981. For the original version, see (12). The version shown here is not currently available; it remains quite common, but (12) will prove easier to find. Length: 3·74in (95mm).

10 1927 Talbot Van, "Ibcam Motoring Festival/August 23, 25, 25, 1980"; MoY Y-5 (4th Issue; unidentified type). A "Models of Yesteryear" van with appropriate paintwork and decals is specifically issued each year for sale at this British festival for motor enthusiasts. The models are always dated, like the example shown, and are fairly eagerly sought by all collectors. Length 3·74in (95mm).

11 1927 Talbot Van, "Dunlop/Tyres & Accessories"; MoY Y-5 (4th Issue; unidentified type). This version of the Talbot Van appears to be unlisted. It may be a limited edition, in which case it will be a scarce item and very collectable. Length: 3·74in (95mm).

12 1927 Talbot Van, "Taystee/Old Fashioned/Enriched Bread"; MoY Y-5 (4th Issue; fourth type). See note at (9): this is the first version, marked as such by its yellow chassis, which first appeared in 1980 and is currently available. Note that a version with yellow body and yellow chassis, with the word "Taystee" in yellow on red (as compared to white on red in the British version shown), was made for sale in the USA. Two other yellow-finished Talbot vans (4th

Issue; fifth and sixth types), with advertising for "Merita Old Fashioned Enriched Bread" and "Langendorf Old Fashioned Enriched Bread", were made only to be sold on the US market. Length: 3·74in (95mm).

13 1927 Talbot Van, "Nestlé's Milk/The Richest in Cream"; MoY Y-5 (4th Issue; seventh type). This version first appeared in 1981; it is not currently available and is among the hardest to find of the Talbot vans. Even more difficult to obtain (outside its intended marketing area) is a version with a lighter grey roof, issued in the same year for the Australian market. Limited. Length: 3·74in (95mm).

14 1927 Talbot Van, "Wright's/Original/Coal Tar/Soap"; MoY Y-5 (4th Issue; ninth type). This version

first appeared in 1982 and is currently available. It may be found with either silver (as shown) or gold plastic spoked wheels. Common. Length: 3·74in (95mm).

15 1927 Talbot Van, "Chivers/&/Sons Ltd./Jams, Jellies & Marmalades"; MoY Y-5 (4th Issue; eighth type). This version first appeared in 1982 and is currently available. Common. Length: 3·74in (95mm).

16 1927 Talbot Van, "Chocolat/Menier"; MoY Y-5 (4th Issue; second type). This was the first variation to appear on the original Talbot van (which bore "Lipton's Tea" advertising; with the words "By Appointment", which were replaced by the firm's address in 1980), and was issued in the same year, 1978. It is currently available. Common. Length: 3·74in (95mm).

1 Double Decker Bus by Dinky Toys, Great Britain; Dinky Toys Reference Number (DT No) 290. The perennially-popular double decker was first issued early in 1938 as DT No 29c—see (5), (8), (9) and (13). It was reissued after World War II, passing through several design changes, as detailed below, and being renumbered DT No 290 in 1955. It remained in production under this number until 1963. The example shown here, finished in green-and-cream, and also produced in red-and-cream, is without a "number box" on the front of its roof, marking it as one produced between c1956, when this feature was deleted—see (2), and 1960, when it was reintroduced. It bears the commonest of the advertising transfers found on this

model: "Dunlop The World's Master Tyre". The Leyland radiator seen on this example featured on models produced between 1948 and 1962. This model is fitted with spun-aluminium wheels with rubber tyres. Limited. Length: 4·055in (103mm).

2 Double Decker Bus; DT No 290. This example is without the roof box; see note at (1). Notice also that the lettering of "Dunlop" is upright, not slanted as at (1). It has the Leyland radiator and, like the examples shown at (3-9), is fitted with ridged cast wheels with rubber tyres. It is a limited item. Length: 4·055in (103mm).

3 Double Decker Bus; DT No 290. This example has the second-type AEC radiator (also called the "Guy" radiator); note that the "V" at the top of the radiator is less pronounced

than at (5) and (9). This radiator was fitted between 1950 and c1956. Limited. Length: as (1).

4 Double Decker Bus; DT No 290. This example, with roof box, is fitted with the Leyland radiator. Limited. Length: 4·055in (103mm).

5 Double Decker Bus; DT No 29c. This is an earlier model with the first-type AEC radiator—note the pronounced "V" at the top of the grille—fitted in the period 1949-59. Limited. Length: 3·937in (100mm).

6 Double Decker Bus; DT No 290. In red-and-cream finish, this has the Leyland-type radiator. Limited. Length: 4·055in (103mm).

7 Double Decker Bus; DT No 290. This example has the second-type AEC radiator. A limited item. Length: 4·055in (103mm).

8 Double Decker Bus; DT No 29c. A

somewhat earlier example than (7), dating from before the renumbering of 1955, but again with the second-type AEC radiator. A limited item. Length: 3·937in (100mm).

9 Double Decker Bus; DT No 29c. This is in the alternative colour finish of red-and-grey and is fitted with the first-type AEC radiator with the pronounced "V". Limited. Length: 3·937in (100mm).

10 Double Decker Bus; DT No 290. This example is fitted with the Leyland radiator and has aluminium wheels. Limited. Length: as (1).

11 Double Decker Bus; DT No 291. This model, based on the Leyland version of No 290, was introduced in 1959 and remained in production until 1963. Finished in red, it bears yellow-and-black "Exide Batteries" decals. The example seen here is

fitted with plastic wheels. Note that the same DT No was used for the Atlantean City Bus of 1974-77; see (15-17), *pages 138-139*. Limited. Length: 4·055in (103mm).

12 Double Decker Bus; DT No 291. As (11), but with ridged cast wheels. Limited. Length: 4·055in (103mm).

13 Double Decker Bus; DT No 29c. A side-view of this model, showing a two-tone green finish: other colour variations may be found. Limited. Length: 3·937in (100mm).

14 Observation Coach, DT No 280. This model was in production from 1954 to 1960; see (15). This one is the post-renumbering version, which appeared in cream with a red flash. It is a limited item. Length: 4·409in (112mm).

15 Observation Coach; DT no 29f. The original form of the model at

(14), first issued in 1950 and in production, in grey with red flash, until it was renumbered 280 in 1954. It may be a little harder to find than (14). Length: as (14).

16-18 Duple Roadmaster Coach; this model was first issued as DT No 29h in 1952, appearing in blue-and-silver, as shown at (16), until 1954. It was then renumbered 282, and remained in production, appearing in red-and-silver (17) and then yellow-and-red (18), until 1960. On later versions, the words "Leyland Royal Tiger" appear on the base plate. The blue- and red-and-silver versions are limited; the yellow-and-red version is scarce. Length: 4·6875in (119mm).

19 B.O.A.C. Coach; DT No 283. This was issued in 1956 and remained in production until 1963. Finished

in blue, with a white roof, it has the decal "British Overseas Airways Corporation" along its upper body, and "B.O.A.C.", with logo, on its side. It is a limited item. Length: 4·724in (120mm).

20-22 Streamline Bus; DT No 29b. This model was first issued in 1936, was in production until 1940, and was reissued in 1948-50. The body is a single casting and, unlike some other Dinky models, it is very rare to find pre-War examples that have been affected by metal fatigue. The major difference between pre- and post-War examples is that the former have a cut-out rear window and the latter have not. The model was made in various two-tone finishes additional to those of the post-War examples shown here.

Post-War versions are limited. Length: 3·465in (88mm).

23-26 Luxury Coach; DT No 29g (renumbered 281). This model was first issued in 1951 and was in production as No 29g, finished in cream with orange flashes, as seen at (25), until 1954. It was then re-named the Modern Coach, renumbered 281, and remained in production until 1960. It is a limited item. Length: 4·449in (113mm).

27-29 Single Deck Bus; DT No 29e. This model was first issued in 1948 and remained in production until 1952. It appeared only in the three colour finishes shown here: cream with blue flash (27); green with dark green flash (28); blue with dark blue flash (29). Limited. Length: 4·449in (113mm).

1   2   3   4   8   14   15   16

1 Berliet Urban Bus (*Berliet Bus urbain*) by Dinky Toys, France; French Dinky Toys Reference Number (FDT No) 889U, issued in 1965 and in production until 1970. Finished in the red-and-cream livery of T.C.L. de Lyon, this model features—as may be seen in the similar model shown at (2)—automatically-opening side doors (operating when the model is pressed firmly downwards), clear plastic windows and a detailed interior. It is fitted with jewelled headlights. It bears a "Pepsi-Cola" decal on the left side and, again as visible at (2), a "Dunlop" decal on the right. Like most models by Dinky Toys, France, it is of limited availability in Great Britain. Length: 8·819in (224mm).

2 Berliet Paris Bus (*Berliet Autobus Parisien*); FDT No 889, issued in 1965 and in production until 1970. Finished in the two-tone green livery of the R.A.T.P., this is in all other respects the same model as that shown at (1), bearing the same decals and here photographed from such an angle as to display more fully its various special features. Limited. Length: 8·819in (224mm).

3 Continental Touring Coach by Dinky Toys, Great Britain; Dinky Toys Reference Number (DT No) 953, issued in January 1963 and in production until 1965. This Dinky Supertoys models is fitted with clear plastic windows and has a detailed interior. It bears "Dinky Continental Tours" decals along its upper sides, and appeared only in pale-blue-and-white. Scarce. Length: 7·677in (195mm).

4 Vega Major Coach; DT No 961, issued in 1973 and in production until 1977. This most attractive model was issued for sale in Switzerland, and bears the appropriate finish; see (5) for the British version. It features battery-powered side-mounted indicator lights that flash when the six-wheeled vehicle is steered to the appropriate side by pressing down on its front (bogey) pair of wheels. It has opening doors and an opening rear luggage compartment; its clear plastic windows include roof-lights. Suspension is fitted. This model is of limited availability. Length: 9·528in (242mm).

5 Vega Major Luxury Coach; DT No 954, issued in 1972 and in production until 1976. This is basically the same model as that shown at (4), but in white finish with a maroon flash, as issued for the British market. Although plastic-lensed indicators are fitted on the sides, they do not flash on this model. On an earlier version— DT No 952, issued in 1964 and in production until 1971; now of limited availability—flashing lights as described at (4) were fitted. The earlier version was finished in grey with a maroon flash. The version shown here is a fairly common item. Length: 9·528in (242mm).

6 Wayne "School Bus"; DT No 949, issued in February 1961 and in production until 1964. Judging from its finish, it is probable that this Dinky Supertoys model was intended to be marketed in the United States, although it was in fact available only in Great Britain. It

has a detailed interior with a separate steering wheel (left-hand drive) and is fitted with clear plastic windows. Its tinplate base plate is stamped with the maker's name and "Wayne Bus". Limited. Length: 7·677in (195mm).

7 Renault Autobus by CIJ, France; dating from the early 1960s. The casting incorporates a roof rack. Limited. Length: 4·921in (125mm).

8 "Red Arrow" Single-Decker Bus; DT No 283, issued in 1971 and in production until 1976. Appearing at first in red finish and later in metallic red, this model is fitted with clear plastic windows, a number plate, a detailed interior, and opening side doors that are worked by a sliding-catch (just visible on the upper side of the vehicle away from the camera) that

also rings a bell. Fairly common. Length: 6·575in (167mm).

9 Mercedes Benz 18-Seater Coach (*Mercedes Benz Autocar 18 places*); FDT No 541, issued in May 1963 and in production until 1971. This model features clear plastic windows, including roof-lights, a detailed interior, and suspension. A limited model. Length: 4·409in (112mm).

10-11 Isobloc Coach (*Isobloc Autocar*); FDT No 29E, issued in 1953 and in production until March 1955. See also (12-13): this is the later version of the model, marked as such by the ribbing on the luggage-rack roof. As in all versions, the ladder at the rear is tinplate. It appeared only in the finishes shown. Limited. Length: 5·00in (127mm).

12-13 Isobloc Coach; FDT No 27E,

issued in 1951 and in production until 1952. An earlier version, with the same number, of the model at (10-11): note the smooth roof. Limited. Length: 5·00in (127mm).

14-15 Chausson Coach (*Chausson Autocar*); FDT No 29F, issued in April 1956, renumbered 571 in 1959, and in production until 1960. This well-detailed model was issued only in the two finishes shown. It is a limited item. Length: 6·063in (154mm).

16 Chausson Trolley Bus by Solido, France; maker's reference number AP52, issued in 1952 and available until 1957. Note the similarity in finish with the French Dinky Toys model shown at (14-15). Limited. Length: 5·591in (142mm).

17 Chausson Coach by Solido, France; issued in 1952 and available until

1957. The same casting is used as in the trolley bus at (16). Limited. Length: 5·591in (142mm).

18 Somua-Panhard Paris Bus (*Autobus parisien Somua-Panhard*); FDT No 29D, issued in January 1952 and renumbered 570 in 1959; production ceased in 1959 but this very popular model remained available until 1961. Limited. Length: 5·629in (143mm).

19 "Midland Red" Motorway Express Coach by Corgi Toys, Great Britain; maker's reference number 1120, issued in 1961 and in production until 1978. Bearing "Derby Birmingham Liverpool" route-board decals on its upper sides, this model has clear plastic windows and an interior with detail that extends even to a lavatory. A limited item. Length: 5·512in (140mm).

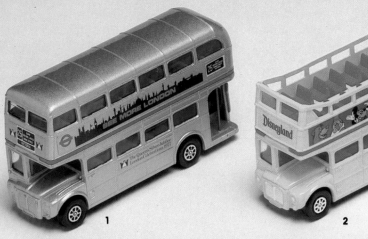

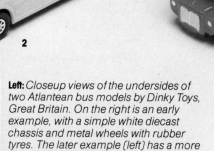

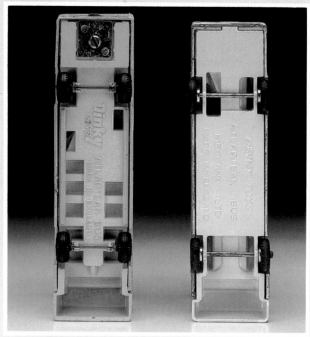

Left: *Closeup views of the undersides of two Atlantean bus models by Dinky Toys, Great Britain. On the right is an early example, with a simple white diecast chassis and metal wheels with rubber tyres. The later example (left) has a more complex yellow diecast chassis and is fitted with plastic speedwheels.*

1 **Routemaster Double Decker Bus,** "Queen's Silver Jubilee", by Corgi Toys, Great Britain; maker's reference number (MRN) 471, issued in 1977. This model has an all-silver body with the decals "See More London", printed in red against a London skyline in black, on its upper body, and "The Queen's Silver Jubilee/London Celebrations", with logo, in black on silver, on its lower body. Like all the Corgi Routemaster models shown on this spread (1-6), it has a plastic chassis and is fitted with plastic whizzwheels. It is fairly common. Length: 4·8425in (123mm).

2 **Routemaster Double Decker Bus,** "Disneyland", by Corgi Toys; MRN 470, dating from 1977. The open-topped Routemaster model first appeared in 1973, when

versions were issued bearing advertising on behalf of "Old Hoborn" (No C469/10, finished in orange); "Blackpool Transport" (No C469/17, finished in cream-and-green); "Manchester United" (No C469/23, finished in red); "Bournemouth" (No C469/30, finished in either orange or yellow); and "Suntrekker" (No C478, finished in orange-and-white). This version, finished in yellow with "Disneyland" in red, has a decal showing Walt Disney's famous cartoon characters along its upper body. A fairly common item. Length: 4·8425in (123mm).

3 **Routemaster Double Decker Bus,** "Swan & Edgar" "London Transport", by Corgi Toys; MRN C469, issued in 1974 and in production until 1980. Finished in

red, it bears the decal "Swan & Edgar Piccadilly Circus" on its upper side, and "London Transport" on its lower side. As on the models shown at (4) and (5), the headboards bear Corgi Toys' name and logo. A fairly common item. Length: 4·8425in (123mm).

4 **Routemaster Double Decker Bus,** "BTA" (British Travel Association) "London Transport", by Corgi Toys; MRN C469, the same as (3), issued in 1975 and currently available. The decal on the upper side reads "BTA Welcome to Britain", with a Union Flag motif; otherwise the finish is as (3). This model is common—but a variant bearing a label advertising the James Bond film "Octopussy", on one side only, is extremely rare. Length: 4·8425in (123mm).

5 **Routemaster Double Decker Bus,** "Selfridges" "London Transport", by Corgi Toys; MRN 467, first issued in 1977 and in production until 1981. The decal on the upper side reads: "There's no place like Selfridges", otherwise the the finish is as (3) and (4)—but note that this model has a Route 12 destination board, whereas (3) and (4) are Route 11. It is fairly common. Length: 4·8425in (123mm).

6 **Routemaster Double Decker Bus,** "Leeds" "Omnibus", by Corgi Toys; MRN C469, the same as (3) and (4), first issued in 1979 and in production until 1981. Finished in dark green and yellow, this bears the decal "Say 'the Leeds' and you're smiling" on the upper side, and "Omnibus", "George Shillibeer 1829 London Transport 1979"

(marking the 150th anniversary of the London bus service) on the lower side. It is one of the less common Routemaster models. Length: 4·8425in (123mm).

7-8 London Routemaster Bus, "Esso Safety Grip tyres", by Dinky Toys, Great Britain; Dinky Toys Reference Number (DT No) 289, first issued in 1970 and in production until 1977. In the familiar red finish of "London Transport", this model was produced with plastic speed-wheels, as shown at (7), or with aluminium wheels fitted with rubber tyres, as shown at (8). Both are fairly common, although the rubber-tyred version will probably be harder to find. Other "advertising" versions of DT No 289 include "Tern Shirts For Crispness" (1964-65); "Ssschweppes" (1965-69); "Festival of London Stores" (c1970; a scarce item); and "Visit Madame Tussaud's" (1977-78). Length: 4·764in (121mm).

9 Atlantean Bus, "BP" "Corporation Transport", by Dinky Toys; DT No 293, first issued in 1963 and in production until 1968. Finished in green-and-white, this bears the decal "BP Is The Key To Better Motoring" on its upper side. Note that it incorporates the figure of a driver. It is of limited availability. Length: 4·764in (121mm).

10 Atlantean Bus, "Ribble", by Dinky Toys; DT No 292, first issued in 1962 and in production until 1966. Finished in red-and-white, this has "Regent for peak pulling power" on its upper side, and "Ribble" on its lower side. A limited item. Length: 4·764in (121mm).

11 Atlantean Bus, "Regent", by Dinky Toys; DT No 292: produced under the same number as (10), from 1962 until 1968, and the same model, save for the fact that "Corporation Transport" and a coat-of-arms replace "Ribble". Limited. Length: 4·764in (121mm).

12 Silver Jubilee Bus (Leyland Atlantean) by Dinky Toys; DT No 297, issued in 1977. Finished in silver, this bears the decal "The Queen's Silver Jubilee 1977" along the upper side, and "National" on the lower side. It has a diecast chassis and is fitted with plastic speedwheels. Fairly common; although a version specially-decalled for Woolworths stores is limited. Length: 4·764in (121mm).

13-14 Atlantean Bus, "Yellow Pages", by Dinky Toys; DT No 295. There are several variants of this model. Two are shown here: (13) is in yellow with a white engine cover; (14) is finished overall in deeper yellow. The major variant is in the earlier versions, in production 1973-74, in which the lettering on the headboards is reversed; later versions, in production 1974-76, are lettered as seen at (14). The earlier version is fairly limited. Length: 4·8425in (123mm).

15-17 Atlantean City Bus, "Kenning", by Dinky Toys; DT No 291, issued in 1974 and in production until 1977. Three colour variants are shown. A fairly common item. Length: 4·8425in (123mm).

18 Atlantean Bus, "Esso Safety Grip tyres" by Dinky Toys; DT No 291. As (15-17), but with unplated wheels and a special finish.

1 Plymouth Yellow Cab by Dinky Toys, Great Britain; Dinky Toys Reference Number (DT No) 278, issued in 1970 and in production until 1980. Using the same casting as the Plymouth Fury Police Car (DT No 244, 1978-79), this appeared in yellow only. It has clear plastic windows, a detailed interior and a plastic whip aerial. It has a plastic chassis and is fitted with plastic speedwheels. Common. Length: 5·276in (134mm).

2 Renault Prairie by CIJ, France; dating from the 1950s. This is a simple one-piece casting and is fitted with white rubber tyres. Length: 3·937in (100mm).

3 Peugeot 404 Taxi by Dinky Toys, France; French Dinky Toys Reference Number (FDT No) 1400, dating from the 1960s. This

model features jewelled headlights, front and rear numberplates, and a detailed interior with steering wheel (left-hand drive). It is a limited item. Length: 3·976in (101mm).

4-5 Taxi with Driver; DT No 36g, first issued in 1948, in production until 1940, and reissued in 1946-49. Appearing as a separate item in the "36 Series" (ie, it was never available as part of a boxed set) this model was made in a variety of colours: the wings, top and interior were always black, but the remainder was finished in green (4), brown (5), blue, yellow, red, grey or fawn. It has a cast "Taxi" sign on the roof and a licence plate at the rear. Pre-War versions have an open rear window and are fitted with smooth wheel hubs; post-War versions are without the rear

window and have ridged wheel hubs. Both versions are limited. Length: 2·835in (72mm).

6 London Taxi Cab by Budgie Toys, Great Britain; dating from the 1960s. This model features a cast "Taxi" sign on the roof, clear plastic windows, plated wheel hubs and rubber tyres. It is a limited item. Length: 4·21in (107mm).

7-8 Austin Taxi; DT No 40h, issued in November 1951, renumbered 254 in 1955, and in production until 1962. This was the only "40 Series" vehicle to have a diecast base, which bears the maker's name, "40H" (on some earlier models) or "254" (after 1955), and "Austin taxi". It has a cast "Taxi" sign on the roof, a taxi meter, numberplates and a steering wheel. The earlier version appeared in blue or yellow

(7); in 1954-56 it was made in dark blue (8) or yellow; in 1956-62 it appeared in green-and-yellow. The earlier version is now limited. Length: 3·70in (94mm).

9 Simca 9 Aronde Taxi by Dinky Toys, France; FDT No 24ut, dating from the mid-1950s. It has a cast "Taxi" sign on the roof and a taxi meter on the bonnet and is fitted with white rubber tyres. A limited item. Length: 3·74in (95mm).

10 Ford Vedette Taxi; FDT No 24xt, dating from 1954-56. Contemporary with (9), this is also based on a car casting (FDT No 24x), with a two-tone finish applied and a sign and meter added. It is a limited item. Length: 4·134in (105mm).

11 Simca Ariane Taxi; FDT No 24zt, dating from the late 1950s. This model is fitted with clear plastic

windows and, like (10), has chromed wheel hubs. Limited. Length: 3·976in (101mm).

12 Opel Rekord Taxi; FDT No 546, dating from the early 1960s. This model, with a cast "Taxi" sign on the roof but no meter, is fitted with clear plastic windows and has a detailed interior complete with steering wheel (left-hand drive). Note the bright "Rekord" lettering on the rear wing. A limited item. Length: 4·134in (105mm).

13 Citroën ID 19 Ambulance; FDT No 556, dating from the mid-1960s. It has a plastic warning light on the roof, a cast roof rack, clear plastic windows, an opening tailgate and a detailed interior. It has "Ambulance Municipale" decals on the front doors. Length: 4·21in (107mm).

14 Renault Prairie Ambulance by CIJ,

France; dating from the 1950s. This simple model makes use of the same casting as (2), but in white finish with filled-in rear side windows, an "Ambulance" decal, and a fabric flag on a chromed staff on the right front wing. Limited. Length: 3·937in (100mm).

15 Renault Ambulance by CIJ, France; dating from the 1950s. This model, with "Ambulance" and red cross decals, has opening rear doors. Limited. Length: 4·21in (107mm).

16 Mercedes Ambulance by Lesney, Great Britain; dating from around 1969. This has opening doors and a detailed interior (left-hand drive). A fairly common model. Length: 4·134in (105mm).

17-18 Daimler Ambulance; DT No 30h. This model was first issued in 1950, appearing as shown at (17),

in cream (later in white) with red crosses, until 1954. It was renumbered 253 in March 1954 and thereafter was in production in cream or white until 1964; later production items, like the example at (18), have clear plastic windows. The tinplate base plate of the earlier version is stamped with the maker's name and "Daimler"; the number "253" is found on some later examples. In 1956 a version in matt green was issued for sale in the USA, where it was marketed as the Army Ambulance (DT No 30hm; later renumbered 624). The earlier version of this long-lived model will be the harder to find. Length: 3·78in (96mm).

19 Vauxhall Victor Ambulance; DT No 278, issued in 1964 and in production until 1968. The casting

for the Vauxhall Victor Estate Car (DT No 141, 1963-67), with the addition of a roof piece incorporating a sign and warning light, was used for this model. It is a fairly common item. Length: 3·425in (87mm).

20 Graham Paige Ambulance by Tootsietoy, USA; dating from the 1930s. This early diecast model has been repainted. It is limited. Length: 3·82in (97mm).

21 Superior Criterion Ambulance; DT No 263, issued in 1962 and in production until 1968. This model features the figures of a driver and nurse, roof-mounted warning lights, opening doors and tailgate, and a detailed interior with the figure of a patient on a stretcher. This model will be fairly easy to find. Length: 5·0in (127mm).

1 Plymouth Fury Police Car by Dinky Toys, Great Britain; Dinky Toys Reference Number (DT No) 244, issued in 1977 and in production until 1980. Like almost all Dinky Toys police vehicles, this was based on a car casting, in this case the Plymouth Stock Car (DT No 201), with the appropriate additions —warning lights, etc—decals and finish. This model has battery-powered flashing lights and a plastic whip aerial; it is fitted with a plastic chassis and plastic wheels. This model will be easy to find. Length: 5·276in (134mm).

2 Chevrolet State Police Car by Corgi Toys, Great Britain; maker's reference number (MRN) 223, issued in 1959 and in production until 1961. This model has a detailed interior (left-hand drive)

and suspension. Common. Length: 4·252in (108mm).

3 U.S.A. Police Car; DT No 258. This model appeared in four different forms between 1960 and 1968. The example shown is that available in 1960-61, based on the De Soto Fireflight (DT No 192, 1958-63). It is fitted with a flashing roof-light. The second version, based on the Dodge Royal Sedan (DT No 191, 1959-64), was available 1961-62. The third version, based on the Ford Fairlane (DT No 148, 1962-65), was available 1960-66. The fourth version, sold as the Cadillac U.S.A. Police Car, was based on the Cadillac 62 (DT No 147, 1962-68) and was available 1966-68. All four versions have black finish with white doors. The first two versions,

although not scarce, will be harder to find. Length: 4·488in (114mm).

4 Oldsmobile Sheriff's Car by Corgi; MRN 237, issued in 1962 and in production until 1966. The model bears "County Sheriff" and badge decals and is fitted with suspension. A common model. Length: 4·252in (108mm).

5 Cadillac R.C.M.P. Car; DT No 264, issued in 1966 and in production until 1968. This model, with Royal Canadian Mounted Police badge decals and with two uniformed "Mounties" inside, is based on the Cadillac 62 (DT No 147) and features a flashing light, suspension and fingertip steering. Two other models appeared with the same number: R.C.M.P. Patrol Car, 1962-66, based on the Ford Fairlane (DT No 148); Rover 3500

Police Car, (DT No 180). Fairly common. Length: 4·37in (111mm).

6 Triumph 2000 Police Car; DT No 135. This model was first issued in non-police finish in November 1963 and was in production until 1968. It has an opening bonnet with detailed engine, opening doors and boot, suspension and fingertip steering. Common. Length: 4·21in (107mm).

7 Riley Police Car by Corgi; MRN 209, issued in 1958 and in production until 1961. Finished in black-and-silver, this model has a metal "Police" sign, spotlight and bell on its roof. It is fairly common. Length: 3·819in (97mm).

8 Ford Zephyr Motorway Patrol by Corgi; MRN 419, issued in 1960 and in production until 1963. The casting incorporates a roof rack. Fairly

common. Length: 3·819in (97mm).
9 Humber Hawk Police Car; DT No 256, issued in December 1960 and in production until 1964. Based on the Humber Hawk (DT No 165, 1959-63), this model was marketed with the figures of a police driver and passenger (driver only is shown) and with the number-plate "PC 49" (the title of a then-popular radio series). It has an aerial and a roof-mounted "Police" sign and is fitted with suspension. It is one of the less common Dinky Toys police vehicles. Length: 4·016in (102mm).
10 Renault 300KG Police Radio Van by CIJ, France; dating from 1952. Note aerial with metal spring fitting. Length: 3·268in (83mm).
11 Peugeot 404 Police Car by Dinky Toys, France; French Dinky Toys

Reference Number (FDT No) 1429. This model is based on the Peugeot 404 Saloon (FDT No 553) which, in civilian finish, was marketed in Great Britain in 1962-63. It is a fairly common item. Length: 4·134in (105mm).
12 Simca 1100 Police Car by Dinky Toys, France; FDT No 1450, dating from the 1960s. A limited item. Length: 3·5625in (90mm).
13 Citroën DS 19 Police Car by Dinky Toys, France; FDT No 530, issued in 1964. This model, which has jewelled headlights, is based on the civilian-finish Citroën DS 19 with the same reference number, which was marketed in Great Britain in 1965-66. It is a limited item. Length: 4·252in (108mm).
14 Volkswagen Police Car by Corgi Toys; MRN 492, issued in 1966 and

in production until 1969. Finished in green-and-white with "Polizei" decals it has jewelled headlights. Fairly common. Length: 3·583in (91mm).
15 Renault 4CV Police Car by CIJ, France; dating from the 1960s. Note the cut-away doors on this small and simple model. A limited item. Length: 3·15in (80mm).
16 Ford Taunus Police Car; FDT No 559, dating from the later 1960s. Limited. Length: 4·055in (103mm).
17 Citroën 1200KG Police Van; FDT No 566, in production from 1965 until 1970. Note the well-modelled radiator, sliding side door and plastic "mesh" windows. Limited. Length: 4·606in (117mm).
18 Police Motor Cyclist; DT No 37b, first issued in June 1938 and in production until 1940, reissued in 1946 and available until 1948.

It is of limited availability. Length: 1·772in (45mm).
19-20 Police Motor Cycle Patrol; DT No 42b, first issued in August 1936 and in production until 1940, re-issued in 1948 and available until 1955. Length: 1·85in (47mm).
21 Point Duty Policeman (in White Coat); DT No 42c, issued in August 1936 and available until 1941. Common. Height: 1·654in (42mm).
22 Point Duty Policeman; DT No 42d, issued in August 1936 and available until 1941. It is a common item. Height: 1·575in (40mm).
23 Police Box; DT No 42a, issued in August 1936 and in production until 1940, reissued after World War II, renumbered 751, and available until 1960. It is a common model. Height: 2·598in (66mm).

1 E.R.F. Fire Tender by Dinky Toys, Great Britain; Dinky Toys Reference Number (DT No) 266, issued in 1976 and in production until 1980. This well-detailed model, with "Fire Service" and crest decals, is fitted with roof-mounted warning lights and bright plated hose drums, clear plastic windows and a detailed interior with steering wheel. It has a well-modelled radiator with an "ERF" logo and is fitted with treaded plastic wheels. The wheeled extending escape ladder, in white plastic, is removable. This model will be easy to find. Length overall: 8·779in (223mm).

2 E.R.F. Airport Fire Rescue Tender; DT No 263, issued in 1978 and in production until 1980. The body casting is the same as that of the E.R.F. Fire Tender at (1), but it is

finished in yellow, with "Airport Rescue" decals on the sides, "Rescue" above the cab and a crest on the doors. It is fitted with a non-extending plastic ladder. Common. Length overall: 6·969in (177mm).

3-4 Turntable Fire Escape; DT No 956, issued in February 1958 and in production until 1973. This handsome model appeared in two forms, the earlier of which is shown at (10). The two examples here are of the type appearing in 1969-73, normally in red-and-silver (4), sometimes in red-and-black, and with minor variations in finish, as at (3). Both have a large Berliet cab (note the marque name on the bright strip above the radiator) with clear plastic windows and a detailed interior. The turntable-mounted ladder, elevated and

extended by crank-handles on its mounting, is common to all versions. The later versions shown here are fairly common models. Length: 7·874in (200mm).

5 Merryweather Marquis Fire Tender; DT No 285, issued in 1969 and in production until 1980. This model, with the same decals as (1), is notable for its operating water pump: a reservoir within the toy is filled via the hatch at the right side of the roof and a press-button pump-action (the button can be seen just in front of the filler-hatch) forces water through the black hose. The three-piece plastic ladder on the roof is removable. The cab is fitted with clear plastic windows and has a detailed interior. It is a fairly common item. Length: 6·969in (177mm).

6-7 Fire Engine with Extending Ladder; DT No 555. This model was first issued by Dinky Supertoys in December 1952, was renumbered 955 in late 1954, and remained in production until 1969. Of the two examples shown, (7) is the earlier version, without plastic windows and fitted with metal wheels with rubber tyres. The example at (6) dates from after renumbering: it has windows and is fitted with plastic wheels. All versions feature a bell, a ladder that can be raised and extended, and a towing-hook. The tinplate base plate is stamped with the maker's name, "555" ("955" later) and "Fire engine". The earlier version is the harder to find. Length: 5·512in (140mm).

8 Fire Engine; DT No 259, issued in November 1961 and in production

until 1969. A Bedford vehicle, with "Fire Brigade" and crest decals on its rear sides, this model is fitted with a bell, a non-detachable ladder and clear plastic windows. It has metal wheels with rubber tyres and a tinplate base plate stamped with the maker's name and "Fire engine". It is fairly common. Length: 4·606in (117mm).

9 Airport Fire Tender; DT No 276, issued in August 1962 and in production until 1969. Another Bedford vehicle, with "Airport Fire Control" decals on its rear sides, it features a bell, a battery-powered flashing light and a rotating foam extinguisher in grey plastic. It has metal wheels with rubber tyres. Like (8), it is fitted with suspension and fingertip steering. Fairly common. Length: 4·606in (117mm).

10 Turntable Fire Escape; DT No 956; see also (3-4). This is the earlier version of the model, made in 1958-69, with a small Bedford S-Type cab and with a differently-cast rear body. It is fitted with a bell to the right of the cab roof, but the ladder and mounting are the same as on (3-4). This earlier version will be harder to find than later ones. Length: 7·874in (200mm).

11 Berliet 770 KE Camiva Fire Engine by Solido, France; maker's reference number (MRN) 352, dating from the 1970s. It is a limited item. Length: 6·496in (165mm).

12 Berliet GBC 34 Fire Engine by Solido, France; MRN 351, dating from the 1970s. It has "Aeroport de Paris" decals and features a bright-plated swivelling foam extinguisher. Length: 5·709in (145mm).

13 Berliet Camiva 4x4 Fire Tender and Motor Pump by Solido, France; MRN 354; dating from the 1970s. Length overall: 5·827in (148mm).

14-15 Savien SG4 Fire Engine by Solido, France; dating from the 1970s. The example at (14) has "Sapeur Pompier" and crest decals and is fitted with plastic wheels; (15) lacks decals and is fitted with metal wheels with rubber tyres. Length: 4·528in (115mm).

16 Hotchkiss H6 G54 Fire Tender by Solido, France; dating from the 1970s. Length: 4·409in (112mm).

17 Citroën C35 V.S.A.B. Fire Truck with Trailer by Solido, France; MRN (truck) 368, (trailer) 371; 1970s. Length overall: 7·677in (195mm).

18-19 Streamline Fire Engine; DT No 25h, first issued in April 1936 and in production until 1940, reissued

in 1948, renumbered 250 in 1954, and finally deleted in 1962. The example at (18) is the pre-War version, a single-piece casting with no base plate, fitted with white rubber tyres; the post-War version (19) utilises the same casting but has a tinplate base plate. The pre-War version is scarce; the post-War version is fairly common. Length: 3·976in (101mm).

20 Dodge 6x6 Fire Truck with Motor Pump by Solido, France; 1970s. Length overall: 6·693in (170mm).

21 Renault 4 Fourgonnette Fire Department Van by Solido, France; MRN 1325, dating from the 1970s. Length: 3·5625in (90mm).

22 Citroën 2CV Fire Department Van by Dinky Toys, France; FDT No 25d, dating from the 1950s. A limited item. Length: 3·307in (84mm).

1 Johnston Road Sweeper by Dinky Toys; Great Britain; Dinky Toys Reference Number (DT No) 451, issued in 1971, renumbered 449 in 1977, and in production until 1980. This model features brushes that revolve as it is pushed along; the hose is black plastic. The earliest version, issued in 1971, has opening doors: this will be harder to find than later examples, as shown, with non-opening doors. It is fairly common. Length: 5·591in (142mm).

2-3 Snow Plough; DT No 958, issued in January 1961 and in production until 1965. This Supertoys model uses the Guy Warrior chassis and is fitted with a blade that lifts back over the cab. It appeared only in yellow-and-black but, as shown, with variations in the colour of the blade.

Limited. Length overall: 7·677in (195mm). Shown just to the right and in front of (3) is the Breakdown Jeep; FDT No 1412, issued in 1968 and in production until 1971. Length: 3·307in (84mm).

4 Mercedes Snow Plough by Dinky Toys, France; French Dinky Toys Reference Number (FDT No) 567, issued in 1967 and in production untill 1970. It features an adjustable blade and a black plastic canopy. Length overall: 5·709in (145mm).

5 Snow Plough with Trailer by Solido, France; maker's reference number 213, dating from the 1970s. It is fitted with plastic wheels. Length overall: 8·189in (208mm).

6 Ford D800 Snow Plough/Tipper; DT No 439, issued in 1970 and in production until 1976. With an adjustable blade and a tipping

back, this model appeared in several finishes, but with the blade always in yellow. The cab has clear plastic windows and opening doors. Fairly common. Length overall: 7·638in (194mm).

7 LMV Road Sweeper; FDT No 596, issued in 1960 and in production until 1963. It is fitted with a brush that revolves and pivots as the vehicle moves. Length: 4·882in (124mm).

8-9 Refuse Wagon; DT No 978, issued in 1964 and in production until 1979. Using the Bedford TK cab and chassis, this appeared in various colours and features a rear body (plastic) that tips forward and back, with opening rear doors. It may be found with or without opening doors to the cab, and with a roof box either of plastic (earlier) or cast (1978-79). Note also the wheel variation in

the two examples shown. Common. Length: 5·984in (152mm).

10-11 Citroën U23 Breakdown Truck; FDT No 35A, issued in 1955, renumbered 582, and in production until 1971. Of the examples shown, (11) has a metal hook and dates from before 1959; (10) has a plastic hook. In both cases, the crane is tinplate and "Dinky Service" is stamped in yellow. Length: 4·921in (125mm).

12 Berliet GAK Breakdown Truck; FDT No 589, issued in 1965 and in production until 1969. It has a plastic aerial and roof-mounted warning light. Length: 4·803in (122mm).

13-14 Bedford TK Crash Truck; DT No 434, issued in April 1964 and in production until 1972. This model is fitted with an operating winch. The version at (14), in green-and-

white with "Top Rank" decals, is the more common; the red-black-and-white "Auto Services" version (13) appeared only for a short time. Length: 4·803in (122mm).

15-17 Commer Breakdown Lorry; originally issued as DT No 25x in September 1950, renumbered 430 in 1954, and in production until 1963. Fitted with an operating winch and a towing-hook, and with "Dinky Service" decals, this model appeared first in brown-and-green and thereafter in other finishes. The example at (15) is a late one, with windows. Fairly common. Length: 4·843in (123mm).

18-20 Bedford Refuse Wagon; DT No 25v, issued in October 1948, renumbered 252 in 1954, and in production until 1964. It has a tipping body with sliding doors. It

was first issued as seen at (19), in fawn-and-green and without windows. The versions at (18) and (20)—note wheel variations—date from after 1954. Fairly common. Length: 4·21in (107mm).

21 R.A.C. Patrol Van; DT No 273, issued in 1965 and in production until 1969. This Mini-Van is fitted with a peg-in plastic roof sign. Common. Length: 3·071in (78mm).

22 R.A.C. Guide at the Salute; DT No 43d, issued in October 1935 and in production until 1940. A common item. Height: 1·417in (36mm).

23-24 R.A.C. Motor Cycle Patrol; DT No 43b, issued in October 1935 and in production until 1940, and reissued in 1948-49. The pre-War version (23) is fitted with white solid rubber wheels and has a driver with a well-detailed uniform; the

post-War version (24) has black solid rubber wheels. The pre-War version is limited; the post-War version is fairly common. Lengths: (pre-War) 1·811in (46mm); (post-War) 1·772in (45mm).

25 R.A.C. Box; DT No 43a, issued in October 1935 and in production until 1940. Lithographed tinplate. Limited. Height: 2·008in (51mm).

26 R.A.C. Guide Directing Traffic; DT No 43c, issued in October 1935 and in production until 1940. Common. Height: 1·457in (37mm).

27 A.A. Box; DT No 44a, issued in October 1935 and in production until 1940. It is of lithographed tinplate, with three tinplate signs. Limited. Length: 3·189in (81mm).

28-30 A.A. Motor Cycle Patrol; DT No 44b, issued in October 1935 and in production until 1940; reissued

in 1946, renumbered 270, and in production until 1963. At (28) is a post-War model, with solid black rubber wheels. (Note that post-renumbering versions have grey plastic wheels.) At (29-30) are pre-War versions, with solid white rubber wheels. Fairly common. Length: 1·811in (46mm).

31 A.A. Guide Saluting; DT No 44d, issued in October 1935 and in production until 1940. A common item. Height: 1·417in (36mm).

32 A.A. Guide Directing Traffic; DT No 44c, issued in October 1935 and in production until 1940. Common. Height: 1·457in (37mm).

33 A.A. Patrol Van; DT No 274, issued in 1964 and in production until 1972. Except for its finish, this is the same model as (21). A common item. Length: 3·071in (78mm).

1 Coles 20-Ton Lorry-Mounted Crane by Dinky Toys, Great Britain; Dinky Toys Reference Number (DT No) 972, issued in May 1955 and in production until 1968. Appearing only in orange-and-yellow, this Supertoys model features the cast figures of drivers in both lorry and crane cabs. The crane body swivels, and the hook is raised or lowered by the crank-handle on the side of the body; the angle of the jib is adjusted by a similar handle on the other side—see (2). It is fitted with six wheels with black rubber tyres and has a tinplate base plate. This is a fairly common item. Length overall: 9·449in (240mm).

2 Coles 20-Ton Lorry-Mounted Crane by Dinky Toys, France; French Dinky Toys Reference Number (FDT No) 972, issued in 1957, renumbered

889, again renumbered 972L, and in production until 1958. The same casting as the British model (1), but with grey rubber tyres.

3 Jones Fleetmaster Cantilever Crane; DT No 970, issued in 1967 and in production until 1976. With a working crane operated by a crank-handle, this model first appeared in red-white-and-yellow, and then, as shown, in metallic red and white. This is a fairly common model. Length overall: 6·85in (174mm).

4 Goods Yard Crane; DT No 752, issued in February 1953, re-numbered 973 in January 1955, and in production until 1959. An interesting and unusual model in that it is not fitted with wheels, this was announced as being for use with Gauge "0" toy railways. An all-diecast model, it has working

crane action with an adjustable jib, controlled by crank-handles on either side. It is fairly common. Length of base: 3·937in (100mm); (height) 7·677in (195mm).

5 Salev Mobile Crane; FDT No 50, issued in April 1957, renumbered 595, and in production until 1959. It has a working crane controlled by crank-handles and is complete with driver. Length: 6·142in (156mm).

6-7 Coles Mobile Crane; DT No 571, issued in December 1949, re-numbered 971 in 1954-55, and in production until 1965. This Supertoys model has a swivelling body and a fully-operating crane controlled by a crank-handle. At (6) is an earlier version, with grey rubber tyres and a brass handle to its crank; (7) has black tyres and a plastic handle. Fairly common.

Length overall: 6·299in (160mm).

8 Berliet GBO Saharien; FDT No 888, issued in 1960, in production until 1966, and briefly reissued in 1968. This model of an oil exploration vehicle has a block-and-tackle operated by a crank-handle. Earlier examples have diecast wheels; later ones will be found with plastic wheels fitted. Length: 6·732in (171mm).

9 Richier Road Scraper; FDT No 886, issued in 1960 and in production until 1965. Fitted with a fairly complex and rather unsatisfactory control system for its swivelling blade, this model has a diecast driver. Length: 6·929in (176mm).

10 Servicing Platform Vehicle; DT No 977, issued in September 1960 and in production until 1964. Parallel wires on either side

support the elevatable platform; the stays on either side may be folded up or down. Common. Length overall: 7·756in (197mm).

11-12 Blaw-Knox Bulldozer; DT No 561, issued in January 1949, renumbered 961 in 1955, and in production until 1964. It has a driver and is equipped with a lifting blade and rubber caterpillar tracks. The example at (11) is the earlier version, which appeared in red only. At (12) is a post-renumbering version in yellow with a grey blade; the model also appeared for a short time in green-and-orange plastic. Fairly common. Length overall: 5·433in (138mm).

13 Blaw-Knox Bulldozer; FDT No 885, issued in October 1959 and in production unti 1961. This resembles the British model (11-12)

in all respects, save that its tinplate base plate is stamped *"Assemblé en France"*. Length: as (11-12).

14 Blaw-Knox Heavy Tractor; DT No 563, issued in August 1948, renumbered 963 in January 1955, and in production until 1959. This is the same casting as the Bulldozer (11-12), minus the blade. Common. Length: 4·567in (116mm).

15 G.M.C. 6x6 Truck by FJ, France; dating from the 1960s. This model is fitted with an adjustable shovel and has a tipping rear. Limited. Length: 5·315in (135mm).

16 Berliet GBO Quarry Truck; FDT No 572, issued in 1970 and in production until 1971. Using the same chassis as the Berliet GBO Saharien, see (8), this model is fitted with a tipping rear body that is made of yellow plastic.

Length: 7·402in (188mm).

17 Coventry-Climax Fork-Lift Truck; DT No 14c, issued in November 1949, renumbered 401 in 1954, and in production until 1964. This has a fork-lift raised by a crank-handle on its side. Fairly common. Length: 4·252in (108mm).

18 Coventry-Climax Fork-Lift Truck; FDT No 597, issued in 1959 and in production until 1961. It uses the same casting as the British model (17), but its tinplate base plate is stamped *"Assemblé en France"*.

19-20 Aveling-Barford Diesel Roller; DT No 25p, issued in February 1948, renumbered 251 in 1954, and in production until 1963. Appearing only in green-and-red but with variations in shades, this has a swivelling front roller. It is fairly common.

Length: 4·3125in (110mm).

21 Richier Diesel Roller; FDT No 90A, issued in 1958, renumbered 830 in 1959, and in production until 1969. It is fitted with a swivelling front roller. Length: 4·409in (112mm).

22 Muir-Hill Dumper Truck; DT No 562, issued in September 1948, renumbered 962 in 1954-55, and in production until 1965. Appearing only in yellow, it has a tipping rear body and is fitted with a towing-hook. A common item. Length: 4·134in (105mm).

23 Muir-Hill Dumper Truck; FDT No 887, issued in 1959 and in production until 1961. This resembles the British model (22) in all save its black rubber tyres and the words *"Assemblé en France"* stamped on its tinplate base plate. Length: 4·134in (105mm).

Diecast Farm Equipment by British Makers, 1930s-1970s

1 Farm Trailer by Britains, Great Britain; Britains Catalogue Number (BCN) 130F, dating from around 1948. The rubber-tyred trailer, fitted with detachable racks and with a tipping rear body with a hinged tailboard, is intended to be towed by a tractor. It is a common item. Length: 4·488in (114mm).

2-3 Halesowen Harvest Trailer by Dinky Toys, Great Britain; Dinky Toys Reference Number (DT No) 27b, issued in June 1949, renumbered 320 in 1954, and in production until 1970. It is fitted with removable racks, a tow-bar and a towing-hook at the rear. An early version with diecast wheels is shown at (2); at (3) is a post-renumbering example, which has plastic wheels fitted with black rubber tyres. A fairly common

model. Length: 4·764in (121mm).

4 Leyland 384 Tractor; DT No 308, issued in 1971 and in production until 1979. This model, which was marketed in a bubble-pack, is fitted with a towing-hook and is shown pulling the Halesowen Harvest Trailer, see (2-3). A common item. Length: 3·386in (86mm).

5 Massey-Ferguson Tractor; DT No 300, and Massey-Harris Spreader, DT No 321. The Tractor was first issued as the Massey-Harris Farm Tractor, DT No 27a, in June 1948; it was renumbered 300 in 1954 and remained in production until 1971. It is fitted with swivelling front wheels. The Manure Spreader was first issued as DT No 27c in October 1949; it was renumbered 321 in 1954 and remained in production until 1973. Note the

working parts at the rear, activated by a metal driveband from the axle. The example shown attached to the tractor is a post-renumbering version; to the right is an earlier version, with diecast wheels. Both models are fairly common. Lengths: (tractor) 3·504in (89mm); (spreader) 4·449in (113mm).

6 Muir-Hill 2WL Loader; DT No 437, issued in February 1962 and in production until 1980. This model has a working shovel. Common. Length: 4·134in (105mm).

7 Timber Carriage with Log; BCN 12F, dating from the 1940s. This was issued as part of a five-piece set, along with two horses and a farmhand. The log is real wood and the carriage has an adjustable chassis. A fairly common item. Length: 8in (203mm).

8 Week's Tipping Farm Trailer; DT No 319, issued in June 1961 and in production until 1970. The two-wheeled trailer is fitted with a tow-bar and has a tipping body with a hinged tailboard. A common item. Length: 4·134in (105mm).

9 Disc Harrow; BCN 135F, dating from c1948. This is a common model. Length: 2·25in (57mm).

10 Four-Furrow Tractor Plough; BCN 138F, dating from about 1948. The red-handled arms are used to adjust the angle of the plough's blades to three different positions. Common. Length: 7·008in (178mm).

11 Farm Tractor and Hay Rake; DT No 27ak. Issued in March 1953, this is a set consisting of the Massey-Harris Farm Tractor, DT No 27a, see (5), and the Hay Rake, DT No 27k. The set was renumbered 310 in 1954

and was in production until 1966. Limited. Length overall: 6·181in (157mm). Shown immediately to the right is a Roller; BCN 136F.

12-13 Field Marshall Farm Tractor; DT No 27n, issued in October 1953, renumbered 301 in 1954, and in production until 1965. It has a swivelling front axle and is fitted with a towing-hook. Limited. Length: 3·11in (79mm).

14-15 David Brown Tractor and Disc Harrow; DT No 325, issued in 1966 as a set consisting of DT No 325 (Tractor) and DT No 322 (Disc Harrow), and available in this form until 1972. At (15) the tractor is shown with its cab removed; note also the variation in colour finish. The Harrow, which has rotating discs, is also shown in two different finishes. Fairly common. Lengths:

(tractor) 3·268in (83mm); (harrow) 3·386in (86mm).

16 Fordson Tractor; BCN 128F, dating from 1948. This model is marked as a later-type issue by its balloon-tyres; see also (17). It is fairly common. Length: 4in (102mm).

17 Fordson Tractor; BCN 127F, dating from the 1940s. Its "spudded" metal wheels show that this is an earlier model than that at (16). Limited. Length: 4in (102mm).

18 Farm Tractor; DT No 22e, one of the original "Modelled Miniatures" announced by Meccano in December 1933. This diminutive tractor, with a cast-in steering wheel, a towing-hook and metal wheels, is based on a Fordson. It remained in production until World War II and is now a rare model. Length: 2·756in (70mm).

19 Fordson Major Tractor; Britains "Lilliput" series, BCN 604, dating from around 1950. A limited item. Length: 1·75in (44mm).

20 Motocart; DT No 27g, issued in December 1949, renumbered 342 in 1954, and in production until 1961. It is a common item. Length: 4·3125in (110mm).

21 Land Rover (Pick Up); DT No 344, issued in 1970 and in production until 1977. It has an opening bonnet and doors. Common. Length: 4·252in (108mm).

22-23 Land Rover; DT No 27d, issued in April 1950, renumbered 340 in 1954, and in production until 1970. Note the tinplate windscreen frame and spare wheel. The model normally appeared in green-and-orange (23); in the paint finish shown at (22), it is scarce.

Length: 3·5625in (90mm).

24 Land Rover; DT No 340, with Land Rover Trailer, DT No 341. The two-wheeled trailer was first issued in 1954 as DT No 27m; it was almost immediately renumbered 341 and remained in production until 1973. Fairly common. Length: 3·11in (79mm).

25 Tumbrel Cart with Horse and Hay Racks; Britains "Lilliput" series, BCN 606, dating from c1950. Limited. Length: 2·75in (70mm).

26 Milk Float and Horse, BCN 605, with Stable Lad, BCN 531; Britains "Lilliput" series, dating from about 1950. Limited. Length (horse and cart): 2·25in (57mm).

27 Dairy Cart with Milkman and Two Churns; BCN 131F, dating from c1950. Limited. Length (horse and cart): 5in (127mm).

4

The magic of railways is strong: to children they are symbols of speed and power and the spell they cast may endure for a lifetime. Thus, it is not surprising that toy trains, with their overwhelmingly nostalgic appeal, should now be among the most sought-after of collectable toys. And it is inevitable, too, that many of the earlier toy trains by such famous makers as Bing, Carette and, especially, Märklin, should now command prices appropriate to the works of art that they are now perceived to be.

The illustrations in this section span the entire history of toy railways, from the early unpowered "floor trains", through the primitive steam-powered "piddlers" and "dribblers" and the clockwork and electric classics of the 1918-1939 period, to the increasingly collectable Gauge "00" models produced in the Hornby Dublo range after World War II. Shown with the locomotives is a fine selection of rolling stock and accessories, including stations and their furniture and lineside equipment.

Toy Trains

European and American "Floor Trains", 1860-1890

Among the earliest of all commercially-produced metal toys, dating from the second half of the 19th century, are tinplate and cast-iron trains of the kind shown here. Since they were usually push-along or pull-along toys and were not meant for operation on a track, they are generally known as "floor trains" or "carpet toys". With the increasing availability towards the turn of the century of steam- or clockwork-driven trains operating on rails and marketed as sets, carpet toy trains lost their popularity and were latterly only produced in the cheap and simple form of "penny toys". Carpet toy trains are still to be found at what are, considering their age and their historical value alone, fairly reasonable prices.

All the trains shown on this spread

were photographed at the London Toy & Model Museum.

1 Carpet Locomotive by a British maker, c1890. This charming tinplate locomotive, which is hand-enamelled and has a brass plate with the impressed designation "Express" affixed to the farther side of the boiler, is powered by a "Hall's Patent" mechanism. When the winding handle that forms an integral part of the rear wheel is wound anti-clockwise, a cord draws back and compresses a large-diameter coil spring (with a sealing washer at its forward end) inside the boiler. When the rear wheels are released, the locomotive is propelled forward and a whistle set in the funnel is sounded by the air forced up the stack by the washer. Length:

10·75in (273mm). Scarce.
2-4 Platform Train by Faivre, France, c1885. This simple pull-along carpet toy is of tinplate with hand-enamelled finish, and consists of three "platforms", or six-wheeled chassis, bearing a very basically designed locomotive and eight passenger coach units. No provision appears to be made for coupling: originally, wire hooks and loops may have been fitted, or the owner may have been expected to improvise couplings of wire or thread. Each of the three platforms is 9·5in (241mm) long. Limited.
5 Platform Train by Faivre; a smaller and even more simple version of the train shown at (2-4), by the same maker and again dating from c1885. The locomotive and two carriage units are mounted on a

four-wheeled platform. Length: 8in (203mm). Limited.
6-8 Pull-Along Locomotive, Tender and Carriages by Wallwork's, Manchester, England, c1890; a cast-iron floor train (but note the flanged wheels, presumably fitted for added realism) of British manufacture—American examples in this material being more common. The semi-scale 4-2-2 locomotive with the cast number "1893" (possibly the date of manufacture) is a reasonably faithful representation of a contemporary railway engine; it has a six-wheeled tender with the cast designation "Express". Simple couplings link these to a six-wheeled carriage (7), the central pair of wheels missing in this example, and a six-wheeled brake composite carriage (8), again with

the central wheels missing. Note the words "Wallwork's Patent" cast along the chassis of the carriages. Limited.

9 Locomotive and Tender by J. & E. Stevens Company, USA; a pull-along toy (with pull-cord attached) of cast-iron construction, dating from about 1890. The 2-2-0 locomotive, with a cowcatcher and a high funnel of the kind associated with American wood-burning locomotives, is a two-piece casting: the front wheels are of a wider gauge (3in, 76mm) than those at the rear (2·25in, 57mm). A matching four-wheeled tender and four-wheeled open wagon, both bearing the embossed letters "UPRR" (Union Pacific Rail Road), are attached by simple couplings. Well known for their cast-iron toys,

notably money banks, the Stevens brothers traded from 1869 onward in association with the pioneer tin toy manufacturer George W. Brown, as the Stevens and Brown Manufacturing Company of Cromwell, Connecticut. After Brown's death in 1889, the Stevens brothers continued business on their own account. Limited.

10 Floor Locomotive by Hess, Nuremburg, Germany, c1885. This tinplate locomotive, with its plated boiler, short chimney, and large, decorative, spoked wheels (note the patent marking and "Made in Germany" on the hub plates), is driven by a flywheel. The cast-iron flywheel, mounted on brackets on the rear platform of the locomotive, is spun by a sharp pull on a string wrapped round its

axle towards the centre: power is transmitted via the ends of the axle, which rest on the locomotive's rear wheels. The Hess company, founded in 1826 and in production until the 1930s, was one of the pioneer manufacturers of metal toys in Germany. Length: 7·25in (184mm). Limited.

11-13 Floor Train by Hess, c1875; an earlier product of the maker noted at (10). This is a simple but most attractive pull-along toy of pressed tin; note the "rivet" details on the boiler. The 2·5in (63·5mm) gauge, 0-4-0 locomotive, with the embossed name "Merkur" ("Mercury"), pulls a rather oversized four-wheeled tender, numbered "No. 10", and First/Second Class enclosed four-wheeled carriages numbered "No. 100" (12) and

"No. 400" (13). The carriages have paper lithographed side details. Note the German patent wording and number around the wheel rims. Scarce.

14-17 Floor Train attributed to Lutz, Germany, c1860. This charming and elegant pull-along carpet toy, an early example of its kind, is of tinplate and diecast construction, with soldered joints; the finish is hand enamelled. The 2·25in (57mm) gauge, four-wheeled locomotive, with a high funnel, a well-detailed boiler, a firebox with opening door, and diecast wheels, is linked by simple wire hooks to a four-wheeled tender, with raised "rivet" detail on its sides, a flat truck (15), a passenger coach (16), and a cattle truck (17). This toy is rare.

Rails for the assembly of circuits on which toy trains could be run in a realistic manner were in general production towards the end of the 19th century. The gauges (ie, the distance between the rails and, hence, between the wheels on the axle of locomotive or rolling stock) took some time to become standardized: in the early period, trains were made in a variety of large gauges, which were eventually standardized to Gauges "0" to "4", followed by the introduction, around 1922, of "table top" railways and the smaller Gauges "00" and "HO" of the type preferred today. (For a detailed explanation of "Gauges", see the Introduction, under "Toy Trains". Most of the early large-gauge locomotives, as shown here, were of

the spirit-fired live-steam type. All the trains shown on this spread were photographed at the London Toy & Model Museum.

1 "3¾" Gauge (3·75in, 95mm) 2-4-0 Locomotive and Six-Wheeled Tender by Bateman, Great Britain, c1880. Note that Gauge "4", largest of the later standardized gauges, was 2¹³⁄₁₆" (2·8125in, 71mm). An excellent example of a spirit-fired live-steam locomotive, constructed of steel and brass. It bears a cast plate identifying it as an engine of the "L&NWR" (London and North-Western Railway) and it is a fine representation of a locomotive of the period. Note such details as the safety valve on the dome, hand rails along the boiler, springs beneath

the boiler, finely cast coupled driving wheels, and chequered footplate. The six-wheeled tender is similarly well detailed, with hand rails, springs, and a painted chassis. Overall length: 22·5in (572mm). Rare.
2 "3¼" Gauge (3·25in, 83mm) First/Third Class Passenger Coach by Stevens Model Dockyard Company, Great Britain, c1885. The hand-enamelled detail of this six-wheeled carriage, in tinplate with soldered joints and finished in L&NWR livery, extends to pull-cords for the window blinds. Note the roof ventilators; the rather crude buffers are probably replacements for the originals. Length: 16in (406mm). Limited.
3 "3¼" Gauge (3·25in, 83mm) 2-2-2 Locomotive by Radiguet, Paris,

France, c1890. It is constructed mainly of brass: Radiguet, in production from 1872 to c1902, was noted for locomotives in this material. Incorporating its own tender, and thus of tank engine type, its detail includes a high chimney (or smoke-stack), a whistle and safety valve on the boiler top, and a drain tap on the boiler front. This spirit-fired live-steam locomotive belongs to a class generally known as "Piddlers" or "Dribblers", so called from their propensity to leave behind them a trail of water from their oscillating cylinders! Length: 9·5in (241mm). Limited.
4 "3⅝" Gauge (3·625in, 92mm) 2-2-0 Locomotive by a French maker, c1890. A fine example of a spirit-fired live-steam locomotive

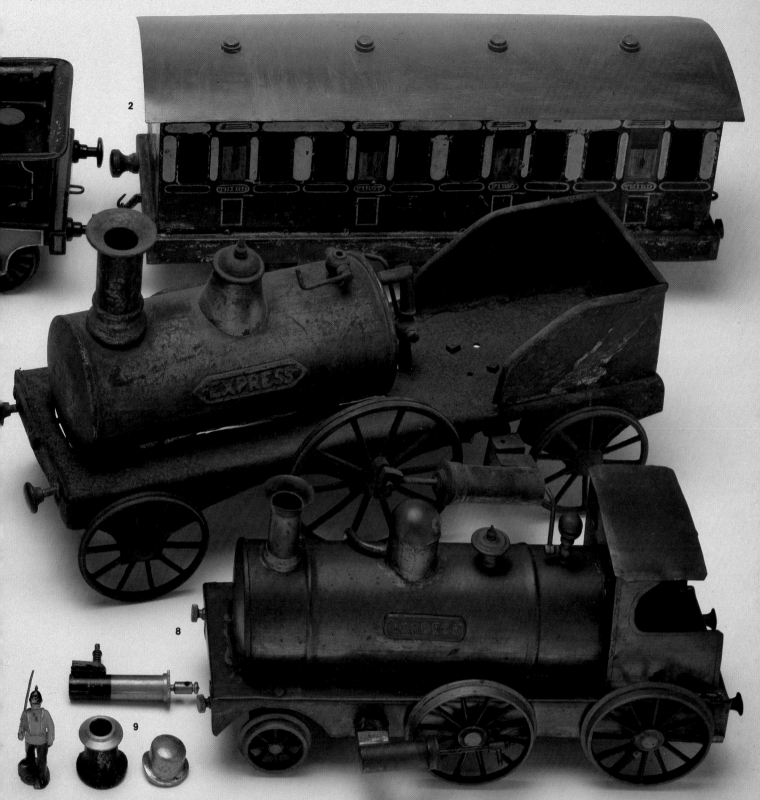

with simple rear-mounted oscillating cylinders, built mainly of brass. The detail is extremely attractive, including a mahogany front buffer beam and a boiler, part-enamelled to simulate lagging, fitted with hand rails and, from front to rear, a high chimney, a pressure dome, a safety valve with a lever-operated regulator, and a whistle (the top part missing from this example). Length: 12·25in (311mm). Limited.

5"4¼" Gauge (4·25in, 108mm) 2-2-2 "Express" Locomotive by Stevens Model Dockyard Company, Great Britain, c1880. Although a spirit-fired live-steam "Dribbler" (with rear-mounted oscillating cylinders), this is a "floor train", not meant to run on rails. It is somewhat crudely constructed of

tin and brass, with a high chimney, pressure dome, and whistle (the top part missing). Length: 14·75in (375mm). Limited.

6"2⅝" Gauge (2·625in, 67mm) 2-2-0 "Vulkan" Locomotive by Ernst Plank, Nuremburg, Germany (with the maker's early trademark on the front of the boiler), c1890. This is one of the earliest locomotives made by a firm founded 1866, and is a spirit-fired live-steam engine, with oscillating cylinders mounted in front of the (rear) driving wheels, of brass and tinplate construction. Note the simple five-spoked wheels, the large pressure dome, and the whistle; the greater part of the narrow funnel is missing from this example. Length: 7in (178mm). Scarce.

7Gauge "1" 0-6-0 Locomotive,

possibly a British maker's prototype, c1890. Constructed mainly of brass, this is a spirit-fired live-steam locomotive with forward-mounted oscillating cylinders driving the front wheels. Detail on the boiler includes hand rails, a pressure dome, and a safety valve. The central pair of wheels is missing — possibly removed by a former owner to enable the locomotive to negotiate tight turns on the track. Length: 7·125in (181mm). Scarce.

8"3¾" Gauge (3·75in, 95mm) 2-4-0 "Express" Locomotive by the British Modelling and Electric Company, c1880. This spirit-fired live-steam locomotive, of mainly brass construction, has oscillating cylinders driving the central pair of wheels. The ribbed boiler is fitted

with a smoke-stack, pressure dome, safety valve, and dome-topped whistle. The front buffers are obviously later items. Length: 11in (270mm). Limited.

9A selection of the parts available from Stevens Model Dockyard Company, Great Britain, around 1890. The oscillating cylinder (top), funnel (left), and pressure dome (right) were among the parts that could be purchased to build or refurbish a model locomotive. Home assembly of toy locomotives by railway enthusiasts, using parts like those shown here, was a hobby followed in Great Britain from around the late 1860s-early 1870s onward, but it does not appear to have been a popular pastime in other European countries or in the USA.

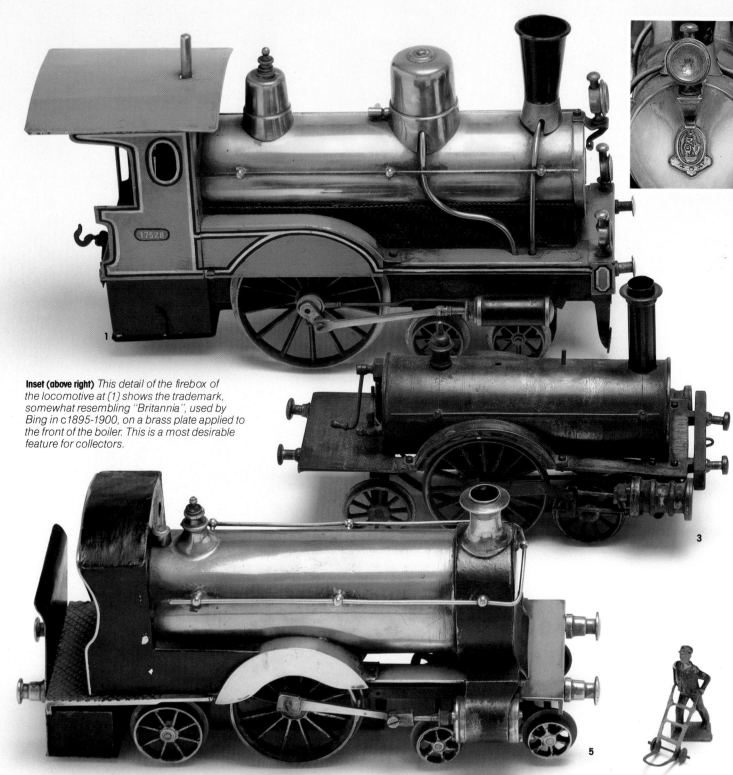

Inset (above right) *This detail of the firebox of the locomotive at (1) shows the trademark, somewhat resembling "Britannia", used by Bing in c1895-1900, on a brass plate applied to the front of the boiler. This is a most desirable feature for collectors.*

1 Gauge "4" 4-2-0 Locomotive, numbered "17528", by Gebrüder Bing, Nuremburg, Germany, dating from c1895. This spirit-fired steam locomotive, in tinplate with a brass boiler and fittings, is of the type popularly known as "Storklegs", a somewhat obscure expression, probably of American origin, referring to its wheel arrangement. The front pairs of wheels are not on a bogie, as the photograph may suggest, but are fixed. Note such detail as the dummy front lamps and the whistle protruding through the cab roof. The locomotive is 15in (38·1cm) long overall and has a maximum height of 8·5in (21·59cm). This example featured in the very popular movie "The Railway Children" (1970), in

which it "blew up" in a spectacular manner — a real possibility if the safety-valve (on the boiler nearest the cab in the photograph) should malfunction. It may be noted that it is possible to find coal-fired locomotives of this type, but these are generally custom-made models and are hardly to be described as toys. The locomotive was offered at £2 10s 0d (£2.50, $3.00) in the 1902 Catalogue of A.W. Gamage, London; a high price in those days. Like all Gauge "4" items by Bing, it is now rare.

2 "3¾" Gauge — but built approximately to ¾in: 1ft (1·9cm: 30·5cm) scale — 2-4-0 Locomotive by J. Bateman & Co., Great Britain, dating from c1880 and based on a London and North-Western

Railway locomotive of the period. It is shown as obtained by the author, without tender, and has a length of 18in (45·72cm). It has no cab, simply a "spectacle plate" as was usual in British locomotives of the time, and is a most sophisticated model, with full boiler fittings, including a Salter-type safety-valve, regulator, pressure-gauge, water-gauge, and reversing gear. A spirit-fired steam model (spirit carried in tender and fed through a drip-feed) it works to high pressure, about 45 p.s.i., and was probably intended for a "garden railway", although in the enormous houses that were favoured by the well-to-do of the Victorian and Edwardian eras, such a model might well have been run indoors. In good working

order, this engine would be quite capable, with its six-wheeled tender, of hauling some 12 pieces of rolling stock (which at that time were often made of polished mahogany). Bateman's model-making firm was established in 1774, and in the 19th century operated as the "Original Model Dockyard".

3 An attractive 2-2-2 "Piddler" or "Dribbler" — so called from their propensity to leave in their wake a trail of moisture from their cylinders — dating from c1880 and catalogued and advertised in Great Britain by Clyde Model Dockyard (basically a retailer rather than a maker). In spirit-fired steam (externally fired, with steam exhausting through the chimney), this is a fairly superior example for its time in that it has

slide-valve cylinders. The pressure dome and whistle are missing, but note the regulator and water-level cock above the foot-plate. With a length of 10in (25·4cm), it is not built to scale: its wheels are pre-set to run on curved track of 3in (7·62cm) width, and it was most likely sold with a circle of track but with no provision for a tender or rolling stock. "Piddlers" were much favoured by collectors in the 1960s, when examples like this might sell for around £150.00 ($180.00): in the 1970s prices fell sharply, but they are now once again becoming popular.

4 A small all-brass "Piddler" by Newton & Co., Great Britain, a scientific instrument maker noted for "Piddlers" of all sizes, of

superior workmanship and finish. Note the range of boiler fittings and the wooden buffer beam on this example, the latter a mark of the good-quality "Piddler", and the water-level cock on the front of the firebox. Of archaic appearance, almost "Rocket"-like, it in fact dates from c1880. A spirit-fired steam locomotive (externally fired, with oscillating cylinders) it is not intended to pull rolling stock, simply to run around a circular track. This example is in "2⅛" (5·4cm) Gauge—there were, of course, no standard gauges at the time of manufacture—and is 7in (17·78cm) long, with a height of 7·5in (19·05cm) to the top of its high funnel.

5 "2¾" Gauge 4-2-2 Locomotive

by Stevens Model Dockyard, Great Britain, dating from c1890: a somewhat simplified but nevertheless recognisable repre-sentation of a Great Northern Railway "Single" (ie, with a large single driving wheel) of the period. It has a copper boiler, which was probably originally painted, and brass fittings. A spirit-fired steam model with slide-valve cylinders, it is semi-internally fired. This example, 12in (30·48cm) long, has undergone some restoration; but note that there was apparently never any provision for couplings.

6 "Dragon", a most attractive 2-2-2 "Piddler" of copper and brass. It is believed by the author to be the work of Radiguet et Massiot, France, a scientific instrument

maker famous for stationary steam engines and toy boats, and was marketed in Britain in the 1880s by Clyde Model Dockyard. Spirit-fired, with oscillating cylinders, it is, like (4), of archaic appearance for its time and has no provision for couplings. Note the whistle and safety-valve (at rear of boiler): identical fittings are found on locomotives by various makers of the period and were probably standard parts made on the continent and imported to Britain. Like many "Piddlers", especially those of Clyde and Stevens Model Dock-yards, this locomotive was available either ready-made or in kit form: kits were sold as early as the 1870s. This example is 9·5in (24·13cm) long.

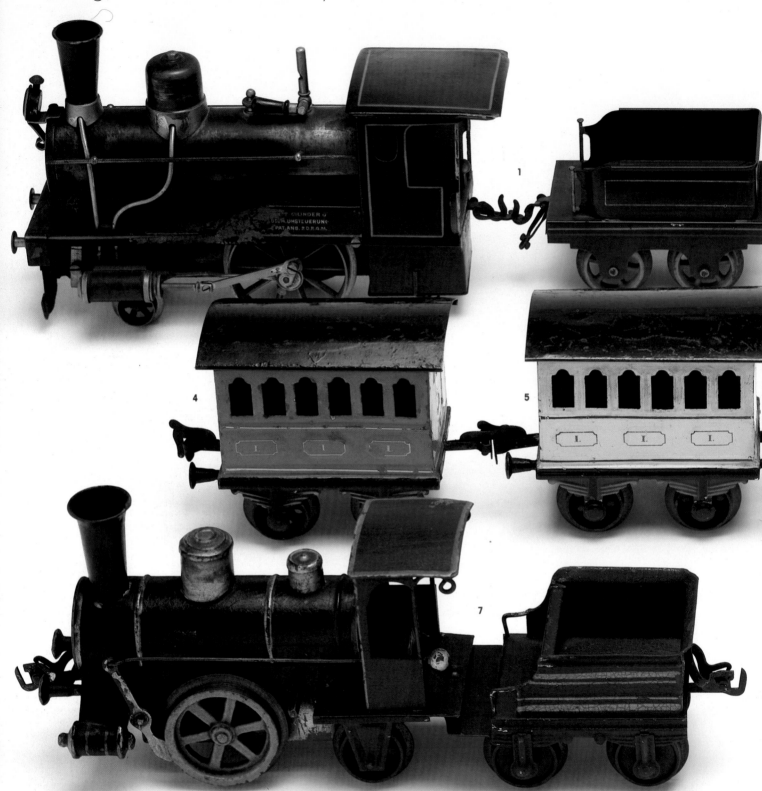

1-3 Gauge "2" Locomotive and Four-Wheeled Tender (1), with rolling stock (2-3), by Gebrüder Bing, Nuremburg, Germany. The locomotive is basically another version of the Gauge "4" 4-2-0 locomotive shown at (1) on *pages 158-159*. However, this smaller locomotive—the overall length of engine and tender is 15in (38·1cm)—has a 2-2-0 wheel arrangement, one pair of leading wheels being thought sufficient by the maker. It can be dated with some certainty to around the same time as the larger locomotive, c1895, since it was found in Sydney, Australia, in the shop of an optician who had received it as a Christmas present when a child, in 1897. Its elderly owner kindly let it go to

the author's "good home", along with six pieces of rolling stock, for a nominal sum—although such items are rare and are generally expensive. The locomotive is tinplate, with an oxidized brass boiler and cast-iron wheels; a spirit-fired steam model, it has the familiar Bing slide-valve cylinders and the usual boiler fittings—pressure dome, safety-valve, and whistle —and is fitted with reversing gear. Note the dummy lamp in front of the chimney (such features are often missing from specimens of this vintage) and the German patent information, now partly obliterated, stamped on the side of the cab. The four-wheeled tender is of the type standard for Bing locomotives of the time.

At the time of manufacture, this item would have been marketed as a boxed set, along with three wagons (or two wagons and a passenger coach) and a circle of track. It is shown here with two pieces of its original rolling stock: a four-wheeled Cattle Truck (2), and a four-wheeled Brake/Goods Wagon (3) with sliding doors at the centre and an attractive and interesting "guard's look-out" cabin, complete with access ladder, at the rear. It is interesting also to note that both wagons are certainly Gauge "1" items that were fitted by Bing with Gauge "2" wheels for sale with the Gauge "2" locomotive. As was usual at this period, all the elements of the set are hand-painted.

4-6 Gauge "1" 0-2-2 Locomotive and Four-Wheeled Tender (6), clockwork-powered, with rolling stock (4-5), by Bing. This particular locomotive has caused considerable interest among collectors: no other example fitted with connecting-rods, as seen here, has yet been found; nor does the locomotive appear ever to have been catalogued in this form. Clockwork locomotives of this period do not usually have connecting-rods—see the typical Märklin engine at (7)—but there is no doubt that these are original fittings: they were certainly not added at a later date. The item can be fairly precisely dated from its most distinctive buffers and couplings, quite unlike those used by Bing at other

times, which the author's researches show to have been fitted only in 1895-97. The powerful clockwork motor, a simple non-reversing mechanism, has all-brass gears giving two "speeds": "Stop" and "Very Fast"! Rim-operating brakes, as seen acting on the large driving wheels, were fitted by both Bing and Märklin at this time. The locomotive is of tinplate with nickel-plated domes and connecting-rods: although the nickel here is in good condition, it may corrode, but it remained in use until the introduction of chrome-plating in the 1920s. Unusually, this example bears no trademark other than the raised "GB" (Gebrüder Bing)—on the boiler side. The overall

length of engine and tender is 13in (33·02cm). The attractive hand-painted Passenger Coaches (4-5) are typical of the period: the shape of their windows provides another dating feature. When sold as a set, with a circle of track, three coaches would have been provided. Like all pre-1900 items, this is rare.

7 Gauge "1" 0-2-2 Locomotive and Four-Wheeled Tender by Gebrüder Märklin, Germany, dating from c1895. It is interesting to compare this clockwork locomotive with that at (6) by Bing, Märklin's great Nuremburg rival. Most collectors seem to believe—although the author does not necessarily agree—that Märklin items of this kind are more desirable than those of

Bing: at any rate, Märklin pieces consistently fetch higher prices at auction. On this tinplate engine, hand-painted with gold-painted domes, note particularly how the coupling of the tender differs from the Bing example: the "stepped" arrangement is a typical Märklin feature. It has a simple non-reversing clockwork mechanism with brass gears and no speed governor. The silver-coloured knob of the brake lever for the rim-brake acting on both sides protrudes from the rear of the cab. A plaque on the boiler, just visible in the photograph, bears the raised figure "1", signifying the gauge. Overall length of engine and tender is 11in (27·94cm).

8 Gauge "1" 0-4-0 Locomotive

and Four-Wheeled Tender, clockwork, by Märklin. This is the same size as the Märklin locomotive at (7) but dates a little later, c1898. Again it is hand-painted and has a Gauge "1" mark on the boiler. However, the gears of the clockwork mechanism are a mixture of brass and steel and, like the Bing example at (6), it has nickel-plated domes: both steel gears and nickel-plating were probably just coming into use at this period. Like the other locomotives on this spread it has spoked wheels, but note that those on the tender have drilled holes. The Märklin trademark of the period—a shield enclosing the letters "GM"—is embossed on the front of the boiler.

All the trains shown on this spread are the property of the author, Ron McCrindell, and are currently on loan to the London Toy and Model Museum, October House, 21/23 Craven Hill, London W2, where they were photographed.

1 Gauge "1" PLM Pacific 2-3-1 Locomotive and Eight-Wheeled Tender by Gebrüder Märklin, Göppingen, Germany. (Note that 2-3-1 is the continental designation for a Pacific locomotive, as opposed to the British and US usage, 4-6-2.) This magnificent tinplate locomotive, clockwork-driven in the case of the example shown here, and a rare and much sought-after collector's item, was first made by Märklin in 1912 and remained available, in steam—see

(1), *pages 180-181*—and electric-driven versions also, for some years. It was still in the maker's catalogue, in electric only, as late as 1930. The locomotive shown here dates from around 1920 and is fitted with Märklin's standard, powerful, six-coupled geared-wind mechanism. Thus driven, it runs very well, unlike the steam version which, like most steam-driven locomotives by Märklin, is much too heavy because of the many castings used in its construction. (Märklin did not make a really satisfactory steam-driven locomotive until its final steam model—a Deutschbahn Pacific made in Gauges "0" and "1". This appeared in 1936 and was made only until 1939, it is, consequently, now very rare). A particular point of interest

on the locomotive shown is the retailer's plate on the side of the cab, indicating that it was supplied by Märklin to "Au Paradis des Enfants", a famous toyshop in Paris, France. This locomotive is modelled on the famous "231A Class" of the Paris-Lyon-Mediterranée (PLM) Railway. These were express engines especially celebrated for their fine performance when hauling the romantically evocative "Blue Train" on the Paris-Monte Carlo run, and they were among the few railway engines to be immortalized in music by a composer of note: Honegger's wonderfully descriptive composition "Pacific 231" vividly recalls the atmosphere of these remarkable locomotives. Some collectors will, perhaps, recall with pleasure a fine

colour-documentary movie issued in the late 1950s which, without spoken commentary, blended Honegger's music with action shots of a PLM Pacific. Length (engine and tender); 27·5in (69·85cm).

2 Gauge "1" "Mitropa" Sleeping Car by Märklin; a very handsome item from the maker's 1920 Series, in tinplate and virtually hand-made, with all joints soldered—no tongue-and-slot construction here! It is hand-painted in simulated wood finish and runs on cast bogies with steel wheels. Interior fittings include beds with reclining plaster figures (peacefully sleeping—not, as in the case of Märklin's sitting passengers, noted on other spreads, impaled on spikes!). Like the PLM Pacific locomotive with which

it is shown, this is a rare and valuable item. Length: 20 866in (53cm).

3-4 "3¼in" Gauge 4-2-2 Locomotive, "Zulu", and Six-Wheeled Tender (3), shown here with an Open Wagon (4), made by Shaw of London, an optical instrument maker. A brass plate on the side of the cab bears the maker's name and the date "1891": it is rare to be able to identify such a model so precisely. This is a good example of the kind of model then being produced to order by the optical instrument makers concentrated in London's West End and, as is usually the case, is of rather archaic appearance (but delightfully so) for its date of manufacture. The copper boiler is spirit-fired and the locomotive has an impressive array of fittings, included cab-operated

Stephenson's link-gear reversing, lever-type regulator, water gauge, pressure gauge, whistle, displacement lubricator, level cocks, and lever safety-valve. The locomotive's wheels are sprung, as are those of the attractive tender, which houses a spirit reservoir. The period wagon is constructed of mahogany, with all brass fittings and leaf springing. Lengths (engine and tender): 25in (63·5cm); (wagon): 13in (33·02cm).

5 Gauge "1" Great Northern "Single" 4-2-2 Locomotive, numbered "266", and Six-Wheeled Tender, made by Gebrüder Bing, Nuremburg, Germany, for Bassett-Lowke, Great Britain, and dating from about 1910. This clockwork-driven model is a good representation of the Ivatt Singles that replaced the Stirling 8-Footers in light, fast passenger

service on the Great Northern Railway. It is typical of the fine true-to-prototype models made by Bing for Bassett-Lowke up to 1914: only a few comparable items appeared after World War I. Well-finished and hand-painted, it has a two-speed mechanism that would, Bassett-Lowke claimed, give a run of over 200ft (60m) on one winding. It was priced in the UK at £3 10s 0d (£3.50, $4.20) in 1911; a very considerable sum for that time. Length (engine and tender): 20in (50·8cm).

6 Gauge "1" London and North-Western Railway (L&NWR) "Cauliflower" 0-6-0 Locomotive, numbered "930", and Six-Wheeled Tender; like (5), this was made by Bing for Bassett-Lowke around 1910, and is fitted with a two-speed

clockwork mechanism. It is modelled on the six-coupled engines designed by Webb for the L&NWR as fast goods locomotives; these were so successful that they were frequently used on passenger services. The L&NWR crest that in real practice featured prominently on the centre driving-wheel splashers of these locomotives (although it is not to be seen on this model) looked, at a distance, like the familiar vegetable — hence, the engines were called "Cauliflowers", a nickname that remained with them all their days and is still used by railway enthusiasts. This model was also available from Bassett-Lowke in less authentic Midland Railway livery, in that case numbered "3044". Length (engine and tender): 18in (45·72cm).

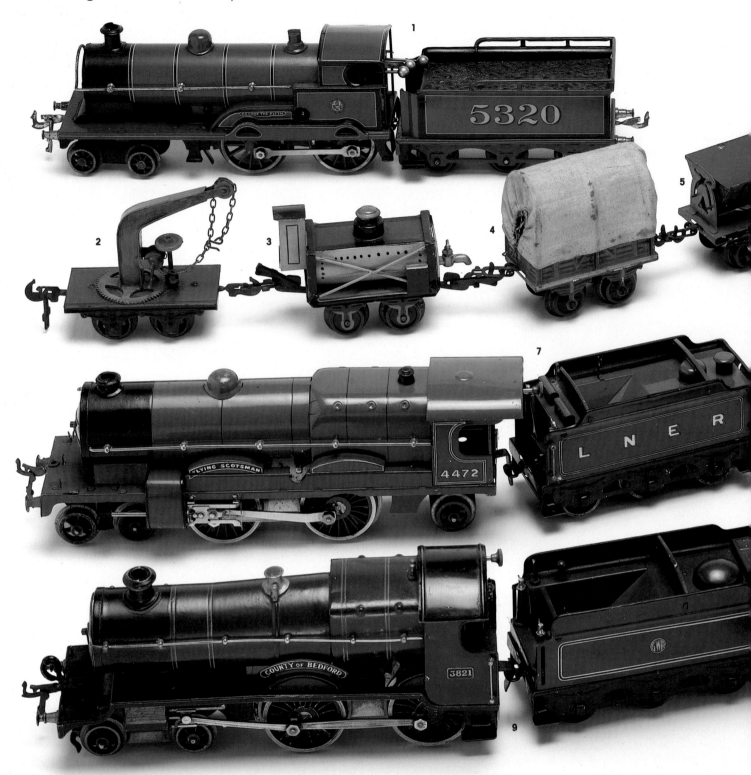

1 Gauge "0" "George the Fifth" Locomotive and Six-Wheeled Tender, numbered "5320", made by Gebrüder Bing, Nuremburg, Germany, for sale in Great Britain by Bassett-Lowke. This example dates from the mid-1920s, but the model was available as early as 1912 and was made in quantity until well into the 1920s. Originally available in black, with the correct number of the prototype, "2663"—see (7-8), *pages 170-171*—it subsequently appeared in several different liveries—the example shown is in London, Midland & Scottish Railway (LMS) colours—and with different names, including "Minerva" and "Queen Mary". It was made in Gauges "0", "1", and "2" (available only in black in

the two larger gauges) and in clockwork, as seen here, and electric: a "de luxe" version with generally superior finish and with better-scaled wheels was available in Gauge "0". It is a most attractive item and, because of its long production run, not too difficult to find. Length (engine and tender): 16in (40·64cm).

2-6 Gauge "0" Steam Train; an early train, dating from around 1895 and featuring models of that period by three great German makers. The simple 0-4-0 Locomotive (6) in spirit-fired steam; with a single cylinder inside the cab and an exterior flywheel, is by Bing, and was catalogued in 1895 at a price of 4s 6d (22½p, 27c). In spite of its age it is in excellent working

order and is regularly run on the author's layout. Length: 6in (15·24cm). The Hopper Wagon (5), with tipping action, and Covered Wagon (4), with a tarpaulin held by a draw-string, are both by Bing; both are 3·5in (8·99cm) long. The Water Wagon (3), with its rear-mounted guard's (look-out) compartment, can be filled through the cap on top and emptied through its tap; made by Märklin, it was also sold as a Tar Wagon. It is 4·75in (12·06cm) long. The Crane Truck (2), with a working, rotatable crane, is by Carette, and is 3·5in (8·89cm) long. All these items are handpainted.

7 Gauge "0" "Flying Scotsman" 4-4-2 Locomotive, numbered "4472", and Six-Wheeled Tender,

made by Hornby, Great Britain; this model had a long production run, from c1928 until 1940. Although the number is that of the real "Flying Scotsman", neither the outline nor the wheel arrangement bear much resemblance to the prototype, which was a Pacific (4-6-2). However, the 4-4-2 arrangement does improve the model's negotiation of sharp curves on the track. Produced as part of Hornby's "No 3 Locomotive Series", which also included "Royal Scot", the model was available in clockwork, as shown, with an excellent long-running mechanism, or electric. Seen here in London and North Eastern Railway (LNER) livery, it was made also in other major

liveries and other names; the tender is the standard one for the series. Length (engine and tender): 16in (40·64cm). A famous model, this is one of the easier Hornby items for collectors to acquire—although it may prove to be expensive.

8 Gauge "0" "Alberta" Hornby No 2 Special Composite Coach, in the Pullman livery of the late 1920s. This bogie coach features opening end and luggage compartment doors, celluloid windows with printed details of lamps, and provision for corridor connections. It was available with other names: "Alberta" is believed to be one of the rarer examples. Length: 13in (33·02cm). See also (10-11).

9 Gauge "0" "County of Bedford" 4-4-0 Locomotive, numbered

"3821", and Six-Wheeled Tender, made by Hornby, Great Britain. This model was an early item in Hornby's "No 2 Special" series, introduced in late 1929. It represented an important advance by Hornby: for the first time, almost true-to-prototype models were produced, beginning with this example in authentic Great Western Railway (GWR) outline, and at later dates including an LMS Midland Compound, Southern Railway (SR) L.1. Class, LNER "Yorkshire" and "Bramham Moor", and SR Schools Class "Eton". All were 4-4-0 locomotives with either four-coupled clockwork mechanism, as shown, or electric. The series proved very popular and its authenticity did much to enhance the appearance

of model railways. The loco-motives were available separately or could be purchased in a boxed set with track and, usually, two Pullman cars, at a price in the early 1930s of £3 5s 0d (£3.25, $3.90) in clockwork or £3 15s 0d (£3.75, $4.50) in electric. Length (engine and tender): 15·25in (38·73cm).

10-11 Gauge "0" Bogie Pullman Cars, "Iolanthe" and "Montana" (the latter one of the rarer names) in the later Pullman livery—compare with (8)—as they appeared from Hornby from the mid-1930s until 1940. Save for lithography and roof colour, they are identical with (8).

12 Gauge "0" 4-4-0 Locomotive, numbered "142", and Eight-Wheeled (two bogies) Tender,

made by Bing for Bassett-Lowke. In Caledonian Railway blue livery, and based on the famous "140 Class" Dunalastaires of the CR, this was felt by Bassett-Lowke to be one of its most realistic models, and it is, indeed, a most attractive and desirable item. First appearing in 1914, it remained in Bassett-Lowke's Catalogue as late as 1927, initially available, as seen here, in clockwork only, but during the 1920s in electric also. The original price of £2 2s 0d (£2.10, $2.52) had risen to £4 4s 0d (£4.20, $5.04) by 1927. It was made in Gauges "0" and "1" and, while now very difficult to find in any gauge, it is, as is usual, rarer in Gauge "0" than in "1". Length (engine and tender): 16in (40·64cm).

1 Gauge "1" 4-4-0 Locomotive and Six-Wheeled Tender made by Gebrüder Bing, Nuremberg, Germany, for sale in Britain by Bassett-Lowke Limited, Northampton, who first catalogued this item in 1903. The example shown is in Midland Railway livery: it was also available in the liveries of the London and North-Western Railway (L&NWR), Great Northern Railway (GNR), and London and South-Western Railway (L&SWR). When obtained by the author it was completely over-painted and, as seen now, is the result of many hours of painstaking restoration. In tinplate with brass domes, it is fitted with a two-speed clockwork mechanism: protruding from the cab are the speed regulator

(fast/slow), and forward and reverse levers. The number "2631" on the tender was used by Bing up to 1914 on a long series of locomotives in Midland livery. The overall length of the locomotive and tender is 19in (48·26cm).

2 Gauge "1" 2-2-2 "Lady of the Lake" Locomotive, numbered "531", made in 1902 by Carette, Nuremburg, Germany, for sale in Britain by Bassett-Lowke—at an original price of £1 11s 0d (£1·55, $1·86) in Gauge "1" or £1 13s 6d (£1.67½, $2.01) in Gauge "2". It is interesting to note that this locomotive was one of the very first commercially-made models to bear a good likeness to its prototype; ie, the real locomotive on which it was

based. "Lady of the Lake" was a famous locomotive of the L&NWR, whose livery it wears, as early as the 1850s; thus, the style of the model is much earlier than its date of manufacture. A spirit-fired steam engine with twin oscillating cylinders (partly concealed by the cylinder casings, in order to give a more realistic appearance when running), it is fitted with the spoked wheels of superior quality that were made available by Bassett-Lowke at a slight extra charge. Note that the leading pair of wheels is mounted on a pony truck (ie, with two pivoted wheels; a bogie has four pivoted wheels) to enable the locomotive to negotiate tight curves on the track. This is an extremely rare item: the

author knows of only four extant examples, of which two (including the example shown, which is seen with a six-wheeled tender by Bing, dating from c1909) do not have the original Carette tender. The overall length of locomotive and tender is 19in (48·26cm).

3-4 Gauge "11" Corridor Car (3) and Dining Car (4) by Märklin, Germany, dating from 1903. These attractively hand-painted tinplate coaches are of somewhat continental appearance: they were marketed by Märklin in Europe in German, French and Swiss railway colours; a Hospital Coach version, with a large red cross on the side, was produced for the continental market, and they were also exported, with appropriate

decoration, to the USA. They were made in all four gauges—"0", "1", "2", "3"—then advertised by Märklin. The version seen here is in L&NWR livery, as supplied for sale in Britain by the famous department store of A. W. Gamage, London. The original price of the corridor car (both were also available in Midland Railway livery) was 10s 6d (52½p, 63c). Both coaches have opening doors and roofs that open on hinges to reveal such detail as: (3), an end lavatory with wash-basin and commode, baggage racks, and seats with spikes on which the terracotta passengers are securely—and seemingly contentedly!—impaled; and (4), tables and seats, with an end kitchen. These coaches,

each 11in (27·94cm) long, are hard to find.

5 Gauge "1" Express Bogie Coach, made by Märklin for sale in Britain by Gamage, 1903, and available also in Gauges "0", "2", and "3". Made of tinplate and hand-painted in Midland Railway livery (it was also available in L&NWR colours), it has opening doors with cast-metal handles, a slide-off roof and, like (3), seats with spikes to accommodate the unfortunate passengers! Note the "steps" at the coach's end, in reality intended to give the conductor access to the roof with its lamp tops. The coach is 12in (30·48cm) long. The legend "Made in Germany" is stamped on its underside, but it bears no Märklin trademark,

which appears irregularly on items of this period. Also unseen in the photograph is an applied plaque with the embossed "Gamage" mark on the coach's end—a most desirable feature for the collector. A rare item.

6-7 Gauge "1" 4-4-0 Locomotive, numbered "593", and Six-Wheeled Tender, with Four-Wheeled Passenger Coach (Third Class), made by Bing for sale in Britain by Basset-Lowke in 1903 —in the same series as the locomotive shown at (1) above. This locomotive and its attractively-lithographed tinplate coach, with the addition of a Brake Van and an oval of track, formed part of a set that was offered by Bassett-Lowke at a price of £1 15s 0d (£1·75, $2·10) in Gauge

"1", or £1 5s 6d (£1·27½, $1·53) in Gauge "0". It was also available in Gauge "2", and could be had in the liveries of the L&SWR, as shown here, L&NWR, Midland Railway, and Great Northern Railway. The coach has non-opening doors. At about the time of manufacture of this item, Bing was introducing a more powerful clockwork mechanism. Note, therefore, that in this example the winding shaft is on the right hand side, whereas in (1) it is on the left: this dates (1) as the later item, probably by a few months, with a more powerful mechanism and heavier wheels. The overall length of the engine and tender is 20in (50·8cm); length of coach: 9·5in (24·13cm).

1 Gauge "3" 0-4-0 Locomotive, numbered "2631" on an applied plate on the cab, and Six-Wheeled Tender, made by Gebrüder Bing, Nuremburg, Germany, and dating—on the evidence of the winding shaft on the left hand side—from *c*1903. Note that the number is the same as that of the Gauge "1" Bing locomotive of the same period shown at (1) on *pages 166-167*. Inside the cab is a Bing trademark of the period: this indicates that the locomotive was made for sale in Great Britain by A. W. Gamage, since Bassett-Lowke preferred to give the impression that the toys it marketed were British-made, and was careful to see that Bing's trademarks did not appear on its products.

This locomotive was available in both clockwork, as shown, and steam models, and in Gauges "4" models run on 3in (7·62cm) track; Gauge "3" on 2·5in (6··35cm) track; and only Gauge "2" on 2in (5.08cm) track as the designation implies.) Gamage's price for this item in the 1903 Catalogue was £2 15s 0d (£2.75, $3.30) in Gauge "3", or £3 3s 0d (£3·15, $3·78) in Gauge "4". This particular example is in well "played-with" condition, with its smokestack and connecting-rods missing, and needs restoration—which would be well worthwhile, since it is a comparatively rare item. It is in Midland Railway livery; it was

available in Britain also in L&NWR livery and, on the continent, in the colours of various European railroads. Gauge "3" and "4" engines were the largest commercially-made trains in which clockwork was employed, and the massive mechanism of this locomotive —two-speed, with forward and reverse gears—takes all an adult's strength to wind. The overall length of engine and tender is 23·6in (60cm).

2 Gauge "1" 0-4-0 Tank Engine by Bing, dating from *c*1902; a fairly accurate representation of a North London Railway tank locomotive of the period, produced to follow the maker's more celebrated Gauge "2" version of 1901. A spirit-fired

steam model, this has a single oscillating cylinder in the cab and, as the author has found over a 20-year period, runs well and is surprisingly powerful for a single-cylinder locomotive. Made of tinplate, it has a brass boiler and fittings and is 11in (27.94cm) long. This locomotive was sold in Britain by both Bassett-Lowke and Gamage, the latter cataloguing it at a price of 14s 9d (73½p, 88c) in Gauge "1", or 9s 9d (48½p, 58c) in Gauge "0".

3 Gauge "1" "Sydney" 4-4-0 Locomotive, numbered "3410", and Six-Wheeled Tender, made by Bing, *c*1905, for sale in Britain by Bassett-Lowke. This is a clockwork model with a two-speed mechanism, with

forward and reverse gears, an automatic brake, and, in the words of Bassett-Lowke's catalogue, "patent governors to prevent derailing when running light". A similar model to the GWR's famous "City of Truro" locomotive, this is attractive and well detailed: note the engine's brass dome and handrail, and the pressed-tin "coal" top of the tender. It was available in Gauges "0", "1", and "2"—at prices of £1 1s 0d (£1·05, $1·26), £2 2s 0d (£2·10, $2·52), and £3 7s 6d (£3·37½, $4·05) respectively—but only, as shown, in the livery of the Great Western Railway (GWR). The overall length of engine and tender is 20in (50·8cm).

4 Gauge "1" "Sir Alexander" 4-4-0 Bogie Express Locomotive, numbered "1014", and Six-Wheeled Tender, made by Bing in 1903, for sale in Britain by Bassett-Lowke. This was described by Bassett-Lowke as the firm's first scale-model locomotive—"an official working model in ⅜in scale"—and although not precisely to scale it is, indeed, very accurate for its period. Based on a Great Central Railway express locomotive of the time, it is finely enamelled—note particularly the "Great Central" crest on the tender—and well detailed: note the dummy vacuum hose brake pipe situated above the front buffers; and the steps forward of the front driving wheels, to the cab, and at either end of the tender. The two-speed clockwork mechanism incorporates a patent governor, reversing gear, and automatic brake. The overall length of engine and tender is 20in (50·8cm). See (6) for a Coach made to match.

5 Gauge "1" Bogie Wagon by Märklin, Germany, dating from the early 1900s; marketed in Britain by Gamage and available in Gauges "0", "1", "2", "3", and "4". It is hand-painted and well detailed, with opening doors, as shown, on both sides, and steps at each end. Length: 8·5in (21·59cm).

6 Gauge "1" "Great Central Railway" Bogie Passenger Coach, made by Bing to match with the locomotive shown at (4). It has opening end doors and a slide-off roof (in this example, a replacement item), but no interior detail. Although both are hard to find, this coach is somewhat rarer than the locomotive it complements. Length: 16in (40·64cm).

7 Gauge "2" Baggage Van, made by Märklin in c1902 for sale in Britain by Gamage, and originally priced at 4s 11d (25p, 30c). Hand-painted in Midland Railway livery, it was catalogued by Gamage in Gauges "2" and "3", and is known to have been available at various times in Gauges "0" and "1" also. It has the legend "Made in Germany" stamped on its underside and, at one end of its upper body, the applied white-metal "Gamage" plaque that is always a desirable addition. Length 10·5in (26·67cm).

1-3 Gauge "0" 4-4-2 Locomotive, numbered "31801", and Eight-Wheeled (two bogies) Tender (3), with Sleeping Car (2) and Dining Car (1), by Hornby; the famous "Blue Train", so called from the colour of its coaches, modelled on the Calais-Mediterranean Express, and in the livery of France's Nord railway. The engine was almost certainly initially produced by Hornby's factory at Bobigny, France, and the locomotive became the prototype for the "No 3 Locomotive Series" that included the "Flying Scotsman"—see (7), *pages 164-165*. Introduced in 1927, it remained in the Hornby Catalogue until the beginning of World War II. The locomotive seen here has no smoke deflectors: this indicates that it is an early item in the production run. The train was available in France in different liveries, including both red and black finishes, and it was sometimes sold along with standard Hornby Pullman coaches with French lettering as described below. Note that the example shown has red driving wheels, an unusual variation—but certainly not a later modification. The locomotive was made in both clockwork, as shown, and electric versions, the latter with a 4-volt (or later a 20-volt) motor: Hornby had by this time abandoned the high-voltage electric motor used in such models as the "Metropolitan Electric" (Although the "Metropolitan Electric" remained in the Catalogue for some years thereafter). This example is in good order and is regularly run by the author (who, when a boy, particularly coveted this model but could never afford it!); however, its wheels show signs of the "metal fatigue" that is all too frequently found on Hornby items (although not invariably: it is found only in models where an incorrect mix of metals was used in casting the wheels). Length (engine and tender): 16·5in (41·91cm). The Sleeping Car (2) and Dining Car (3) are modelled on the luxury coaches provided by the International Sleeping Car Company to suit the needs of wealthy travellers to the fashionable French resorts served by the "Blue Train". Hornby's models finely reproduce the opulence of the prototypes, with exterior finished in royal blue with gold lining and the company's famous lettering—"Compagnie Internationale des Wagons-Lits et des Grands Express Europeens" —faithfully reproduced. Both coaches have two bogies, opening end doors, working corridor connections, and celluloid windows, with printed detail of lamps on the windows of the Dining Car. Length (coach): 13in (33·02cm). The "Blue Train" is one of the most desirable items of the Hornby range and although it was in production over a long period it is now not particularly easy to find, especially in good condition, and tends to command a comparatively high price.

4-6 Gauge "0" 0-4-0 Locomotive,

numbered "1902", and Four-Wheeled Tender (6), with Twin-Bogie Passenger Coach (5), First Class, numbered "1985", and Twin-Bogie Brake Van (4); made by Gebrüder Bing, Nuremburg, Germany, and dating from around 1903. Although the coaches do not appear to be in scale with the locomotive, these items were definitely marketed together as a set. The locomotive is in spirit-fired steam (it was also available in clockwork), and its somewhat over-scale proportions were doubtless intended to give it a more powerful, longer-running performance: it is capable of running for 15-20 minutes on one filling of methylated spirit and water. Length (engine and tender): 12·75in (32·38cm). The

set shown is in London and North-Western Railway (L&NWR) livery: it was available also in the other major liveries of the period. The tinplate coaches, each with three opening doors on either side, and with interior detail of seats and compartment divisions in the Passenger Coach, are printed: in larger gauges, Bing coaches of this period were still hand-painted. Length (coach): 6·75in (17·14cm).
7-8 Gauge "0" "George the Fifth" Locomotive, numbered "2663", and Six-Wheeled Tender (8), in clockwork, by Bing: the original version, in the true-to-prototype black livery of the L&NWR and with the correct number, of the model fully described at (1) on *pages 164-165*. It is shown

here with a Brake Coach (7), numbered "1921", Third Class, of Bing's 1921 Series. These items were sold as a set, with the addition of a Passenger Coach and an oval of track. The twin-bogie coach is fitted with corridor connections and has dummy gas cylinders on its underside; it has non-opening doors and no interior detail. Length (coach): 13in (33·02cm).
9 Gauge "0" 4-4-2 Tank Locomotive, numbered "1784", by Hornby, Great Britain; this model, known as the "No 2 Special Tank", first appeared in the late 1920s and remained in production until the beginning of World War II. The example shown here is clockwork-powered, having the standard Hornby mechanism

with forward and reverse gears and brake (note the long control levers protruding from the rear of the cab), and is in the livery of the London and North Eastern Railway (LNER). The model was also available with an electric motor, and in the liveries of the other major British railway companies of the period: the London, Midland & Scottish (LMS), Great Western Railway (GWR), and Southern Railway (SR). This was a very popular Hornby item and remained in production throughout the 1930s. It is, therefore, a model that is fairly easy for the collector now to find — although it is not often to be found in the pristine condition of the example shown here. Length: 10·5in (21·94cm).

1 Gauge "1" Great Northern Railway 4-4-2 Atlantic Locomotive (note that the term "Atlantic" is applied to any locomotive with a 4-4-2 wheel arrangement), made by Gebrüder Bing, Nuremberg, Germany, for sale in Britain by Bassett-Lowke. This example dates from 1909, when a series of Bing models based on British prototypes and commissioned by Bassett-Lowke began to appear. These models were accurate representations of their prototypes, with very pleasing proportions. The locomotive shown was available in Gauges "0" and "1", powered by clockwork or steam. This spirit-fired steam model has twin piston-valve cylinders; Bassett-Lowke's Catalogue specifies its fittings as "covered saftey-valve, bell whistle, spring buffers, try cock, regulator in cab, vapourising spirit lamp and steam superheater", and adds that "the cylinders are lubricated by special automatic lubricator in smokebox". Length (engine and tender): 23in (58·42cm).

2 Gauge "1" Great Northern Railway 0-6-2 Tank Locomotive, numbered "190", made by Bing for Bassett-Lowke and dating from 1909. This is based on a very powerful British prototype intended for heavy suburban traffic, and Bing's careful attention to detail is apparent in the photograph. On the real loco-motive, the boiler mountings had to be cut down to allow it to pass through the Metropolitan tunnels to London's Moorgate Station: this feature appears on the model. Further, since the real locomotive had to condense its own steam, again because of passing through the tunnels, a condenser pipe (the fat, black pipe at the sides) features on the model—although it is clockwork-powered and was not, in fact, available in steam. It has a two-speed, geared-wind clockwork mechanism; ie, it is wound not with a key but with a fairly sizeable crank handle—an easier, if somewhat more time-consuming, way of winding such a powerful mechanism. Although this example is in GNR livery, all Bassett-Lowke models could, for a small extra payment, be modified to suit the customer's requirements in livery and numbering. This model was available in Gauges "1" and "2", and it is interesting to note that a fair number of Gauge "2" examples in fine condition have appeared for sale in recent years. Length: 13·75in (34·92cm).

3 Gauge "1" 0-4-0 Tank Engine, by Bing for Bassett-Lowke. This is the Gauge "1" version, 10in (25·4cm) long, of the celebrated "No 112" tank locomotive available in Gauges "0", "1", and "2", in steam, clockwork, and electric, from c1910 until 1930. Like all steam models, which obviously must withstand hard wear, this example is hand-painted. It was originally available in the liveries of the Midland; London and North-Western (L&NWR); Great Northern (GNR); and

Caledonian (blue) Railways, and later in the colours of the London, Midland & Scottish (LMS); London and North Eastern (LNER); Great Western (GWR); and Southern (SR) Railways. This example has obviously been well-steamed, but it is still apparent that it is in SR livery, dating it to the mid-1920s after the regrouping of the British railway companies. Note the large control levers at the rear of the cab: a thoughtful provision to save the owner from burned hands. Another interesting point is that the number "112" is the number of Bassett-Lowke's store in High Holborn, London.

4 Gauge "1" Lancashire & Yorkshire Railway 4-6-0 Locomotive, numbered "1510", and Six-

Wheeled Tender, made by Bing for Bassett-Lowke. A most pleasing representation of an Aspinall-designed prototype, this is a very rare item: it was first catalogued in 1915, very soon after the appearance of the prototype, and it is believed that only 100 were made. Of the six examples encountered by the author, all were in excellent condition, showing that this was a model that was treasured right from the start. It was available in clockwork only, with a powerful two-speed, six-coupled (ie, driving all six of the larger wheels) geared-wind mechanism. As on the prototype the driving wheels are comparatively small, giving excellent hauling power. Overall length of engine and tender:

22in (55·88cm).

5 Gauge "1" 0-4-0 Peckett Saddle Tank Locomotive, numbered "101". This is the early and very desirable version made by Carette, Nuremberg, and dating from 1906, of a powerful shunting engine built by Peckett of Bristol. Carette ceased production in 1917, and Bing later made a version for Bassett-Lowke using parts acquired from Carette. It was made by Carette in Gauges "0", "1", and "2"; by Bing probably only in Gauges "0" and "1". This example, 11in (27·94cm) long, is in Midland Railway livery and has a particularly long-running clockwork mechanism. The Carette version is rare; the Bing version is more common.

6 Gauge "1" 4-4-2 Atlantic Tank Locomotive in London, Brighton & South Coast Railway livery, numbered "11", by Bing for Bassett-Lowke. Available also in Gauge "0", this model had a long run, appearing in c1912 and remaining in Bassett-Lowke's Catalogue (with a break, of course, during World War I) until the late 1920s, when it was available in SR livery. It has a powerful two-speed, four-coupled clockwork mechanism and is well-detailed. Märklin produced a similar model, in Gauges "0" and "1", which is a less accurate representation and has a more "toy-like" quality, making it generally more desirable to collectors. This Bing version, which is 15·75in (40cm) long, is not particularly rare.

1 Gauge "1" Gotthard 0-4-4-0 BO-BO Locomotive of Swiss Railways, numbered "1802", made by Gebrüder Märklin, Germany, immediately after World War I. ("BO-BO" refers to the wheel arrangement and signifies that the locomotive has two bogies, each with four wheels). This model was first catalogued by Märklin in 1919 and was available also in Gauge "0"; production continued throughout the 1920s, but it was probably not made in any great quantity: production is more likely to be numbered in the hundreds rather than thousands. A massive and imposing model for three-rail electric operation, it is hand-painted and nicely detailed, with working headlights, opening doors at the ends, and dummy pantographs on the roof. The roof lifts off to give access to the powerful 110-220 volt electric motor. This model was made primarily for the continental market, but it is now much in demand by collectors all over the world and is particularly popular with American collectors: an attractive, desirable, and rare item. Length: 17·7in (45cm).

2-4 Gauge "1" Steeple-Cab 0-4-0 Locomotive (2), numbered "V 1021"; with (3) Four-Wheeled Suburban Coach ("Personen-wagen"), numbered "18071", made by Märklin in Gauges "O" and "1" from c1930 until World War II; and (4), Four-Wheeled Passenger Luggage Van, numbered "18081". This train in continental livery was made by Märklin around 1930. The Steeple-Cab is based on a locomotive of the Paris-Orleans Railway: the prototype was, of course, electric, but the model is clockwork, with a very powerful Märklin two-speed mechanism: note the brake and forward/reverse controls protruding from the cab, and the speed regulator on the roof. The locomotive's detail includes cast-metal headlights and chrome-plated handrails. The Passenger Luggage Van (4) has sliding doors centrally and opening doors towards its end, and is fitted with red rearlights that can be illuminated. The raised part of its roof accommodates a guard's lookout. Lengths (locomotive): 10in (25·4cm); (rolling stock): 10·5in (26·67cm).

5 Gauge "1" tinplate Four-Wheeled Crane Truck by Gebrüder Bing, Nuremburg, Germany; the odd one out on this spread, where all other items are by Bing's great rival Märklin. This model was sold in Great Britain by A.W. Gamage, London: in Gamage's 1906 Catalogue it was listed in Gauges "0", "1", "2", and "3"; the Gauge "1" version being priced at 2s 3d (11p, 13c). As usual for its period, it is hand-painted. As is apparent, the crane is fully pivoted on the truck body; mounted just behind the bottom of the jib is a counterbalance weight that moves forward or back on a slide. The hook (missing from this example) is raised and lowered manually

4

6

8

by a crank handle. Lengths (truck body): 5·5in (13·97cm); (overall, including jib arm): 8·75in (22·2cm).

6 Gauge "1" tinplate Cattle Truck by Märklin, catalogued by Gamage's in 1906 in Gauges "0", "1", and "2", and priced then at 5s 6d (27½p, 33c) in Gauge "1". Hand-painted, it has sliding doors centrally on either side and a hinged roof; the ubiquitous Märklin bogies of the period are seen to advantage in the photograph. The legend "Made in Germany" is stamped on the base. The example shown is of particular interest to American collectors, since it was intended for the US market, with the letters "P.R.R." ("Pennsylvania Railroad") stamped at each end. Length: 9·5in

(24·13cm).

7 Gauge "1" North British Railway Atlantic (4-4-2) Locomotive, numbered "4021" and Six-Wheeled Tender, first catalogued by Märklin in 1919. This example was obviously intended for the British market, but Märklin also produced it for the continental market in German (*Deutschbahn*) livery of black with red wheels. However, why Märklin should have chosen a prototype from a comparatively obscure British railway of the period remains something of a mystery. This model was available in steam, as shown here, clockwork, and electric versions, in Gauges "0" and "1". It has the unfortunate Märklin characteristic of being extremely heavy and, in consequence, is not a good

runner, seeming only just able to drag itself around the track! Nevertheless, it is an impressive and quite handsome locomotive, with such detail as brass handrails and simulated coal in the tender. Note the oiling caps situated on top of the cylinders, a typical Märklin feature. Length (engine and tender): 23in (58·42cm).

8 Gauge "1" 0-6-0 Tank Locomotive; a somewhat rare version, as explained below, of a popular model first made by Märklin after 1918 and produced in Gauges "0" and "1" over a long period. This example is in clockwork: note the large control levers (only one visible here) protruding from the sides of the cab, and the rim brakes (just visible) acting on the front pair of wheels. It is

12in (30·48cm) long. First appearing immediately after World War I, it was probably available in the liveries of all the major British railway companies—certainly in those of the Great Western Railway (GWR) and London and North Eastern Railway (LNER)— but the author has not been able to locate any instance of the example shown here, in Great Eastern Railway (GER) livery, having been catalogued. The model was sold in Great Britain by both Gamage's and by Bond's ("Bond's o' Euston Road"), London: up to World War I, Gamage's appear to have had a near-exclusive arrangement for marketing Märklin's products in London, but after the War Bond's were also selling Märklin's models.

1-4 Gauge "0" "American Flyer Lines" 2-4-2 Locomotive and Bogie Tender (4), with Gondola (3), Breakdown Crane (2), and Caboose (1). This train by the American Flyer company, USA, is in near-mint condition and dates from about 1929. The locomotive, for three-rail electric operation, has a diecast body with a brass handrail and domes and piping in copper-coloured tinplate. It is fitted with forward and reverse mechanism and has a working headlight. The tender, with two bogies, is tinplate, with copper-coloured detail and a top that simulates coal. The tinplate, two-bogie Gondola has a dummy brakewheel at its forward end. The Breakdown Crane, again tinplate with two bogies, has a jib

that can be raised and lowered and is held in the desired position by a latch that engages with holes pierced in the cab roof. The tinplate, two-bogie Caboose features a conductor's lookout; when the train is running, the rear bogie picks up current from the track to illuminate the interior of the caboose. Like the locomotive and tender, the brightly painted (ie, dipped) rolling stock is liberally adorned with "American Flyer Lines" transfers. American collectors, to whom this item will be of most interest, will probably be able to find models of this kind without great difficulty, but they are not widely collected outside the USA. Lengths (engine and tender): 15·5in (39·37cm); (rolling stock,

each): 10in (25·4cm).

5-6 Gauge "0" Coaches by Gebrüder Bing, Nuremburg, Germany; described as "Pullmans", these appeared in Bing's English-language Catalogue of 1926. The pair comprises a Pullman Dining Coach (5), numbered "3295", and a Composite Passenger and Guards Van (6), numbered "3296". They were available in the liveries of the Great Western Railway (GWR), as shown, London, Midland & Scottish Railway (LMS), and London and North Eastern Railway (LNER). It is of interest to compare these with the earlier Bing coaches and to note that even at this comparatively late date, the coaches still have detailed interiors with tables and chairs

(with spikes for passengers, although passenger figures had not been available for some years), and opening doors. Length: 12in (30·48cm).

7 Gauge "0" "Duke of York" 4-4-0 Locomotive and Six-Wheeled Tender, numbered "1931", made by Bing for Bassett-Lowke, Great Britain. Made both in clockwork, as shown (note key on tender), and electric, this model was first issued in 1927 and was produced under an arrangement with B.D.V. Cigarettes: the locomotive and tender, wagons, coaches, rails, and accessories, could be obtained by collecting coupons given to the purchasers of the cigarettes—the locomotive "cost" 260 coupons, the tender 150 coupons. Locomotive and tender

could be purchased in the normal way at an inclusive price of £1 5s 0d (£1.25, $1.50), or £1 16s 0d (£1.80, $2.16) for a locomotive fitted with Bassett-Lowke's "Permag" electric motor. The number "1931" may be taken as the date of production: the model is also found with the numbers "1927", "1928", "1929", and "1930". Shown in LMS livery, it was also available in the colours of the GWR, LNER, and Southern Railway (SR). This model was made by Winteringham, Bassett-Lowke's Northampton-based subsidiary. Length (engine and tender): 14·75in (37·46cm).

8-10 Gauge "0" 0-4-0 Locomotive and Four-Wheeled Tender, both numbered "504", with two Four-Wheeled Passenger Coaches

(9-10), First Class, both numbered "3747"; from a fairly late series made by Bing for the British market, 1926. These were sold in the UK as a boxed set, with an oval of track, at a price of £1 3s 0d (£1.15, $1.38), and were available in the major railway liveries; the example shown is in LNER colours. The clockwork-powered locomotive has forward/reverse mechanism. Note the unusual couplings on the coaches, a feature that appeared on a number of items around this time. The same coaches, but finished in the livery of a Germany railway, appeared in Bing's German catalogue. Lengths (engine and tender): 11·5in (29·21cm); (coach): 4·75in (12·06cm).

11 Gauge "0" "Vulcan" 0-4-0

clockwork Locomotive, numbered "3433" and Four-Wheeled Tender, by Bing; much like (8) and dating from the same period, but of slightly heavier construction with a pleasing brass dome and sturdy polished handrails. Like (7), this was available by an arrangement with B.D.V. Cigarettes and could be obtained by collecting coupons. The example shown is in GWR livery. Length (engine and tender): 11·5in (29·21cm).

12-14 Gauge "0" "King Edward VII" 0-4-0 clockwork Locomotive, numbered "1902", and Four-Wheeled Tender (14), with Four-Wheeled Passenger Coach (13), and Brake Van (12); again by Bing, but considerably earlier than (8-10) or (11), and

probably dating from about 1906. It is in London and North-Western Railway (L&NWR) livery. Lengths (engine and tender): 10·75in (27·3cm); (coaches): 5in (12·7cm).

15-16 Gauge "0" "Minerva" 0-4-0 (no connecting rods) clockwork Locomotive, numbered "3410", and Four-Wheeled Tender (16), with a Four-Wheeled Passenger Coach (15), First/Third Class; another simple model produced by Bing in the mid-1920s. These are in LNER livery. Lengths (engine and tender): 9in (22·86cm); (coach): 4·75in (12·06cm). Compare the locomotive with the simple 0-4-0 clockwork engine of Bing's earlier period, dating from about 1906, in L&NWR livery, shown just behind and to the rear of the coach at (16).

Inset (above) *The rear of the tender of the locomotive shown at (3) bears a transfer with the Bassett-Lowke "LOWKO" trademark. This trademark was used before 1914 and, from time to time, in the 1920s; however, not all items marketed in Great Britain by Bassett-Lowke bear the firm's mark.*

1 Gauge "1" 4-4-4 Bavarian State Railway Locomotive and Eight-Wheeled Tender, made by Gebrüder Bing, Nuremberg, Germany, from 1912 until World War I and again, although only in limited numbers, in the early 1920s, in Gauge "1" only and probably from parts made before the War. This large—overall length with tender: 27·5in (69·85cm)—and powerful locomotive is an externally-spirit-fired steam model with a vaporising burner; ie, the spirit is vaporised before it is ignited, which is, in theory at any rate, a more efficient system. Built for the continental market and available in Gauges "0" and "1", steam only, it was not generally sold in Great Britain. However, although production of this model was not resumed by Bing after World War I, it made a brief appearance in the Bassett-Lowke Catalogue for 1924: the "bargain price" of £6 6s 0d (£6·30, $7·56), reduced from £8 8s 0d (£8·40, $10·08), suggests that there was little demand in Britain, where it remains a rare item in Gauge "1", and

extremely rare in Gauge "0", for a German-style locomotive.

2 Gauge "1" 4-6-0 Locomotive, named "Sir Sam Fay" and numbered "423", and Six-Wheeled Tender, made by Bing for sale in Great Britain by Bassett-Lowke. Catalogued immediately prior to the outbreak of World War I in 1914, at about the same time as the appearance of its prototype (a Great Central Railway locomotive bearing the name of a director of that railway), it did not appear in any quantity until the 1920s. Unusually for items made by Bing for Bassett-Lowke, this example bears beneath the tender a Bing trademark, with the words "Made in Bavaria". It was available in both clockwork and electric versions, in Gauge "1"

only: the example shown has a powerful six-coupled, geared-wind clockwork mechanism, with the usual control levers protruding from the rear of the cab. As with several other models made by Bing for Bassett-Lowke at this period, no tinplate coaches were produced to go with the locomotive—although customers could have matching rolling stock painted to order by Bassett-Lowke, usually from the standard Bing/Bassett-Lowke coaches of the time and most likely in GWR form, of which Bassett-Lowke then appears to have had a surfeit. The attractively-finished model proved popular: it is believed that up to 1,000 examples were made, and it is thus an item that the collector may well

encounter. When the example shown came into the author's possession it was in a poor state: as seen now, it is the result of careful professional restoration, which included the repainting of the entire boiler, the side frames, and nameplates. Overall length of engine and tender: 24·25in (61·6cm).

3 Gauge "1" 0-6-0 Locomotive and Six-Wheeled Tender, numbered "3044", made by Bing for Bassett-Lowke. First catalogued in 1911, and available in Gauge "0" and "1", clockwork-powered versions only, it was then priced at £3 3s 0d (£3·15, $3·78). It did not reappear after World War I, and is thus a fairly rare item. Based on the L&NWR so-called "Cauliflower" locomotive,

and available, as shown, authentically in L&NWR livery, it has a two-speed mechanism with forward-reverse gears and brake. On the example shown the original mechanism has been modified with a Van Reimsdijk speed-control system, enabling the locomotive to be run at a very slow speed and thus giving a most realistic effect with a long line of wagons. Overall length of engine and tender: 18·5in (47cm).

4 Gauge "1" 4-4-0 Great Western Railway (GWR) Locomotive, named "County of Northampton", and Six-Wheeled Tender, made by Bing for Bassett-Lowke and dating from 1909. It was made as a steam model only, in Gauges "1" and "2" (with a very small number made in Gauge

"3"). Total production is believed to have been around 500 models, the majority in Gauge "1", and although fairly rare it may be found at auction from time to time. It may be noted that the GWR had, in reality, no locomotive named "County of Northampton", for the lines of that railway ran nowhere near the East Midlands' county; however, Bassett-Lowke's factory was situated in Northampton and the firm doubtless desired to honour the locality in this manner! The example shown here is of particular interest in that it formed part of the estate of the late Victor Harrison, a member of a famous printing family and a personal friend of Wenman J. Bassett-Lowke. This

loco, among the first of the series, was sent by Bing to Bassett-Lowke for evaluation and was presented by W. J. Bassett-Lowke to his old friend. It has been regularly run throughout its long life: since coming into the author's possession some twenty years ago, it has steamed many thousand Gauge "1" miles and is still in splendid working order. The overall length of engine and tender is 21in (53·34cm).

5 Gauge "1" Coal Wagon by Bing, made for the German market in c1906. This four-wheeled tinplate wagon in attractive orange livery has a pressed-tin top painted to simulate a full load of coal; stamped on the side is the legend "10000Kg", indicating its capacity. It is 8in (20·32cm) long.

1 Gauge "1" 4-6-2 PLM (Paris, Lyon and Mediterranée Railway) Pacific Locomotive (any locomotive with a 4-6-2 wheel arangement is designated a Pacific) and Eight-Wheeled Tender, (twin bogies), made by Märklin, Germany. This model first appeared in 1912 and was available in various forms—in Gauges "0" and "1", and in steam (as shown), clockwork, and electric versions—until 1930. It was generally marketed only on the continent—although it could be ordered in Great Britain through A. W. Gamage, London—and it appeared both in dark green livery, as shown, and in black. The locomotive is of typical continental appearance and is well-detailed. However,

Märklin have been inclined to spoil the realism of an otherwise pleasing model by incongruously siting the filler and safety valves on top of the domes instead of directly on the boiler as in the prototype. Note the automatic lubricators for the cylinders above the front bogies. The miniature spring-loaded hand pump on the side of the locomotive is used to pump water from a track-side tank to the boiler, via a length of rubber tubing: in practice, it does not work very well. Note also the screw-cap on the tender: spirit is poured in here and fed through rubber tubing from the inlet pipe (see *Inset*) in the cab; the wheel at the front of the tender controls the admission of the

spirit. Although most attractive and impressive in their steam versions, these large Märklin locomotives do not run very satisfactorily because of their excessive weight, the frames being of cast metal. Nevertheless, they are much desired by collectors and are rare in Britain. Overall length of engine and tender is 28·75in (73cm).
2 Gauge "1" 4-6-2 Maffei Pacific Locomotive and Eight-Wheeled Tender (twin bogies), by Gebrüder Bing, Nuremburg, dating from 1912. It is a splendid model, based on a prototype by the German builder Maffei and finished in the black-and-red livery of the Bavarian State Railway —and this particular example is of especial interest. The pointed

top of the cab is typical of the type and, in a continental-style locomotive, one would expect the boiler front also to be pointed —as in the Gebrüder Bing 4-4-0 Bavarian State Railway locomotive shown at (1) on *pages 178-179*—instead of rounded, as seen here. The author has never seen the model catalogued in the form shown here and, indeed, has encountered no other expert who has. It is the author's opinion that this particular example was intended for the North American market, where it would have appeared without buffers and with the addition of a cowcatcher. However, the tender, which is almost certainly the one originally supplied, is of

typically German appearance. This model must, therefore, be described as an interesting hybrid, the exact nature of which remains something of a mystery. In its usual form, with a pointed boiler, it had a long production run in Gauges "0" and "1": it was made in steam, electric, and clockwork versions, and the Gauge "1" version in steam was still being catalogued by Bing in 1927. The six-coupled mechanism of the example shown is driven by a simple electric motor of the early type, and it features electric headlights. Note that the central pair of driving wheels is unflanged to enable it to negotiate sharp curves: this is a common feature on larger Bing locomotives of the period but it does not appear in equivalent models by Märklin. Bassett-Lowke always insisted that locomotives made in Germany for the British market should have unflanged central wheels, and when Bing, in 1910, produced a Mogul (ie, with 2-6-0 wheel arrangement) with flanged central wheels it was rejected by Bassett-Lowke and was marketed instead by Gamage's. Length of engine and tender: 27in (68·58cm).

3 Gauge "1" 4-6-2 Locomotive and Eight-Wheeled Tender by Märklin, made for the British market and dating from the late 1920s. This is Märklin's massive and somewhat freelance representation of the famous "Flying Scotsman" of the London and North Eastern Railway (LNER): it is an example of Märklin's usual cavalier attitude to both the prototype and to numbering. Although some attempt has been made with the tapered boiler to give a characteristic LNER appearance, neither the cab nor the twin-bogie tender bear any resemblance to the prototype. The number "1021" is the Märklin code referring to the gauge (shown by the final digit): the number of the prototype was "4472". It is, nevertheless, a most impressive model, with an overall length (engine and tender) of 29in (73·66cm). It was made in Gauges "0" and "1", in steam only: its mechanism is much like that of the PLM Pacific shown at (1), incorporating Märklin's unique firing system with its vaporising spirit lamp. First catalogued by Gamage's in 1928, it remained available only until the early 1930s, and because of this short production run is now very rare. It is a much-desired item.

Inset (top right) *A closeup view of the cab of the Märklin PLM Pacific locomotive shown at (1) shows the steam pressure gauge (bearing the initials "GM&Co.", and with a water gauge hidden behind it); speed regulator; inlet pipe for spirit (see main caption); and try cock. The last-named — the curved pipe descending to the right in the photograph — is used to test the pressure of the steam.*

1 Gauge "0" Eight-Wheeled Bogie Passenger Coach, in SCNF (French National Railways) colours, issued by Hornby, Bobigny-Seine, France, after World War II to complement the streamlined, steam-outline 4-4-2 locomotive of the period. This vehicle, with its distinctive windows, appears a little low in proportion but is a fairly accurate model of a contemporary French coach. It is strange that whereas the Gauge "0" production of Hornby, Great Britain, was severely limited after World War II, French Hornby's Gauge "0" programme continued to thrive for some years. Like most French Hornby items, these coaches are quite eagerly sought after and are not very easy to find. Length: 12in (30·48cm).

2 Gauge "0" Wagons-Lits Pullman Dining Car, by Jep, France, made throughout the 1930s and again, briefly, after World War II. The famous French "Flèche d'Or" (Golden Arrow) express ran a unique set of Wagons-Lits Pullmans, and the "golden arrows" are evident on the waist of this model, one of Jep's finest items. Although a little over-scale and somewhat short, this fully captures the spirit of its prototype, with the aid of fine lithographed detail and good door-end design. Like their companion "Nord" locomotives, these coaches are extremely collectable and quite hard for the collector to find. Length: 14in (35·56cm).

3 Gauge "0" "Nord" Bogie Baggage Container Vehicle, "Flèche d'Or",

by Jep; like (2), this was available throughout the 1930s and again, briefly, post-War. This vehicle, delightfully modelled by Jep, was unique to the "Flèche d'Or" express: it had detachable end baggage containers which were shipped across the Channel to run on the British "Golden Arrow" from Dover to Victoria, London. Quite rare, this model is equally as collectable as (2); indeed, they may almost be seen as a matching set. Length: 10·5in (26·67cm).

4 Gauge "0" Four-Wheeled Electric P.O.E1.31 Locomotive by Hornby, France. These Bobigny-made 20-volt electric models, based on a type used on the Paris-Orleans-Midi Railway, were made from the early 1930s until World War II, and were reissued post-War in more

jazzy colours. The body pressings are among the most elaborate ever undertaken by French Hornby, with a wealth of detail that includes louvres, rivets and springs. The model was marketed for a time in Britain—see (8). The pre-War dark-green version shown here is fairly scarce; the brighter post-War versions are more common. Length: 8·25in (20·955cm).

5 Gauge "0" Four-Wheeled Goods Van, "DSB", by Hornby, Britain, issued in c1934-35. This vehicle, with hinged opening doors, is one of those lettered by Hornby in foreign liveries, in this case, the Danish State Railway. It must be remembered that Hornby exported many such items: they may be found in various European liveries and in those of South Africa, New

Zealand, South America, and the USA. They are unlikely to be found outside the countries for which they were intended, but most collectors would not go to great lengths to obtain such "oddballs". Length: 5·5in (13·97cm).

6 Gauge "0" Single-Barrel Wine Wagon. This rather garish wagon is by far the rarer of the wine wagons originated by French Hornby but issued in Britain in 1928-29. The double-barrelled version, with ladder and service platform but lacking the brake hut, is much easier to find: it replaced the single-barrelled version in the early 1930s, both items having for a while been issued concurrently. Length: 5·5in (13·97cm).

7 Gauge "0" No 2 Bogie Cattle Truck, "DSB"; another Hornby

vehicle intended for Denmark—see (5). Like the No 2 Luggage Van, this was one of Hornby's earlier goods vehicles. It was available in form almost unchanged (except for liveries) from the 1920s until World War II, and is easy enough to find in British liveries. Length: 9in (22·86cm).

8 Gauge "0" No LEC1 Locomotive, numbered "10655" and lettered for Swiss Federal Railways, by Hornby, dating from the 1930s. This is a clockwork, reversing model, based on the P.O.E1 seen at (4); a 20-volt AC version, No LE1/20, was also available in Great Britain. Note that this version for the British market has done away with the dummy skirting, axle-boxes and springs of the French version shown at

(4), evidently to suggest a Swiss appearance by leaving the wheels mostly exposed. Basically, this may be described as a French model of a Swiss type with a "Made in England" transfer! Length: 8·25in (20·955cm).

9 Gauge "0" Four-Wheeled "Wagons-Lits" Blue Pullman, by Hornby, France, mid-1930s. This odd little vehicle is probably French Hornby's version of the British company's M1 Pullman, although the vehicles differ in dimensions, and suggests some planning cooperation between the British and French companies. Length: 4·75in (12cm).

10 Gauge "0" Covered Wagon, "Nord"; a French-style vehicle by Hornby, issued in the mid-1930s. Based on the British No 1 version,

this wagon was fitted with a tarpaulin on hoops (missing here). Quite a number of French-style vehicles, all lettered "Nord", were issued for the British market, but no French locomotive appropriate to these vehicles was ever put on the market. Length: 5·5in (13·97cm).

11 Gauge "0" Two-Car Diesel Articulated Set, electric, by Jep, France, available during the late 1930s and again after World War II. Although not a particularly inspiring model, it is characteristic of the little local trains so common in France and is very robustly made and quite well proportioned. It is fairly rare, although not avidly sought after by collectors. Length (overall): 12·25in (31·1cm).

1 Gauge "0" 4-4-4 Tank Locomotive, numbered "1534", by Hornby, Great Britain. This famous Hornby locomotive is shown here in its early form, dating from 1923, complete with its original box of embossed cardboard. It has a polished brass dome and is fitted with cast-iron wheels. This model, now most collectable and a "must" for Hornby enthusiasts, was made in clockwork only, and appeared in the liveries of the major British railway companies. The locomotive shown here is in the livery of the London and North Eastern Railway (L&NER; note that the ampersand marks this as an early example, since the form "LNER" was introduced in the early 1920s). As is the case with many Hornby items, examples in Southern Railway (SR) livery are hard to find. Length: 10·5in (26·67cm).

2 Gauge "0" 0-4-0 Tank Locomotive, numbered "623" and in London, Midland & Scottish Railway (LMS) livery, by Hornby. This is one of the rare permanent-magnet 6-volt No 1 locomotives, introduced in 1929, and is shown here in its original "Hornby Series" box, complete with its DC current forward-and-reverse speed controller. It is interesting to note that the Meccano company never took DC locomotives very seriously and later concentrated on AC current locomotives with elaborate reversing gear. This very attractive tank engine was produced in the colours of the four major British railway companies, and in "goods black". Length: 7in (17·78cm).

3 Gauge "0" 0-4-0 No 1 Tank
Locomotive, in Great Western
Railway (GWR) livery, by Hornby;
one of the firm's earliest
production models, appearing in
the early 1920s. Early examples are
of bolted construction, but the
more usual tabbed assembly was
later adopted. The model underwent
some refinement in the late 1920s,
and a version was produced
bearing the name "Zulu". A tender
variety—see (8)—was also
available. The locomotive was made
in the major British and many
continental liveries. The example
shown is clockwork, with the usual
brake and forward/reverse control
knobs protruding from the rear of
the cab: it was later made in
electric versions, and most
collectors find the 6-volt electric

model much more attractive than
its EPM16 successor. Length:
6·5in (16·51cm).
4 Gauge "0" Snow Plough, lettered
"Snow Plough" and in GWR colours;
an early mid-series Hornby item.
Especially heavy wheels were
fitted to this model, and a spring
belt ran around a V-pulley on the
leading axle to drive the Meccano
fan, or "snow pusher". The cast
lamp above the fan appears only on
the earlier versions; nor do the
sliding doors feature on later
models. The snow plough was
made in many different colour
schemes, finally appearing in bright
yellow and blue in a late, post-
World War II version. Length (with
plough): 7in (17·78cm).
5 Gauge "0" Private Owner Van,
"Carr's Biscuits", by Hornby;

an early version with a spindly
chassis and link couplings.
Note that these early vans are
fitted with hinged, opening doors;
later versions have sliding doors.
It is interesting to compare the
"Hornby Series" rectangle on this
van's solebar with the later
version seen on the control unit
at (2). Length: 5·5in (13·97cm).
6-7 Gauge "0" Four-Wheeled Coach,
Third Class (6), and Guard's Van
(7), by Hornby, dating from the
late 1920s. Note that these coaches
have clerestory roofs: on later
coaches, elliptical roofs were
fitted, but removal of these will
reveal the turned-over end of the
earlier clerestory versions. These
coaches were available in the four
major British liveries: the examples
shown are in LMS colours and,

again, SR versions are the hardest to
find. Length: 6in (15·24cm).
8 Gauge "0" 0-4-0 No 1 Tender
Locomotive, with Four-Wheeled
Tender numbered "2710", clockwork, by Hornby; one of the earliest
production models—see also (3).
A non-reversing version with an
identical body was also available.
Later versions had longer splashers
and had tenders that were lettered
for the railway companies rather
than with the number "2710". This
example is in the livery of the
London and North Eastern Railway
(LNER); note the characteristic
Hornby "Forward" crest on the cab
side, and the Hornby "garter"
behind the polished dome (a
little shabby on this "play-worn"
example). Length (engine and
tender): 10·25in (26·035cm).

On this spread are shown Hornby locomotives of the type generally known as "Number 3", denoting 4-4-2 locomotives of a type initiated at the Meccano factory at Bobigny, France. It is thought that, after production of the initial "Nord" French locomotive for the "Blue Train"—see (1)— Hornby of Britain decided to use the French body-pressings, with minor modifications, for locomotives in the liveries of the four major British railways. Early models in the series retained typically French "stove-pipe" funnels, but these were soon replaced by a more British equivalent. In the caes of all the locomotives shown here, it would appear that the locomotive body pressings only

were of French origin; in fact, it is possible that it was only the body press-tools that were shipped from Bobigny to Liverpool, rather than great quantities of unpainted body casings.

1 Gauge "0" E320 4-4-2 "Riviera Blue" Locomotive and Eight-Wheeled Tender, both numbered "3.1290" and in "Nord" finish. This is one of the last of the long run, a 20-volt electric model in the matt finish of the immediate pre-War period, with the improved tender bogies and characteristic smoke deflectors of the later examples. This style of locomotive probably underwent more changes and colour variations than any other Hornby item. Representing the

famous "Blue Train" that ran from Calais to the Riviera via Paris, it was originated by Hornby of France but was also very popular in Britain. The locomotive first appeared in 1926, in clockwork or 4-volt electric, and then had a polished brass boiler dome, a fixed headlamp, and smaller driving wheels made of cast-iron. The 1930s saw models in 6-volt electric, No 2 Special clockwork, and, later still, No 2 20-volt automatic reversing motors. The polished domes soon disappeared in favour of black- or brown-painted versions, and the smoke deflectors were added around 1936. Many different numbers were used—it is now not unusual to find specimens with non-matching tender numbers

—and Hornby, France, produced these locomotives in most French railway liveries, some highly inappropriate. They are not too difficult to find in one form or another and are a most important feature of any Hornby collection. Note that a locomotive of French origin will display on its tender-mounted gold rectangle: "Série Hornby/Fab. par/ Meccano, Paris"; the British model will have: "Made in England/by/ Meccano Ltd./Hornby Series". Length: (engine and tender): 16·5in (41·91cm).
2 Gauge "0" E320 4-4-2 "Lord Nelson" Locomotive and Six-Wheeled Tender, numbered "850" and in Southern Railway (SR) colours. The example shown is a late model in 20-volt electric. Earlier models

in the series, made before 1930, had a tender quite different from that seen here: the early No 2 tender, as for the type "2711", with distinctive coal rails around the top. These were superseded by the far more elaborate and accurately-detailed tender seen here. But both the earlier and later tenders were also sold as separate items, to suit the numbering of the locomotives; thus, the finish seen here might also feature on an earlier tender. "Lord Nelson" is one of the rarer names in the series; pre-1930 versions are very rare, although mid-1930s examples are not too difficult to find. Length (engine and tender): 16in (40·64cm).

3 Gauge "0" E320 4-4-2 "Royal Scot" Locomotive, numbered "6100", and Six-Wheeled Tender, in London, Midland & Scottish Railway (LMS) livery; a late 1930s version in 20-volt electric. Both "Royal Scot" and "Flying Scotsman" (5) were made in great numbers in clockwork and electric: the famous names alone must have sold these models, which are not at all true-to-prototype. The earlier French-influenced version was interesting in that it had the "6100" number on the tender, the cab side bearing a large, round LMS coat-of-arms. It may be that "red" locomotives had the greatest appeal, since significantly more examples were sold in LMS colours than any other. LMS colours were also chosen for such markets as India and South Africa, although the name was then

deleted and the appropriate railway companies' initials replaced "LMS". These models are not at all rare, although a mint specimen is most collectable. Length (engine and tender): 16in (40·64cm).

4 Gauge "0" E320 4-4-2 "Caerphilly Castle" Locomotive, numbered "4073", and Six-Wheeled Tender, in Great Western Railway (GWR) colours. This 20-volt electric version displays three minor modifications when compared to other locomotives of the same series at (3) and (5). A somewhat larger chimney has replaced the earlier "stove-pipe"; a strange-looking brass version of the typical GWR safety-valve is fitted halfway along the boiler; and the usual French-type safety-valve

immediately in front of the cab has been replaced by a brass whistle. "Caerphilly Castle" is slightly rarer than "Royal Scot" or "Flying Scotsman". Length (engine and tender): 16in (40·64cm).

5 Gauge "0" E320 4-4-2 "Flying Scotsman" Locomotive, numbered "4472", and Six-Wheeled Tender, in 20-volt electric, by Hornby. It can be said that this model looks even less like the locomotive whose name it bears than any other in the series: save for its name, number, and its London and North Eastern Railway (LNER) livery, it has no features in common with its prototype. An extremely popular model, it remains easy to find. Length (engine and tender): 16in (40·64cm).

1-4 Gauge "0" No 1 0-4-0 Tank Locomotive, numbered "667", in Southern Railway (SR) colours. This Hornby locomotive of the late 1920s, available in the liveries of the major British railway companies, is shown here hauling a train of contemporary Hornby goods vehicles: "Colman's Mustard" Van (2); "Seccotine Sticks Everything" Van (3); and "United Dairies" Milk Tank Wagon (4). The locomotive shown here is clockwork, with brake and reversing gear: it is quite a scarce item in this form, but is much rarer in the later 6-volt electric version. Note the characteristically large handrails and knobs, the fixed dummy front lamps, and the over-height buffer level. The wheels of these early Hornby locomotives

are of lead-alloy, or cast-iron in some of the larger models, so they are not liable to the fatigue often encountered in the mazac (zinc-alloy) wheels of some later models. Of the rolling stock in this train, "Colman's Mustard" is probably the rarest of all Hornby vans, and "Seccotine" the next rarest. On "Seccotine", note Hornby's advertising rectangle to the right of the sole-bar, and compare this typical mark of the later 1920s with the earlier "Meccano" oval on the "Shell" tank wagon at (7). The "United Dairies" milk tank wagon is perhaps the most popular model of its type. Note that all three vehicles are of the earlier type, dating from before c1931, with open chassis and link couplings.

Lengths (locomotive: 6·5in (16·51cm); (each wagon): 5·5in (13·97cm).

5 Gauge "0" No 0 Clockwork Tender Locomotive, 0-4-0, and Four-Wheeled Tender, numbered "2710", in Great Western Railway (GWR) colours. A very early Hornby series, issued in the early 1920s, in non-reversing clockwork with brake, these locomotives were produced with various changes up to the early 1930s. The number "2710" marks the earlier production run. This was priced in the 1930s at 10s 6d (52½p, 63c), the tender being 2s 6d (12½p, 15c) extra, and, as in some cheaper models, the hand-rail knobs were diecast, the entire hand-rail assembly being painted gold. Length (engine and tender): 10·5in (26·67cm).

6 Gauge "0" Open Wagon, Hornby, 1920s. This is the earliest form of Hornby's open wagon, of bolted construction, with blank axle-guards, turned-brass buffers and brass link couplings, and with the letters "LNWR" (London and North-Western Railway) individually pressed and clipped on. Length: 5·5in (13·97cm).

7 Gauge "0" Tank Wagon, "Shell", Hornby, 1920s. Hornby produced many private owner tank wagons based on this very early version, with its plain axle-guards and locomotive-valve-style filler. As in (6), its underside bears the early press-stamped marking "MLDL (the "D" superimposed above the horizontal stroke of the first "L"), England ("Meccano Limited, Liverpool, England"). This is a rare item.

Length: 5·5in (13·97cm).

8 Gauge "0" No 2 Corridor Coach, LNER, Hornby, 1930s. This is one of a series that appeared in the four major liveries as both coaches and brake ends. Somewhat under-scale, they represent the maker's first attempt to break away from all-Pullman mainline trains, and illustrate also the use of lithographed tinplate to keep down cost. Note "The Queen of Scots" title-board (which properly belongs on an LNER Pullman): most Hornby corridor coaches of the 1930s were provided with brackets to hold destination- or title-boards, which were available in great variety as separate items. Length: 11·75in (29·845cm).

9 Gauge "0" No 2 Special 4-4-0 Locomotive, "Yorkshire", and Six-Wheeled Tender, numbered "234", in LNER livery. This was the first of the famous No 2 Special Loco-motives which appeared around 1929. For a fuller account of this series see *pages 194-195*, where the later version of this locomotive, "Bramham Moor", is shown at (4). This example can be distinguished as one of the first series by the fact that the number "234" and letters "LNER" both appear on the tender side: on later models, "234" appears on the cab side. Length: 14·625in (37·15cm).

10 Gauge "0" Metropolitan Brake Coach, Hornby, 1920s. This brake coach, and a matching passenger coach, was issued to complement the Metropolitan Electric locomotive shown at (11); the items were boxed in sets from the outset. A well-lithographed representation of its prototype, it features an intriguing interior lighting system via brass roller-pickups to the track. All Metropolitan coach roofs are fitted with the knurled nut system, and this coach always retained the early, rigid, pressed bogie, although compensated bogies were fitted to other coaches. Length: 13in (33·02cm).

11 Gauge "0" Metropolitan Electric Locomotive; this item was first issued by Hornby in *c*1926 as a high-voltage model running at 110 volts AC, the controller being in series with a 60-watt lamp. This system was obviously dangerous—indeed, it is thought that the British authorities planned to legislate against it!—and a 4-volt version to work off an accumulator soon appeared, along with a clockwork version. In the 1930s the model was classified as "Series 3", and improved 6-volt and, finally, 20-volt automatic reversing versions appeared. Production ended in 1939. The all-lithographed body is a well-proportioned representation of a prototype used on London's Metropolitan Railway at the time of the Wembley Exhibition of 1926, but so far as the wheel arrangement is concerned, this model of a BO-BO electric locomotive is, in fact, an 0-4-0 disguised by a pressed skirt, making it rather unconvincing if viewed at track level. It is a most collectable item in any form. Length: 9·7in (24·765cm).

The collecting hobby may be pursued in many different ways, and some toy train collectors will choose to specialize in one aspect only of the wide range open to them. As shown here, a collection of Hornby tank wagons, with their many variations, would certainly make a good show. Generally speaking, wagons are among the easiest Hornby items to collect, although some have now achieved parity in desirability—and in value—with certain Hornby locomotives. Seen here is a good selection of tank wagons produced by Hornby from the 1920s until World War II. All the wagons shown on this spread are in Gauge "0", and all are of the same length (measured over buffers): 5·625in (14·29cm).

1 Milk Tank Wagon, "Nestlés Milk", in production from the mid-1930s until World War II. This wagon succeeded the "United Dairies" model shown at (3); both have the late-type chassis and automatic couplings, but "United Dairies" is also to be found with the early chassis and couplings, as shown at (4).

2 Bitumen Tank Wagon, "Colas", available up to World War II. The model is similar to (1), but lacks a ladder. The "Colas" wagon in red, as seen, is quite rare; the earlier blue one is more common.

3 Milk Tank Wagon, "United Dairies"; a high-quality model of the early 1930s. Dating between the earlier "United Dairies" (4) and the "Nestlés Milk" wagon (1), this is a little rarer than other

milk tank wagons; it has the late chassis and automatic couplings, and chassis and trimmings are finished in blue.

4 Milk Tank Wagon, "United Dairies"; late 1920s. This is the earlier model: note the early-type chassis with open axle-guards, link couplings, and the grey finish of chassis and trimmings. These early Hornby wagons have a higher, over-scale buffer height.

5 Petrol Tank Wagon, "Pratts"; a standard tank wagon of the early 1930s, with the later pressed chassis and automatic couplings. This is not hard to find.

6 Petrol Tank Wagon, "Esso"; an example from the late 1930s, not particularly rare, in which the nicely-detailed cast tank filler top seen on (5) and on other earlier

models on this spread has been replaced by one embossed in the tinplate dome.

7 Petrol Tank Wagon No 1, "Power Ethyl"; another late model, but one of the most attractive in the series, and not so easy to find. Note that this example is wrongly fitted with link couplings; they should be automatic.

8 Petrol Tank Wagon No 1, "Pool"; the last of the pre-War run. "Pool" petrol, replacing the familiar named brands, was introduced as a wartime measure, which suggests that production of this wagon extended into the early stages of World War II.

9 Motor Spirit Tank Wagon, "National Benzole"; one of the early series, dating from the 1920s, with the early chassis and

large-link couplings. Note that the tank ends had a considerably greater return than on later models. Not too hard to find.

10 Petrol Tank Wagon, "Redline-Glico"; one of the first austere-detail tank wagons, lacking the cast filler top, of the early 1930s. It is not hard to find; see also (18).

11 Petrol Tank Wagon, "Shell"; one of the most common tank wagons, available from the mid-1930s until World War II. This example is one of the non-buffered versions that were used in certain Hornby "M Series" sets.

12 Petrol Tank Wagon "BP". This had a long run for one of the less colourful items, and may be found with either link or automatic couplings. Good examples of this

wagon are fairly common.

13 Petrol Tank Wagon, "Pratts". A yellow-ochre finish replaced the earlier green—see (14)—in this model of the early 1930s, but the lettering layout remained almost identical. Although having the later pressed chassis, this wagon is still fitted with link couplings and probably marks the transitional period. It is less easy to find than (14).

14 Petrol Tank Wagon, "Pratts"; the earlier green version, dating from the 1920s. This wagon had a reasonably long production run and is easier to find than the later version shown at (13).

15 Oil Tank Wagon, "Mobiloil"; one of the last series, dating from 1939-40, and with the austere top. It is interesting to note

that Hornby never truly established a standard location for its own advertising rectangle. It appears on this and most other later items at one end, where it does not affect the side lettering, but on earlier models—for example, (3), (5), and (12)—its position varies. This model is not one of the easiest of the Hornby wagons for the collector to find.

16 Petrol Tank Wagon, "BP". This model of the mid-1930s retains the cast filler top into the period of the late chassis and automatic couplings; it may prove to be rather harder to find than some others in the series.

17 Oil Tank Wagon, "Castrol"; a rather poor example of a mid-1930s Hornby wagon that is still easy to find.

18 Petrol Tank Wagon, "Redline"; the predecessor of (10), dating from the early 1930s. As seen here, with automatic couplings, this wagon seems to be rather harder to find that the earlier version with open chassis and with large-link couplings.

19 Oil Tank Wagon, "Royal Daylight", dating from the later 1930s. This is one of the most common of Hornby's pre-War tank wagons: the collector should only accept a good example and should not bother with the purchase and subsequent restoration of one in poor condition.

20 Petrol Tank Wagon No 1 "Motor Spirit" ("Shell" and "BP"); one of the most attractive of the late series, this tank wagon is comparatively rare.

1 Gauge "0" E120 Special Electric 0-4-0 Locomotive and Four-Wheeled Tender, numbered "179", by Hornby, Great Britain. This No 1 Special locomotive was first available in clockwork in 1929; the electric version seen here appeared in the early 1930s, and production continued until World War II. The example shown is one of the de luxe 0-4-0s, a desirable item for Hornby collectors. It was available in the liveries of the four major British companies: the Southern Railway (SR) version shown here seems to be by far the scarcest. With apparent design affinity to the Hornby No 2 Special 4-4-0 "Yorkshire"/"Bramham Moor", this locomotive was quite highly priced: in 1937 it was catalogued at £1 7s 6d (£1.37½,

$1.65) in electric, or 15s 9d (78½p, 94c) in clockwork; the tender being 3s 3d (16p, 19c) extra in either version. The locomotive was also boxed with three four-wheeled coaches in exotic-sounding passenger sets: "Comet" for the LMS; "Queen of Scots" for the LNER; "Torbay Express" for the GWR; and "Bournemouth Belle" for the SR, as shown here (less one Pullman) at (1-3.) Length (engine and tender): 11·75in (29·845cm).
2-3 Gauge "0" No 1 Pullman Coach (2), "Cynthia", also available as "Corsair"; and Pullman Coach Composite (3), "Ansonia", also available as "Aurora". These small vehicles were issued by Hornby in sets with the No 1 Special tender-type locomotive (1). Earlier versions have opening end and

baggage doors and are fitted with link couplings. Desirable for the Hornby collector, they are not rare. Length: 6·625in (16·83cm).
4 Gauge "0" Type 101 0-4-0 Tank Locomotive, numbered "2270", by Hornby, c1954. This locomotive can only be distinguished from its pre-War counterpart by the style of its "Hornby" label (not visible here) and the size of its funnel (smaller in the pre-War version). Pre-War locomotives should also have bright-red wheels. It was made in clockwork, as seen, and electric versions and appeared in the four major liveries—the SR and GWR versions being the scarcer—and finally in British Railways (BR) black. Electric models are harder to find than clockwork ones, but none of the

series should be difficult to come by. Length: 6·5in (16·51cm).
5-6 Gauge "0" Four-Wheeled Coaches, in London and North-Western Railway (L&NWR) livery; these are early Hornby vehicles, dating from around 1924. At this time, vehicles bore no "Hornby" label; instead, the undersides are marked with the letters "MLLD" (the "D" being superimposed on the horizontal of the first "L") above the word "England"—signifying "Meccano Limited, Liverpool, England". These early items are hard to find. Length: 5·5in (13·97cm).
7 Gauge "0" No 1 0-4-0 Locomotive and Four-Wheeled Tender, numbered "2710". This clockwork model is another early Hornby item, first issued in the 1920s in a fairly plain form. The example

shown is in LMS colours; they appeared in various liveries but no SR version was made and examples in GWR or Caledonian Railway blue liveries are rarer than others. However, examples of this reasonably collectable locomotive should not be too hard to find. Length (engine and tender): 10·5in (26·67cm).

8 Gauge "O" M1 0-4-0 Locomotive and Four-Wheeled Tender, numbered "3435", made by Hornby from the early 1930s until World War II and again post-War. This little clockwork, reversing locomotive was catalogued at 4s 6d (22½p, 27c) in 1937, with the tender 9d (3½p, 4c) extra. In its red and bright-green versions it was sold in great quantity and should be easy to find. Some pre-War colours may

be more difficult to acquire, and 6-volt and 20-volt electric models are the scarcest of all. Post-War production—all clockwork, like all post-1945 Hornby Gauge "O" models—included a much-altered version in BR colours. Length (engine and tender): 9in (22·86cm).

9-10 Gauge "O" M1 Pullman Coaches, "Marjorie" (9) and "Aurelia" (10), also found as "Viking", made by Hornby from the early 1930s to complement, among other models, the M1 locomotive (8). These are among the most common Hornby coaches: they were marketed in many boxed sets and were available separately at a price, in 1937, of 1s 0d (5p, 6c) each. Length: 4·75in (12·065cm).

11 Gauge "O" E120 Special Electric 0-40 Tank Locomotive, numbered

"5500". This Hornby model was made in clockwork from 1929 until World War II, the electric version appearing in c1934. The companion to the No 1 Special Tender locomotive at (1), this was available in the four major liveries: the GWR version is shown here. This tank engine seems to be far more common than the tender variety, even in SR colours, but, as with most Hornby locomotives, electric models are far scarcer than clockwork: for every ten clockwork models, the collector may only encounter one electric specimen. In any form, it is an important addition to a Hornby collection. Length: 7·125in (18·097cm).

12-14 Gauge "O" 0-4-0 Locomotive and Four-Wheeled Tender (14), numbered "6161", with M0 Pullman

Coaches, "Joan" (12) and "Zena" (13). This little set, made in non-reversing clockwork only, was introduced by Hornby in the early 1930s and reappeared after World War II. The passenger set was priced in 1933 at 5s 9d (28½p, 34c). Unlike the post-War example seen here, the earlier locomotive had no cylinders or motion (side-rods). Pre-War versions, in which a fixed key appeared, were numbered "4472" in green or "6100" in red. Post-War versions continued into a more convincing BR passenger livery. As well as coaches, some wagons were made to complement the locomotive. Apart from the earliest versions, all components of this set are fairly easy to find. Lengths (engine and tender): 8·5in (21·59cm); (coach): 4in (10·16cm).

With the exception of (5), the Hornby locomotives shown here belong to the No 2 Special series of express passenger trains which first appeared around 1929, representing Hornby's first attempts at near-scale modelling. They are well-made and finely-proportioned representations of 4-4-0 locomotives in the liveries of the four major British railway companies of the time. They continued in production, with minor changes, until World War II, but, like most of Hornby's better Gauge "0" models, did not reappear thereafter. They were originally available in clockwork, appearing in electric versions, as shown here, from around 1934.
It should be noted that none of the locomotives shown here has the smokebox headlamp that, in the opinion of many collectors, disfigured these otherwise pleasing models in their electric versions. The locomotives were made in the style shown for one year only: sales fell, and the ugly headlamp was restored—but the locomotives remained available without headlamp to special order. Hornby No 2 Special locomotives are not too difficult for the collector to find, although they are very scarce in good condition. They were popular toys, and most surviving examples have been well "play-worn". They would grace any general collection and are a "must" for the Hornby specialist.

1 Gauge "0", Hornby No 2 Special, 4-4-0 Standard Compound Loco-motive, numbered "1185", and Six-Wheeled Tender, London, Midland & Scottish Railway (LMS); 20-volt electric. Like the other No 2 Special locomotives shown here, this model formed part of an express passenger train set—for full details of set make-up, see (4)—in this case hauling "The Yorkshireman". As is usually the case with Hornby models, the LMS version was made and sold in considerably larger numbers than its companions. Length (engine and tender): 15in (38·1cm).
2 Gauge "0" Hornby No 2 Special, 4-4-0 "County of Bedford" Locomotive, numbered "3821", and Six-Wheeled Tender, Great Western Railway (GWR); 20-volt electric. This locomotive featured in "The Bristolian" express passenger train set. Length: as (1).
3 Gauge "0", Hornby No 2 Special, 4-4-0 "L1 Class" Locomotive and Six-Wheeled Tender, numbered "1759", Southern Railway (SR); 20-volt electric. Hauling the "Folkestone Flyer" express passenger train set, this was, in terms of sales, certainly the least popular of the series—and is therefore now the scarcest and the most sought after by collectors. Length: as (1).
4 Gauge "0", Hornby No 2 Special, 4-4-0 "Bramham Moor" Locomotive, numbered "201", and Six-Wheeled Tender, London and North Eastern Railway (LNER); 20-volt electric. This model represents an up-date on "Yorkshire", the first of the No 2 Special locomotives, and it featured in the express passenger

train set named "Scarborough Flier". From the mid-1930s, the No 2 Special sets were available in either clockwork or electric. In clockwork, the No 2 Special set consisted of a reversing locomotive with tender; one No 2 Corridor Coach; one No 2 Corridor Composite Coach; twelve A2 Curved Rails, one B1 Straight Rail, and one BBR Straight Brake and Reverse Rail, making up a 5ft 4in x 4ft 6in (1·625m x 1·37m) layout. The E220 Special set in 20-volt electric consisted of an automatic reversing locomotive, with electric headlamp (not present in the examples shown; see introductory note), and tender; two No 2 Corridor Coaches; one No 2 Corridor Composite Coach; and twelve curved and two straight rails, again making up a

layout 5ft 4in x 4ft 6in (1·625m x 1·37m). Sets were priced at £2 12s 0d (£2.60, $3.12) in clockwork, or £3 12s 0d (£3.60, $4.32) in electric. The locomotives and the other set components could, of course, also be purchased as separate items: the electric locomotive, without tender, was priced at £1 17s 6d (£1.87½, $2.25); the clockwork version, without tender, at £1 7s 6d (£1.37½, $1.65); and the tender at 7s 6d (37½p, 45c) for either version. Length: 14·625in (37·15cm).

5 Gauge "0" 4-4-0 "Eton" Locomotive and Six-Wheeled Tender, numbered "900", by Hornby. This representation of a "Schools Class" locomotive of the SR does not belong to the No 2 Special series: it is classified as Series

4, of which it is the only example. Based on No 2 Special components, it is a markedly foreshortened model but is surprisingly convincing in its general proportions and is an interesting example of Hornby's approach to the upper end of its market, with a model nearer-to-prototype and of less "toy-like" quality. Note that it does not have the ugly smokebox headlamp that was fitted on most of the No 2 Special locomotives beneath the "Hornby" label—the latter visible at (1); and note also the effective use of polished brass fittings, an innovation for Hornby at this time. This model was produced only from 1937 until World War II and was available as the E420 20-volt electric model with remote

control (a control lever on the transformer allowed the train to be started, stopped, or reversed, and speed varied to suit the layout), as shown here; or as the No 4C clockwork version. It was priced at £2 2s 6d (£2.12½, ($2.55) in electric, or £1 15s 0d (£1.75, $2.10) in clockwork; the tender being 6s 0d (30p, 36c) extra for either version. Although it had only a comparatively short production run, this locomotive is not particularly rare. However, it is avidly sought after by Hornby collectors, and it will probably prove to be difficult to find a Series 4 locomotive that is in the fine condition of the example shown here. Length (engine and tender): 14·75in (37·465cm).

1-3 Gauge "00" Surburban Southern Electric Set by Triang, Great Britain; comprising R156 Suburban Motor Coach with Powered Bogie Unit (1), and R225 Dummy Suburban Motor Coach, Un-Powered (3); here seen with an additional First Class Coach (2). The two-car Southern Region set was produced in the late 1950s and is an excellent representation, in plastic, of a British commuter train. Triang trains are made by Rovex Models, Margate. The early LMS Pacifics were crude, but quality improved through the 1960s. For a time, items were produced under the Triang-Hornby name: the Hornby name prevailed, and Triang continues to produce excellent Gauge "00" models under the Hornby mark. The set shown is

keenly sought and is not easy to find. Length (each coach): 8·9375in (22·7cm).

4 Gauge "00" Tank Wagon, "Standard" and "Esso" (other side: "Standard" and "Essolub"), tinplate, by Gebrüder Märklin, (West) Germany, dating from either 1939-40 or post-War (it incorporates the automatic coupling introduced in 1939). Many items in Märklin's Gauge "00" series are mirror-images of their Gauge "0" equivalents. Note on this wagon such detail as the brake hut and ladder. Length: 3·75in (9·5cm).

5 Gauge "00" Timber Wagon with Brake Hut, tinplate, by Märklin; again with automatic coupling, dating as (4), and another most attractive continental-style wagon. Length: 3·75in (9·5cm).

6 Gauge "00" Banana Van, "Fyffes", tinplate, by Märklin; a pre-1939 item with claw-type buckeye couplings rather than the automatic couplings seen on (4) and (5). Length: 3·35in (8·5cm).

7 Gauge "00" 2-6-2 Prairie Tank Locomotive, Great Western Railway (GWR), electric, by Graham Farish, Great Britain. This maker appeared in the late 1940s and continued in production into the 1950s. The locomotive shown has a diecast body and metal-rimmed plastic wheels: plastics were used more extensively in other Graham Farish locomotives, which included a Western Region "King Class", Southern Region "West Country" and "Merchant Navy" types, and a Midland Region "Class 5". These models were much inferior to their

Hornby counterparts, although their two-rail electric operation looked vastly better than Hornby's printed-tin track. The wheels were inferior to Hornby castings, permitting no daylight to be seen between the spokes. The locomotives suffered from mechanical defects and, structurally, from warping mazac (zinc alloy). Tender locomotives were motorised in the tender, with a universal coupling to the locomotive gearing. The firm also produced some plastic-bodied Pullman Cars with diecast floors and interiors: these were good models—but the plastic had a tendency to "banana" and the castings were subject to fatigue. Certain Graham Farish items, especially those in Southern Region colours, are now quite

eagerly sought by collectors.
Length: 6·5in (16·51cm).
8 Gauge "00" "Mitropa" Sleeping
Car by Märklin, dating from the
mid-1930s; one of Märklin's earlier
series in this scale, produced
until World War II and, unlike the
nearer-scale vehicles at (11-12),
painted, lined, and transferred.
The attractive little vehicles were
made in many non-German liveries,
including British ones, and are
quite collectable items. Length:
6·9in (17·5cm).
9 Gauge "00" Pullman Coach with
Lights by Trix Twin, Great Britain.
Produced immediately before World
War II and again from the later
1940s, this was one of Trix's
better-looking passenger vehicles
and, like most Trix vehicles, was
lithographed by Winteringham.

Length: 8·75in (22·22cm).
10 Gauge "00" Southern Railway
Passenger Coach by Trix Twin.
Again lithographed by Winteringham,
this example has hook-and-loop
couplings that date it from pre-
1940; the model was reissued
post-War—see (14-15). These short
vehicles were made to complement
Trix's 0-4-0 locomotives; rather
unattractive models, they are
sought only by Trix enthusiasts.
Length: 7in (17·78cm).
11-12 Gauge "00" "Wagons-Lits"
Dining Car (11) and Sleeping Car
(12) by Märklin. These are the
maker's better-length vehicles of
the late 1930s, with a high
standard of detail and convincingly
lithographed in a famous livery.
Many collectors concentrate entirely
on Märklin's Gauge "00" models.

Length: 8·86in (22·5cm).
13 Gauge "00" 4-4-0 Standard LMS
Compound Locomotive, numbered
"1168", and Six-Wheeled Tender,
electric, by Trix Twin. This is a
pre-War specimen of a model that
appeared in the late 1930s and was
reissued after World War II, lasting
into the British Railways period.
Disproportionate in comparison with
its Hornby Dublo equivalents,
this 4-4-0 series included an
LNER "Hunt Class" and an SR
"Schools Class". Trix models are
increasingly collected, but their
appeal is limited. Length (engine
and tender): 8·5in (21·59cm).
14-15 Gauge "00" LMS Passenger
Coaches by Trix Twin; post-War
examples of the short coach at (10),
seen here in different livery.
Length: 7in (17·78cm).

16-20 Gauge "00" "Table Top" 2-4-0
Tank Locomotive (16) by Gebrüder
Bing, Germany; shown with a train
of which (17) may not be by Bing;
(18) and (19) are Bing GWR coaches;
and (20) is a Bing LNER coach. All
these items are a little shabby
but could be restored; this would
be well worthwhile, as Bing "Table
Top Railways", dating from the
mid-1920s to the early 1930s, are
now quite collectable. The
locomotives were made in
clockwork, as shown, or electric.
Lengths (locomotive): 3·75in
(9·5cm); (coach): 3·25in (8·25cm).
21 Gauge "00" Caboose by Trix Twin,
Great Britain, c1953. This is a
more than usually interesting Trix
item, since it depicts one of the
caboose cars so popular with US
collectors. Length: 4·5in (11·43cm).

SPARE PARTS FOR BOWMAN LOCOS, 300 & 265

REPAIRS.

BOWMAN MODELS.
DEREHAM, NORFOLK.

1 Gauge "0" Four-Wheeled Tank Locomotive, Model "300" and numbered thus, made by Bowman, Norwich, Great Britain. All sizes of the Gauge "0" steam trains made by Bowman from the 1920s until production ended in the late 1930s are shown on this spread. In London and North Eastern Railway (LNER) livery—it was also available in London, Midland & Scottish (LMS) colours—this locomotive is fitted with oscillating cylinders, a safety-valve, and a water-level cock on the firebox. It is shown in its original wooden box—which bears the pencilled price "21/-" (£1 1s 0d, £1.05, $1.26)—with its instruction leaflet. Length: 8·5in (21·59cm). As is apparent from this and the other Bowman

items shown, these locomotives, although excellent runners, tend to be of clumsy appearance and generally over-scale. The firm was originally known for its stationary steam engines made to drive Meccano models, and also produced a popular series of wooden-hulled steamboats.

2 Gauge "0" 4-4-2 Locomotive and Six-Wheeled Tender, numbered "4472", by Bowman; supposedly a representation of the "Flying Scotsman", in LNER livery and bearing that famous locomotive's number—but there the resemblance ends! A massive and unwieldy spirit-fired steam model, it is nevertheless a splendid performer: it was introduced in 1927 at the British Industries Fair, London, where, according

to Bowman's publicitiy, it ran continuously for 187 *real* miles (300km) hauling six tinplate coaches. The copper steam-pipe leading to the cylinders, and the typical Bowman safety-valve, used on all the maker's models, are seen to advantage in the photograph. For some reason, possibly to make them appear to be cheaper, engine and tender were sold in separate boxes, priced at £1 7s 6d (£1.37½, $1.65) and 7s 6d (37½p, 45c) respectively. Length (engine and tender): 19·25in (48·89cm).

3 Gauge "0" 0-6-0 Tank Locomotive (a type popularly known as a "Jinty"), numbered "489" and in Great Western Railway (GWR) livery, by Archangel Models, Great Britain. This model of a

locomotive of c1900 dates from the mid-1970s and its maker is still in production. The well-proportioned locomotive is fitted with a twin-burner spirit lamp, has an inside cylinder with displacement lubrication, and features slip-eccentric reversing. Note the large throttle handle at the rear of the cab. Its small, turned cast-iron wheels—the central pair unflanged to enable it to negotiate sharp curves—give it excellent pulling power: it will run for 15-20 minutes with a train of up to six bogie coaches or 12 goods wagons. Length: 9·5in (24·13cm).

4 Gauge "0" 4-4-0 Locomotive and Six-Wheeled Tender, numbered "6285", made by Winteringham, Bassett-Lowke's Northampton-

based subsidiary. This model, made in steam only, was called "Enterprise" by Bassett-Lowke and first appeared in the late 1920s: it was later available in kit form, as well as ready-made, and remained in the Catalogue until the 1960s. It is equipped with displacement lubrication; ie, water pressure in the boiler is utilized, via a tube, to force oil into the cylinders. It has piston-valve cylinders and is, in the opinion of the author, who has run this example regularly for some 20 years, the most efficient Gauge "0" locomotive ever made commercially in respect of power and long-running: it will haul six tinplate bogie coaches for 45 minutes on a single filling. Length (engine and

tender): 18in (45·72cm). Note the the number of the tender refers not to a real locomotive but, in fact, to the telephone number at the time of production of Bassett-Lowke's shop in High Holborn, London!

5 Gauge "0" Four-Wheeled Locomotive in LNER livery by Bowman, the smallest of the firm's range, only 7in (17·78cm) long. With a single oscillating cylinder in the cab, it is in spite of its diminutive size a fairly efficient runner, travelling for 10-12 minutes on a single filling. It was sold in a wooden box (like all Bowman models), complete with filling funnel, lubricating oil, and instruction leaflet, at a price of 10s 6d (52½p, 63c) in the late 1920s-1930s.

6 Gauge "0" 0-4-0 Locomotive and Six-Wheeled Tender by Bassett-Lowke: a model with a pronounced Carette appearance and, in fact, made for Bassett-Lowke in Northampton in the 1920s from pressings acquired from Germany after the French-owned, Nuremburg-based firm of Carette went out of business during World War I. Produced also in Gauge "1", and in steam only, it was available in the liveries of the Midland Railway, as shown, GWR, L&NWR, and Caledonian Railway (blue). It has a vaporising spirit lamp, piston-valve cylinders, displacement lubrication, and unusually for Bassett-Lowke at this time, slip-eccentric reversing. Length (engine

and tender): 13in (33·02cm).
7 Gauge "0" 0-4-0 Tank Locomotive, numbered "265" and in LNER livery, by Bowman. The over-scale character of Bowman's models is particularly evident here: with a length of 11in (27·94cm) and a maximum height of nearly 5in (12·7cm), this model is virtually in 9mm scale, rather than the 7mm scale normal for Gauge "0". Aesthetically, Bowman's locomotives have little to offer, but they were nevertheless very popular with collectors in the 1970s, when prices rocketed. They are presently out of fashion (although, in the author's opinion, only temporarily) and the would-be collector should hesitate before paying excessive sums for these items.

1 Gauge "0" 2-6-2 Suburban Tank Locomotive, Great Western Railway (GWR), numbered "6105"; available from Bassett-Lowke from the late 1930s until World War II. This model, almost entirely handmade and well-proportioned although plain, was made in 8-10 volt DC, 20-volt AC, and clockwork, and incorporates such distinctive features as a brass safety-valve casing and a copper chimney-top. In these models, sheet-steel was soft-soldered with the use of an acid flux, and it may be found that, because of insufficient cleaning at the time of manufacture, "bubbling" has occurred on the paintwork in areas of complex detail. Although this sign of rusting can look unpleasant,

especially on the underside or interior, there is no need to fear further corrosion provided the model is kept in a dry place. If the condition is very bad, however, it is advisable to take steps to neutralize or cover it. This is quite a rare model. Length: 11·375in (28·89cm).

2 Gauge "0" 4-6-0 "Royal Scot" Locomotive, numbered "6100", and Six-Wheeled Tender, London, Midland & Scottish Railway (LMS). This 12-volt electric model dating from c1937 is the final version of Bassett-Lowke's standard tinplate lithographed model, now slightly improved, hand-painted, fitted with smoke deflectors, and with a new Stanier-type high-sided tender. Both lithographed and hand-painted versions are

not too hard to find; the former seem to manifest a considerable range of LMS reds, from a rather garish bright shade to a near-correct crimson. Available in electric or clockwork, it reappeared after World War II in clockwork only and in a black, red-lined LMS livery. Later, Bassett-Lowke totally altered the model, introducing a taper-boiler and firebox and a new front end. Length (engine and tender): 18·375in (46·67cm).

3 Gauge "0" 4-4-0 LMS Standard Compound Locomotive, numbered "1063", and Six-Wheeled Tender. This model was available from the early 1930s in clockwork or electric: the one shown is an electric version, entirely lithographed, dating from c1949.

This Bassett-Lowke model was a good representation of its prototype, but post-War versions are generally of a much better colour than pre-War examples. However, a run of post-War lithographed models (not including the example shown) appeared in a totally spurious brown livery. Bassett-Lowke Compounds are by no means rare. Length (engine and tender): 15·75in (40·005cm).

4 Gauge "0" 2-6-4 LMS Standard Tank Locomotive, numbered "2603". This Bassett-Lowke model was available in electric or clockwork from the late 1903s, succeeding a rarer Märklin-bodied counterpart —see note at (6). The example shown is an electric version dating from c1949: it is

Right: *The close-up front view of the Märklin-bodied Bassett-Lowke 5XP-Type "Newfoundland" locomotive at (6) shows how the polished smokebox hinges contribute to the effect of this excellent model. Note that the buffer-beam on the Märklin-bodied locomotive does not feature Bassett-Lowke's usual ugly coupling and slot.*

interesting to note that the price rose from around £9 0s 0d (£9.00, $10.80) pre-War to £23 6s 0d (£23.30, $27.96) in 1949, and to more than £60 0s 0d (£60.00, $72.00) in the 1960s. Length: 12·75in (32·385cm).

5 Gauge "0" 4-6-0 "Arsenal" Locomotive, numbered "2848", and Six-Wheeled Tender, London and North Eastern Railway (LNER), available in electric, as shown, or clockwork, from the mid-1930s until World War II. This most convincing model by Bassett-Lowke of a "Sandringham"-type locomotive of the Eastern Region of the LNER is one of the "Football" series: another of the models was named "Huddersfield Town", and the non-football choice "Melton Hall" also appeared.

Probably not many were made — and surviving examples tend to be in truly terrible condition. The example shown has been restored professionally by its present owner from a poor state. With shabby or poorly-repainted models, there is little alternative other than to strip and repaint, although it is sometimes possible to retrieve and restore the original paintwork. Collectors differ on this subject: some advocate no restoration, but this seems unacceptable in the case of badly chipped paintwork, lettering rubbed away, visible areas of rust, soldered seams split, dents, or badly enamel-painted patches. How does restoration affect value? For an unrestored model, we may say that

if the mint original is worth 100 per cent, a slightly used example may be worth 70 per cent; a shabby one, 50 per cent or less; and a really bad example around 25 per cent. A professionally-restored model, capturing fully the style and finish of the maker's original, should fall into, or even above, the 70 per cent bracket. This is a rule-of-thumb: there will be many exceptions in the areas both of steam and of very rare models. The locomotive shown here is avidly sought by collectors. Length (engine and tender): 17·25in (43·815cm).

6 Gauge "0" 4-6-0 "Newfoundland" 5XP-Type Locomotive, numbered "5573", and Six-Wheeled Tender, LMS, electric. Around the mid-

1930s, Bassett-Lowke engaged Märklin to produce the upper bodywork for certain runs of its more expensive models: a GWR "King", an SR "Schools", an LMS Tank Locomotive — see note at (4), and the 5XP-Type seen here. Most 5XPs were not named, but "Newfoundland" was added in accordance with LMS practice, and a black "Silver Jubilee" also appeared. All the Märklin-bodied models are very highly valued and rare, and the example shown is likely to be one of the more difficult to acquire. Bassett-Lowke's British-made versions of a later period, named "Conqueror" and then "Victory", are likely to be easier to find. Length (engine and tender): 18·25in (46·355cm).

All the trains shown on this spread were photographed at the London Toy and Model Museum, October House, 21/23 Craven Hill, London W2.

1-3 Cast-Iron Floor Train by a American toymaker, dating from around 1880. This is, of course, very much an "odd one out" on this spread, but it is interesting to study this early item in contrast to the much later trains by American makers also shown here. It is possible that this train was made by the Kenton Hardware Company, Kenton, Ohio, a noted maker of cast-iron toys, but precise identification of these unpowered, pull/push-along toys in a material so favoured by American toymakers is difficult, since they were extremely

popular during the later 19th century and were produced by many makers throughout the United States, few of them bearing any manufacturer's mark. The train shown here, made in a scale slightly smaller than Gauge "1", is headed by a 4-4-0 Baldwin "Wild West"-type Locomotive (3), with a Four-Wheeled Tender, hauling two eight-wheeled cars: a Parlour Car (2) and a Combine (Brake End) (3), both of which are attractively embossed "Chicago, Rock Island and Pacific Railroad Co". This is a rare item. Lengths (locomotive and tender): 14in (35·56cm); (each car): 12in (30·48cm).
4-6 Gauge "0" "English Flyer" Clockwork Train Set, made for the British market by American Flyer, USA, and dating from around

1925. This is an unusual and somewhat rare item, since it apparently represents an isolated attempt by American Flyer to break into the British market then dominated by Bing/Bassett-Lowke and Hornby. The small four-wheeled Locomotive (6) is made of cast-iron; the four-wheeled Tender numbered "No.120", the Passenger Coach (5), and the Mail Van (4), are all in lithographed tinplate. All the items are in the livery of the Great Northern Railway (GNR), and the legend "English Flyer" appears on the carriage ends and on the buffer beam of the locomotive. Note, however, that no buffers are fitted to any of the items in the set. This simple clockwork train, which was marketed as a boxed set complete with a circle of tinplate track,

resembles the category of cheaper toy trains that were produced at this time by British and other makers in competition with Hornby. These are generally of less appeal to the collector than Hornby items—although this particular set, as noted above, is both interesting and unusual and would be well worth having. Cheaper sets in this category were produced in Great Britain by Chad Valley, Mettoy and other makers. Length (train overall): 21in (53·34cm).
7-10 Gauge "00" Electric Train Set by the Lionel Corporation, New York, USA. This item illustrates a most interesting, and short-lived, development: Lionel's venture into Gauge "00". Lionel trains in this gauge—built to "00" scale but running on track of 19mm (0·75in)

gauge — appeared in the late 1930s and early 1940s but, unfortunately, did not reappear after World War II, although Lionel then became busy on the Gauge "H0" scene, working in that field in conjunction with Rivarossi from 1959 (the year in which Lionel became part of the Roy M. Cohn Group, continuing production thereafter as The Lionel Toy Corporation). The attractive and well-detailed diecast train shown here is headed by a 4-6-4 Hudson Locomotive, numbered "5432", and Twelve-Wheeled Tender (10), finished for the New York Central Railroad. This model was inspired by Lionel's famous, earlier fine-scale Hudson locomotive in Gauge "0". It was made in Gauge "00", to a scale of 4mm, in 1938, when it was fitted for three-rail

electric traction (as in the example shown). From 1939 until 1942, when production ceased following the entry of the United States into World War II, it was issued with a two-rail pickup: The train it is here shown hauling consists of a High-Sided Gondola (9) of the Southern Pacific Lines; a Box Car (8), "Lionel Lines"; and a Caboose (7), of the Pennsylvania Railroad. The Hudson, the premier locomotive used on the New York-Chicago run, occupies about the same place in the affections of American railway buffs as, say, the "Flying Scotsman" does in those of British railway enthusiasts. Many manufacturers produced models of this locomotive, the largest probably being the "2½in" Gauge non-motorised version by Gilbert,

USA. In the smaller scales, probably the most sought-after and valuable Hudson is that made in Gauge "0" by Märklin, Germany, in the late 1930s, although Märklin's version has few pretensions towards scale. In Gauge "H0", models were produced by Graham Farish, Great Britain, probably in an attempt to break into the American market, and by Rivarossi, Italy, the latter being a very fine streamlined model. Length (train overall): 33in (83·82cm).

11-12 Gauge "0" Twin-Unit Diesel Locomotive of the Western Pacific Railroad, by Lionel, maker's catalogue number 2355A, dating from 1953. It is modelled on an "F3 Type" Diesel locomotive and is fitted with "Magnatraction", a magnetic device patented by Lionel that was

designed to provide for greater rail adhesion, and thus give increased hauling capability. Although it is a fairly late item, fitted for three-rail electric operation, this Lionel model, constructed mainly of diecast alloy, is nicely detailed and well finished. Length (overall): 26in (66·04cm).

13-16 Gauge "0" "Lionel Lines" "Streamliner" (thus catalogued by the maker, and numbered "1700"; but sometimes known as the "Burlington Zephyr"), made by Lionel in 1935-37. Lionel's version of the streamline diesel train as a four-car articulated unit is in aluminized tinplate finish. It is fitted for three-rail electric operation. Such sets are quite hard to find outside the USA. Length (train overall): 40in (101·6cm).

All the trains shown on this spread were photographed at the London Toy and Model Museum, October House, 21/23 Craven Hill, London W2.

1 and **7** "Standard Gauge" Electric Locomotive (1), maker's number 402E, and Combine Pullman Car (7), by Lionel, USA, dating from around 1920. A familiar item to all collectors of American trains, this massive locomotive in the maker's Standard Gauge, of 2·125in (54mm) measured between the rails, is made of tinplate. It is on twin trucks (bogies), one of which is powered for a three-rail pickup. Although it is not apparent in the example shown here, this model is usually to be found lettered "N.Y.C.

Lines' (New York Central), although neither the locomotive nor the Pullman car is in that railway's colours. The strangely unorthodox livery is believed to have resulted from Lionel's employment of an Italian designer who apparently knew a great deal about Italian railways but little of American lines! Nevertheless, both locomotive and Pullman car are by no means unattractive items and they are eagerly sought after by American collectors in particular. In Great Britain, too, interest in Lionel's models is increasing and there are now, to the author's knowledge, several British enthusiasts who collect and run Lionel trains. Lengths (locomotive): 16·5in (41·91cm); (Pullman car): 18in (45·72cm).

2-3 "Standard Gauge" Four-Wheeled Electric Locomotive (3) and Twin-Truck Pullman Car (2), "Pleasant View", numbered "790", by Dorfan, USA, dating from 1926. The locomotive is of diecast zinc alloy; the Pullman car is tinplate. The Dorfan company was founded in Newark, New Jersey, in the early 1920s by the Forchheimer Brothers, formerly of the Kraus Toy Factory, Nuremburg, Germany. The Forchheimers brought with them to the United States John Koerber, formerly a craftsman with Gebrüder Bing. Dorfan initially made electric trains in Gauge "0", and from 1926 in Standard Gauge, the latter items by Dorfan's newly-developed process of pressure diecasting in zinc alloy. The method of construc-

tion of this toy is, therefore, of interest. The locomotive body was cast in two halves, each shell containing all the necessary axle bearings, lugs and fittings to accommodate the electric motor and wheel assembly. This was simply inserted into one half, which was then firmly pressed into conjunction with the other half, making a tight fit that required no nuts or bolts to secure it. An interesting refinement in Dorfan locomotives was the use of ball bearings on the motor drive and as axle bearings. Dorfan was a victim of the Depression, and although production continued into the 1930s it then consisted only of cheap toy trains in Gauge "0", none of the attractive Standard Gauge items reappearing.

The underside of the Pullman car seen here bears the label: "Dorfan Co, Newark, New Jersey"; it is, however, possible that this pleasing vehicle may have been made for Dorfan by Kraus in Nuremburg. Lengths (locomotive): 12in (30.48cm); (Pullman car): 13.5in (34.29cm).

4 Gauge "0" Buffet Car, numbered "No.130", 'The Ives Railway Lines"; this car forms part of the Ives train shown at (5-6). It may be noted here that Ives was an early entrant into the Gauge "0" scene in the United States and was very successful in the earlier years of this gauge. However, when Lionel concentrated its efforts on Standard Gauge, Ives chose to put emphasis on Gauge "1". The company only entered the Standard

Gauge market at a later date, around 1921, when it was more or less forced to do so by the market pressure exerted by Lionel, American Flyer, and Dorfan. The Ives company suffered badly during the market slump of 1929 and these problems resulted in its takeover by its major competitors, Lionel, Hafner, and American Flyer. Lionel alone continued to produce Ives models—as Lionel-Ives, at Irvington, New Jersey—in 1931-32, but in the latter year the famous name of Ives vanished from the market. Length: 9in (22.86cm).

5-6 Gauge "0" Four-Wheeled Electric Locomotive (6), numbered "3258", and Parlour Car (5), "Saratoga", numbered "No.129"; with the Buffet Car shown at (4), these items make up an electric

train set made by Ives, Bridgeport, Conn., USA, and dating from around 1912. The locomotive, lettered "The Ives Railway Lines" and "NYC & HR" (New York Central & Hudson Railroad), is constructed chiefly of cast-iron and, despite its four-wheel arrangement, is not unlike its prototype. The parlour car and buffet car are both in printed tinplate. It is interesting to note that this locomotive was available also in clockwork, a feature unique to Ives among American makers of toy trains at that time. Lengths (locomotive): 8.5in (21.59cm); (each car): 9in (22.86cm).

7 "Standard Gauge" Combine Pullman Car by Lionel; see note at (1), above, for details.

8 Floor Toy Train, probably dating from the mid-1950s and by

a maker of unknown nationality identified only as "Zak". Something of a mystery item, this appears at first glance to be an attractive and well-proportioned Gauge "0" train. It is, indeed an attractive and well-made toy of pleasing proportions—but it is actually a friction-powered floor toy, made of tinplate and with rubber wheels. It represents the Union Pacific Railroad's famous "Flying Yankee" as a twin articulated unit and is lettered "Union Pacific" and "New York-S.Francisco". The ends of the units bear the maker's mark "Zak", which will probably mean as little to other collectors of railway toys as it does to the present author. It is, possibly, a Japanese-made item. Length (overall): 23in (58.42cm).

Gauge "O" Trains by Lionel, USA, 1930-1940

1 Gauge "O" Caboose, Maker's Catalogue Number 657 (all Lionel items display a serial number, visible on the side of this vehicle), by The Lionel Corporation, New York, USA, dating from the 1930s. Note also the "Lionel Lines" plaque on this eight-wheeled (two bogies) caboose. Throughout the 1930s and early 1940s, and again after World War II, Lionel produced a wide range of very robustly built rolling stock in pressed steel, both in Gauge "O" and in the much larger "Standard Gauge". Although perhaps not as attractive in appearance as some of their European-made contemporaries, these are well-made vehicles, incorporating brass trimmings and such detail as brake handles, axle boxes, end ladders,

pressed rivets, and the like. It is interesting to note that exported items sold at comparatively high prices in Great Britain: the caboose shown here was priced at 10s 0d (50p, 60c) in the late 1930s. Most of these vehicles, including the later, better-proportioned, plastic-bodied examples, are sought by Lionel collectors, particularly in the USA. Length: 6·75in (17·145cm).
2 Gauge "O" Flat Car (Lumber Wagon), Catalogue No 651, by Lionel, 1930s. The eight-wheeled (two bogies) wagon is loaded with lumber that may be removed and replaced with other freight. Lumber wagons of this type, and shorter four-wheeled versions, were boxed in some of Lionel's smaller freight train sets. These wagons are very easy

for the collector to find, even outside the USA. The wagon shown was priced at 9s 6d (47½p, 57c) in Britain in 1940; a major British retailer was Gamage's, London, and many veteran British collectors will remember with affection that store's famous operating Lionel railway. Length: 6·75in (17.145cm).
3 Gauge "O" 2-4-2 Locomotive and Twelve-Wheeled Oil Tender, Catalogue No 255E, by Lionel. Produced throughout the 1930s, and electric-powered like all Lionel locomotives, this is one of the maker's de luxe models: extremely strongly built, comparatively well proportioned, and of truly impressive appearance. It is fitted with an operating headlamp and illuminated firebox, and, on the example shown, a whistle mechanism in the tender

(although according to Lionel's Catalogue, model 255E had no whistle; No 255W being thus equipped). These models incorporated a large amount of mazac (zinc alloy): this material in its pre-War form was liable to fatigue, and some of these fine locomotives will now be found with areas warped, cracked, or missing. However, many replacement parts are available in the USA, and these splendid machines are eagerly collected items. Length (engine and tender): 19in (48·26cm).
4 Gauge "O" Remote Control Streamline Outfit (less one unit; see below), Catalogue No 751E, by Lionel, 1930s. Based on the famous "City of Portland" of the Union Pacific Railroad, this finely-made pressed steel and diecast set

is perhaps one of Lionel's most convincing models, faithfully reproducing the detail of the prototype. It incorporates illuminated cars, coloured tail warning lights, and a remote-controlled whistle mechanism. Ingenious snap-fix articulated joints make the units easily detachable—and the tail car has been omitted from this photograph for reasons of space. The remote-controlled 20-volt front unit is only just powerful enough to pull the heavy train from rest—but once it is really rolling, its performance is truly impressive. A silver-coloured version was also produced. The whole of the front end, rear end, and floors of the train are largely of mazac construction and are subject to

fatigue, but in good structural condition these sets are highly desirable and are quite rare, especially outside the USA. Length (as shown): 46in (116·84cm).

5 Gauge "0" Super Detail Scale Model "Hudson", numbered "5344", and Twelve-Wheeled Tender, Catalogue No 700E, by Lionel, 1930s. This is one of the most important items for the Lionel collector: a truly magnificent model of a 4-6-4 locomotive of the New York Central Railroad, the engine is fitted with a working headlamp, illuminated firebox, and operating tender whistle. The 15-volt AC motor and the gearing are of exceptionally high quality, giving a marvellous performance. Lionel used an all-diecast set of components on this model, so the first consideration

for any collector is to check the condition of all cast parts. Fatigue, and missing pieces, are all too common; but spares are available. The example shown, although an excellent one, displays signs of fatigue on the smokebox door, as well as lacking the boiler-mounted hooter and the coal deck on the tender. Beautifully-made cars were issued to run with this locomotive, thus making up the Lionel "Rail Chief", and it was also later produced in a slightly cheaper version. A Gauge "00" version was also made: the only locomotive in that gauge made by Lionel in the 1930s. Number 700E "Hudsons" are very rare and consequently are extremely valuable items. Length (engine and tender): 23·5in (59·69cm).

6 Gauge "0" Illuminated Observation Car, Catalogue No 614, by Lionel, dating from around 1940. Like the maker's freight rolling stock—see (1)—Lionel passenger cars, usually finished in red or blue, were made of pressed steel and appeared in both Gauge "0" and the larger "Standard Gauge". The range included Pullman Cars and Baggage Vans. Lionel passenger vehicles of the type shown here are distinctly under-length, although they present an acceptable appearance when running with the shorter electric- or steam-outline locomotives. None of the shorter-length vehicles is scarce, but some of the larger, de luxe passenger vehicles are highly-prized collector's items. Length: 10·5in (26·67cm).

All the trains and accessories shown on this spread were photographed at the London Toy and Model Museum, October House, 21/23 Craven Hill, London W2.

Toy train collectors of a purist turn of mind may be moved to protest that two of the items shown on this spread—the "Easter Bunny Express" by Marx (5), and the "Donald Duck Hand Car" by Lionel (6)—are not trains at all, but rather mechanical novelty toys. To which objection, the author makes reply that both these items were supplied with tinplate track and were fitted with flanged wheels to run on it: they are trains—of a sort!—and it would be a pity if a book devoted to all kinds of toy trains could not find room for

such attractive and amusing (and very collectable) oddities. Nevertheless, it must be admitted that their appeal is likely to be to the collector of tinplate toys in general, rather than to the dedicated railway enthusiast.

1 Standard Gauge "Lionel Corporation" Power House, made by The Lionel Corporation, New York, USA, and believed to date from around 1926. This nicely-proportioned tinplate building is intended realistically to accommodate the transformer used to supply electric power to a Lionel Standard Gauge railway layout. It is interesting to compare this item with the similar approach to such an invaluable accessory adopted by Jep, France; see (1),

pages 214-215. This is obviously a most desirable item for any collector who wishes to run Lionel trains. Dimensions of base: 10in x 9in (25·4cm x 22·86cm).
2 Standard Gauge "Lionel Flagman", made by Lionel at around the same time as the "Power House" at (1), in the mid-1920s. The tinplate warning sign is lettered "Railroad Crossing/Look Out for the Locomotive", and the arm of the tinplate flagman is articulated. Maximum height of sign: 7in (17·78cm).
3 "Railway Crossing" Post, made by American Flyer, USA (lettered on its cross-arm "American Flyer R.R."), and dating from around 1920. This tinplate accessory is suitable for use with Standard Gauge layouts. Height: 6·75in (17·145cm).

4 Standard Gauge "Railway Crossing" Post, by Lionel, dating from the mid-1920s. This tinplate accessory, rather more elaborate than the American Flyer version at (3), is electrically wired to display a green or a red light, and bears the legend: "Stop on Red Signal". Height: 6·5in (16·51cm).
5 "Easter Bunny Express", made by the Louis Marx company, New York, USA, in 1936. This novelty train in brightly-lithographed tinplate was made only for sale at Easter 1936: the Bunny and its four open wagons, each marked "Bunny Express" and bearing a design of Easter chicks, were marketed as a boxed set complete with an oval of tinplate track (note the flanged wheels). The wagons, it may be noted, are of a suitable shape to

3

4

5

6

7

carry a freight of chocolate eggs! The Bunny itself is clockwork-driven, with a fixed key protruding from its side. The example shown is a complete set—and is believed to be the only complete specimen yet located. It will be appreciated, therefore, that the "Bunny Express" is an extremely rare item and very desirable. The Marx company, founded in 1920, had become one of the largest toy companies in the world by the 1930s, when a British subsidiary was also in production; see (7). Marx is especially known to collectors for tinplate novelty toys and clockwork trains of the cheaper kind. Overall length of "Bunny Express": 30in (76·2cm).

6 Gauge "0" "Donald Duck Hand Car", made by Lionel, in association with the Walt Disney

organization, in 1936-37: the red label above the winding aperture on the kennel side proclaims: "Donald Duck Hand Car/Walt Disney (copyright mark)/Lionel Corporation of America". This amusing clockwork-driven novelty toy in tinplate, showing Pluto pointing the way from his kennel while Donald Duck steers the car, may seem to represent a rather curious departure for a "serious" model railway maker like Lionel; however, such is the appeal of Walt Disney's characters— which have continued to feature in popular toys up to the present day—that the success of this item was most welcome to Lionel at a time when the sales of conventional toy trains were sagging. The car has flanged

wheels and was marketed complete with a circle of Gauge "0" tinplate track. This toy is quite rare and is much desired by collectors, particularly in the United States. Length: 11in (27·94cm).

7 Gauge "0" "Silver Jubilee" Clockwork Train Set, made by Marx, Great Britain, and dating from around 1936. This streamlined "LNER" (London and North Eastern Railway) engine with its articulated "Pullman Streamline" "Coach" and "Coach Buffet" was brought out by the British subsidiary of the Marx company of New York, USA, at a time when Sir Nigel Gresley's striking all-silver express locomotive "Silver Link", hauling the all-streamlined train designed to mark the Silver Jubilee

of King George V and Queen Mary in 1935, had captured the public imagination and was very much in the news. The toy train is of the cheaper variety generally associated with this maker and, like Marx's products in the USA, was chiefly marketed through the cheaper chain-stores, but it is nevertheless a rather attractive item and is certainly most evocative of its period. It was produced also in green livery, and in blue livery with the lettering "LMS" (London, Midland & Scottish Railway). It is interesting to note the strong American influence apparent in the design and finish of the Pullman units, which are in a style more reminiscent of the New York Central Railroad than of the LNER! Length overall: 32in (81·28cm).

1-3 Gauge "00" EDP2 Passenger Electric Train Set, London, Midland & Scottish Railway (LMS). The example shown dates from 1951; the set was first catalogued in 1939 but was not in fact issued until after World War II. It represents a really magnificent attempt by Hornby Dublo at true scale modelling. The diecast 4-6-2 locomotive, numbered "6231", is a faithful representation of a "Duchess Class" then in use by the LMS, with a most comprehensive set of Walschaerts valve gear. This example is named "Duchess of Atholl". The six-wheeled tender has a diecast chassis, tinplate upper half, and plastic coal deck. The bogie coaches also represented a great advance for Hornby Dublo, since although

lithographed they have transparent windows and are fitted with side corridors. Although most collectable when boxed in fine condition, these sets are by no means rare. Lengths (engine and tender): 12in (30·48cm); (coach): 9·0625in (23·02cm).
4 Gauge "00" Southern Railway (SR) Brake Van, c1950. Based on a pre-War model, this is rarer than most Hornby Dublo brake vans. The main difference between pre- and post-War examples is that on the later versions a type of half-buckeye automatic coupling was fitted, whereas a strange, flat, horizontal-sprung device coupled pre-War models. Length: 4·3125in (10·95cm).
5 Gauge "00" High Capacity Brick Wagon. In both pre- and early

post-War versions this was lettered "NE", but it is more often found with the British Railways (BR) prefix "E" only. It is easy to find. Length: 5·75in (14·6cm).
6 Gauge "00" Hornby Dublo EDLT20 "Bristol Castle" Locomotive, numbered "7013", and Six-Wheeled Tender, in BR (Western Region) livery. This model was announced at Christmas 1957, the first addition to the range for some time. Unlike other Hornby Dublo tender locomotives, it has an all-diecast tender, joined to the locomotive by a drawbar. Centre-rail current collectors are fitted beneath the tender. With a new electric motor that had to fit into a reduced space, these locomotives were somewhat underpowered, but later "Castles" had an improved

ring-field motor which extended well into the cab. In the main, the "Castles" are easy to find in three-rail or later two-rail versions. Length (engine and tender): 10·25in (26·035cm).
7 Gauge "00" D20 Composite Restaurant Car. Following soon after (6), this may be found in Western Region chocolate-and-cream or standard BR plum-and-cream. It has a quite convincing interior. These vehicles are easy to find. Length: 9·0625in (23·02cm).
8 Gauge "00" D21 Corridor Coach, Brake Second. Lithographed in Western Region colours for "The Bristolian" train sets, this was made to complement (6) and was a re-lithograph of an LMS item—see (3). It is easy to find. Length: 9·0625in (23·02cm).

9 Gauge "00" 0-6-2 Tank Locomotive, numbered "6699", Great Western Railway (GWR), electric; an item of 1950, from boxed set EDG7, in which the wagons at (10) and (18) also featured. It was made in large numbers both pre- and post-War (available also in clockwork in the former case) in all four major liveries. The GWR and SR versions are the rarer, and clockwork versions in any livery are scarce. Length: 5·5in (13·97cm).

10 Gauge "00" D1 Open Wagon, GWR; an early model, made in great quantity and boxed in most Hornby Dublo freight sets. Length: 3·5in (8·89cm).

11 Gauge "00" D1 Meat Van; a post-War version of an SR vehicle produced pre-War and with a short post-War run. Like many SR items, it is comparatively scarce. Length: 3·5in (8·89cm).

12 Gauge "00" D1 Cattle Truck, GWR; produced both pre- and post-War. In this instance, the LMS version seems hardest to find. Length: 3·5in (8·89cm).

13 Gauge "00" D1 Petrol Tank Wagon, "Power Ethyl". Available in 1939-40 and for a short time post-War, this is one of the rarer Hornby Dublo wagons. Length: 3·5in (8·89cm).

14 Gauge "00" D1 Petrol Tank Wagon, "Esso". Available as (13), this is one of the most attractive and probably one of the rarest of Hornby Dublo wagons. Length: 3·5in (8·89cm).

15 Gauge "00" D1 Goods Brake Van, GWR. This appeared in all major liveries both pre- and post-War, with a later BR version. GWR versions are quite hard to find. Length: 4·3125in (10·95cm).

16 Gauge "00" D1 Oil Tank Wagon, "Royal Daylight". As shown, with the "Esso" oval, the wagon is common; an earlier version, lithographed "Royal Daylight" only, is much harder to find. Length: 3·5in (8·89cm).

17 Gauge "00" D1 Tank Wagon, "Esso Petroleum Company"; produced in the mid-1960s as one of a variety of "Esso" colour schemes, and fairly common. Length: 3·5in (8·89cm).

18 Gauge "00" D1 Tank Wagon, "Power Petrol". Available from the early 1950s as a replacement for (13), this is fairly easy to find. Length: 3·5in (8·89cm).

19 Gauge "00" D1 Tank Wagon, "Esso"; a common item, available from the mid-1950s. Many of these wagons had two-rail plastic wheels fitted when two-rail traction was introduced in the early 1960s. Length: 3·5in (8·89cm).

20 Gauge "00" D1 Tank Wagon, "Shell Lubricating Oil"; available from the mid-1950s, and very easy to find. Length: 3·5in (8·89cm).

21 Gauge "00" EDL18 2-6-4 Tank Locomotive, numbered "80054", BR; available from the mid-1950s and still easy to find in both two- and three-rail versions. Length: 7in (17·78cm).

22-23 Gauge "00" D13 Coaches: Suburban First/Third (22), and Suburban Brake/Third (23), both BR. These were brought out to complement (21), and were later re-tooled with transparent windows. They are easy to find. Length: 7·9375in (20·16cm).

1 Gauge "0" Buffers, tinplate, made by Gebrüder Bing, Nuremburg, Germany. This hand-painted accessory dates from around 1906, when it was catalogued by A.W. Gamage, London, at a price of 1s 3d (6p, 7c) in Gauge "0", 1s 6d (7½p, 9c) in Gauge "1", and 1s 9d (8½p, 10c) in Gauge "2". A Bing trademark is stamped between the rails. Length of base: 4·5in (11·43cm).

2 Station, tinplate, for use with Gauge "0" trains, made by Bing and first catalogued by Gamage's in 1913, when it was described as "a realistic model English railway station, in fine polychrome japanning with advertisements in correct colours . . . 22 inches (55·88cm) long . . . 3s 11d (19½p, 23c)." A larger version, 26in (66·04cm) long, was also available at a price of 5s 11d (29½p, 35c). This model remained in Gamage's Catalogue well into the 1920s, and was listed in Bing's own English-language Catalogue as late as 1928, by which time the price of the version shown here had risen to 6s 9d (33½p, 40c). The front of the station is shown here; the rear is equally well-detailed. It is, indeed a most attractive specimen, made even more interesting and desirable by the wealth of contemporary advertising signs, a feature much appreciated by all toy collectors. The base is pierced to allow the insertion of lighted candles to illuminate the buildings, with an added touch of realism then provided with smoke from the chimneys.

3 Train Indicator, tinplate, by an unidentified German maker and dating from about 1910. The accessory is in continental style, but this example, showing British towns as destinations, was obviously made for the UK market —although no railway normally served stations so widely separated as Glasgow, Blackpool, Liverpool, Southport, Birmingham, and Brighton! The same model, with appropriate destinations, was produced for the European market. Base: 4·5in x 2·75in (11·43cm x 6·98cm); maximum height: 8in (20·32cm).

4 Gauge "0" Tunnel by an unidentified German maker; an early railway accessory dating from around 1900. It is of tinplate and is constructed in two halves for easier packaging, and is attractively hand-painted with landscape details. Length: 8·5in (21·59cm); width: 5in (12·7cm); maximum height: 8·5in (21·59cm). The train seen approaching the tunnel is a Gauge "0" 0-4-0 "Vulcan" Great Western Railway locomotive and tender, with two passenger coaches, made by Bing in the mid-1920s.

5 Station for Gauge "0" trains, by an unidentified German maker and dating from around 1900, or possibly earlier. This very simple accessory of hand-painted tinplate is no more than a station façade on a base; nevertheless, it has a certain elegance and is a desirable item. Length of base: 7·25in

3

4

Next Train to

LIVERPOOL

BRIGHTON

BOVRIL

ZEBRA
THE
BLACKLEAD

OXO

BOVRIL

ROBIN
STARCH

LUX
WONT SHRINK
WOOLLENS

11 12 13 14 15 16 17 18 19 20

(18·41cm); maximum height: 7·25in (18·41cm).

6 Railway Sign, "Stop when the Gates are closed"; a simple lineside accessory in handpainted tinplate by Bing, Germany, dating from around 1900. Height: 7in (17·78cm).

7 Clock and Indicator, tinplate on a tinplate stand, by an unidentified German maker and dating from around 1900. Since the destination board shows "Southampton-Portsmouth-Exeter", this example was obviously intended for the British market; as with (3), the same model would have been produced with appropriate destinations for sale on the continent. Like a number of other accessories on this spread, it is in no particular

scale and is intended for use with toy railways of any gauge. Height: 7·75in (19·68cm).

8 Wayside Station by Bing; a most pleasingly lithographed tinplate item, again with interesting advertisements of the period, including the ubiquitous "Oxo" and "Bovril" along with other present-day survivors such as "Lux" (soap) and "Wright's Coal Tar Soap" —as well as the now-vanished "Zebra the Blacklead" (for cleaning fire-grates). It is nicely proportioned and the station building, as shown here, has an opening door. This accessory was listed in Bing's English-language Catalogue for 1928 at a price of 4s 9d (23½p, 28c). Length overall: 19·5in (49·53cm); maximum

height: 7·5in (19·05cm).

9 "Victoria Station" by Bing; a small but colourfully lithographed tinplate model—somewhat incongruously named, since Victoria is a major London terminus—listed in Gamage's 1906 Catalogue, as a "Local Railway Station", at a price of 0s 9d (3½p, 4c). The lithographed detail is identical on both sides: again, there are a number of interesting advertisements. Note particularly the "Smith & Sons Bookstall"—the bookstalls of W.H. Smith are still a prominent feature on many British stations —and the "Gentlemen" (lavatory) to the right. This model like (2), could be illuminated with candles. Length of base: 10·75in (27·3cm); width: 3·25in (8·25cm); height: 3·5in (8·89cm).

10 Porter's Hand Barrow, a tinplate accessory, probably of German manufacture, listed in Gamage's 1902 Catalogue at a price of 1s 0d (5p, 6c). It is immediately obvious that this large model is completely out of scale with any toy train. Length overall: 5·25in (13·33cm).

11-20 Figures and Station Furniture, dating approximately between 1910 and 1935. The Bench and Passenger at (11) and (12), the Nurse (16), Lady in Edwardian Dress (17), Passenger (18), Lady in 1920s Dress (19), and Clergyman (20), are all hollow-cast figures made by Britains, Great Britain. The Platform Machine (13), Weighing Machine (14), and Chocolate Vending Machine (15), are by unidentified makers.

1 Transformer Unit by Jep, France, dating from the 1920s-30s. This quaint hut is an excellent method of disguising an essential but utilitarian component of an electric train set. Some other makers produced similar items, and it is surprising that the idea was not more widely adopted. Items of this kind are very collectable and are quite hard to find.

2 Oil Lamp Standard by Bing, Germany c1905. This delightful model has a paraffin reservoir in a tube concealed down its length and a wick in its ventilated glass lantern. Like many of the accessories shown on this spread, it is in no particular scale. Collectors place a high value on these oil lamps; they are hard to acquire, since their appeal is not

limited to railway enthusiasts.
3 Electric Lamp Standard by Bing, 1920s. This small lamp is one of many varieties of electric lamp produced by both Bing and Märklin. Another very desirable collector's item of wide appeal.
4 Train Indicator and Clock Pedestal by Bing, made for the British market (note lettering of boards) in the late 1920s. Bing produced many items of station furniture of this kind. This would be in place only on a platform of huge scale—but is probable that play-value was the maker's primary consideration.
5 Train Route Indicator, in continental style, by Märklin, Germany, dating from c1930. Hand-painted and with rubber-stamped lettering, this is one of

Märklin's many delightful, high-quality accessories and, like many similar items that were perhaps not so highly valued in their time, it is rare.
6 Gauge "0" Distant Bracket Signal by Bassett-Lowke, Great Britain; an accessory made both before and after World War II. These Northampton-made signals have a nearer-scale appearance than their Hornby counterparts, and although not highly prized, they certainly would look better on a vintage layout.
7 Indication Post by Märklin, 1930s; a rather unusual-looking item of continental-style track furniture. Like all Märklin items, it is collectable, although not highly desirable.
8 Gauge "0" No 2 Signal Cabin

by Hornby, Great Britain; made both before and after World War II. The roof opens to give access to the lever frame, see (13). There was also a cheaper No 1 version. These are among the most common Hornby buildings.
9 Gauge "0" Junction Sign by Jep, mid-1930s; an electrically-lit accessory in French style. Not particularly valuable, but of interest to Jep collectors.
10 Luggage Weighing Post by Kibri, Germany, 1930s. Again, an accessory in which play-value is the primary consideration, with working scales. Kibri's range of buildings and accessories does not occupy a high place in the attention of most collectors.
11 Gauge "00" "Table-Top" Signal Box by Bing: one of the attractive

little buildings produced in the 1920s to complement the maker's compact Gauge "00" systems in electric and clockwork. This equipment has recently increased in collecting popularity.

12 Gauge "00" "Table-Top" Level Crossing by Bing, c 1927. This is for the clockwork system: electric items are more difficult to find.

13 Gauge "0" Lever Frame by Hornby, made from the mid-1920s until World War II. This well-made accessory could operate from a signal cabin—see (13)—to control trains on the track. These items, with black or blue bases, are eagerly sought and are scarce.

14 Gauge "1" Hydraulic Buffers by Bing, mid-1920s. This Gauge "1" version is quite rare, although Gauge "0" hydraulic buffers by

Bing, Hornby, and Bassett-Lowke are among the more easily-found "unusual" accessories.

15-16 Gauge "0" Railway Accessories No 8: Notice Boards, by Hornby; items from a boxed set of six pieces, available from the late 1920s until World War II. As boxed sets, these Hornby items are rare and most desirable.

17 Gauge "1" Gateman's Hut; this pre-1914 item may be by Carette, Germany, although it shows strong Märklin influence. Although charming, it is not of great collectable importance. Nor is the item shown immediately below it: a Gauge "0" Platform Water Crane by Exley, Great Britain, first catalogued in the mid-1930s. Made of brass, this is a simple model of high quality.

18 Gauge "0" Railway Accessories No 7: Workman's Hut, Brazier, Shovel and Poker, by Hornby; a delightful accessory, not often found complete, made from c1930 until World War II.

19 Gauge "0" Railway Accessories No 2: Gradient Posts and Mile Posts; a Hornby accessory made from 1929 until World War II. A boxed set is hard to find.

20 Gauge "0" Platform Accessories No 1: Miniature Luggage; made by Hornby until World War II. Complete with porter's barrow, this is a most collectable set, and not particularly rare.

21 Hall's Distemper Advertisement, Dinky Toys No 13, made by Meccano for its Gauge "0" Hornby layouts. This is a highly-prized lineside accessory, consisting of two lead

figures with a cardboard sign, and is exceptionally hard to find in complete condition.

22 Gauge "0" "Table-Top" Passenger Station, Bing, 1927. One of the larger "Table-Top" items, this is made in three pieces, with side clips to hold it at the right distance from the track. A "must" for Bing collectors; not very scarce.

23 Gauge "00" Table-Top" Locomotive Shed, Bing, mid-to-late 1920s. Made in both electric and clockwork versions (the latter shown here), it is one of the rarer "Table-Top" items.

24 Gauge "0" M Wayside Station, available from Hornby throughout the 1930s, and made to complement the maker's cheap "M Series" train sets. This is easy to find.

5

As the merest glance at the illustrations in this section will show, toy boats are among the most beautiful and desirable of all toys. Sadly, they are also among the scarcest and most costly. The finest specimens were "luxury" toys, made in limited numbers to sell at very high prices: the Liner by Märklin shown at (3), *pages 224-225*, was marketed in Britain before World War I at a price equivalent to about one month's pay for the average worker. And many toy boats that would now be the pride of any collection must lie rusting on the beds of lakes and ponds, the victims of long-ago shipwrecks. Even the surviving examples will seldom be found without restoration or replacement parts, for their fittings, such as ships' boats, anchors, flags, masts and rigging, were fragile and subject to loss.

Our selection ranges from "carpet toys" to near ocean-going examples, and from rowing boats to battleships and submarines. German makers are particularly distinguished in this field (as in others), and we include fine toys from Bing, Carette, Fleischmann and Märklin, dating from the "golden age", as well as more modern examples by the West German firm of Arnold, last upholder of a great tradition.

Toy Ships and Boats

All the boats shown on this spread were photographed at the London Toy & Model Museum. The warship shown *Inset* is from the collection of Ron McCrindell.

1-7 Carpet Toy Battleship & Flotilla, lightweight tinplate, by Hess, Nuremburg, Germany, c1910. The two-funnelled battleship (6), with the White Ensign of the Royal Navy at its masthead, is powered by clockwork. Concealed beneath its hull are three eccentric wheels which give a pitching-and-rolling effect as it moves. It is linked by jointed rods—detached example at (7)—to five gunboats (1-5) of differing types, each with a peg at bow and stern to fit into an aperture on a rod. Note that the rods are provided with several apertures so

that the gunboats may be arranged in varying formations. The battleship and the individual gunboats could be bought as separate items. Lengths: (battleship) 8·25in (21cm), (gunboat) 5·5in (14cm).

8 Carpet Toy Battleship "New York", cast iron with tinplate masts, by Arcade, USA, c1912. This impressive pull-along toy is attractive in its disproportion—note particularly the large figure of the captain on the bridge—for many collectors feel that "toy-like" items like this have greater charm than more faithful models. The ship bristles with guns, although some gun barrels are missing from the sponsoned turrets to both port and starboard. Length: 20·375in (52cm). Limited.

9 Carpet Toy River Boat, cast iron, certainly by an American maker (probably Kenton), c1910. The hand-enamelled finish is rather less "play-worn" than that of (8). The central wheels are concealed within the paddle boxes; the beam on the central deck is connected to the cranked axle of the main wheels and rocks as the boat is pulled along. Length: 10in (25cm). Limited.

10 Novelty Boat, tinplate, possibly by a French maker, dating from c1900; an unusual pull-along toy. As the boat is pulled, a striker operating from the cranked axle hits the two bells. Length: 4·75in (12cm). Limited.

11 "Toc-Toc" Boat, tinplate, British-made and dating from around 1900. This toy was

patented by Thomas Pilot in 1898 and was probably the first of its kind: it is propelled by water-jets from a heated coil—see note at (9) on *pages 226-227*—and its name derives from the sound made by its propulsion unit. This example bears a brass tablet impressed: "J. Robinson & Sons, Opticians & Photographers, 172 Regent St."; this London retailer specialized in late 19th century optical and other "scientific" toys. Length: 9·75in (25cm). Scarce.

12 Gunboat "Mikasa", tinplate, by Bing, Germany, dating from c1904 and perhaps inspired by the Russo-Japanese War of that time. Its operation is ingenious: as the clockwork motor runs down it activates a cap-firing mechanism in the gun turret; one gun fires and

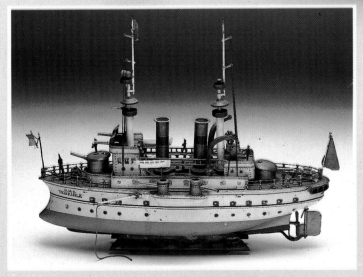

the boat changes course by 90°; the second gun fires and the course alters a further 90° to return the boat to its launching point. The bridge section hinges back to allow the guns to be loaded. The Japanese battle-flag at the stern is a replacement; the original would have been a smaller tinplate flag. Length: 19·5in (50cm). Scarce.

Battleship, "HMS Terrible", tinplate, by Märklin, Germany; a magnificent toy dating from no later than 1905, probably earlier. Concealed beneath the superstructure is a maker's number "7": the present owner believes that this may indicate very limited production. It is, in any case, extremely rare. Length: 24·5in (62cm).

13 Torpedo by Ernst Plank, Nuremburg, Germany, c1902. An unusual clockwork toy, of soldered tinplate and with an enamelled finish, which operated semi-submerged, directed by its adjustable rudder. The hatch amidships is unscrewed to give access to the winder. Note the applied Plank trademark forward of the hatch and patent number aft. Length: 12in (30cm). Rare.

14 Two-Man Racing Motorboat by Bing, Germany, c1910. This tinplate toy is more fully noted at (6) and (13) on pages 226-227, where an example with a different pennant number is shown. Length: 8·5in (21·5cm). Limited.

15 Lifeboatman, a diecast figure by Britains, Britain, dating from c1935. Height: 3in (76mm).

In comparison with toys of other kinds, boats are both fragile and liable to accidental loss during play. Therefore, all tinplate boats of the kind shown here and on the three following spreads — almost all of which are of pre-1939 manufacture and in fine condition — may be properly described, in the terms of the classification system used throughout this book, as "Rare". No classification has, therefore, been applied to most of the items shown.

All the boats shown on this spread are from the collection of Ron McCrindell, London.

1 Torpedo Boat by Gebrüder Bing, Germany; first catalogued in 1902 and offered by the famous store of Gamage's, London, in that year at

a price of 9s 11d (49½p, 70c). This boat is clockwork-powered, running for about five minutes on one winding (winder in funnel), but it was also available in steam and is, indeed, described in Gamage's Catalogue as a "Steam Torpedo Boat". It is a pleasing and fairly accurate model and, like all this early series, rare. Note the original cradle, or trolley, 9in (23cm) long; this was supplied with the boat and incorporates a ring through which a cord could be tied temporarily to convert the craft to a pull-along toy. The boat was made in three sizes: 15in (38cm); 20in (50cm), as shown here; and 24in (60cm), as shown at (2).

2 Torpedo Boat by Bing, c1902: the de luxe version, catalogued as a "Steam Torpedo Division Boat", of

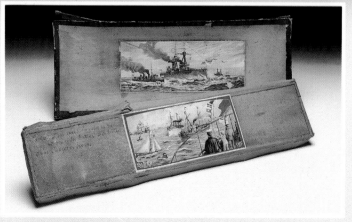

Box lids for Bing boats of the pre-1914 period: (top) for the Dreadnought Battleship shown at (10) on pages 222-223; (bottom) for the Large Torpedo Boat with three funnels shown at (4) on this spread.

the boat shown at (1). This example is clockwork, it was available also in steam, and was sold in Britain by Gamage's at a price of 15s 0d (75p, $1.07). This example is in excellent original condition, with no restoration. Note the detail, including the original lithographed tinplate flag, wire rigging, anchor and chain, and wheel that turns rudder. It rests on its original 14in (36cm) cradle. Length: 24in (60cm).

3 Torpedo Boat by Bing, dating from c1906 and probably available until World War I. A more utilitarian model than those of the 1902 series shown at (1) and (2), this has its original tinplate Italian tricolour at the stern and original tinplate mast. The two-funnelled example shown is 27·5in (70cm)

long and is powered by clockwork; it was also available in steam, and was made in a larger, three-funnelled version; see (4).

4 Large Torpedo Boat, "No 121", by Bing, catalogued by Gamage's at £1 17s 6d (£1.87½p, $2.66) in 1908. It is powered by clockwork and was also available in steam. It is a later, larger, three-funnelled version of the boat shown at (3). Length: 39·5in (100cm).

5 Gunboat (Canonenboot in the maker's catalogue) by Bing, first catalogued in 1902 and originally named (for the British market) "King Edward". This example is clockwork, the powerful motor giving about ten minutes' run on one winding; it was also available in steam. It has undergone minor restoration: two lifeboats are

missing (it is rare to find a boat of this vintage with all accessories intact), but the masts are the original rolled tinplate. The boat shown is 30in (75cm) long: it was made also in a 24in (60cm) version, with two funnels and this smaller version has only two lifeboats. The sailors are contemporary small "flats" by a Nuremburg maker.

6 Large Coasting Cruiser (maker's catalogue description) by Georges Carette, a French maker working until World War I at Nuremburg, Germany. Dating from 1911, when it sold in Britain at 11s 6d (57½p, 82c), this boat was made only in clockwork. The mast of this example is wood: the original would have been tinplate. Note the simple bracket-stand on the hull

forward, a feature later adopted by Bing. The boat shown is 18in (46cm) long; it was also made in 14in (36cm), 20in (50cm), and "fully detailed" 24in (60cm) versions.

7 Coastal Gun, tinplate, by Marklin, Germany, catalogued in 1902. As an explosive cap is fired in the breech, a spring launches a white metal shell from the muzzle. The gun may be elevated, depressed, and fully traversed by means of the control wheels seen in the photograph; note the small flanged wheels of the traversing mechanism running on a track around the base. Base diameter: 10in (25cm); maximum height: 9in (23cm). The sailors are British-made Britains figures of c1935.

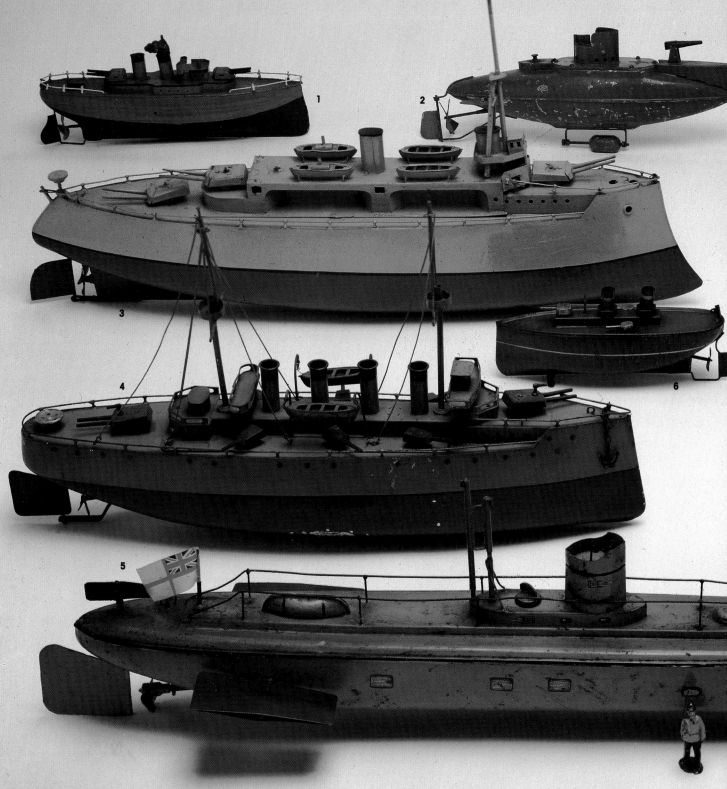

All the boats shown on this spread are from the collection of Ron McCrindell, London.

1 Warship by Fleischmann, Germany, dating from the mid-1930s. Note the "funnel-smoke" winder for the clockwork, one of several Carette features that appeared on Fleischmann boats following the acquisition of Carette's boat division after 1917. Fleischmann often used Carette hull pressings, but the original Carette products can be identified by the styles of guns and ships' boats. The single mast is missing from this example. Length: 12in (30cm).

2 Submarine by a British maker, dating from the World War I period. Note the balance weight that is moved along a screw thread to adjust the trim. This simple toy dives on launching and surfaces when its clockwork motor runs down. Length: 15in (38cm).

3 Battleship, clockwork, by Bing, Germany, issued before World War I but still catalogued in Britain (as "HMS Neptune") by Bassett-Lowke in the 1920s. This example has undergone some restoration and repainting: the anchors, after tripod mast, and two gun turrets originally sited under the flying bridge are missing. It was available in three sizes: 12in (30cm), without anchors; 20in (50cm), with anchors; and 26in (65cm), as shown here.

4 British Armoured Cruiser (Gamage's 1913 Catalogue description) by Bing, 1912: an interesting example of a later Bing series. It is clockwork, Bing having almost abandoned steam-propelled boats by this time, and was made in no fewer than seven sizes: the example shown is 22in (55cm) long. Of the five sizes listed in Gamage's Catalogue, the largest is 37·5in (95cm). This boat is in very good condition, although the rigging needs attention.

5 Submarine by Märklin, Germany: the largest toy submarine produced commercially. This had a long production run, from c1914 until the late 1920s, but it is rarer than many other Märklin boats—all of which are eagerly sought by collectors. This example is complete and in fine original condition. Note the transfer detail of port-holes and machine-gun positions, and the brass hatch aft the conning tower; the latter forms a waterproof seal over the clockwork mechanism and is unscrewed for winding. The action is realistic: the diving vanes are geared to the clockwork mechanism to make the boat submerge and surface alternately. Length: 31·5in (80cm); also available in smaller sizes.

6 Warship by Arnold, Germany, dating from the mid-1920s. This simple, two-funnelled clockwork ship (from which the single mast and flag are missing) was sold in Britain at around 1s 0d (5p, 7c). Length: 9in (23cm).

7 Three-Funnelled Destroyer by Bing, probably dating from the early 1920s. It is more attractively coloured than many boats of its

period. Well detailed, it has tinplate flags; the flag from the after mast is missing. This example is 16·5in (42cm) long — probably the largest size in which this clockwork boat was produced; it was also available in a smaller, two-funnelled version.

8 Battleship, clockwork, by Fleischmann, mid-1930s. As its flags show, this was intended for the US market; it was also produced with German and British flags. It is 20·5in (52cm) long: Fleischmann's standard 52cm hull was used for a number of different boats, and although production of the series ended in 1939, it made a brief reappearance in almost identical form in 1955-56.

9 Submarine by Bing: the largest submarine by this maker and a very rare specimen. It was first

catalogued as early as 1902 and was available in the large size shown until 1910, or possibly a little later. A most attractive design, it is simple in operation, diving after launch and surfacing when the clockwork runs down. Note the very large, original, key: the powerful motor is wound through a separate compartment reached by unscrewing the small turret forward of the conning tower. This example has been restored to close to original condition: such restoration is acceptable, especially in the case of such a rare boat. Gamage's, London, listed this toy in three sizes in the 1902 Catalogue: the largest, as seen here, 27in (68cm) long, priced at £1 17s 6d (£1.87½p, $2.66); 18in (46cm); and 13·5in (34cm). Only

the two smaller sizes remained in the Catalogue in 1913.

10 Battleship by Bing, c1913, modelled on the Royal Navy's revolutionary "all big gun" HMS *Dreadnought.* This is a fairly plain, utilitarian model — the anchors are soldered on and the superstructure cannot be raised to give access to the clockwork — but a solid and pleasing toy. It has triple screws: only the central shaft is driven, but the outer screws revolve as the boat moves through the water. Note the metal plaque with the Bing trademark on the central superstructure. Length: 19·5in (50cm).

11 Submarine by Arnold, dating from soon after World War II (it is stamped "Made in US Zone,

Germany"). A simple clockwork-powered toy, winding through the turret, it is in fully original condition and, despite being relatively recent, is scarce. Length: 12in (30cm).

12 Warship by Carette, dating from c1905 or possibly earlier: an extremely simple boat, with no rudder, which sold in Britain at 0s 6d (2½p, 4c). Note the "funnel smoke" winder — see also (1) — and, even on so basic a design, the readily identifiable Carette guns and, especially, the single-ring stand (just visible beneath the hull forward) which was a feature of almost all Carette boats. The hull is not tinplate but zinc, as found in some other earlier boats, and the paint is now flaking away. This example is complete, apart from a flag aft. Length: 5·75in (15cm).

All the boats shown on this spread are from the collection of Ron McCrindell, London.

1 "Viking" Liner by Arnold, Germany, dating from the 1930s, when this simple clockwork toy sold in Britain for about 0s 7½d (3p, 4c). The lithographed deck fittings—hatchways, ropes, and winches—typical of Arnold boats are just visible; the foremast is missing. Length: 8in (20cm).

2 Liner by Fleischmann, Germany, dating from the 1920s. As in the case of the Battleship at (1) on *pages 222-223*, this boat shows many features adopted from Carette: the hull is a Carette pressing and the masts, the shape of the rudder, and much of the superstructure are of Carette type.

The lifeboats and flags, however, are characteristic of Fleischmann. This is therefore an interesting "borderline" case. Length: 17in (42cm).

3 Liner by Märklin; a very large and grand model—and of surprisingly modern appearance for its date of origin, c1910. It was available for some years, making a brief reappearance after World War I. This impressive craft surely pushes the classification of "toy" to an extreme: it sold in Britain for around £25 0s 0d (£25.00, $35.50) at a time when that sum probably represented more than one month's pay for the average worker. The excellent detail is evident: the boats are hand-painted, as is usual on larger models, and the "deck planking" effect is also

the result of hand-painting. The large and powerful two-speed clockwork motor, driving two propellers, gives a running time of 15-20 minutes. This liner is in good order: it took part in a regatta on the Round Pond, London, in 1983. Length: 39·5in (100cm).

4 Tanker by Fleischmann, dating from the mid-1930s. This clockwork boat is based on the maker's favoured 52cm hull—a Carette pressing—but is unusual in being one of the few toy tankers. Note the attractive detail; also the Fleischmann trademark, "GFN" in a triangle, in the bows. Length: 20·5in (52cm).

5 Liner by Märklin, Germany, dating from immediately after World War I. A Märklin (Wittenburg) trademark stamped on the rudder is

part-visible. This most attractive boat, well-proportioned, interestingly-detailed, and nicely finished (the port-holes on the hull are "rubber-stamped"), is in excellent original condition, with its large key shown in place. It is a pity that this series, which included both liners and warships, had only a short production run. Length: 14in (36cm).

6 Liner by Arnold. This clockwork boat is not unlike the "Viking" Liner shown at (1); it dates from the same period but is a little larger and has a differently-designed superstructure. Again, the foremast is missing. The Arnold trademark stamped on the deck aft is just visible. Length: 9in (23cm).

7 Liner by Fleischmann, dating from the 1930s and based on the 52cm

Set of Liners by Arnold. The boxes in which these clockwork boats were sold are marked "Made in Germany, US Zone", but the boats are probably of pre-World War II manufacture, re-packaged and tactfully fitted with Swiss flags for sale post-1945. The two larger boats have twin propellers; the two smaller, single propellers. They are of especial interest in being among the last of the "quality" tinplate boats in the great German tradition. Lengths: 18in (46cm); 14·5in (37cm); 12in (30cm); 9in (23cm).

hull favoured by this maker. This clockwork boat appeared in the Fleischmann 1936 Catalogue, was made until 1939, and made a brief reappearance in 1955-56.

Note particularly the lifeboats: their simple design is a Fleischmann characteristic. Length: 20·5in (52cm).

8 Liner by Bing, Germany, dating from the mid-1920s. Most Bing liners of this later period have black-and-red hulls; this is unusual in having a lower hull of light copper colour. The yellow deck is, however, typical of Bing boats of the period, as is the lifeboat pattern. The propeller and after mast are missing from this boat, but note the Bing trademark stamped forward of the fore-funnel. This simple, three-funnelled, clockwork boat was made in several sizes: the example shown is 14in (36cm) long; a smaller, two-funnelled version was 9in (23cm) long.

All the boats shown on this spread are from the collection of Ron McCrindell, London.

1 Steam Launch by Jean Schoenner, Nuremburg, Germany, c1900; a rare example of the work of a maker who appears to have ceased production around 1906. The simplicity of the design is typical of Schoenner, as is the power unit: a methylated spirit burner firing a vertical boiler with a single oscillating cylinder. The tinplate ensign at the stern is the Stars and Stripes. The graceful hull of the launch has an overall length of 12in (30cm).

2 Swamp Craft by Bing, Germany, mid-1920s. This rare and interesting toy, probably aimed at the American market, is clockwork-driven via a large traction propeller. The winder can be seen just forward of the driver; the rudder is between the floats. Length: 7in (18cm).

3 Paddle Steamer by Carette, Germany, catalogued in 1911 but probably dating from some years earlier. It has been restored to near-original condition and finish, although the fore and aft masts are missing. Note that the winding aperture, with key in position, is very near the waterline: operation in all but a dead calm would be hazardous! This boat was available in several sizes: the example shown was the largest, with a length of 21in (53cm).

4 Speedboat made in the USSR (Moscow) in the late 1940s—and strikingly similar to the Jep speedboat at (5). Although slightly smaller than the more beamy Jep boat, it is definitely a copy, although it is not known whether the design was pirated or whether Jep sold pressings to Eastern Europe. Even the driver (a composition half-figure) is similar, although in this Soviet model he is better-proportioned and protected by a celluloid windscreen. The cockpit cover and the clockwork motor beneath it may be lifted out as one piece for servicing. Length: 14in (36cm).

5 Speedboat, "Ruban Bleu No 1", by Jep (Jouets en Paris), France, mid-1930s. Compare with the Soviet copy at (4) and with the contemporary Hornby "Venture" at (8). Note the large key in winding position: clockwork engines for speedboats have fewer gears than conventional mechanisms, to give "high revs", and it is not advisable to let the clockwork run while the boat is out of water. The central cockpit section lifts out to give access to the mechanism: if a spring broke, a new engine could be purchased and easily fitted. The half-figure of the driver is composition. This example of a boat available in several different sizes and colour schemes is 14·5in (37cm) long.

6 Two-Man Racing Motorboat by Bing, c1910. A most attractive clockwork toy, sold in Britain at 2s 3d (11½p, 16c), this example is the middle size of the range, at 8·5in (21·5cm). It was also available at 10·5in (26·5cm) and 7·5in (19cm); see also (13).

7 Speedboat, "JEP 3", by Jep; a simpler and cheaper toy than the Jep boat at (5), dating from the 1950s. The hull is flat-bottomed and there is no access to the clockwork mechanism (note fixed key) except by removing the tabbed and slotted deck. The composition driver and the windscreen are typically Jep. The boat's name refers to its size: the model was available in other sizes, "JEP 1" being the smallest. Length: 15in (38cm).

8 Limousine Boat No 4, "Venture", a clockwork boat by Hornby, Britain, available from the late 1920s until World War II. This attractive saloon version (note seat and steering wheel) of the Hornby series was available in three different colour schemes. Length: 16·5in (42cm).

9 "Toc-Toc" Boat, marked "Made in US Zone, Germany" and thus dating from c1946 or later. This simple toy takes its name from its water-jet propulsion: the two ends of a coil tube protrude from the stern and a candle in the cabin heats the coil until water is sucked into one end of the tube and forced out of the other with a "toc-toc" noise. Length: 5in (13cm).

10 Paddle Steamer by Märklin, Germany, c1910. Paddle steamers of this series are particularly rare, and although this example has undergone some small restoration it is in near-original condition. The composition figures on the benches aft are of the type made for use with contemporary Märklin trains. This splendid clockwork boat is 20in (50cm) long.

11 Steam Motor Racing Boat by Bing, Germany. The early Bing trademark on the stern decking suggests a date of c1908, by which time the simple bracket-stand on the hull forward had replaced the wheeled cradle supplied with earlier models. The superstructure hinges towards the stern to give access to the steam engine, with its brass boiler and brass oscillating cylinder. Provision is made for a peg-in driver, but no such figure is known to have been supplied. The boat was listed by Gamage's, London, in 1913 at 14s 6d (72½p, $1.03) for the 22in (55cm) model, as shown, or 8s 6d (42½p, 60c) for an 18in (46cm) version.

12 Rowing Boat by Arnold, West Germany, dating from after World War II. The oars are tinplate, but the rower is composition, an unusual feature at this period when tin figures were more common. Length: 8in (20cm).

13 One-Man Racing Motorboat by Bing, c1910. This smaller version of the toy shown at (6) has undergone some restoration. Length: 7·5in (19cm).

14 Turbine Steamboat by Bing, c1906. Another rare boat, and a particularly interesting one in that it is driven by a tiny steam turbine, with a boiler fired by methylated spirit. As the canopy, Bing used a stamping for a model railway station, and the cabin aft is, in fact, a Bing Gauge "0" railway carriage, minus wheels. This boat was made in three sizes, one larger and one smaller than the example shown, which is 16in (41cm) long.

6

Aeronautical toys based on balloons and dirigibles were available in the latter part of the 19th century, but it was not until the powers of the Wright Brothers' invention had been displayed in Europe, around 1908, that German makers such as Günthermann, Lehmann and Märklin began to feature aeroplanes in their catalogues. The earliest toy aeroplanes, fairly fragile constructions, are now extremely rare and valuable, and the interest of the collector of tinplate toys is likely to centre on the tinplate aeroplanes produced in the 1920s-1930s by such makers as Fleischmann and Günthermann of Germany, Jep of France and Cardini of Italy, or, after World War II, by Arnold and Tipp of Germany, all of whom are represented in this section.

Japanese makers have also been active in this field: some earlier examples of their work are shown on *pages 230-231*, along with a number of more recent battery-powered and friction-driven models, now increasingly collectable, on *pages 232-233*. Nor should the collector overlook the ingenious "flying" helicopters shown on *pages 236-237*.

Diecast aeroplanes were once "unfashionable" among collectors but are now receiving increasing attention. The opportunities for an excellent thematic collection in this field, at moderate cost, are considerable.

Toy Aeroplanes

From the very beginning of man's attempts to fly, toy manufacturers have reflected the romance of the conquest of the air, their products ranging from toy balloons and airships to futuristic models like the Flying Car shown at (2) below — and, of course, in more recent times, space vehicles. As may be seen here, most tinplate aircraft (unlike the diecast models that are shown on *pages 238-241*) are only loosely based on the real thing. The collector may find it hard to acquire examples in the generally fine condition seen here — the efforts of children to "fly" such non-flying models may have something to do with this!
All the aircraft shown on this spread were photographed at the London Toy & Model Museum.

1 Flying Boat by J. Fleischmann, Nuremburg, Germany, *c*1937. It is based on a contemporary Dornier type, with a raised tailplane assembly and aerofoil floats that resemble stub wings. It is appropriate that this large and impressive — although plainly finished — tinplate aircraft should be the work of a company best known for its toy boats, for it is designed to float. The six engines with tractor/pusher propellers mounted on the upper wing are unpowered, but the large and rather clumsy propeller at the nose is driven by clockwork (note winding shaft in fuselage just forward of the upper wing) and pulls the model across the water, albeit somewhat slowly. Length: 17·25in (44cm). Limited.

2 Flying Car by Blomer & Schüler, West Germany, dating from *c*1948-50 and no doubt inspired by reports of immediate post-War attempts by US designers to make such a vehicle a reality. It is clockwork-powered; the wings fold back into the body, springing out when the brake (note lever on boot) is released. Length: 7·5in (19cm). Wingspan: 8in (20cm).

3 Supermarine Spitfire, marked "Empire Made" (possibly in Hong Kong), *c*1950. Of tinplate construction, with printed "camouflage" and Royal Air Force roundels, it is a "push-and-go" toy, with an axle geared to a heavy flywheel which maintains momentum after an initial push. The propeller is plastic. Note that this is a "clipped wing" Spitfire

of the type once built for low-altitude use during the later stages of World War II. Length: 9·875in (25cm).

4 Lockheed Monoplane by E.T.Co., Japan, dating from the 1930s. In tinplate, with a plated cowl to simulate a radial engine, this representation of an American two-seater has colourful printed detail, including the registration letters "J-BAMC" on wing and fuselage, and is crewed by two pressed-tin aviators. It has a fixed undercarriage with the wheels concealed by fairings. Clockwork-powered, it could be suspended by a cord through the loop just in front of the windscreen and, with the aid of its large plastic propeller (now broken), "flown" in a circle. Wingspan: 14in (35·5cm).

5 Military Monoplane by "PW", Germany, c1938. This twin-engined low-wing aeroplane is of tinplate construction and has printed "splinter" camouflage and German national markings. Both the wheels and the tin propellors are driven by clockwork; note the suspension loop aft the printed cockpit. Wingspan: 14in (35·5cm). Limited.

6 Airliner by S. Günthermann, Nuremburg, Germany, c1935. Undoubtedly based on the famous civilian and military Junkers Ju 52 transport, this triple-engined tinplate aeroplane has printed lines to represent the corrugated construction of the real thing; note the wealth of further printed detail, including registration marks. The open cockpit contains two tin

aviators, and a battery-operated headlight is fitted on the nose. Clockwork drives the wheels and the large central propeller; a wire suspension loop is fitted atop the fuselage. Wingspan: 20·25in (52cm). Limited.

7 Racing Seaplane by Jep (Jouets en Paris), France, mid-1930s. This fine tinplate toy is most attractively finished, with detail including French national markings and squadron insignia. A floating toy, it is powered by clockwork (note the large removable key in winding position) driving the four-bladed propeller; the floats have rudders. Wingspan: 19in (48cm). Limited.

8 Airliner by Cardini, Italy, mid-1920s. This biplane has wings of aluminium and a tin fuselage with printed detail (note "Nord-Sud"

legend above cabin). The wings fold to allow storage in its box, which was designed as a hangar. The propeller is clockwork-driven and a raised wire suspension attachment is fitted above the wing. Wingspan: 10in (25·4cm). Limited.

9 Twin-Engined Bomber by "TN" (Nomura Toys Ltd), Tokyo, Japan, c1930. The tinplate body is printed in four-colour camouflage with French national markings, and the plane is crewed by tin figures of a gunner (in the nose, behind a revolving gun turret), pilot, and observer, all in open cockpits. The wheels are driven by clockwork. Wingspan: 15·75in (40cm).

10 Racing Seaplane, British-made and dating from c1927. This single-sided, stand-up, pressed-tin

representation of a Supermarine S.5 Seaplane (one of a series of Schneider Trophy winners of the time) was distributed free as a promotional ploy by the British juvenile publication Modern Boy (Number 3, 1927). The magazine also distributed similar models of various locomotives and of Segrave's "Sunbeam" world land speed record car of 1927. Length: 5in (13cm).

11 Large-scale hand luggage, probably of German origin (since the basket-work case bears the printed message Glückliche Reise, "Lucky Journey") and dating from the 1930s: attractive accessories for the proud owner of a large tinplate aircraft or ship.

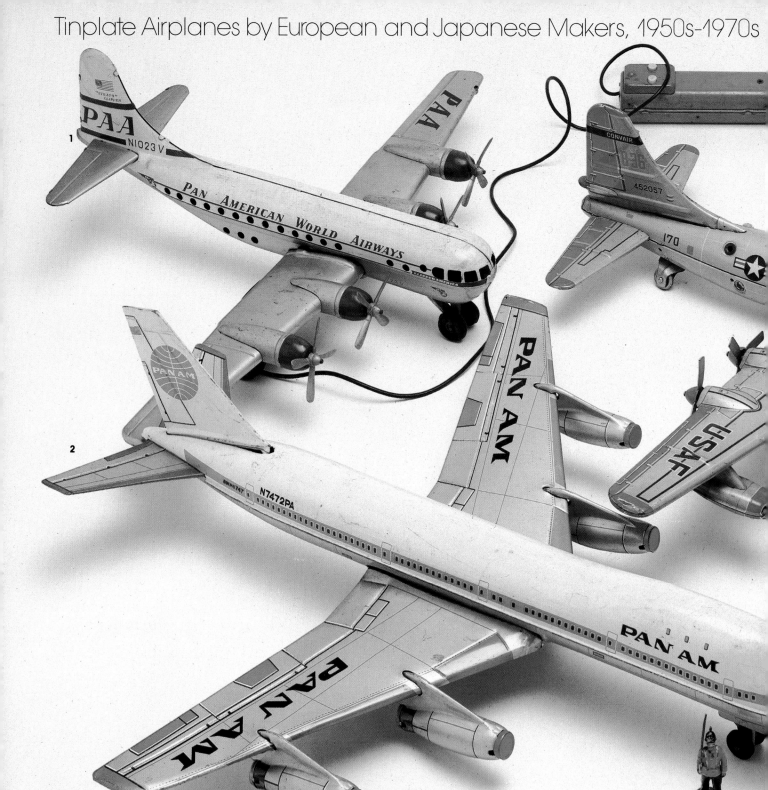

The boom in civil aviation since World War II has seen the appearance of long-range airliners of ever-increasing size. Japanese makers have been particularly active in producing toys—latterly often of part-metal part-plastic construction, and usually battery-powered or friction-driven—based on these giant aircraft. Such models are likely to gain in popularity with collectors as the aeroplanes they depict become a part of aviation history.
All the aircraft shown on this spread were photographed at the London Toy & Model Museum.

1 "Pan American World Airways" Boeing 377 Stratocruiser by a German maker (it is marked only "Made in Western Germany"), dating from the mid-1950s. The four-engined airliner has a tinplate fuselage and wings with printed detail (it is identified beneath the US flag on the tail fin as a "Strato Clipper") and plastic propellers. It is battery-operated and, as seen here, has a remote-control hand-set that starts the motor and taxies the airplane. Wingspan: 19in (48cm).
2 "Pan Am" Boeing 747, a four-engined Jumbo Jet by "ATC" (Asahi Toy Company), Tokyo, Japan, dating from the 1970s. This tinplate airliner with printed detail is a toy of a kind especially popular in gift shops at major air terminals. Although well-modelled, it may be felt to lack the charm of the earlier aircraft shown on *pages 230-231*. Wingspan: 26in (66cm).

3 Convair (General Dynamics) B-36 Heavy Bomber by "E.T. Co.", Japan, dating from the mid-1950s. This is a fine model of the largest and most powerful aeroplane of its time. The B-36 had an interesting history. Designed early in World War II, it was intended to be able to bomb European targets from bases in Canada, in case Britain should be occupied by German forces. As this eventuality became increasingly remote, work on the long-range monster slowed and it did not make its first flight until 1946, remaining in service thereafter until early 1959. The six-engined bomber (with twin-jet booster pods beneath the wings, as seen here) has a tinplate fuselage and wings, with printed detail that includes US Air Force

markings. Note the green plastic blister canopy at the nose and the smaller blisters (one missing towards the tail) for identification lights on this battery-powered model. Wingspan: 26in (66cm).

"BOAC" (British Overseas Airways Corporation) Concorde Airliner by a Japanese maker, dating from the 1960s. This is an interesting example of a toymaker's desire to be up-to-date outrunning reality: by the time the real Concorde entered service, BOAC was no longer in existence. This friction-drive model has a tinplate body and wings with printed detail (the wings are detachable; note the plastic turnbuckles), and has its nose permanently fixed in the "up" position. Length: 14in (36cm).

4 "American Airlines" "Electra II" Airliner by "TN" (Nomura Toys Ltd), Tokyo, Japan (with trademark visible just beneath the tailplane), dating from the 1950s. In tinplate with printed detail, and with plastic engine cowlings and propellers, this model is battery-powered. Wingspan: 16·5in (42cm).

5 "B.O.A.C." (British Overseas Airways Corporation) Vickers Viscount Airliner by Schuco (Schreyer and Company), West Germany, dating from the 1950s; note the name of the maker, well known both before and after World War II for mechanical toys of fine quality, prominently printed on the upper wing and tailplane. This battery-powered model has a tinplate fuselage and wings, with printed detail that includes registration markings, and plastic engine nacelles and propellers. A bubble canopy of clear plastic through which the plastic figures of the pilot and co-pilot can be clearly seen is fitted at the nose. Wingspan: 19in (48cm).

6 Delta-Winged Jet Fighter by Joustra, France, dating from the mid-1950s. This friction-driven aeroplane is of tinplate construction with printed detail that includes French national markings. It incorporates a novelty based on a feature that was being generally fitted to real aeroplanes of this type at the time of manufacture. When the nose-cone is pressed, a spring-loaded mechanism ejects the pilot, complete with parachute. Wingspan: 7·25in (18cm).

1 Douglas DC-6B Airliner by Arnold, West Germany; dating from c1951 (ie, the model appeared at about the same time that the prototype entered airline service). This tinplate airliner is shown in KLM livery, with the legend "De Vliegende Hollander" along the starboard fuselage and its English equivalent, "The Flying Dutchman", to port; see also (3). The identification letters "PE-DFY" appear on the upper and lower starboard wing surfaces and on the tailplane. The model is clockwork-powered, with drive to the rubber main wheels, with a winding aperture on the port side of the nose. Small control knobs on the underside of the fuselage, between the main wheels, allow for the aircraft to be stationary with the inner propellers

turning, or moving forward with all propellers turning. The propellers and the nose-wheel are plastic. Unlike some of the other models shown on this spread, the wing section is not detachable. Length: 9·75in (24·765cm); wingspan: 11·5in (29·21cm).

2 Air Transport Service Car Ferry by HWM, West Germany; dating from c1956. This most pleasing tinplate and plastic toy, with the maker's name on one wingtip and the number "S-72" on the other, is in three sections which are fitted together with the aid of spring-clips: a cabin section, with a clear plastic "bubble" loading bay; a wing section; and a twin-boom with tailplane assembly (with red plastic engine nacelles). A friction-drive mechanism in the lower part of the

cabin section drives rubber wheels and produces a siren sound. The plastic bubble opens to allow a toy vehicle (a push-along DUKW of green plastic) to be run in and out. Length: 9·5in (24·13cm); wingspan: 13·5in (34·29cm).

3 Twin-Engined Airliner by Tipp and Company, West Germany; dating from c1956. The finish is almost identical with that of the four-engined airliner by Arnold, shown at (1), but the identification letters differ. This toy is more fully described at (6), pages 306-307, where its packaging is shown. Length: 9·75in (24·765cm); wingspan: 12·375in (31·43cm).

4 Passenger Plane by an unidentified maker, People's Republic of China; dating from c1958. This fairly simple tinplate model of a

twin-piston-engined airliner bears the legend "International Express" on the fuselage and has beneath the wing section a paper sticker with "Made in China" in both English and Chinese characters. The upper wing bears the identification "MF 036". A rather clumsy friction motor drives both the rubber wheels and, via a coiled-wire drive, the propellers. The wing section is detachable. Length: 7·125in (18·097cm); wingspan: 9·75in (24·765cm).

5 B.O.A.C. Comet 4 Airliner by Tipp and Company, West Germany; dating from 1958. This is possibly a prototype model rather than a production toy, since it is finished to an unusually high standard: it is apparently hand-painted, with fine detailing of wing panels etc. Friction

drives the main wheels (plastic, with rubber tyres) and produces sparks beneath the clear plastic covers of the engine nacelles. The wing section is detachable. Length: 11·75in (29·845cm); wingspan: 12·25in (31·115cm).

6 Viscount Airliner by Tomy, Japan; dating from c1956. This ingenious toy has a tinplate upper fuselage and tailplane and a plastic lower fuselage and wing section. The plastic engine nacelles have bright metal bands; the propellers are plastic and the main wheels are rubber with metal discs. It is powered by three 1·5-volt batteries in the fuselage forward. The lever on the nose opens the plastic canopy over the cockpit. The levers in front of the plastic half-figures of the pilots are the primary on/off

control (centre) and the controls to start or stop the port and starboard propellers, which revolve with a realistic sound while the wing-lights flash. The nose wheels are steerable, and as the aircraft moves forward the track-mounted figure of a stewardess moves up and down between the rows of moulded plastic passengers. Length: 17·75in (45·085cm); wingspan: 19in (48·26cm).

7 Bristol Bulldog Airplane by Straco, Japan; dating from 1958-59. This toy is fully described at (4), *pages 32-33,* where it is shown with its original packaging.

8 Training Plane by an unidentified maker, People's Republic of China; dating from c1958. This simple tinplate novelty is clockwork-powered with a permanent winder.

A springloaded lever beneath the fuselage drives the aeroplane along in a series of somersaults. Length: 3·37in (8·57cm); wingspan: 4·125in (10·48cm).

9 Air France Caravelle by Arnold, West Germany; dating from c1959. This fairly simple, but well-made and pleasingly-designed model is tinplate throughout, with rubber tyres on its metal wheels. The maker's trademark and "Made in Germany" are printed on the underside of the fuselage, between the pressed-tin engine nacelles. Friction drives the main wheels. The model was boxed with a fold-out brochure detailing the history and specifications of the aircraft and extolling the virtues of Air France: it was probably intended to be sold primarily at Air

France offices and airport shops. Length: 14·25in (36·195cm); wingspan: 14·5in (36·83cm).

10 Air Plane by an unidentified maker, People's Republic of China; dating from c1958. This cheap and simple friction-driven tinplate toy has two plastic propellers. Length: 6·375in (16·19cm); wingspan: 6·625in (16·83cm).

11 T.W.A. Boeing 727 Jet Airplane by an unidentified Japanese maker; dating from c1961. This large but simple model, rather crude as regards press-work but with much printed detail, is tinplate throughout and has rubber main wheels which are friction-driven. The words "Made in Japan" are stamped below the tailplane on either side. Length: 14·5in (36·83cm); wingspan: 12·25in (31·115cm).

1

2

6

7

1 Patrol Police Helicopter by an unidentified Japanese maker; dating from c1957. Note the applied "Foreign" sticker across the badge on the helicopter's side; the words "Made in Japan" are printed below the "Police" legend on the side away from the camera. The body and main rotor of the toy are tinplate with printed details; the tail rotor is plastic and the cabin is fitted with red plastic windows. The rubber wheels are fitted with metal discs. It is clockwork-powered, with a permanent winder on the side of the undercarriage away from the camera. When it is wound and released, it moves forward with its main rotor (which is removable and may be folded for packaging) turning and the cabin lit up by a sparking mechanism.

The swivel-mounted front wheel of the tricycle undercarriage causes it to steer a quite erratic course. Length: 9·5in (24·13cm); rotor diameter: 11in (27·94cm).
2 Control Tower and Remote-Control Helicopter by Arnold, West Germany; dating from c1955. The "Idlewild Airport" tower is of good-quality tinplate, attractively printed with national flags, control room details and, around its base, a world map. The pressed-tin helicopter, with plastic rotor and wheels, is in "Sabena" finish. It is powered by Arnold's own remote-control system, using a manually-cranked handset that transmits power through a cored cable; this is fully described at (5), pages 306-307. Details of Arnold's patents are printed on both the handset

and the underside of the tower. The end of the core of the cable running to the helicopter is fitted into the socket on top of the tower, and when the handset is cranked the helicopter takes off and flies most realistically around the tower. Like the other Arnold "flying toys" seen here, it is obviously not suitable for use in a small room! Height of tower: 9in (22·86cm); length of tower-helicopter cable: 27in (68·58cm); length of helicopter: 5·5in 913·97cm); rotor diameter: 7in (17·78cm).
3 Helicopter by an unidentified West German maker; dating from c1953. The serial number "HK 565" is printed beneath the rotor—see also (4)—and the words "Made in Germany" are printed on the side of the fuselage

away from the camera. This simple, colourfully-printed tinplate toy is clockwork-powered (note the winding shaft just forward of the large rubber main wheels); the folding rotor blades are plastic, as is the small rear wheel. Length: 10·25in (26·035cm); rotor diameter: 9·625in (24·48cm).
4 Helicopter by an unidentified West German maker; dating from c1959. Bearing the serial number "HK-570", this simple toy of tab-and-slot construction is obviously by the same maker and of the same period as (4). Its folding blades are metal and its wheels are plastic. It is friction-driven. Length: 7·75in (19·685cm); rotor diameter: 7in (17·78cm).
5 Astra Copter by an unidentified Japanese maker; dating from

Inset (above): Closeup detail of the side of the Japanese-made Astra Copter shown at (4). When the intermittent "stop" mechanism operates, the side hatch springs open and the printed pressed-tin astronaut waves his jointed arm.

c1959. Tinplate throughout, save for the clear plastic tail rotor (with "spinning" markings), this was one of the earlier Japanese tinplate toys made specifically for export. It bears US Navy markings, and is battery-powered with bump-and-go action. The mechanism incorporates an intermittent stop: when this operates, the side hatch opens; see *Inset*. The red plastic light mounted atop the rotor flashes while the toy is in motion. Length: 12in (30·48cm); rotor diameter: 15·5in (39·37cm).

6 Remote-Control Helibus by Arnold, West Germany; dating from c1956. Since this is a "flying" model using Arnold's remote-control system, the body of the helibus is made of very lightweight tinplate; the wing and tail sections, propellers, rotors and wheels are plastic. The legend "Fairey Autodyne' is printed along the sides. Length: 8·5in (21·59cm); rotor diameter: 11in (27·94cm); control cable: 32in (81·28cm).

7 Remote-Control Satellite by Arnold, West Germany; dating from late 1957. This fascinating toy is fully described at (5), *pages 306-307*, where its packaging is shown. Vane diameter: 6·75in (17·145cm); control cable: 31in (78·74cm).

8 Remote-Control Piccolo Helicopter by Arnold, West Germany; dating from c1954. In blue-and-white "Sabena" printed livery, this lightweight tinplate toy is another of Arnold's "flying" models powered by a remote-control handset. As the speed of the hand-cranking is increased, the helicopter takes off from the ground; it can be made to change course, climb or dive by altering the angle at which the handset is held—and can be made to fly backwards by cranking in reverse! The pitch of the rotor blades can also be altered, to improve lifting power, by twisting around the metal sockets of the plastic vanes with pliers. Length: 5·5in (13·97cm); rotor diameter: 7in (17·78cm); length of control cable: 31in (78·74cm).

9 Helicopter by Biller, West Germany; dating from 1958-59. This is a quite fascinating novelty toy of printed tinplate. Both the helicopter itself, with plastic rotor, and its landing base are clockwork-powered. When both are wound, the helicopter is placed on the "Start" section of the base. When the speed-control lever on the "Start" side, at the end of the base, is moved forward, the helicopter takes off, its rotor turning, and flies on its wire supporting arm around the globe-mounted "radar dish", its movement registering on the plastic-shielded screen between the control levers. The lever on the "Landing" side of the base controls the height. Length of helicopter: 3·75in (9·525cm); rotor diameter: 4·25in (10·795cm); length of base: 9·75in (24·765cm).

Inset (above): *Closeup detail of the side of the Japanese-made Astra Copter shown at (4). When the intermittent "stop" mechanism operates, the side hatch springs open and the printed pressed-tin astronaut waves his jointed arm.*

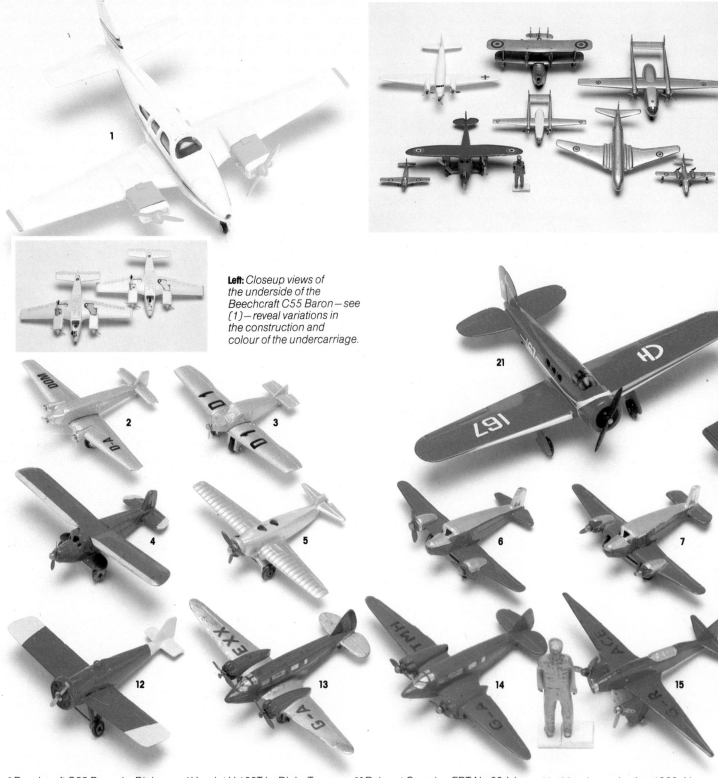

Left: *Closeup views of the underside of the Beechcraft C55 Baron—see (1)—reveal variations in the construction and colour of the undercarriage.*

1 Beechcraft C55 Baron by Dinky Toys, Great Britain; Dinky Toys Reference Number (DT No) 715, in production 1968-76. This model, featuring detachable engine covers and a retractable undercarriage, appeared also in military green finish as the US Army T.42A (DT No 712, 1972-77). A common item. Wingspan: 5·8125in (148mm).

2 Junkers Ju 52 Airliner by Schuco, West Germany; maker's reference number (MRN) 335784, dating from around 1970. It has metal wheels that are fitted with rubber tyres. Wingspan: 2·875in (73mm).

3 Junkers F13 Monoplane by Schuco, West Germany; MRN 335779, dating from around 1970. It has metal wheels that, as at (2), are fitted with rubber tyres. Wingspan: 2·75in (70mm).

4 Henriot H 180T by Dinky Toys, France; French Dinky Toys Reference Number (FDT No) 60c, in production around 1935-40. Wingspan: 3·15in (80mm).

5 Farman F360; FDT No 61c, in production 1938-40. A limited item. Wingspan: 2·75in (70mm).

6-7 Potez 56; FDT No 61b, in production c1938-40. The two versions shown illustrate colour and casting variants: (6) has a tapered tailplane, while the tailplane of (7) is squared off. Wingspan: 2·75in (70mm).

8 Dewoitine 500; FDT No 60e, in production 1935-40. A limited item. Wingspan: 3·15in (80mm).

9 Potez 58; FDT No 60b, in production 1935-40. The example shown has been repainted. Wingspan: 2·99in (76mm).

10 Bréguet Corsaire; FDT No 60d, in production from 1935 until 1940. Wingspan: 3·125in (79mm).

11 General Monospar Plane; DT No 60e. The version shown, in silver, was in production 1936-40. It was made also in gold-and-red finish in 1934-36. Limited availability. Wingspan: 3·15in (80mm).

12 Low Wing Monoplane; DT No 60d. This aircraft was made in red-and-cream, without pilot, in 1934-36, and appeared in orange, with pilot and registration letters "G-A VYP", in 1936-40. The aircraft shown appears to be a repainted later version. A limited item. Wingspan: 3·03in (77mm).

13 King's Aeroplane (Airspeed Envoy); DT No 62k, in production 1938-41. Limited. Wingspan: 3·62in (92mm).

14 Airspeed Envoy Monoplane; DT No 62m, in production 1938-41. The same casting as (20), but easier to find in this finish. Wingspan: 3·62in (92mm).

15 Light Racer (D.H. Comet); DT No 60g. This model appeared in this and other finishes with the letters "G-R ACE" in 1946-49. It was made in red-and-gold in 1935-37, and in silver in 1937-40. All versions are limited. Wingspan: 3·375in (86mm).

16 Percival Gull (Amy Mollinson's); DT No 60k. The model appeared as seen here, in blue-and-silver with the letters "G-A DZO" in blue, in 1936. It was marketed in a special box commemorating Amy Mollinson's record-breaking flight to Capetown and back. It appeared in the same finish, but with "G-A DZO" in black, in

1937-40, to mark H.L. Brook's South African flight. See also (17) and (18). Both versions are limited. Wingspan: 2·99in (76mm).

17 Percival Gull Light Tourer; DT No 60k, the post-War reissue of (16) and (18), appearing in single-colour finishes in 1946-48. Fairly common. Wingspan: 2·99in (76mm).

18 Percival Gull; DT No 60c. The first version of this aircraft, appearing in white-and-blue in 1934-37. It was made in single-colour finishes with the letters "G-A DZO" in 1937-40. Easier to find than (16).

19 D.H. Leopard Moth; DT No 60b. This was made in various finishes in 1934-36, and in silver only in 1936-40. The earlier versions are rarer. Wingspan: 2·99in (76mm).

20 Messerschmitt Me 108 Noregrin (in civil livery) by CIJ, France. Wingspan: 2·375in (60mm).

21 Lockheed Orion by NZG, West Germany; dating from around 1965. This large, well-detailed model is fitted with plastic windows, wheels and propeller. Wingspan: 5·25in (133mm).

22-23 Beechcraft Bonanza S35; DT No 710, in production 1965-76. Two colour finishes are shown. This is a quite common item. Wingspan: 5·0625in (129mm).

24 Hawker Siddeley HS 125; DT No 723, in production 1970-75. It has a retractable undercarriage. It is easily available. Wingspan: 5·1875in (132mm).

25 Lear Jet 25B by Schuco, West Germany; MRN 335794, dating from around 1960. It has metal wheels that are fitted with rubber tyres. Wingspan: 2·0625in (52mm).

26 Sikorsky S58 Helicopter; FDT No 60D, issued in May 1957, renumbered 802 in 1959, in production until 1961. Limited. Fuselage length: 3·15in (80mm); rotor diameter: 3·44in (87mm).

27 Sikorsky Float Helicopter by Solido, France; c1960. Limited. Fuselage length: 3in (76mm); rotor diameter: 3·3125in (84mm).

28 Bell Police Helicopter; DT No 732, in production 1974-80. It was also made in "Police Crash Squad" (DT No 299) and "Commando Squad" (DT No 303) versions. It is a common item. Fuselage length: 8·307in (211mm).

29 Bristol 173 Helicopter; DT No 715 — note that it bears the same number as the Beechcraft C55 Baron at (1) — in production 1956-62. A fairly common model. Fuselage length: 5·00in (127mm).

30 Westland Sikorsky S51 Helicopter; DT No 716, in production 1957-62. Fuselage length: 3·504in (89mm).

31 Cierva Autogiro; DT No 60f, in production 1934-41. It appeared also in camouflage finish (DT No 66f; 1940-41). Limited availability. Fuselage length: 2·008in (51mm).

Inset (top left): *(Back row) Fiat G212 Tri-Motor by Mercury, Italy; "Singapore" Flying Boat, DT No 60h, 1936-40; SNCAN Noratlas, FDT No 804, first issued 1960. (Centre) SNCAN Noratlas by CIJ, France. (Front row) Messerschmitt Me 108 Noregrin by CIJ, France; Tri-Motor High-Wing Monoplane by an unidentified French maker; Comet 4 Airliner by Lone Star, Great Britain; Piaggio 136 Seaplane by Mercury, Italy.*

1 Shetland Flying Boat by Dinky Toys, Great Britain; Dinky Toys Reference Number (DT No) 701. This model was first issued in 1947 and remained in production until 1949. The example shown has been repainted: the model originally bore the registration letters "G-A GVD" and "BX". A fairly scarce item. Wingspan: 9·25in (235mm).

2 Empire Flying Boat; DT No 60r, first issued in 1937, in production until 1940, and reissued after World War II. This model appeared with fifteen different sets of registration letters and names: the letters "G-A DHM" on the example shown mark it as the "Caledonia", first of the series. See also (5). This example has been refitted with four-bladed propellers; as seen at (5), three-bladed propellers were

originally fitted. A limited item. Wingspan: 6·18in (157mm).

3 Mayo Composite Aircraft; DT No 63, first issued in 1939 and in production until 1941. These two aircraft were issued both in composite form, as seen here, and as separate items. The composite model is by far the hardest to find and may be described as fairly scarce. Wingspans: (upper) 3·976in (101mm); (lower) 6·18in (157mm).

4 Seaplane "Mercury"; DT No 63b. The upper component of the Mayo Composite shown at (3); this was available as a separate item in 1939-41, and again after World War II until 1954. A limited item. Wingspan: 3·976in (101mm).

5 Empire Flying Boat; DT No 60r. This version of the model described at (2) is fitted with propellers of the

original type. The letters "G-A DUV" mark it as the version named "Cambria". A limited item. Wingspan: 6·18in (157mm).

6 Flying Boat "Clipper III"; DT No 60w, first issued in 1938-40 and available post-War from 1946 until 1948. This example has been repainted: it was issued by the maker in silver only. The pre-War version, which bears registration letters, will be fairly hard to find. Wingspan: 6·46in (164mm).

7-8 Armstrong Whitworth Air Liner; DT No 62p. As seen at (7), in silver finish, this model first appeared in 1938 and until 1941 was available with six different letterings and names: this example has the letters "G-A DSV", marking it as "Explorer". It was reissued in 1946-49, when it was available

either in silver or in two-tone finish as seen at (8). Neither version will now be particularly hard to find. Wingspan: 6·81in (173mm).

9-10 Vickers Viking Airliner; DT No 70c, first issued in 1947, later renumbered 705, and in production until 1962. Earlier versions, as seen at (9), are finished in silver; later ones, as seen at (10), in grey. Both versions bear the letters "G-A GOL", and neither is hard to find. Wingspan: 5·51in (140mm).

11 Four-engined Air Liner; DT No 60r, first issued in 1946 and in production until 1949. See also (20). The model was originally available, with the same number, as the D.H. Albatross Mail Liner, in 1939-41. The pre-War version bore the letters "G-A EVV". Neither version is hard to find, but the

pre-War aeroplane is the rarer. Wingspan: 5·7in (145mm).

12 Dewoitine D338 Tri-Motor by Dinky Toys, France; French Dinky Toys Reference Number (FDT No) 61a, first issued in 1938 and available until 1940. Limited. Wingspan: 5·275in (134mm).

13 Lockheed Super 6 Constellation; FDT No 60c. This model in "Air France" livery was first issued in 1959 and was in production until 1962. It is a limited item. Wingspan: 7·87in (200mm).

14 Bristol Britannia; DT No 998, first issued in 1959 and in production until 1965. It appeared only in "Canadian Pacific" livery, as shown; but see (18) for a colour variation. This is a limited item. Wingspan: 8·86in (225mm).

15 Vickers Viscount Airliner; DT No 708, first issued in 1957 and in production until 1965. In "British European Airways" livery, this example is finished in silver, white and red; in some later production models, silver is replaced by grey. It is of limited availability. Wingspan: 5·87in (149mm).

16 Vickers Viscount Airliner; DT No 706, first issued in 1956 and in production until 1957. This is in "Air France" finish but otherwise resembles (15). It was produced for only a short time and may be hard to find. Wingspan: 5·87in (149mm).

17 Douglas DC3; DT No 60t, first issued in 1938 and in production until 1940. Note the small hole in the centre of the fuselage, provided for what a leaflet packed by Dinky Toys with many of its pre-War aeroplanes called "Gliding". A string was passed through the looped top of a split-pin inserted into the hole; with the string suitably secured at both ends the model could be glided, with the aid of another string fixed to its tail, to a stable landing. Only models made up to early 1940 have the "gliding hole". It is a limited item. Wingspan: 5·197in (132mm).

18 Bristol Britannia; DT No 998. As (14) in all respects save one: a blue stripe replaces the red stripe on the sides and tailfin.

19 Vickers Viscount Airliner; this appears to be DT No 708 — see (15) — but is a "Nicky Toy", made in India from obsolete dies sold by Meccano c1968-70.

20 Four-Engined Air Liner; DT No 62r. This is a colour variation of the model shown at (11).

21 Avro York Airliner; DT No 70a, first issued in 1946, later renumbered 704, and in production until 1959. it is a fairly common model. Wingspan: 6·29in (160mm).

22 Junkers Ju90 Airliner; DT No 62n, first issued in 1939 and in production until 1941. Note the "gliding hole". See also (23). Fairly scarce. Wingspan: 6·22in (158mm).

23 Giant High Speed Monoplane; DT No 62y, first issued in 1946 and in production until 1949. It is a fairly easily available model. Wingspan: 6·22in (158mm).

24 Vickers Viscount Airliner; FDT No 60e, first issued in 1959, later renumbered 803, and in production until 1961. Compare this model with the version by Dinky Toys, Great Britain, at (16). Scarce. Wingspan: 5·87in (149mm).

7

Toy soldiers have perhaps the longest history of any kind of toy, for miniature figures of fighting men were being produced — although not always as toys — as long as 4,000 years ago; children of the Roman era played with lead soldiers; and medieval princes were provided with toy armies with which to further their military studies.

The toy soldier as we know it, however, had its origins in the flat tin figures produced by German craftsmen from the 18th century onwards. "Flats" of a slightly later date are shown on *pages 244-245* and the photographs in this section go on to illustrate in detail the development of toy soldiers over the last 100 years, in a colourful parade of the infantry, cavalry, artillery and air and naval arms of many countries, along with their equipment and vehicles.

For many collectors all over the world, the words "toy soldier" are near-synonymous with the name of Britains of Great Britain, dominant in the production of hollow-cast figures from the 1890s until the "plastic revolution" after World War II. It is certainly fitting that the armies of Britains should dominate the pages we devote to this fascinating branch of toy collecting.

Toy Soldiers

"Flat" Figures by German Makers

The earliest toy soldiers produced commercially in any quantity were "flats", first made by the tinsmiths of Nuremberg from the 1730s onwards. The earliest identifiable maker was Johann Gottfried Hilpert, who by the 1770s was making miniatures of the Army of Frederick the Great and some of its opponents. A lot of the early figures were poorly proportioned, and there was no standardization of scale.
Ernst Heinrichsen, who set up in business in 1839, produced an enormous range of figures in several sizes, but his most influential achievement was the introduction in 1848 of the standard 30mm (1.8in) figure. The "Nuremberg Scale" soon caught on, and was adopted by many

other soldier manufacturers. Although they were also produced in other countries, "flats" have always found most favour in Germany, where they have remained popular to this day. In 1925 Aloys Ochel of Kiel brought out their "Kilia" and "Oki" ranges, aimed at the serious collector as much as at the toy trade. Flats are still being designed and produced, but they are usually sold as unpainted castings to be finished by the purchaser — sometimes to a superb standard of realism.

1-13 French Revolutionary troops of 1796; by Heinrichsen, 1870s. Note both the vigorous action poses of (1-5) and the casual stance of (7-10). In contrast the

wounded figure (6) is rather naïvely portrayed. Items (11-13) are mounted officers. The kneeling firing infantryman (5) has a blob of lead at the muzzle of his musket to represent smoke.
14-16 Prussian cavalry of 1813; by Heinrichsen, 1870s. (14-15) show both sides of the same pose, and (16) is a trumpeter.
17 French horse artilleryman; by Heinrichsen, 1860s. This is from the "Sham Fight" set (see *inset*).
18-30 French foot guards, 1840s uniform; by Heinrichsen, c1860. (18-20) are foot guards marching at the shoulder arms. (21-22) are pioneers with axes, wearing their traditional beards and long aprons. (23-29) are bandsmen, including some playing interesting early brass instruments (23-24).

(30) is a mounted guards officer.
31-34 French hussars, 1860s period; by Heinrichsen, 1860s. From the "Sham Fight" set (see *inset*).
35-37 Chasseurs à Cheval of the late 1840s; by Heinrichsen, c1870.
38-48 Scottish Highlanders; by Heinrichsen; c1870. The label on the box lid (see *inset*) identifies them as "Ecossais Montagnards" thus confusing Highlanders with mountain troops. Accordingly they are equipped with mountain artillery pieces carried on mules. They wear rather brief kilts, also spartanly worn by the mounted officer! (41) and (47) show two views of the foot officer; the standard bearer (45) appears to be carrying an Austrian flag.
49-62 The Abyssinian Expedition of 1868; by Heinrichsen, c1870. The

244

63 64 65 66 67 68 69 70 71 72 73

74 75 76 77 78 79 80 81 82

86 87 88 89 90 91 83 84 85

92 93 94 95 96

97 98 99

Inset (above): *Heinrichsen boxes. The large paper-covered wooden box has a sliding lid with a print of a battle scene entitled "The Sham Fight". It contains artillery, consisting of fully three-dimensional limbers and cannons pulled by flat horses — see (17) — and hussars as illustrated at (51-54). The split pine boxes on the right are typical of the packaging used for flats in the 18th and 19th centuries. The right-hand box is labelled "Extra fine tin composition figures — silver prize medal". The medal is illustrated, showing the head of King Ludwig I of Bavaria. The number of pieces is handwritten, as is the title "The Abyssinian Expedition" — the latter in German, French and English. At the bottom of the label is printed "E. Heinrichsen in Nürnberg". The label on the other box is similar but shows a gold prize medal with the head of Ludwig II, and the handwritten title "Ecossais Montagnards".*

infantrymen carry their rifles in three different positions, each shown from either side at (51-53) and (55-57). Three sappers with slung rifles carry an axe, pickaxe and shovel (58-60). Note the officer (50) puffing on a cigar. While all ranks wear the Havelock — a Foreign Legion style cap — an alternative drummer (49) has a sun helmet.

63-70 Austrian infantry of 1680-1700; from the "Kilia" range of Aloys Ochel, *c*1930. These figures capture rather well the late 17th-century uniforms. A more accurate semi-matt paint finish is used, but to the collector this does not have the charm of the glowing semi-translucent colours of the earlier figures.

71-73 Bavarian infantry of the 1830s.

These attractive 48mm (1.9in) figures were produced in Bavaria in the 1960s, from old moulds — demonstrating something of the difficulty involved in trying to date such figures accurately.

74-85 Richard the Lionheart, 1190; by Heinrichsen, *c*1930. A splendidly colourful set of a battle between Crusaders (77-85) and Saracens (74-76). Note particularly the Crusader with a captured Saracen (78), and the Crusader assisting a comrade (83).

86-91 British rocket battery, 1880; by Heinrichsen, *c*1930. These notoriously unreliable weapons, introduced by Congreve during the Napoleonic Wars, were still being used (with modifications) in the British Army until the 1890s. The officer (89) and crew are

shown in a variety of relaxed poses; the man in shirt sleeves firing the rocket (90) is sometimes painted wearing a scarlet jacket.

92-99 British infantry and Gatling gun, Zulu War, 1879; by Heinrichsen, *c*1930. Note the traditional feature of the smoke

from the rifles of the two firing figures (96 and 98). The good variety of poses includes two different infantrymen kneeling with fixed bayonets (94 and 99). The sailor crew for the Gatling gun have been given red jackets, as though they were infantry.

Semi-flats, or semi-solids (*halb massif* in German) are thicker than flats, giving a rounded appearance when viewed from the side. They are rather looked down on by most collectors, and indeed at their worst they can be very crude and uninspired. This is not helped by the fact that many semi-flat moulds were sold for home casting in the 1900s by firms such as Gebrüder Schneider of Leipzig. They were very popular in the USA, where the moulds themselves are collected. The result has been that some very poorly cast semi-flats have found their way on to the market; the dating of the figures has also been made difficult. Despite this there are many exceptions, with a charm

and character of their own, combining the pictorial quality of the flat with a pleasing solidity.

1-7 Austrian cavalry bivouac; *c*1900. Some of the attractive figures from a set currently produced by Kober of Vienna from old moulds by Wollner. A cavalryman in shirtsleeves (1) grooms his horse; (2-4) are dragoons, while (6-7) are hussars.
8 British officer surprised by Zulus. This imaginative piece is by an unknown German maker, *c*1890.
9-14 Austrian artillery, 1880s; by Kober. These Austrian gunners in their distinctive brown tunics serve a fully three-dimensional artillery piece in an attractive group cast from old Wollner moulds. Austrian cannon were

traditionally painted yellow.
15-18 Austrian Army field hospital, *c*1900; by Kober. Some of the charming figures from a set produced by Kober from Wollner moulds: (15) a surgeon bandaging the head of a soldier supported by an orderly; (16) a nurse of possibly later design — judging by her raised hemline; (17) an

Inset (above) Old metal home-cast moulds, of designs originally produced by Gebrüder Schneider of Leipzig, together with finished and painted examples of the figures they produce. In the foreground are the British officer, infantryman and Highlander (62-64), and behind are the advancing and marching sailors and the naval officer (50-52).

orderly bandaging a soldier's leg, assisted by a nurse; and (18) two orderlies carrying a wounded man without using a stretcher.
19-26 German sailors, *c*1900; by Schweizer. This German family firm was founded by Adam Schweizer in 1796, and still produces a range of flats and semi-flats in varying sizes, of both military and civilian subjects. (19) depicts a German sailor catching up on the news while leaning against a palm tree and puffing on his pipe. In a smaller scale, (20-26) show a German naval officer supervising sailors going about their tasks and raising the ensign, while other relax.
27-30 The French firm of Mignot, better known for its 54mm (2.12in) solids, also produced an

28 29 30 31 32 33 34 35 36 37 38

40 41 42 43 44 45 46 47 48

50 51 52 53 54 55

57 58 59 60 61 62 63 64

attractive and distinctive range of 40mm (1.57in) semi-flat (*demi ronde bosse*) figures, often available in multi-tiered display boxes including buildings, trees and accessories. These are "Turcos" — French Algerian troops of *c*1900.

31-38 Allied troops of 1914 by Mignot: (31) French line infantryman marching, parade dress. (32) French line infantryman charging in greatcoat. (33) Belgian infantryman standing firing. (34) Belgian infantryman marching. (35) Russian infantryman marching, parade dress. (36) Russian infantryman advancing in greatcoat. (37-38) British infantry advancing and standing firing. The least satisfactory of an

otherwise good series, the British "Tommies" are in fact Japanese infantry originally designed to oppose (35-36) in a Russo-Japanese war setting, but hurriedly turned out in khaki for World War I. Mignot have never been at their best when portraying British troops!

39-43 French infantry, Franco-Prussian War; by an unknown German maker, *c*1880. Virtually the same figures were produced in dark blue with German *picklehaubes* (spiked helmets) as Prussians, or in scarlet tunics as British infantry.

44-48 Prussian infantry in action; cast from Schneider moulds of the 1900s. These figures are still being produced commercially on a small scale in England, packed

in cartons and drums marked "Victorian Toy Soldiers".

49 A Prussian bandsman from a Schneider mould, painted as a British soldier.

50-52 German sailors; from an old Schneider mould, recently home-cast and painted (see *inset*).

53-54 A Prussian artilleryman on a draught horse, and an ornate field gun; cast from Schneider moulds by the same firm as (44-48).

55 A small-scale khaki British infantryman of 1914, from a Schneider mould.

56 18th-century infantryman advancing; from a range designed by Holger Eriksson and cast from a modern "Prince August" rubber home-cast mould.

57 A steel-helmeted Swedish cavalryman, designed by Holger

Eriksson and cast from a "Prince August" mould of the 1970s.

58-59 A very basic Soviet soldier at attention with slung sub-machine gun (58), and a trumpeter from a small range of bandsmen (59), made in the USSR in the 1960s.

60-61 Prussian infantry standing and kneeling firing; from a home-cast rubber mould in the "Zinn Brigade" range by Schildkrot. These figures are almost fully round. Home-cast moulds are popular in Germany and available in most large toy shops today. Sadly, the Zinn Brigade range seems to have been discontinued.

62-64 British infantryman and officer, from the Zulu War period, and a Highlander in full dress; commercially produced from a Schneider mould (see *inset*).

247

Solid Figures by Lucotte, France

While the Germans were producing flat figures in tin the French were developing the fully round solid figure in lead. The earliest known firm, Lucotte, is said to have been founded at about the time of the French Revolution in 1789. Their later amalgamation with C.B.G. Mignot gives the latter firm the distinction of being the oldest toy soldier maker in continuous existence. The bulk of Lucotte's production was devoted to the French Army of the Revolutionary and the First Empire periods. The figures are of excellent quality and have great style; of almost model standard, rather than toys, they must have been expensive playthings. Some fine examples can be seen in museums, and in collections

such as that of the Duke of Marlborough which is on show at Blenheim Palace.
It is difficult to put a date earlier than the 1860s on most of these pieces. Various dates have been put forward for Lucotte's amalgamation with C.B.G. Mignot, but it can be said that soldiers were being produced in the distinctive Lucotte style until after World War I.
Lucotte figures have a longer stride and a lighter step than those by Mignot. They have plug-in heads, and whereas Mignot arms are bent into position those of Lucotte figures are cast separately and fitted over lugs at the shoulder to be soldered in position. The cavalry horses are more elegant than those of

Mignot, with long tails, and the movable reins are applied separately and held in place by pieces of wire. The saddles are removable and have stirrups, although they usually hang too low for the riders' feet to engage in them. Some Lucotte bases are marked with an Imperial Bee flanked by the letters "LC".
From time to time Mignot, who hold Lucotte moulds amongst their vast collection, re-issue such items as Napoleon and his staff or a set of cavalry kettle-drummers — at a high price. Some of the items in Mignot's personality range are of Lucotte origin, such as Marshal Foch (22). For a direct comparison between Lucotte and Mignot figures see the illustration on *page 10*.

1-7 Musicians from the band of the Imperial Guard. Note that two different figures are used — (1, 5, 6), and (2-4). The musicians are: (1) bass drummer; (2) clarinettist; (3) glockenspiel player; (4) clarinettist; (5) serpent player (this was a cumbersome instrument of wood bound in leather); (6) trombone player. The splendid tall figure in the extravagantly plumed hat and red boots (7), missing most of his staff in this example, is in fact a portrait figure of Drum Major Senot who served with the band of the Imperial Guard throughout the Napoleonic period.
8 Napoleonic lancer of the Vistula Legion. Note that this excellent figure of a Polish lancer and all the following Lucotte cavalry have separate saddles and also

18 **19** **20**

21 **22** **23**

24 **25** **26** **27** **28** **29** **30**

feature separate movable reins.
9 Trooper of the 5th Hussars. He wears a separately cast pelisse (fur-trimmed jacket) hanging from the left shoulder.
10 Officer of the 5th Hussars. He is dressed similarly to the trooper, but correctly wears a fur busby rather than a shako and has a different pattern saddle cloth.
11 British infantryman, Waterloo period. Note the particularly jaunty step of this and some of the other figures.
12 A British infantry drummer in ''reverse'' colours: his jacket is in green facing colour rather than red, and trimmed with distinctive ''drummer's lace''
13 French line infantryman of the Napoleonic period, marching at the slope.

14 French infantryman, in the white uniform of 1806. This uses the same body casting as (13) but with a taller plumed shako.
15 French infantryman, in white uniform, at the present arms.
16 Standard-bearer of the Flanqueurs of the Imperial Guard, 1812-14.
17 Flanqueur, marching at the shoulder arms.
18-22 A series of mounted personality figures of World War I. Note that the next five models all have the same horse and rider casting; apart from the painting only the portrait head and sometimes the saddlery varies. (18) King George V in the World War I khaki service dress of a general officer. (19) General Cadorna, Commander-in-Chief of

the Italian Army, in pre-war style uniform. (20) King Peter of Serbia. (21) General John Pershing, Commander of the First US Army, in campaign hat. (22) Marshal Foch; interestingly, this is a figure currently available from C.B.G. Mignot in their personality range, but unlike most of the series it is entirely Lucotte in design, the base of the horse being marked with an Imperial Bee flanked by the letters LC.
23 Indian Army cavalry trooper, in khaki World War I uniform.
24 Indian Army sepoy, in World War I khaki, marching on the slope. A Mignot sepoy was also made.
25 Chasseur Alpin (or mountain light infantryman), standing firing. This casting, rather shorter than most Lucotte figures, was also issued

in khaki with a steel helmet as a British Tommy.
26 Chasseur Alpin, kneeling firing. Mignot also produced figures of Chasseurs Alpin.
27 French infantryman, prone firing, in ''Adrian'' helmet and horizon blue greatcoat. Compare with the similar Mignot figure shown at (41) *page 250*.
28 French standard-bearer, in horizon blue tunic. The Mignot equivalent to this figure is shown at (4) *page 250*.
29 French infantry bugler, in ''Adrian'' pattern helmet and horizon blue greatcoat. Note the separately applied *fouragerre* or lanyard on the left shoulder.
30 French infantryman, in horizon blue uniform, depicted at the order arms position.

The firm of C.B.G. Mignot of Paris, with a lineage dating back via takeovers and their absorption of Lucotte to the period of the French Revolution, can claim to be the oldest toy soldier maker still in existence. C.B.G. stands for Cuperly, Blondel and Gerbeau — three early 19th-century makers who amalgamated and were taken over by Mignot. A large part of the Mignot range depicts Napoleonic troops, but it has also covered the spectrum from Ancient Greeks, Romans, Gauls and Huns to the Israeli Army of the 1950s. The 54mm (2.12in) solid range of figures is the most important, but Mignot also made 40mm (1.57in) semi-flats — see *(27-38) page 247* — some large hollow-casts, aluminium figures,

and second-grade 54mm (2.12in) hollow-casts, as well as an extensive range of flats which are still produced. Hand-cast in bronze moulds, their 54mm (2.12in) solid figures emerge from the mould headless and with arms outspread. After cleaning the casting a suitable head is plugged in, and the arms are "animated" or bent into position to receive a weapon or musical instrument which is soldered on. The figures are then painted. In the past, infantry were issued in sets of 12, with an officer, standard bearer and drummer or bugler. Cavalry were in boxes of six. Cavalry are now five to a box, and infantry are in sets of 12 or eight figures — still in shiny red boxes. Infantry are also sold in

clear plastic-fronted boxes of four. Figures dating from the 1900s have dark green bases and a particularly good-quality paint finish, and contemporary troops carry the Chassepot rifle which has a more prominent sword bayonet than the later Lebel rifle. In the 1930s a very light sand colour was used for bases, and the facial detail which is such a feature of Mignot soldiers was not always so well painted. In the 1970s a rather "thin" full-gloss painting was adopted, and the bases were painted very dark brown. From about 1979 a semi-matt or satin finish painting has been used. Current figures have "C.B.G. Made in France" or just "Made in France" impressed into the base.

1 Monaco Carabinier at attention; white summer uniform.
2 Gun team with 75mm gun. This version with artillerymen in dark blue was produced in the 1970s.
3 French Army De Dion Bouton staff car, with driver, officer in kepi and NCO in greatcoat holding a map. This is a recent revival of a c1905 item.
4 French World War I standard bearer, in horizon blue uniform.
5 Marshal Joffre. This personality figure, produced c1930, is not just a head change, as he has the authentic portly figure!
6 A personality figure of Marshal Lyautey, produced c1980 in gloss finish. Strangely this figure uses the same body casing as that used for a Hindou.
7 A personality figure of Lyautey as

Governor-General of Morocco, in an Arab cloak.

8 Officer of hussars, in 1900s full dress, in current production.

9 Chasseur à Cheval, produced c1930, in 1915 horizon blue.

10 St Cyr cadet, from the mounted squadron in current production.

11 Officer of Dragons, 1900, in cloak; in current production.

12-15 Artillerymen in horizon blue, currently available.

16 Fortress cannon, an impressive item, recently discontinued.

17 World War I motor truck, of recent production.

18-29 The well-known Hommes de Corvée, or fatigue party. Note that these are infantrymen — not engineers as they are sometimes incorrectly described. Apart from the NCO (18) they all use the

same casting with an undress cap and a typically French canvas smock. Among the items carried are a side of bacon (22) and a broom with real twigs (24). This is a 1970s gloss-paint production. These figures have appeared with a number of different paint finishes and heads — see (30).

30 British soldier in fatigue dress with shovel.

31-33 British artillery of the 1900s, produced c1905. This interesting piece uses the same gun team as (2), including the famous French "75" gun, but with mounted artillerymen in khaki foreign service helmets as worn in the South African War. The gunners seated on the limber and the two marching figures (32 and 33) wear the peaked caps introduced

into the British Army in 1905.

34 Mounted British artillery officer, to accompany the gun team. Based on the same casting as (8), but in khaki with a foreign service helmet, he has inappropriate frogging cast on his tunic.

35 Italian lancer, World War I.

36 Italian dragoon, World War I.

37 French line infantryman advancing, 1914.

38 French horizon blue infantryman in greatcoat, kneeling firing; of recent manufacture.

39 French horizon blue infantryman advancing; recent manufacture. This is the same figure as (37) but with a steel helmet.

40 French horizon blue infantryman in greatcoat, standing firing.

41 French horizon blue infantryman in greatcoat, prone firing.

42 French horizon blue infantryman, standing firing; unusually in a tunic rather than a greatcoat.

43 French horizon blue machine-gunner; of recent manufacture.

44 French Foreign Legionnaire, advancing; recently re-issued.

45 US infantryman, standing firing, 1917.

46 US infantryman, advancing.

47 Chasseur Alpin ski trooper; a recent re-issue, also available in dark blue uniform.

48 French horizon blue despatch rider, on what is a virtually flat motorcycle; 1970s.

49 Monaco cannon; to accompany the Monaco Carabiniers.

50 Mountain gun. Despite its list description, this strange looking weapon is quite different from the Mignot mountain battery gun.

Although solid (and semi-solid) figures had been produced sporadically in Germany since the 18th century, the home market was dominated by the flat tin soldier. In the early 1870s, however, perhaps influenced by the success of the excellent solid figures produced by Lucotte and Mignot, Georg Heyde of Dresden started producing solid lead soldiers on a regular basis. Despite the charm of his figures he never really threatened the position of the "flat" in his own country, and had his greatest success with exports to countries such as Britain and the USA. Heyde produced figures in a bewildering variety of styles and scales — seven main infantry sizes from 43-120mm (1.7-4.7in),

the most numerous being the 43mm (1.7in) followed by the 52mm (2in) sizes. As with Mignot figures a fairly small number of different malleable soft lead bodies and plug-in heads with suitable paint finishes were able to represent almost any uniform or pose desired, but whatever the army represented, the figure retained a "Germanic" look. Heyde's smaller-scale soldiers were often lumpy, ill-proportioned little things, but his great achievement was in the imaginative uses to which he put them. Ordinary marching and firing figures were certainly produced, but what Heyde is most noted for are great ceremonial parades, and working parties going about their chores,

launching observation balloons, or following more tranquil occupations in a bivouac.

1 Scottish piper at attention. A good figure of a Gordon Highlander, only marred by a rather odd-shaped glengarry. This is to 52mm (2in) scale, the remainder of the figures shown — except (26) — being in the smaller 43mm (1.7in) size.
2 British Guardsman at attention.
3 Guards colour bearer, with the usual rather strange interpretation of the Union Flag.
4 Guards side drummer, with drummer's lace, but also a German-style backpack.
5 Marching Guards officer.
6 Guardsman, marching with his rifle at the slope.

7 Guards officer, in action with drawn sword.
8 Guardsman, standing firing.
9 Guardsman, kneeling firing.
10-18 German Navy working party, comprising: (10) sailor walking empty-handed; (11) sailor scrubbing the deck with a broom; (12) sailor with a coil of rope over his arm; (13) sailor coiling a rope on the deck; (14) sailor carrying a bucket; (15) sailor carrying a barrel; (16) sailor carrying a box on his shoulder; (17) sailor emptying a bucket; (18) sailor with a broom over his arm.
19 British line infantryman, marching with fixed bayonet in a white foreign service helmet.
20 British line infantry colour bearer, in spiked helmet.
21 British line infantryman, in foreign

service helmet, standing firing.
22-23 Variations of (19).
24 Line infantryman, marching at the slope in spiked helmet.
25 Line infantry officer, in action with drawn sword.
26 British Army cyclist, in scarlet jacket and glengarry; 52mm (2in) size. Heyde produced at least two quite distinct patterns of bicycle.
27-36 Luftwaffe pilot and ground crew. The German air force or Luftwaffe was formed in 1935. The figures here are: (27) pilot, using US "doughboy" body with a flying-helmet head; (28) airman walking empty-handed; (29) airman walking with spanner; (30) airman kneeling with spanner; (31) airman carrying a propeller; (32) airman kneeling with pliers; (33) airman carrying papers; (34)

Luftwaffe officer — this uses the same casting as the men, but with a "Sam Browne" cross-belt painted in, a white shirt, and a silver pilot badge; (35) airman carrying a large hammer; (36) airman emptying a petrol can.
37-49 British World War I working party, comprising: (37) British officer — very much a Prussian figure in British uniform; (38) British soldier with slung rifle holding the lead of a guard dog; (39) British soldier carrying a sandbag on his shoulder — this figure and (41-42, 44-45) use a US Army "doughboy" casting; (40) British soldier patrolling with rifle at the ready; (41-42) two soldiers carrying spools of telephone cable; (43) an empty-handed figure which probably

carried a shovel originally; (44) soldier carrying two buckets; (45) soldier carrying a nicely-modelled bow-saw; (46) soldier with a pick-axe; (47) soldier kneeling to unleash a guard dog; (48) soldier trudging along with rifle at the slope; (49) a very German-looking British officer in a soft peaked cap, with a walking stick.
50-54 American War of

Independence British Army bivouac. Some individual figures from the scene featured on the endpapers of this book: (50) infantryman carrying a bale of hay; (51) bare-headed soldier carrying buckets; (52) grenadier on guard duty; (53) grenadier off duty walking with his hands behind his back; (54) off-duty infantryman smoking a pipe.

Inset (above): *In the foreground Lord Kitchener rides up to discuss the progress of the battle with his officers of, from left to right, infantry, dragoons, hussars and lancers. Behind them nurses care for the wounded under the supervision of a medical officer, while an orderly brings water. In the background a FANY nurse gallops off, side-saddle, to rescue a wounded soldier from the battlefield. In 1907 the First Aid Nursing Yeomanry (FANY) was formed of women to be trained in first aid and riding. Only Heyde depicted them in their intended role — no British manufacturer did. In fact the FANY personnel served as ambulance drivers during World War I.*

Compared with other toy soldier makers Britains made quite a feature of military bands. These are very popular with collectors.

1 Band of the Coldstream Guards; set 37 This version was produced from 1895-1910, but a Coldstream Guard band remained in the catalogue until 1959. The figures have unmarked oval bases, gaiters and ''slotted arms'' — the instrument arms are fitted into slots in the body and held rigidly in position by solder. This was always a 21-piece set; the band shown is missing one trombone. The drum major's mace is cast integrally, but on later bands the mace is longer and cast separately, being riveted on which allows some movement.

The bombardon (extreme left, third row of musicians) was a feature of the early bands, being replaced in 1910 by a bass horn. From 1933 one euphonium and one trumpet were deleted and replaced by a tenor horn and a double bass horn.
2 Band of the Royal Scots Greys; set 1721. This excellent 12-piece band (one of the trumpeters had gone on sick parade when the photograph was taken) was only available in 1939-40. The seven-piece set 1720 introduced at the same time reappeared post-war and remained available until 1965. It contained the following instruments: kettle drums, cymbals, tuba, clarinet, bassoon, trombone and trumpet. Note that the kettle drummer alone rides a

black horse and has a white ''bearskin'', said to have been presented by Tsar Nicholas II of Russia. All the musicians have red plumes over the tops of their caps, rather than the usual white.
3 Royal Marine bandsmen. Not a complete band, these musicians are from the very popular 12- and 21-piece sets introduced in 1934. The 12-piece set 1291 contained: a drum major, two trombonists, two trumpeters, two euphonium players, one fifer, one cymbalist, two side drummers and a bass drummer. The 21-piece set 1288 had additionally: one tenor horn player, one bass horn player and one double-bass horn player, two clarinettists, one bassoonist, one extra trumpeter and two extra side drummers. Reflecting actual

Royal Marine practice, both bands had more side drummers than other sets. In 1956, for one year only, set 2115: Drums and Bugles of the Royal Marines replaced the 12-piece set. This consisted of a drum major, bass drummer, a cymbalist, three side drummers, a tenor drummer, and five buglers. This does not seem to have been a popular set, as it was replaced the following year (making it very scarce) by a new 12-piece band with plastic drums: set 2153. This band, which lasted only until 1960, contained a drum major, one trombonist, one euphonium player, one clarinettist, one bassoonist, one fifer, one cymbalist, three side drummers, one bass drummer, and a tenor drummer. The gaitered bass

drummer shown is unusual, in that drummers and drum majors in gaiters were given full trousers to match the musician figures very soon after the introduction of the Royal Marine bands in 1934.

4 Band of the Life Guards; set 101. A mounted Life Guard band in state dress was available from 1899, the first version having "slotted arm" musicians. There was also a Horse Guards band: set 103, but this was fairly short-lived. The magnificent gold-laced state dress dates back to the time of Charles II, except for the "jockey cap" which is Victorian. It is really a Royal livery, only worn on state occasions; at other times regimental dress is worn. For the record a state occasion is a parade or ceremony at which

the sovereign (or his or her personal representative) is present, a ceremony celebrating the sovereign's birthday, or a ceremony held in the presence of a member of the Royal Family and which is designated as such. This splendid band, from the 1930s, consists of: one kettle drummer on a piebald horse, two trombonists, one cymbalist, three clarinettists (more usually two clarinettists and one fifer), one bassoonist, two trumpeters, one bass horn player and one euphonium player. In the post-war version re-introduced in 1953 the musicians lost their swords, and the fifer was deleted in favour of a director of music in regimental dress of white plumed helmet and scarlet tunic carrying a baton.

The set was available until 1965.
5 Band of the Line; set 27. The first version (1895-1910) of the first band listed by Britains, with unmarked oval bases and slotted arms, using the same figures as the Coldstream Guards band but with infantry spiked helmets. The composition of the band is: drum major, two euphonium and trombone players, one cymbalist, a bass drummer and side drummer, three trumpeters and a fifer, which was sometimes substituted for a bombardon player. The bandsmen have white facings (collars and cuffs), so they can represent almost any English line regiment of the period which is not a "Royal" regiment. Since 1881 Royal regiments had blue facings while other

regiments had white facings; over the years many regained their cherished original distinctive colours. Set 30, Drums and Bugles of the Line, originally comprised a drum major, bass drummer, two side drummers, and four buglers, and had blue facings, thus representing a Royal regiment. Over the years the set dwindled to five pieces. From 1910 the bandsmen were slightly taller, with movable arms and square bases. Musicians became straight-trousered soon afterwards, but drum majors, bass drummers and side drummers kept their gaiters until c1935 giving the bands of the intervening period a rather ill-matched look. For later bands, see *pages 280-281*.

Britains' first two sets were 1: The Life Guards and set 2: The Horse Guards of the Household Cavalry. These were the same castings with different painting details.

1 Life Guard of 1837. This is the second-version Life Guard produced in 1897, with fixed arm and tin-strip sword. It is from an unnumbered box of 12 Life Guards issued to celebrate Queen Victoria's Diamond Jubilee (1837-97). Half the figures wear the uniform of 1897, much the same as that worn today, and the others wear this magnificent "Romanesque" helmet and have the white paint of their breeches taken up to waist level.

2 The 1902 version Life Guard, now with a movable arm. Note the aiguillettes on the chest, discontinued a few years later.

3-4 The very first versions of Britains Life Guards and Horse Guards from 1893. Note the small horse, tin-strip sword and generally "Continental" look. The earliest sets have five figures of the same casting, and the officer is distinguished only by a gold waist sash. These figures are not as uncommon as might be expected, because although replaced in the first-quality sets by 1897, they continued to be sold in simpler packaging in the "X" series for a number of years.

5 Horse Guards officer, on prancing "one-eared" horse, with tin-strip sword and wedge-shaped base, c1894. This impressive figure replaced the trooper with gold sash initially used to represent an officer in sets 1 and 2. He was also used, with scarlet jacket and red and white plume, in set 3: The 5th Dragoon Guards, and for this purpose the casting included a throat plume dangling from the reins. This was normally snipped off for Household Cavalry.

6 Horse Guards trooper of 1897-1902. This is similar to much later figures but with aiguillettes, a fixed arm holding a tin-strip sword and a "one-eared" horse — for ease of casting there is no indentation between the horse's ears, a feature which Britains corrected on later versions.

7 Life Guard Trumpeter in State Dress. Available in sets 2067, 2085 and as a Picture Pack, this is a much later figure than those discussed so far, not appearing until 1953. Like many other figures this was inspired by the coronation of Queen Elizabeth II.

8 Life Guards officer on rearing horse; set 1, issued 1946-53. The officer casting (5) was converted to a movable-armed figure in 1902, and then replaced by this casting in 1909. The paint style shows this to be a post-war example, made before 1953 when it was replaced by an officer on a more sedately trotting horse more suitable for a coronation procession. Interestingly, although revived at this date, the Horse Guards officer did not receive the new horse.

9 2nd Life Guards trooper galloping with carbine; set 43, early 1930s. Until 1922, when they

4　　　　　5　　　　　6

10　　　　　11　　　　　12

17　　18　　　　19　　　　20

amalgamated, there had been
two regiments of Life Guards.
These were most readily
identifiable by their sheepskin
saddle covers: the 1st's were
black, and the 2nd's were white.
After the amalgamation white
sheepskins were worn. Britains
produced the 2nd Life Guards
right up to World War II.

10 Horse Guards trooper at the
gallop with sword. This figure was
only available as part of the
squadron of Royal Horse Guards
riding with a complete company
of Coldstream Guards in a
71-piece Display Set, no. 93.
Some unusual figures could be
obtained only in the larger sets.
This trooper dates from the late
1930s. See also (12).

11 Horse Guards trooper; set 2. He

is mounted on the perfected
horse introduced in 1912 which
no longer has a carbine on the
saddle and now has two ears! His
rather thin sword compared with
(2) puts him later than 1925, and
the fact that Britains have not
given him a red collar, which they
did in 1935, neatly dates him to
around 1930.

12 Horse Guards trooper at the
gallop with lance; set 93, c1900.
This is the first version with a
slightly "Germanic" look; note
that because his scabbard is
moulded as empty he has in
effect lost his sword. See (10).

13 Life Guards Farrier Corporal of
Horse, available in set 2067 from
1953-66, and in Picture Pack
1270B from 1954-59. Despite first
appearances this figure with a

ceremonial axe is a Life Guard,
and is distinguished from a Horse
Guard farrier by his black hanging
plume and white sheepskin.

14 Life Guard in winter cloak, set
400. This simple, elegant figure
first appeared in 1930 and
remained in the catalogue until
the end of production in 1966. The
officer used the same casting
with an empty-handed arm, rather
than the outstretched sword arm.

15 Life Guards trooper; set 1. This
shows the new walking horse with
head up, introduced in 1953, as
well as the new head with falling
plume of the same date.

16 Life Guard foot sentry; set 2029.
One of the foot figures from a set
comprising two mounted Life
Guards at the halt, and four
dismounted troopers. The set was

produced from 1949 until the end,
but lost one foot sentry in 1960.

17-18 Horse Guards Sentry on Foot,
and Horse Guards Trooper at the
Halt; Picture Packs 1340B and
1336B. Oddly, unlike the Life
Guards these figures were never
combined in a set, but were only
available individually in 1954-59.

19 Royal Horse Guards trooper in
winter dress; set 1343.
Introduced four years after the
Life Guards in cloaks, and
discontinued in 1959 — thus
making them slightly more scarce
— this example can be dated to
the late 1930s. Note that the reins
were not painted post-war.

20 Horse Guards Standard Bearer at
the Halt. Using the same casting
as the trooper, this was only
available in Picture Pack 1339B.

257

Lancers by Britains, UK

1

2

3

7

8

9

13

14

15

Lancers were introduced into the British Army just after the Napoleonic Wars, the British having observed the effectiveness of the lance in the hands of Napoleon's Polish Lancers. The light dragoons converted to lancers adopted the Polish square-topped cap as their distinctive headgear and later wore a panel of cloth in facing colour on the front of the tunic, known as a plastron.

1 12th Lancers trooper. This is the very earliest type of Britains lancer, smaller than standard size, on a galloping horse with a plug-in arm that goes right through the torso. This rare figure with red plume and plastron represents a trooper from a set of

nine without a number which included an officer and trumpeter.
2 5th Royal Irish Lancers trooper; set 23. Identified by the green plume, this trooper at the halt on the first-version horse was produced from 1894-1903. With the lance and arm as an integral part of the figure, this is an accomplished piece of casting, although the horse's rear legs are rather two-dimensional.
3 Lancer officer. No excuses are needed for showing three examples of the Britains lancer officer turned in the saddle, based on a painting by the eminent Victorian military artist Richard Simkin. This excellent casting was available with only minor alterations right through from 1894-1966, retaining the tin-strip

sword throughout. This particular item is an oddity, purporting to be a post-war green-plumed 5th Lancer officer, but Britains did not produce this regiment after the war. Close examination reveals that this is probably a 12th Lancers officer from Picture Pack 1349B with the distinguishing red plume carefully overpainted in green. It is typical of the problems encountered when identifying Britains figures.
4 5th Lancers Trooper; set 23. This is a second-version lancer with movable lance arm, on the improved horse at the halt. Introduced in 1903, this set was dropped in the early 1930s, the 5th Lancers having amalgamated with the 16th Lancers.
5 9th Queen's Royal Lancers

officer; set 24. A post-war officer turned in the saddle, identifiable by the black and white plume. Still with the tin-strip sword, this example dates from the 1960s.
6 9th Lancers trooper at the halt; set 24 (post-war). This set had previously used the same castings as (2) from 1894-1903, and then those of (4) from 1903-40, with the lance at the carry. When reintroduced after World War II the 9th troopers carried slung lances as shown.
7 12th Lancers trooper; set 128. This set, produced from 1902-40, had troopers on cantering horses and an officer on a trotting grey.
8 12th Lancers; set 2076. This new set of 12th Lancers was introduced in 1953. Like other sets of that period, the troopers

were on two patterns of horse — cantering and trotting — and held their lances at the carry. In contrast to the pre-war version the officer rides a cantering grey with his sword vertical.

9 12th Lancers officer; set 128. Unlike the officer from set 2076 at (8) this officer from the late 1930s has an outstretched sword arm and rides a grey at the trot.

10 16th Lancers trooper; set 33. While all other British lancer regiments wore basically dark blue uniforms the 16th were resplendent in red tunics with blue plastrons. This is the first version at the halt, produced from 1895-1903, with a fixed arm, and is the same basic casting as (2).

11 16th/5th Lancers trooper; set 33. In contrast with (10), a late

version trooper from this very attractive set's brief post-war revival from 1946-52.

12 16th/5th Lancers officer; set 33. The magnificent officer turned in the saddle, this time in the red tunic of the 16th Lancers in a post-war issue. Note that the 16th Lancers had amalgamated with the 5th Lancers in 1922 and Britains dropped the latter from the range a few years later. The 16th took precedence in the amalgamated title because of some indiscretion committed by the 5th Lancers in the past.

13 21st Empress of India's Lancers in Full Dress; set 100. A trooper in the attractive blue/grey plastron and white plume of this famous regiment, dating from the 1930s.

14 21st Lancers trumpeter; set 100.

This set contained a trumpeter on a grey cantering horse, rather than an officer.

15 21st Lancers trooper, armed with a sword! This oddity turns up from time to time and is original — he does not have a replacement arm, and does not appear to be intended as an officer as he has neither gold trim nor an extended sword arm. He was probably intended for sale singly as a second-grade figure. Two distinct versions of the 21st Lancers in service dress were also available under set number 94: as ''Heroes of Omdurman and Khartoum'' in khaki with foreign service helmets, from 1898, not shown here, and later in World War I steel helmets as at (18, 19) *pages 282-283.*

16 17th Lancers trooper in active service dress; set 81. Known as Ulundi Lancers as they depict the 17th Lancers at that battle in the Zulu War, this set was first introduced in 1897. They are in white foreign service helmets, but otherwise in full dress with their distinctive white plastrons.

17 17th Lancers trumpeter; set 81. This set normally included a trumpeter on a trotting bay rather than an officer. When an officer was included the excellent casting of an officer turned in the saddle was used, complete with a full dress lancer cap. These two figures date from shortly before the set's deletion in 1940. 17th Lancers were also available in full dress with lancer caps in the Display Set 73.

259

The excellent gun teams produced by Britains in different versions have always been very popular with collectors.

1 Royal Horse Artillery Gun Team at the Gallop; set 39. This is the version produced from 1895-1906, the distinctive features being the shafted limber and the gunners riding on the gun and limber. Whereas all later limbers have a centre pole only, in this pattern the offside wheeler (the unridden horse nearest to the limber) is harnessed between a central shaft and a side shaft running forward from the right-hand wheel hub. The hinged limber top has valises at the ends, and slots to hold two seated gunners. Plug-in seats on the axle

tree of the gun also hold seated gunners. The gun resembles a 15-pounder of the period.

2-5 Royal Horse Artillery Gun Team; set 39, second version (1906-25). This revised version reflected changes in real artillery practice. The limber was altered to a centrepole type, shown at (7), and to lighten the load the seated gunners were replaced by mounted outriders. A mounted officer was also added. The outriders on trotting horses (2-4) carry short carbines and look like hussars, but they have short jackets — note the red trouser stripe continued up to the waist — and their horses have painted-on breast harness. The RHA mounted officer (5) is a fixed-arm figure with frogging detail cast on

his jacket, on a galloping horse.

6 Royal Field Artillery; set 144. This represents heavier artillery than the RHA, and a walking team is used. The mounted gunners have two patterns of movable whip arm. The men seated on the gun were soon dropped, but the men on the limber were retained, no mounted outriders being provided with this set. A mounted officer (not shown) rode a brown cantering horse.

7-12 Royal Horse Artillery Khaki Gun Team; set 39a (later 1339). Introduced in 1919, this set depicts the RHA in the service uniform of World War I. The only change to the castings is the replacement of busbies by peaked caps, although the magnificence of full dress has

Right: *Mountain Gun of the Royal Artillery; set 28. This is a late example, from 1965, of a very popular and attractive set that was introduced in 1895. The set comprised a mounted officer and six gunners in white foreign service helmets, dark blue tunics and pale khaki breeches, with four mules carrying the three parts of the mountain gun and a load of ammunition.*

been replaced by khaki. Apart from the peaked cap, the officer (8) is the same casting as the full-dress version, resulting in incorrect frogging cast on his khaki tunic. The outriders (9-12) follow the same formula; note that they have the longer carbines newly introduced by Britains.

13-18 King's Troop Royal Artillery; set 39. This early post-war example uses a finely-detailed limber with a hinged rear section, and a gun loosely based on a late 18-pounder, both introduced in 1930. The horses wear the light breast harness which replaced the heavy collar harness on Britains gun teams in 1925, and are linked by plain wire. In about 1950 this was replaced by light brown painted H-shaped clips which could be readily removed and replaced. The trotting outriders have been replaced by figures at the full gallop (14-17), similar to the 4th Hussars. This set still has the original pattern officer (18) but about this time a new officer with a plain movable arm was introduced.

19-24 Royal Horse Artillery, Active Service; (B series) set 126. From about 1898 Britains produced a range of soldiers smaller than their "standard" infantryman size of 54mm (2.12in), known as the B series. In this range (dealt with more fully on *pages 284-285*), infantrymen were 44mm (1.73in) high. This set, and the full dress gun team, set 125, appeared in 1901. The field gun has a strip of spring steel which can be flexed to fire projectiles. The officer (20) rides a grey at the gallop, and has a movable outstretched sword arm. The outriders (21-24) use the same casting, but with a carbine arm and black or brown horses. The full dress outrider is shown at (32) on *page 285*. Both sets stayed in the catalogue until 1939.

1 2 3 4 5 6 7

11 12 13 14 15 16

24 25 26 27 28 29 30

Britains Foot Guards have always been popular sellers, with the result that they are some of the commonest figures to be found today. The identifying plume colours of the Guards are: Grenadier Guards: white plume on the left. Coldstream Guards: red plume on the right. Scots Guards: no plume. Irish Guards: blue plume on the right — but note Britains at first used green. Welsh Guards: white plume with green bar across, on the left.

1 Grenadier Guards, Standing Firing; set 34. This is the first version, fixed-arm officer with gaiters, on an oval base, who was accompanied by eight guardsmen firing and a drummer boy in the original 1895-1901 set. See (4).

2 Colours and Pioneers of the Scots Guards; set 82. A first-version (1897-1905) pioneer from a set of seven with a colour bearer.
3 Irish Guards; set 107. This first-version Irish Guardsman, marching at the slope with (incorrect) green plume, was introduced soon after the regiment's actual formation in 1900. Note this is the same as (2) but with a "droopy sling" rifle.
4 Grenadier Guards, Standing Firing; set 34. This is the first-version firing Guardsman of 1895-1901, "volley firing".
5 Scots Guards; set 75. This third-version square-based marching Scots Guardsman of about 1908, date-stamped 1.8.1905, which refers to the same figure on an oval base.

6 Scots Guards, Running at the Trail; set 70. Introduced in 1899, this was a short-lived set, using the first-version running figure.
7 Irish Guardsman running at the trail, from display set 102. This is the final-version running at the trail figure, with the left arm close to the body.
8 Coldstream Guards officer on "sway-back" horse. This figure usually appeared in set 111, as a Grenadier Guards officer with men at attention. As a Coldstream it is probably from Display Set 93.
9 Irish Guards officer; from set 102, see also (7). A rather battered figure, dated 1.1.1901, based on the cavalry horse at the gallop.
10 Scots Guards officer, mounted on a brown version of the Scots Greys' horse. This interesting

piece is probably from set 130, introduced in 1902, which contained 118 Scots Guards.
11-12 Grenadier Guards in Winter Overcoats; set 312. An officer and man from 1929-66.
13-15 Grenadier Guards Firing; set 34. The different items from a nine-piece version of this set, from the late 1930s. Compare with (1) and (4).
16 Kneeling Guards officer. Up to 1940 this officer could be found with a red plume in set 120: Coldstream Guards Kneeling Firing, or with a blue plume in set 124: Irish Guards Lying Firing. As a Scots Guards officer this may be from set 130 — see (10).
17-18 Coldstream Guards at Present; set 205. The two versions of Guardsmen presenting arms

8

9

10

17　18　19

20　21

22　23

31　32　33　34　35　36　37

produced from 1923-40; (17) has the feet together while the later version (18) has the right foot brought back at an angle.

19-22 Grenadier Guards Colour Party; set 460. The two ensigns and two of the colour sergeants from a set of seven pieces produced as Grenadier Guards from 1932-35, and then with the same set number as Scots Guards until 1940.

23 An unusual Scots Guards officer based on a Guardsman casting. This rather battered example has a plain left arm, maroon waist sash, gold collar and cuffs, and brown gloves, and is presumably from set 130.

24-25 Scots Guards; set 75. A 1930s Guardsman and officer from a set that lasted from 1897-1965. A

piper (27) was also included.

26 Scots Guards pioneer with axe; set 82, final version, from the 1946-59 period. Compare with (2).

27 Scots Guards piper; set 76. To avoid confusion with Black Watch pipers, note that while both have feather bonnets with red hackles and Royal Stuart tartan, the Scots Guards pipers have dark blue doublets and the Black Watch dark green.

28 One of six pipers from set 2096: Drum and Pipe Band of the Irish Guards. This unusual figure wears a dark green tunic and caubeen from which a small blue plume is missing on this example, and a plain brown kilt. This set was produced from 1954-65.

29 Scots Guardsman at attention. Up to 1940 this figure was

produced as a grenadier in set 111, while from 1954 the pose was used to represent Coldstream Guards in set 2082. A Scots Guardsman was available post-war in a Picture Pack, but that shown here is in the pre-war paint style so must be from the large Display Set 130.

30 Coldstream Guardsman at ease; set 314, produced from 1929-40. Post-war this casting was used for the Welsh Guards in set 2083.

31-32 The Rifle Brigade; set 9, produced from 1897-1915. From their formation in the Napoleonic Wars to carry rifled weapons rather than smooth-bore muskets, the rifle regiments have been associated with dark green uniforms. Britains produced the Rifle Brigade with black facings,

and the Rifle Corps with red facings. This officer and man have square bases dated 16.11.1905 and 1.8.1905 respectively.

33-35 The Kings Royal Rifle Corps; set 98, introduced in 1899. (33) and (34) are the square-based first-version rifleman and officer with a gap between the left arm and the body. (35) is the later, rather inferior casting with the left arm tight against the body.

36-37 Kings Royal Rifle Corps Marching at the Trail; set 2072. After a brief post-war revival, set 98 was replaced in 1953 by this set of riflemen marching at the trail. The officer (36) uses the standard 1930 body while the rifleman (37) is based on the US Marine casting.

The full dress uniform of the British line infantry, as worn from 1879-1914, and depicted by Britains, consisted of scarlet tunic, dark blue trousers and spiked helmet. The fusiliers — whose name derives from an early improved musket, the fusil, which was only issued to special units — had as their distinctive headgear a cap similar to the Guards' bearskin, but smaller and and made of seal or racoon skin.

1 The "Plug-handed Fusilier" Possibly the first foot figure to be produced by Britains, this rare 60mm (2.36in) fusilier steps off on the right foot on a plain square base, and has a separate rifle that plugs into the left cuff. The only figure with which it is compatible

is that of a large Scots Grey trooper, which, on a brown horse, was used as an officer in an unnumbered set with fusiliers.
2 Royal Sussex Regiment; set 36. This figure is rather undersized at 50mm (2in), oval-based, but without gaiters, and commits the military sin of sloping arms on the right shoulder.
3 Infantry officer. This is the first-version fixed-arm officer with medal detail and the very small head sometimes used at this time. Probably from the Buffs (11-13), but Britains did not put facing colours on their officers, making identification difficult.
4-5 7th Royal Fusiliers; set 7. Two views of the 1897-1905 round-based movable-arm figure.
6 The Royal West Surrey Regiment.

The 1905 infantry figure with Slade-Wallace equipment and oval base, replaced by a square base three years later. The Surreys were normally portrayed "at the ready" with fixed bayonets, but were also marching at the slope in Display Set 29.
7-10 Somersetshire Light Infantry; set 17. The elements of a ten-piece set that contained an officer, bugler, four standing and four kneeling figures, introduced in 1894, but with the short-lived movable-arm "wasp waisted" officer introduced about four years later. The SLI have green Light Infantry helmets.
11-13 The Buffs (East Kent Regiment); set 16. Another ten-piece set, containing an officer, bugler, drummer boy and seven

men at the ready, with buff facings. The officer (11) is the improved 1905 figure matching the infantryman at (6).
14-15 The Warwickshire Regiment at the Present; set 206. An officer and man presenting arms, from an eight-piece set. The first, 1923 version had the legs at attention, but this second version has the right leg brought back.
16-17 East Yorkshire Regiment; set 113. (16) is the first version, introduced in 1901, of a set of eight round-based gaitered infantrymen at attention, each with a right-angled arm holding the rifle near the muzzle. A later square-based version (17) was introduced c1908, with the final-type straight arm holding the rifle into the side of the body.

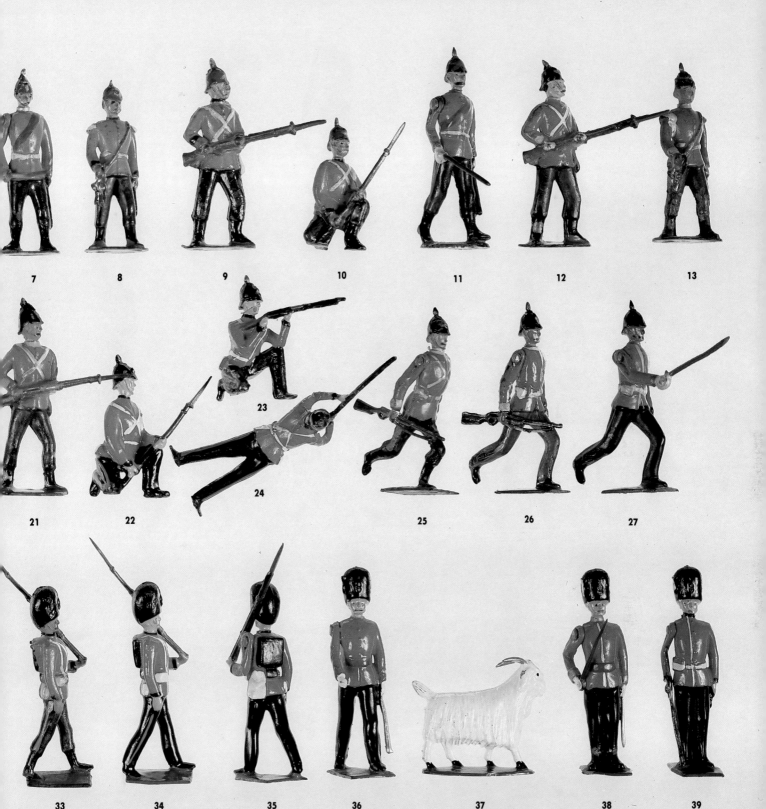

7   8   9   10   11   12   13

21   22   23   24   25   26   27

33   34   35   36   37   38   39

18-20 Royal Irish Regiment, Standing, Kneeling and Lying Firing; set 156. A set of ten, later eight line infantry with blue facings. These gaitered figures are the first version of 1908.

21 The Buffs; set 16. The second-version square-based "on guard" figure with gaiters of 1910-30.

22 The Worcestershire Regiment; set 18. Using the same castings as set 17 (7-10) this set was usually distinguished by white helmets and facings. This unusual late example, "kneeling to receive cavalry", has a blue helmet and dark green facings.

23-24 Queens Royal Regiment (West Surrey); set 2086. Post-war, the full-trousered infantrymen in firing positions introduced about 1930 were available in this 16-piece

set, with an officer holding binoculars. Note that the full-trousered lying figure (24) has the legs splayed, unlike the earlier gaitered figure.

25-27 The York and Lancaster Regiment Running at the Trail; set 96. (25) is the "pigeon-chested" first version introduced in 1899, but note that this example is later as it does not have the earlier magazine rifle. The second version (26) has full trousers and "daylight" between the left arm and the body. The officer (27) is the same figure as the man but with an outstretched sword arm and gold facings.

28-29 The Middlesex Regiment; set 76. This post-war officer and man, produced until 1963, are from a set introduced in 1897. They use

the final form of marching figure.

30 Royal Sussex Regiment; set 36. An early example of the 1910 marching infantryman figure, with a "droopy sling" rifle, blue facings and the white helmet in which Britains were to portray the Royal Sussex until 1940.

31-32 Royal Sussex Regiment; set 36. An infantryman and mounted officer from the post-war set of six men and an officer, now with blue helmets. The officer uses the heavy ADC's horse.

33 Fusilier; a gaitered square-based version from the late 1920s. Britains made no distinction between their 7th Royal Fusiliers, set 7, and Royal Welch Fusiliers, set 74, except for the inclusion of a goat mascot with the latter. The Royal Welch Fusiliers lasted

right through to the end, but the Royal Fusiliers set was discontinued in 1940.

34-36 Royal Welch Fusiliers; set 74. (34-35) are two views of the final pattern fusilier produced in about 1930. Note that the fusiliers kept their full equipment when they lost their gaiters. (36) is the final-pattern officer, full-trousered and empty-handed, from the 1930s.

37 The splendid long-haired goat mascot of the Royal Welch Fusiliers, with gilded horns and a shield on his forehead.

38-39 The Royal Welch Fusiliers at Attention; from set 2124. This rare set contained an officer, two men and the goat mascot, and was only produced from 1957-59. Note that the fusilier (39) is used as the scale man in this book.

1   2   3   4   5   6   7

16   17   18   19   20

27   28   29   30   31

1-2 The Black Watch; set 11. These rather stocky figures running at the trail on plain oval bases are from Britains' first set of Highlanders. Note that the same casting is used for officer and man; they have weapons with hands that plug into the cuff of the figure. The Black Watch are distinguished by red hackles in their bonnets and dark green kilts with black hatching. This version was produced from 1893-1903.

3 The Argyll and Sutherland Highlanders; set 15. As set 11, but with yellow facings and a dark green kilt with light green stripes.

4 The Seaforth Highlanders; set 112. This marching Highlander in full equipment with movable arm is from a set without an officer introduced in 1901. Seaforths

have red and white stripes over dark green kilts.

5 Gordon Highlanders; set 77. A private from a set introduced in 1897 which included two pipers. Gordons have yellow cross-hatching over dark green kilts.

6 Cameron Highlanders (Active Service); set 114. Introduced in 1901 during the Boer War, this set uses the same body casting as (4-5) but with a foreign service helmet and khaki jacket. This example has the early smooth helmet, which was soon replaced. The Camerons have dark blue kilts with red and yellow stripes.

7 Black Watch Highlanders; set 122. An early undated oval-based figure from a set available from 1901-40, consisting initially of nine men standing firing and a

standing officer with binoculars.

8-12 The Cameron Highlanders; set 89. This 30-piece set containing the new Highlander figures in firing positions was introduced in 1901. Available until 1940, it consisted of a standing officer with binoculars (8), a kneeling officer (10), six men standing firing (9), nine men kneeling firing (11), ten men lying firing (12), and two pipers in glengarries.

13-15 The Gordon Highlanders; these were available as lying firing figures from 1901 in set 118 (15), and in all three firing positions from 1908 in set 157.

16 Argyll and Sutherland Highlanders; set 15. In 1903 the "plug handed" Highlander was replaced by a vigorously charging figure. The oval base changed to

a square base in 1908, this example dating from the 1930s.

17 The Black Watch; set 11. The same casting as (16), from a post-war set reduced to five charging Highlanders, but with the addition of the marching piper (34).

18-20 Seaforth Highlanders Charging with Mounted Officer and Pipers; set 2062. The pre-war large set of Seaforths, no. 88, was not reinstated after the war, but replaced in 1952 by this set of 14 charging Highlanders (18), two pipers in dark green doublets and glengarries (19) and the excellent mounted officer (20).

21-22 Officers of the Gordon Highlanders; set 437. When first produced, these excellent figures of Highland officers mounted in trews, and marching in kilt and

plaid, were only available as
Gordons, and were not
introduced into the existing sets
of Highlanders. They were
available from 1932-40.

23 Officer of the Argyll and
Sutherland Highlanders. This is a
Britains special painting, just the
same as the Gordon officer (22),
but with light green cross-
hatching on kilt and plaid.

24 Gordon Highlander Officer;
Picture Pack 461B. A direct
comparison can be made
between this post-war version,
only available in a Picture Pack,
and the same figure from the pre-
war set 437 (22).

25 Seaforth Highlander officer. This
post-war figure is something of a
puzzle as Britains did not
normally produce a marching

Seaforth officer; he is from set
1323 which normally contained
Royal Fusiliers and Royal Sussex
Regiment with officers, and
Seaforth Highlanders without —
but occasionally, as here, a
Seaforth officer was included.

26 Seaforth Highlanders; set 112.
This is the bulkier figure without
equipment which replaced the
earlier marching Highlander (4)
just before World War I.

27 Highlander; 34N. This is the
standing firing Highlander in a
second-grade khaki paint finish.

28-29 Highlanders in khaki, running.
These Highlanders in glengarries,
charging in two positions and
slightly over-scale, are pre-war
second-grade items.

30-31 Highlanders, Khaki, Charging
with Bayonets; Shrapnel-proof

Helmets. These are the same as
(28-29) but with steel helmets.

32 Cameron Highlanders (Active
Service); set 114. Like the
marching full dress Highlanders
this set also changed to the
bigger figure without equipment in
about 1914, but with a foreign
service helmet and khaki tunic.
Available until 1940, and 1946-47.

33 Black Watch Highlander; set 449.
A rare paint version of the
marching Highlander, issued
briefly in the 1930s.

34 Black Watch piper: this post-war
piper was available in set 11 with
five charging Black Watch from
1946, in Display Set 73, and set
2109: Highland Pipe Band of the
Black Watch, shown on *page 281*.

35 Black Watch marching officer; an
extra-fine quality ''special''

painting of the Highland officer.

36 Highland Light Infantry; set 213.
In 1924 Britains produced a figure
in Scottish doublet and trews to
represent the non-kilted Scottish
regiments. The HLI have their
distinctive shakoes and green
trews with red and white stripes.
Not available post-war.

37 The Royal Scots; set 212.
Introduced at the same time as
the HLI, this set used the same
body with a Kilmarnock bonnet.
Early examples have yellow criss-
cross stripes over dark green on
the trews. This later version has
red and white stripes over green.

38 Royal Scots piper. When set 212
was revived in 1948, reduced to
five pieces, it included this piper
in green doublet, Royal Stuart
tartan and a glengarry.

Inset (above): *On the left is a very unusual medical orderly, based on the first-version RAF airman from set 240 (centre), but in khaki uniform with a Red Cross emblem on the left arm, a brown belt and white gloves. This figure is possibly from a special khaki version of the large RAMC display set 1300. On the right is the quite scarce military policeman, only available in the station set 1R from 1954-59.*

Britains' first portrayal of army medical personnel came in 1905 with the 24-piece set 137. This contained one Senior Medical Officer (1), two doctors (2), three pairs of stretcher bearers with stretchers (5-6), and eight wounded men; two with arms in

slings (7), three with bandaged heads (8), and three with hands behind heads (9).

1 Senior Medical Officer; he stands in a relaxed pose in a dark blue uniform, with a general's pattern cocked hat with falling plumes.
2 The doctor wears the same uniform as (1), but with a ball-topped helmet. Note that (1) and (2) remained round-based throughout production.
3-4 Nurses, first version. These small nurses wear red capes and white aprons over grey floor-length dresses.
5-6 Stretcher bearers. The first stretcher bearers had oval bases; these are square-based but still with gaiters. Their uniform is dark blue with red facings, with a ball-

topped helmet of which two versions are shown here, (6) being the earlier pattern.
7-9 Wounded soldiers; (7) has his right arm in a sling, with his jacket open to reveal his grey shirt, and a white helmet on the back of his head; (8) has a bandaged head, and appears to lie at attention; while (9), although with a bandaged left leg, seems far more relaxed — his hands are behind his head and his helmet is tipped forward over his eyes.
10-11 Stretcher bearers, 1930s. During this period the stretcher bearers lost their gaiters and became straight-trousered, this version remaining until the end of production in 1940.
12 Nurse, second version, 1930s. A taller figure with a wide white

head-dress, white apron, red cape and grey dress, with black-stockinged legs now visible. Included in a number of sets, this nurse was available up to 1961 in set 1723, with battledress stretcher bearers.
13 An unusual and attractive good second-grade nurse in a blue cape and dress. Not listed, and presumably for sale singly, this may be a navy or air force nurse.
14 RAMC nurse; no. 122P. A rather basic second-grade painting of the nurse from the New Crown range, first issued in 1956.
15-16 Stretcher Party Unit of the Royal Army Medical Corps, Steel Helmets; set 1719. Available in 1939-40, rapidly being replaced by the more up-to-date battledress figures, these men in

service dress and steel helmets replaced the same figures in peaked caps.

17-18 Casualties. The figure on the stretcher, and the one in the tent, are both castings of a civilian casualty. He is straight-trousered with an open-necked jacket with shirt and tie underneath, but painted khaki. The figure which probably should go with (15-16) is shown at (24) painted as a wounded civilian!

19-21 Stretcher bearers, battledress. These were available concurrently with the service dress figures just before World War II, and were available in set 1723 and others until 1961. The wounded man with his arm in a sling (21) is an interesting re-working of (7) with a bandaged

head and a map pocket on his trousers, which are straight rather than gaitered.

22-24 Air Raid Precautions Stretcher Squad; set 1759. This grim set, portraying one of the horrors of war which happily did not materialize, contained two stretcher bearer teams, and a man leaning forward with a gas detector stick (not shown). All except the casualties wear black anti-gas suits and respirators. The civilian casualty is a repainting of (8), complete with gaiters.

25 Military Policeman. This figure talking to the ambulance driver is actually from a post-war railway set no. 1R (see also *Inset*).

26 Royal Army Medical Corps, With Ambulance Wagon; set 145. The splendid horse-drawn ambulance

in review order was introduced in 1906, the example shown being the same except for the later breast harness on the horses, which replaced collar harness in about 1925. The basic vehicle was the same as the more common no. 146 General Service Wagon, but with a cloth tilt supported on wires, and an extra pair of horses. This set had a brief revival from 1954-59. From 1919-40 a khaki version was available numbered 145A, later 145O, the men being in khaki uniforms with peaked caps.

27 Army Ambulance, with Driver, Wounded and Stretcher; set 1512. Britain's first motor ambulance, introduced in 1937, using the cab, bonnet and chassis of the series of lorries known as

"square radiator type", first available in 1934. The van-type body is made of tinplate. Note that this and the later model both have reversed colour roundels, suggesting Swiss markings rather than red crosses!

28 Ambulance; set 1512. The post-war vehicle with a round-nosed radiator and a more streamlined look. On this model, produced from 1946-56, the driver's door opens. The final version produced from 1957-60 had a new cab unit without opening doors, a split windscreen, and a fixed driver in a beret with movable arms.

29 A small Red Cross tent, on a wire frame, of unknown make.

30 "Royal Seamless" tent; from a range of 20 different shapes and sizes listed by Britains.

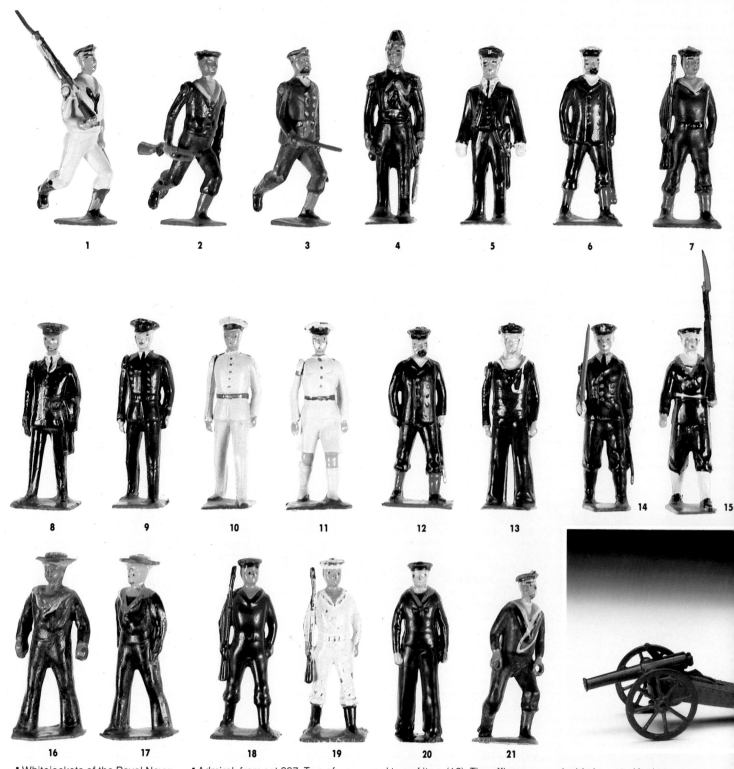

1 Whitejackets of the Royal Navy; set 80. An early-version sailor with rifle at the slope, from a set of eight which included a petty officer (3), produced from 1897-1940. Later variations have square bases, larger heads, and rifles carried at the trail.

2 Bluejackets of the Royal Navy; set 78. This set has the same history as set 80, although rifles at the trail were carried throughout. This is a later figure with square base, larger head, and a rifle without a magazine.

3 ''Petty officer'' running with sword extended; used with sets 78, 79 (*inset*) and 80. Although usually referred to as a petty officer, his buttons, in two rows of four rather than two rows of three, are correct for an officer.

4 Admiral; from set 207. Two of these officers were available from 1923-40 in an eight-piece set of Officers and Petty Officers of the Royal Navy.

5 Midshipman; set 207. He wears a short pea-jacket and an Eton collar, and carries a naval dirk.

6-7 Royal Naval Reserve; set 151. From its inception in 1907 to 1940 this was always a square-based set, with fixed-arm sailors (7) at the shoulder arms. A rare early version of the officer (6) with a movable right arm also exists.

8-12 Officers and Petty Officers of the Royal Navy, in Blue Uniforms, and in White Uniforms; set 1911. Produced in 1940, and post-war until 1959, this seven-piece set contained one of item (8), two of item (9), one each of (10) and (11)

and two of item (12). The officer with overcoat (8) is based on the yachtsman from set 168. (9) is the least satisfactory figure; it uses the US Marine casting shown at (2) *page 278*, and the white shirt, tie and double row of buttons are painted over a closed collar and single-breasted tunic. In contrast the same casting as used for (10) works quite well. The officer in shorts (11) uses the second-version scout-master casting. The petty officer (12) uses the pre-war RNVR casting, but with a blue-topped cap and green gaiters.

13 British Sailors, Regulation Dress; set 1510. An eight-piece set without an officer, produced in 1937-40 and 1946-59.

14-15 Royal Navy, Marching at the Slope; set 2080. The officer (14) in

a double-breasted jacket wears black leather gaiters, while the sailor (15) wears regulation dress with the white web belt and long gaiters. Available from 1953-61.

16-17 These rather Victorian-looking sailors in straw hats, with fixed arms and hexagonal bases, were for sale singly from the 1920s to 1940. There are two versions: the earlier, no. 26C with the arms away from the body (16), and a later one, no. 19N, with the arms close to the body (17).

18 Royal Navy Bluejacket; no. 49N. A simple second-grade painting of the RNVR figure.

19 Royal Navy Whitejacket; no. 50N. A second-grade painting.

20 British Bluejacket; no. 116P in the post-war New Crown range, and in set 1081A pre-war.

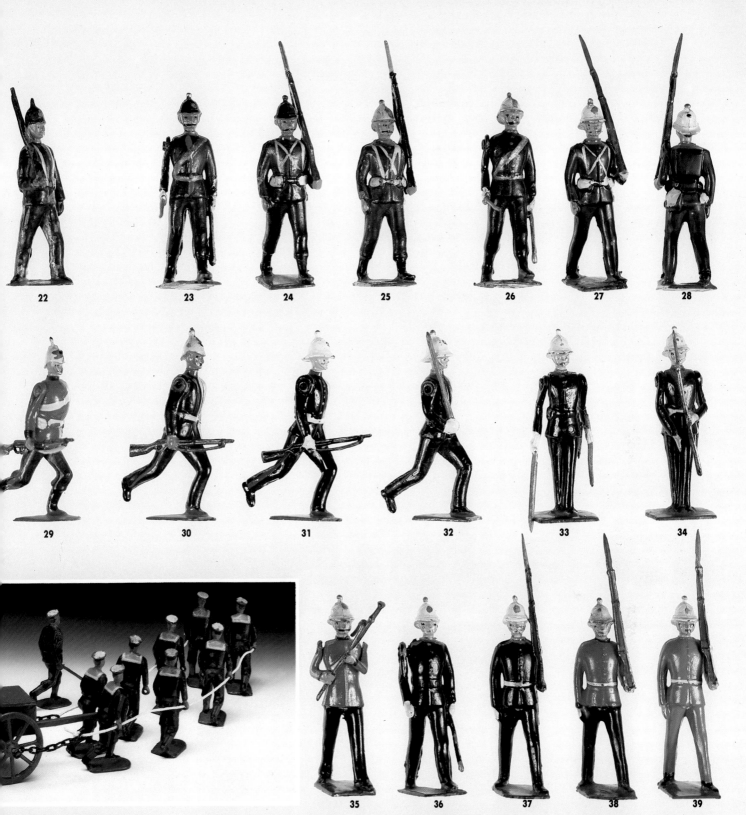

22   23   24   25   26   27   28

29   30   31   32   33   34

35   36   37   38   39

Inset (above): *Royal Navy Landing Party with Limber and Gun; set 79. In this attractive set, eight sailors (21) led by an officer (3) haul a gun and a small limber with an opening hinged lid. It was available from 1897-1940, and post-war from 1952-63.*

21 Sailor, Royal Navy Landing Party with Gun; set 79 (see *inset*).

22 Royal Marine Artilleryman; a second-grade painting from the "X" series, using the 1895-1910 Royal Sussex figure shown at (2) *page 264*. Until 1922 the marines were divided into Royal Marine Artillery, in blue uniforms, and Royal Marine Light Infantry who wore infantry-style uniforms. From 1905 both branches adopted the white foreign service

helmet for home service use.

23-24 Royal Marine Artillery; set 35. This officer (23) and man (24) are the third version with square bases and gaiters, *c*1908.

25 Royal Marine Artillery; set 35. The same figure from a year or two later, now with a white helmet.

26 Royal Marine officer; set 35. Still gaitered, and with an artillery-type gold cross-belt, this officer has the larger marine-pattern helmet introduced *c*1928.

27-28 Royal Marines; set 35. Front and back views of the Royal Marine produced from 1930-36 which, like the fusiliers at (34-35) *page 265*, became straight-trousered but kept the pack and full equipment.

29 Royal Marine Light Infantry; set 97. This set of seven men and an

officer, using the same casting with an extended sword arm, was introduced in 1899. It used the same figure as the York and Lancaster Regiment shown at (25-27) *page 265*.

30 Royal Marines, Running at the Trail; set 97. An early running marine, produced after the change of set title from RMLI but still with the infantry-type helmet.

31-32 Royal Marines, Marching at the Slope and Running at the Trail, with Officers; set 1284. This set, containing eight of each type, was produced from 1933-61 with the usual break. These figures differ from the pre-war marines in set 97 only by slight differences in painting style, and the officer's sword (32) at the carry.

33-34 Royal Marines Presenting

Arms; set 2071. From the seven-piece set available from 1953-60.

35 Band of the Royal Marine Light Infantry; set 1622. An example of a musician from the rare and colourful 21-piece band only available from 1938-40.

36-37 Royal Marines Marching at the Slope; set 35. This set adopted the standard 1910 marching figure rather than the fusilier-type body in 1937.

38 Royal Marine Light Infantry at the Slope; set 1620. This is a rare retrospective figure, in effect the 1936 Royal Marine in a scarlet jacket, only available from 1938-40.

39 Royal Marines at the Slope in Tropical Dress; set 1619. Like (38) but in a pale khaki uniform with white helmet, this rare figure was only available from 1938-40.

1 Britains monoplane: no. 433. A slightly battered example of a rare piece. The fuselage is hollow-cast with tinplate wings and tail, and detachable pilot.

2 Walking pilot. This figure giving a "thumbs up" sign is of unknown make, but similar in style to the pilot by Cresent (9).

3 Pilot in Sidcot suit; a Britains second-grade figure, similar to (37) but with a fixed arm.

4-6 RAF figures from the 1950s, by Crescent. (4) is a pilot in peaked cap and windcheater with map case, while (5) is a RAF Regiment figure marching at the slope; these are both rather undersized. (6) is the science-fiction hero Dan Dare, usually in pale green but here, with "50 mission hat" and medals, in RAF service!

7 Airman in battledress, by Johillco. This figure with a steel helmet slung at his hip is more usually found as a soldier in khaki.

8 WAAF (Womens Auxilliary Air Force) by Johillco.

9 Pilot in flying suit holding a map case; Crescent no. B185.

10 Ground crew with petrol can; Crescent no. A83.

11 RAF airman in service dress, of unknown make.

12 Airman by Crescent, quaintly listed as "A81: RAF Infantry".

13 Airman in service dress; from Britains 22-piece set 2011, 1948-59, which contained nearly all the RAF figures.

14 World War I style pilot. This tall figure was available in a boxed set from Crescent in 1948.

15 A solid World War I pilot made from a home-cast mould of (25).

16-17 Officer and man, from Britains set 240: Royal Air Force, produced from 1925-40. These attractive movable-arm empty-handed figures wear the uniform of the early RAF.

18 A pilot in full flying kit, by the US firm Moulded Miniatures.

19-21 RAF Regiment, by Britains. These were only available in Display Set 2011 and as individual pieces in Picture Packs. Set 2011 included: one officer (19), a Bren gunner (21) and six men with slung rifles (20).

22 Airman in peaked cap holding a swagger stick, by Crescent.

23 Fire-fighter of the Royal Air Force, by Britains. A set of eight, no. 1758, was issued in 1939-40, and two were included in set 2011.

Left: *The Timpo Airport. A rare but remarkably crude set of airfield buildings by Timpo, believed to be for export! The upper two buildings, of fibreboard nailed together, are freestanding. Note that the four pilots made of resin are only about 20mm (0.78in) high, and in turn dwarf the two diecast B17 bombers.*

24 RAF pilot; Johillco 267PC. This is really a World War I figure in a heavy leather overcoat.

25 A pilot in World War I style leather jacket and breeches, but painted dark RAF blue; probably by Taylor and Barrett.

26 RAF rigger; Johillco 267RC.

27 RAF mechanic; Johillco 267MC. Both (26) and (27) were probably designed as RFC men.

28 World War II pilot, by Johillco.

29 The same as (28) but in white.

30-31 These odd figures are based on the Crescent airmen in jacket and in greatcoat, but have German-style helmets. Possibly they are meant to be Luftwaffe.

32 RAF airman in overcoat; Crescent A82. Note the similarity to Britains figure (33).

33 RAF airman in greatcoat, by Britains, available in set 2011, based on set 331: US Army Air Force Officers in Overcoats.

34-35 Pilots running to their planes, by Johillco.

36 RAF pilot in full flying kit, by Britains. Available in 1940-41 in set 1894, and set 1906 with ground staff and fire fighters. After the war two pilots were included in set 2011 and were

also available as a Picture Pack.

37 Pilot in Sidcot suit, from Britains set 2011.

38 RAF officer in battledress with document; Britains set 2011. This was based on the Home Guard shown at (25) *page 283*.

39 RAF despatch rider, by Britains, only available in set 2011.

40-41 Royal Air Force Marching at the Slope with Officer; Britains set 2073. These figures are from an eight-piece set produced from 1953, in time for the coronation of Elizabeth II, until 1959. The officer (40) uses the same casting as the man, but with a sheathed sword in the left hand.

42 RAF Commodore; Britains Picture Pack 1081B. Like the naval officer at (8) *page 270*, this figure uses the civilian yachtsman casting.

43 WAAF by Britains. Two WAAFs were included with the pilots (36) in set 1894 before the war. Post-war, as a WRAF (Womens Royal Air Force), she was available in a Picture Pack, and in set 2011.

44 Band of the RAF; set 1527. This attractive 12-piece band (the fife player is missing from this example) used the same figures and instrumentation as set 1290: Khaki Band, and set 1301: US Band. Available from 1937-40 and intermittently post-war.

45 Aeroplane by Mignot. From a display set first produced *c*1920, this aircraft is from a limited re-issue produced in 1983.

46 A very basic RAF airfield layout by an unknown maker; 1940s.

47 A tinplate biplane fighter by the Italian firm of Ingap, *c*1938.

1-2 Infanterie de Ligne; set 141. Both the officer (2) and man (1) of the line infantry are first-version figures, clearly stamped 9.5.1905 on their oval bases.

3 This excellent French line infantryman, in "grande tenue" or parade dress of a tunic and a kepi with pom-pom — but still with pouches and pack — was only available from the Paris Office.

4 Zouaves; set 142. This splendid figure of a French North African soldier at the charge, in turbaned fez, open short jacket and baggy trousers, was to have a long life from 1905 right through to 1966. The marching officer (2) was included in the first eight-piece set of round-based figures, but this was soon dropped in favour of another charging man. In 1954

a mounted officer (23) replaced two of the men.

5 Turcos; set 191. This set uses the same figure as the Zouaves, but in pale blue with yellow trim. Introduced in 1913, it was discontinued in 1940, and was only available post-war from 1957-59 in a rare "half set" containing two Turcos and a mounted officer (23). Turcos, so-called because of their Turkish style dress, were more properly the Tirailleur Algeriens, or Algerian sharpshooters.

6 Infanterie de Ligne (Shrapnel-proof Helmets); set 192. This figure, depicting the new horizon blue uniform and "Adrian" steel helmet introduced in 1915, is based on the early infantry of the line casting, with a modified pack

and a new head. It was available from c1916-40.

7-10 Infanterie Firing, Standing, Kneeling and Lying, and Machine-gunners; set 215. This fine 14-piece set of French infantrymen in action, introduced in 1924, contained four each of items (7), (8) and (9), and two machine-gunners.

11 Dragons; set 140. The French cavalry sets introduced in 1905 used modified versions of the existing cavalry horses, with bulky saddle-bags and blanket rolls on the saddlery, and fuller breeches and boots on the mounted figures. The Dragons (dragoons) are armed with lances (the tip is missing from this example), and early versions have a separate carbine which clips

into the back of the rider's body and is held in place by the falling plume. The officer, as for all the French cavalry, uses the cantering horse (23) in grey. The rarest of the French cavalry, they were not available after 1940.

12 Cuirassiers; set 138. The French heavy cavalry, in breastplates and helmets with flowing plumes, ride walking "Scots Grey" type horses and are armed with swords. The commonest of the French cavalry figures, they were available right through to 1966.

13-14 Infanterie de Ligne; set 141. The later square-based gaitered French line infantryman (13), in an almost grey rather than blue greatcoat and red kepi, replaced (1) and remained in production alongside the horizon blue figures

in steel helmets. See also (27). The rather attractive movable-arm officer (14) replaced the fixed-arm officer (2) for a while, until being dropped altogether.

15,22 French Foreign Legion Marching at the Slope, with Mounted Officer; set 1711. This set, available from 1939-40 and then from 1948-66, was perhaps inspired by Hollywood. The infantryman from set 141 (13) was used, but with a white-topped kepi and, oddly, white cuffs.

16-20 French Foreign Legion, Firing and Charging with Officer and Machine-gunner; set 2095. This 14-piece set used the body castings from set 215 (7-10), with kepis instead of steel helmets, but with two additions. One of the machine-gunners was replaced

by a kneeling officer with a pair of binoculars, and two of the kneeling figures were replaced by two charging legionnaires which were revived from a much earlier Paris Office figure.

21 Chasseurs à Cheval; set 139. These attractive cavalry in plumed shakoes and tunics with black frogging were introduced in 1905. They carry carbines, and are mounted on trotting horses; the officer rides a cantering grey.

22 French Foreign Legion officer, mounted at the halt. This empty-handed figure, mounted on the standing horse used for the Dragons, was included in the set of marching legionnaires (15) and late sets of the Foreign Legion in action (16-20); it was also available as a Picture Pack.

23 Zouave officer. With the appropriate head and paint finish this figure on a cantering horse has served as the officer for all the French cavalry. In 1954 he replaced two of the charging Zouaves in set 142; in the rare "half set" no. 2138 he led two Turcos into action, but in Picture Pack 1329B he was a Foreign Legion officer — a most varied military career.

24-25 Matelots; set 143. Based on the running British sailors, but with a French sailor's cap with red pom-pom, all versions of this set are very rare. The first, 1905 version (24) carries a Lebel rifle at the slope (the bayonet missing from this example), but this was soon changed to the standard Britains arm with rifle at the trail.

(25) is from the brief post-war revival of this set.

26 Troops of the Algerian Spahis; set 2172. A rare late set of French Colonial cavalry troopers on grey horses, of unique design. A standard bearer rode a brown horse. A five-piece set, it was only produced from 1958-60.

27 Infanterie de Ligne; set 141. In late examples of this set the kepi is finished in a medium blue, representing the cloth cover that the French troops wore in 1914. It was available until 1940.

28 French Foreign Legion Officer; Picture Pack 1367B. This figure was only available post-war in a Picture Pack. Previously, with a pom-pom on his kepi, this officer had accompanied the Paris Office infantry in parade dress (3).

1   2   3   4   5

13   14   15   16

22   23   24   25   26   27

1-4 United States Infantry; set
91.The first figures depicting US
infantry were introduced, along
with set 92 which depicted
Spanish Infantry in 1898
during the Spanish-American
War. The figures use the valise
equipment casting with a
campaign hat (1). The first fixed-
arm, bemedalled officer was soon
replaced by this version (2) with a
movable sword arm. In 1906 a
new fixed-arm figure at the
shoulder arms, using the same
casting as the Boer infantryman
of set 26, was introduced.
Shortly after this a third type
appeared, on guard with fixed
bayonet (3), with an officer using
the CIV casting (4); they remained
in production until 1940.
5 This interesting US cavalryman

at the gallop, using the same
casting as the fixed-arm Boer
cavalryman of set 6, is probably
a special painting.
See also (16).
6-12 American Soldiers; set 149.
These rare figures are from a
"Military Display and Game" set,
introduced in 1907 at the same
time as set 148: The Royal
Lancaster Regiment, which used
the same castings but with
foreign service helmets. The
game consisted of a card tray
with hinged metal clips attached,
into which the bases of the
soldiers could slide — this
feature necessitating the change
from oval to rectangular bases.
The figures having all been shot
down by matchstick gun, or
worse, (helping to account for

their rarity today!) they could be
brought back to life by flipping
them back upright. The figures in
the set, based on castings
already available, but with small-
crowned peaked caps, were as
follows: one mounted officer (6),
two gunners (7) with the gun from
the B-size artillery — (19) *page 47*
— one officer (12), one colour
bearer (8), one bugler (11), three
men running at the slope (9) and
three at the trail (10). The set was
available until about 1922.
13-14 US Infantry, Service Dress; set
227. This set, issued in 1925-40
and 1946-48, captures the look of
the World War I "doughboy"
rather well (14). The fixed-arm
officer (13) wears a peaked cap.
15,17 United States Cavalry, Service
Dress, Mounted at the Walk; set

229. This set used the new
casting, of a figure in a patch-
pocket tunic on a walking "Scots
Grey" type cavalry horse. (15)
shows the early light brown-khaki
finish, while (17) is a late example
in a grey-green uniform. The
cavalrymen were available in set
229 in 1925-40 and 1946-59, and
as Picture Pack 31B in 1954-59.
16 US Cavalry, Service Dress,
Galloping; set 276. Introduced in
1928, this figure uses the same
casting as the South African
mounted infantryman of set 38
(not shown) which replaced the
former fixed-arm type at this time.
It was produced until 1940, and
as Picture Pack 39B in 1954-59.
18 USA Air Force Officers in Short
Coats; set 330. Introduced in
1929, this set contained eight

khaki officers as shown.
19 USA Air Force Officers in Flying Kit and Short Coats; set 332. This attractive figure was only produced as an American pilot, and never as an RAF figure.
20-21 United States Air Corps, 1949-pattern Blue Uniform; set 2044. Produced from 1950-65, this set used the same castings as a set of figures showing Australian infantry in blue dress. The men differ from the RAF figures at (41) *page 273* by having slung carbines and buff waist belts.
22 A post-war example of a second-grade US cavalryman, available from the 1930s onwards either boxed or for retail singly.
23-24 Second-grade US infantry. Note that the officer (23) is the same as (13) but in a simplified

paint finish, while the infantryman (24) is a fixed-arm figure.
25-26 Second-grade US infantry, standing and lying firing. There was also a kneeling firing figure. The standing figure (25) is based on the Gloucestershire Regiment casting of set 119, complete with a campaign hat, but the kneeling and lying figures with puttees are unique.
27 A Second-grade US infantryman "at the ready". Unlike (25-26) the figure is based on the gaitered British line infantry casting.
28 United States Military Police; set 2021. Oddly, when Britains brought out an up-to-date American soldier after the war it was specifically a "snowdrop", as the MPs were known, complete with cast-in armband

and holster, rather than an infantryman. Available from 1948-65, the set was reduced to seven pieces in 1960.
29-30 United States Infantry, Service Dress with Steel Helmets; set 2033 Replacing the "doughboys" of set 227, this set used the same rather slim casting as the Military Policeman. Because of this all ranks have superfluous armbands and cross-belts, and the men have pistol holsters, although these items are not painted in. Produced from 1949-66, the set was reduced to seven pieces in 1960.
31 Band of the United States Army in Khaki; set 2117. This bassoon player is from the new 12-piece band introduced in 1956, to replace the former peaked-cap United States Military Band, set

1301. New features included white steel helmets and plastic drums. Available until 1961.
32 United States Military Band in Full Dress Uniform; set 2110. A saxophonist from this colourful 25-piece band, produced from 1956-59 and then as set 9478 from 1961-63.
33 West Point Cadets, Winter Dress; set 226. These attractive and popular figures of the famous US military academy were available as a set of eight, without an officer, from 1925-40. Post-war they were included in set 232 from 1946-66.
34 West Point Cadets, Summer Dress; set 299. This is the same as set 226 (33), but with white trousers. Available from 1929-40, and 1946-66, and quite common.

1 2 3 4 5 6

13 14 15

16 17 18 19 20 21

1-2 United States Marines, Blue Uniform; set 228. A post-war officer and man from a set first introduced in 1925. In pre-war sets dark blue caps were worn and no officer was included, but one of the marines had red rank chevrons and trouser stripes to indicate a sergeant. Available from 1925-40 and 1946-66.

2-5 United States Marine Corps Colour Guard; set 2101. This was a four-figure set, as shown, with a special box illustrated at (10) *pages 308-309.* The escort (2 and 5) are just standard marine figures. The colour bearers are special castings, similar to the standard marine, but with the distinctive harness moulded on to the figures. The colours are cast metal, stencil painted, the USMC

flag red with the eagle, globe and anchor emblem.

6 A trumpeter from the Full Band of the United States Marine Corps, Summer Dress; set 2112. See *page 280* for the full set.

7 US Marine in Review Order; a second-grade figure, originally issued singly as no. 31C, but also available in a bewildering variety of "A" series sets and other categories at different times.

8 US Bluejacket; no. 92P in the New Crown range introduced in 1956. This late second-grade item is very similar overall to (9), but is a fixed-arm figure.

9 US Sailors (Bluejackets); set 230. This attractive set of eight US sailors in blue was available from 1925-40 but never included an officer. It is uncommon.

10-12 US Sailors (Whitejackets); set 1253. The sailors in white did not appear until 1933, but lasted right through until 1966. The first paint scheme included a blue collar and brown ammunition belt and gaiters (10), but soon after the post-war reappearance of this set the collar became white and the belt and gaiters a pale green (11). Originally a set of eight sailors only, an officer (12) was introduced from 1948, using the standard marching officer casting with a peaked cap, like the US Marine Corps officer at (1). The set was available from 1933-40 and 1946-66, and is more common than the bluejackets.

13 Union Cavalry Trooper at the halt, with Carbine; Picture Pack 1360B. This interesting

figure, which was not included in the ordinary Civil War cavalry sets, is based on the "Continental" horse at the halt — see (11) *page 274.* It was available from 1954-59.

14-15 Union Cavalry; set 2056. An officer and trooper from a set of five cavalry that also included a trumpeter. The officer, wearing a kepi and riding a grey horse, is based on an earlier Indian cavalry figure (not shown). The troopers (14) wear slouch hats, carry carbines and sit the "Chasseurs à Cheval" type horse — see (21) *page 274.* Made from 1951-66, the set was reduced to four pieces in 1960.

16-21 Union Infantry with Officer, Standard and Bugler; set 2059. This seven-piece set used

7 8 9 10 11 12

22 23 24 28 29

25 26 27

castings derived from the range of line infantry figures, with the officer based on that of the CIV. The standard bearer (16) is at attention with the "Stars and Stripes" at his side, the bugler (17) being the same figure with a straight bugle arm. The standing firing figure (18) uses the straight-trousered line infantryman casting. The set also included a kneeling firing man, as (22) but with a dark blue kepi and tunic; this was dropped in 1960. The figure standing at the ready (19) had gaiters, while the officer (20) can be distinguished from that in the early US infantry set — see (4) page 276 — by the black hat and boots rather than brown. The set was completed by a figure kneeling to receive cavalry (21).

Available from 1951-66, the set was reduced to six figures in 1960; all the figures were also available as Picture Packs. An officer kneeling with binoculars was only available as a Picture Pack 1361B. A rare figure produced from 1954-56 was Picture Pack 1362B: Union Zouave charging; this was basically a late version of (4) page 274, with gold trouser stripes and a black top to his head-dress.

22-27 Confederate Infantry with Officer, Standard and Bugler; set 2060. Basically this seven-piece set used the same figures as the Union infantry, but with grey tunics and light blue tops to the kepis. One difference was that the Confederate infantryman at the ready (not shown), had a grey

slouch hat, brown "butter nut" tunic and white "socks". The set was produced from 1951-66, the Confederate kneeling to receive cavalry (21) being dropped when it was reduced to six pieces in 1960. All the Confederate infantry figures were issued individually in

Inset(above): *Confederate Artillery; set 2058. This, and the Union artillery set 2057, saw the reappearance of the pre-1930 field gun—see (7) page 261. These sets were available from 1951-66. The two Confederate gunners, correctly, have red facings, trouser stripes and kepi tops. The two Union artillerymen used the same castings but were dressed as (16-17) with the addition of red trouser stripes.*

Picture Packs, as was a kneeling officer with binoculars.
28 Confederate Cavalry Trooper at the Halt, with Carbine; Picture Pack 1365B. This was the equivalent of the Union cavalryman at the halt (13), but in a kepi. Also issued in Picture Packs, and using the same casting, were an officer with an extended sword arm on a grey horse, and a trumpeter. This was the only way to obtain a trumpeter; the Confederate cavalry set 2055 did not include one, containing only an officer similar to (15) and four troopers like (14) but with kepis.
29 An unusual second-grade Confederate cavalryman, available in some of the Crown range sets produced in the 1950s.

279

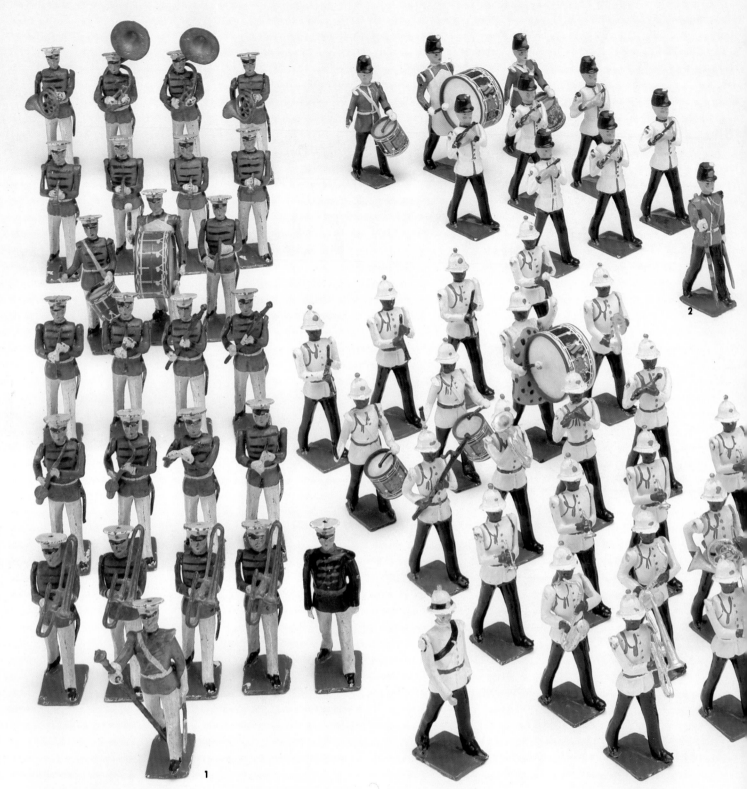

1

2

1 Full Band of the United States Marine Corps, Summer Dress; set 2112. This magnificent 25-piece band was only available from 1956-60, making it both rare and sought-after. While the rest of the Marine Corps had dark blue tunics in full dress, the band traditionally wore red with black frogging, and in summer dress — as depicted by this band — white trousers. The exception was the band leader, who wore a dark blue tunic with gold frogging. Britains based him on their adult bugler figure, but empty-handed. The drum major is based on the standard type, with peaked cap, red tunic with gold frogging, and staff. The musicians are playing, from the front: four trombones, two saxophones, one fife, three clarinets, two bassoons, a side drum and bass drum in plastic, cymbals, four trumpets, two French horns and two sousaphones. This set replaced an earlier USMC band in review order: set 2014, available from 1948-55. This 21-piece band featured men in blue trousers, and metal drums.

2 Fort Henry Guards Band; set 2178. In 1959 two Fort Henry bands were introduced; they were really fife and drum corps. Set 2177 contained only five pieces — a drum major, bass drummer, side drummer and two fife players. This set was not listed in the main catalogue, but appears to have been sold at Fort Henry until 1966. Set 2178, illustrated, contains 10 pieces, and was only produced very briefly. The drum major is based on the standard casting carrying a long mace, but with the black, slightly conical shako with a red and white pom-pom worn by all the Fort Henry guard figures. The six fife players are based on the usual musicians, with the short bandsman's sword, but wear white tunics as worn by British Army bands up to 1873. The boy side drummers and bass drummer have plastic drums.

3 Highland Pipe Band of the Black Watch; set 2109. This magnificent and colourful 20-piece band was introduced in 1956 and remained on sale until a year before lead soldier production ceased. It was based around 12 of the Black Watch pipers already available in set 11 — see (34) *page 267* — but also introduced several new figures. The drum major is similar in style to the Highland officer on foot — see (22) *page 267* — but has a fixed right arm holding a mace, and the plaid billows out from the body. The pipers have black feather bonnets, a feature which they share only with the Scots Guards (all the other pipers wear glengarries). Whereas the rest of the band wear dark green Black Watch kilts the pipers have kilts and plaids in the bright Royal Stuart tartan. The bass drummer is a fixed-arm figure with his right arm raised above his head; he wears a tiger skin for an apron. The two tenor drummers also have tiger skin aprons; they have outstretched fixed arms and carry plastic drums of larger diameter

3

4

5

than those of the side drummers. The side drummers are of adult size, with movable left arms, and have yellow aiguillettes across their chests. This is an example of a set produced relatively recently and over a 10-year period, yet highly valued by collectors.

4 Bahamas Police Band; set 2186. The last band produced by Britains, this is very rare indeed, although not strictly military! With a composition of 26 pieces it was also the largest, but would appear to have been for export only, not being sold in the United Kingdom. The bandsmen were based on the Royal Marine castings — see (3) *pages 254-255* — but have white tunics and dark brown skins, and silver instruments rather than brass. The bandmaster has a

European complexion, and is based on the adult bugler figure, but empty-handed, with a painted-on black pouch belt and a band round his helmet. The drum major has a red sash and medals, and the musicians have red aiguillettes. The bass drummer has a leopardskin apron, and both he and the two side drummers have plastic drums. The percussion line is completed by a cymbalist. As displayed here the rest of the instruments are: front rank — four trombones; second rank — two saxophones and two French horns; third rank — four trumpets; fourth rank — one bassoon, one euphonium and two fifes; rear rank — four clarinets. This set was produced only in 1959. There was also a smaller

version of the band in set 2185.

5 Band of the Royal Berkshire Regiment; set 2093. Produced at the same time as a series of figures in 1953 Coronation Dress this was Britains' only band that was shown in the blue No. 1 Dress. The usual band figures were used, in dark blue with red bands around their peaked caps to denote a Royal regiment. The bandmaster is the usual officer casting, marching empty-handed. The drum major has a gold baldrick, or cross belt, and a red waist belt like the rest of the band. The top of his mace is missing in this example. This band has an interesting selection of brass instruments. The composition is: front rank — two tenor horns and two trombones; second and third

ranks — six clarinets, one fife and one bassoon; fourth rank — four trumpets; fifth rank — one fixed-arm boy side drummer and one bass drummer, both with metal drums, and a cymbalist. Plastic drums were introduced in 1956. The rear rank has, from the left, two euphoniums, a bass tuba and a double bass tuba. Sadly this fine 25-piece band was produced only from 1954-59, making it hard to find. The keen collector should note that there are two main versions of this band — one with metal drums, and the later version from 1956 with plastic drums and a boy fife player instead of an adult one. All Britains bands are collectable, and those illustrated here are particularly sought-after.

1 Territorial Infantry; set 160. Introduced in 1980, this set had six peaked-cap infantrymen at the trail based on the Dublin Fusiliers figure of set 109, 1901 and a mounted officer like (17) but on a dark brown horse. With the outbreak of World War I the title soon changed to the British Expeditionary Force.

2-3 British Expeditionary Force; set 160. During World War I the contents of set 160 changed to these more accurate figures — a fixed-arm officer (2) and seven men (3) in peaked caps, service dress and 1908 webbing equipment. The name of this set reverted to Territorial Infantry in the early 1920s, and remained in the catalogue until 1940.

4-5 Infantry of the Line, Shrapnel-proof Helmets; set 195. These use the same casting as (3) but with a steel-helmet head; the officer carries a short ball-topped cane. Available from 1919-40, and post-war from 1946-59.

6 Royal Tank Corps; set 1250. This interesting figure also used the World War I infantry casting but with the Tank Corps' distinctive black beret. The set was produced from 1933-40.

7 The Devonshire Regiment; set 110. The early versions of the Dublin Fusiliers and Devonshires, sets 109 and 110, could be distinguished by their different rifle positions. However, after World War I they were both depicted at the trail, using the new broader figure in 1908 webbing, the Dublin Fusiliers

being distinguished by sand-coloured trousers and helmets. The set was available until 1940 without an officer.

8-9 British Infantry, Tropical Service Dress; set 1294. These attractive figures, stepping off on the right foot, were available from 1934-40. The officer (8) uses the same casting as the man, but with a plain left arm.

10 Infantry in Steel Helmets and Gas Masks; set 258. A set of eight of these infantrymen, a modification of (3), without an officer, was produced from 1928-40.

11-15 A series of sets of "British Infantry in Steel Helmets and Gas Masks" was introduced in 1937. Set 1611 had seven prone figures and the flamboyant officer (15). Set 1612 had seven men throwing

grenades (13) and an officer (15). Both sets were available until 1940. Set 1613 was a seven-piece set of six charging figures (14) and an officer (15). It was available right through to 1966, latterly as a six-piece set. The unusual digging figure (11) was only available in Display Sets 1614 (until 1966) and 1615.

16-17 Yeomanry, Territorial Army; set 159. This set had five khaki cavalrymen in peaked caps, an officer with extended sword arm on a cantering grey horse (17) and four troopers with swords at the carry on trotting horses. It was produced from 1908-40.

18-19 21st Lancers; set 94. Originally issued in foreign service helmets as set 94 in 1898, these figures were given steel helmets

during World War I. This quite
uncommon set had a trumpeter
on a grey horse (19) and four
troopers holding lances with
furled pennants, and was
produced until 1940.

20 Machine-gun Section, Lying; set
194. This set contained six prone
machine-gunners in peaked caps.
Announced by Britains in 1916, it
was available until 1940.

21 Machine-gun Section, Sitting; set
198. On its introduction in 1920
this set contained four seated
machine-gunners and their guns,
but was increased to six units in
the 1930s. The set was produced
until 1940.

22-23 Infantry with Peaked Caps,
Standing, Kneeling and Lying
Firing; set 1260. Introduced in
1933, the first figures had gaiters,

but these were soon changed to
the full-trousered type. (22) shows
a very unusual transitional form, a
gaitered prone figure with splayed
legs; the figure in gaiters usually
has the legs together, while the
full-trousered type has the legs
splayed. (23) shows the later full-
trousered kneeling figure.

24 British Infantry in Battledress, At
Ease; set 1828. This unusual
figure (actually in service dress) is
based on the operator for the
sound locator and predictor —
see (17) *page 299* — but with the
right arm holding a rifle in the "at
ease" position and a plain left
arm. The set is very rare.

25 The Home Guard Marching, with
Slung Rifles; set 1918. This figure
is in battledress without any
equipment. The officer had a

plain left arm and a dark blue red-
topped field service cap.

26-34 British Infantry (Steel Helmets)
with Rifles and Tommy-guns, and
Officer; set 1898. Most of the
battledress soldiers shown here
(26-34) were sold as second-
grade figures, but set 1898,
available in 1940 and post-war
until 1963, contained four
riflemen at the ready (26), an
officer (27) and three tommy-
gunners (31). Items (29) and (31)
are particularly unusual; although
hollow-cast battledress figures in
identical poses were available,
these two are solid mazak (zinc
alloy) castings, probably
produced in the 1950s to meet
Australian toy safety regulations.
(32-34) have large 1950s helmets.

35-36 Machine-gun Section (Lying

and Sitting); set 1318. This set
combined a re-working of (21) —
the seated machine-gunner now
having an airborne forces-type
rimless helmet and anklets —
with the steel-helmeted version of
the prone machine-gunner. The
set was available until 1966.

37-38 British Infantry, wearing Full
Battledress; set 1858. The officer
(37) carries a baton in his right
hand. The set was introduced in
1939; a Bren-gunner was added
after the war, the set remaining
available until 1959.

39-41 Airborne Infantry; set 2010.
Introduced in 1948, this set was
derived from the battledress
infantry in set 1858 but with the
Parachute Regiment's red beret.
It included a man carrying a Bren
gun and was available until 1960.

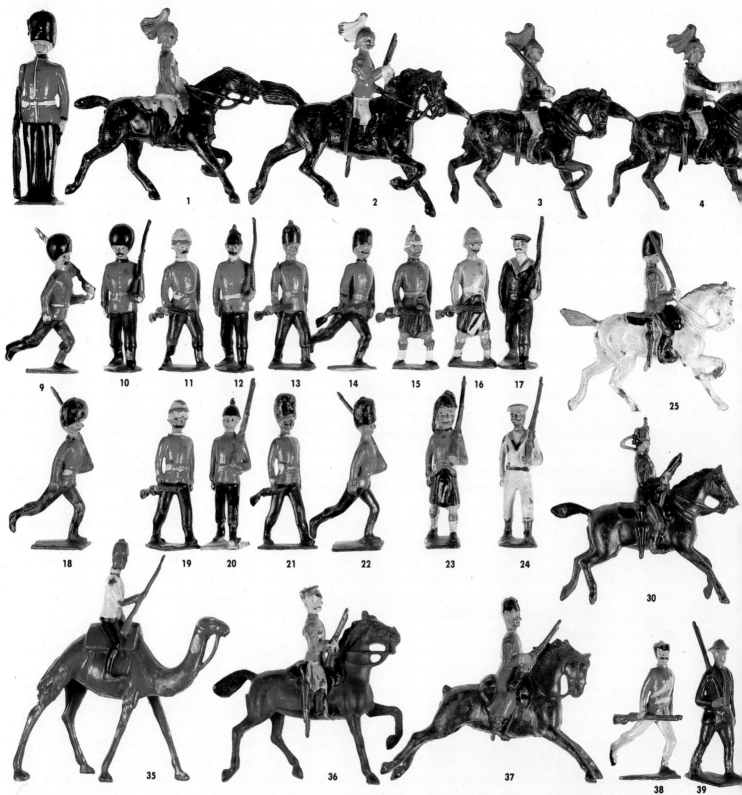

From 1896 until 1940 Britains produced a range of small-size figures, the infantry being about 44mm (1.73in) high and the cavalry 55mm (2.16in), known as the "B" and later the "W" series.

1 Trooper of the 1st Life Guards; set 1B. This is a late fixed-arm figure.

2 Trooper, 2nd Life Guards; set 7B. He has a movable carbine arm.

3 Horse Guards trooper; set 2B. His sword blade rests on his shoulder, and he rides a smaller horse than (2).

4 Horse Guards officer; set 2B. Basically the same figure as (3), but with an extended sword arm.

5 1st Dragoon Guards trooper; set 5B; with the early short carbine.

6 A later 1st Dragoon Guard on a larger "walk-march" horse.

7 This mystery figure has the black plume and blue facings of the 1st Royal Dragoons, although Britains did not list this regiment in their "B" series.

8 16th Lancers (Active Service) trooper; set 12B. Usually depicted in khaki — see (28-29) — this variant wears the 16th Lancers full dress scarlet tunic.

9 Grenadier Guards, Running, Slope Arms; set 18B. Note the "daylight" between the body and the slope rifle — compare (18).

10 Coldstream Guards, Marching at the Slope; set 16B. The same figures were produced as Scots Guards in Display Set 85.

11 Northumberland Fusiliers, Active Service Order; set 21B. An officer figure was produced by snipping away the rifle.

12 The Manchester Regiment, at the Slope; set 20B. A line infantryman in spiked helmet — see also (20).

13 Lancashire Fusiliers, Marching at the Trail; set 17B. The box for this set is shown at (7) *pages 308-309*.

14 Royal Dublin Fusiliers, Running at the Trail; set 19B. The "B" range was well endowed with fusilier regiments.

15 Cameron Highlander, in red doublet and white spiked helmet rather than the usual active service version (16).

16 The Queen's Own Cameron Highlanders, Active Service Order; set 23B. Strangely the figures in this set always seem to be painted with Black Watch kilts.

17 Bluejackets of the Royal Navy; set 22B. These sailors at the slope were also produced as

whitejackets in set 24B. See (24).

18 Grenadier Guards; 11W, later 161W. The slightly taller but simpler "W" version of Grenadier. Note that the numbering system of the "W" series changed in the 1930s from single and double figure numbers to a sequence starting at 145W.

19 Northumberland Fusiliers; set 21B. This is the later, taller square-based version of (11).

20 Infantry of the Line; 10W or 151W. This set was still sometimes labelled as the Manchester Regiment. Compare with (12).

21 Lancashire Fusiliers; 17B. A late version of the "B" series figure — compare with (13).

22 Running fusilier. Apparently an early "W" series figure, although fusiliers were deleted from this

range at a relatively early date.
23 Cameron Highlander, Full Dress;
23B. A late "B" series Highlander
marching at the slope, with a
feather bonnet. This casting was
also in the "W" series.
24 Whitejackets of the Royal Navy;
set 24B. This is the later version
sailor — compare with (17).
25-26 Royal Scots Greys; set 6B.
Two versions of the Scots Greys,
on trotting (25) and galloping (26)
horses — there were sometimes
several different types of horse
within a "B" series cavalry set.
27 An outrider from an RHA Active
Service Gun Team; no. 126B. See
(19-24) *pages 260-261.*
28 16th Lancers, Active Service
Order; set 12B. The 16th Lancers
trooper in the more usual all-khaki
uniform — compare with (8).

29 16th Lancers, Active Service
Order; set 12B. A late-version
trooper on the large "walk-
march" horse — see also (6).
30 11th Hussars; set 10B. An early
trooper with short carbine.
31 11th Hussars; set 10B. A late-
version trooper with a long
carbine, on a large horse.
32 An outrider from the RHA Review
Order Gun Team; set 125B. This
used the same gun and limber as
(19-24) *pages 260-261.*
33 Mounted Infantry; set 15B. An
interesting figure in a scarlet
tunic, khaki breeches and blue
field service cap.
34 17th Lancers; set 13B. A trooper
in full dress.
35 Egyptian Camel Corps; set 68N.
Although compatible in size with
the "W" range, this figure was

listed in the "N" range of second-
grade standard-size figures.
36 Japanese Cavalry; set 11B. The
only "foreign" troops in the
original "B" series were
Japanese and Russians — who
were at war in 1904-5.
37 Russian Cavalry (Cossacks); 14B.
Although based on the galloping
horse, this is a unique figure. The
tail is missing from this example.
38 Japanese Infantry; set 25B. This
late-version Japanese soldier
uses the Dublin Fusilier (14) with
a head-change.
39 US Infantry (Service Dress); 55W,
later 158W. A miniature version of
the standard-size second-grade
"doughboy" — see (24) *page 276.*
40 Russian Infantry; set 26B. Based
on the running Grenadier Guard
figure, Russian infantry are also

found marching at the trail.
41 French infantryman in greatcoat,
from Britains' Paris Office.
42 A Belgian infantryman from the
Paris Office. This is a different
paint version of (41).
43 French infantryman in tunic, from
the Paris Office. An officer was
produced by snipping off the rifle.
44 French Infanterie Coloniale from
the Paris Office. An ingenious re-
use of (19) with the correct double
row of buttons painted on.
45 A German infantryman, also from
the Paris Office, and based on the
later Manchester Regiment (20).
46-48 A cowboy and two North
American Indians, included
because they are quite rare "W"
figures. (46) and (48) are
miniature versions of figures in
the "A" series.

At the beginning of the century the British public in general were proud of the feats of arms achieved by the British forces in the many small colonial wars and campaigns fought throughout the 19th century. The use of artillery was often a decisive factor in these conflicts, and most British manufacturers were quick to realize that, as a major arm of the forces, the gunners needed to be reproduced in model form. Although variable in quality, these cannons and field guns were, from the earliest releases, often quite realistic in appearance and effective in operation.

All the larger British toy soldier manufacturers listed field pieces in their ranges. They were, when combined with figures or complete horse teams to draw them, usually among the most prestigious items in their catalogues as well as the most expensive. Lavishly boxed and presented they represented, then as now, a major acquisition for the keen collector.

Based usually on British Army units of the Royal Horse or Royal Field Artillery, and Royal Navy landing party crews, they appealed strongly to a public who had often seen the real-life counterparts in action — if only at the annual Royal Military Tournament in London.

Their obvious fragility, and the rough use often meted out to them — quite apart from the limited numbers in which, as expensive toys, they were sold — makes all gun teams among the rarest toy soldiers found today. Due to the variable quality of the models made by companies other than Britains, however, this is not always reflected in their value. The occasional foray into gun teams of countries other than the UK was usually accomplished by a simple repainting of an existing casting, or at most, the provision of an alternative head moulding. Some companies used a pre-existing cavalry horse as the basis for their artillery draught horses, in an attempt to reduce the high cost of moulds which would otherwise be relatively little used. One maker used a simple pin to transform a marching figure into one capable of holding a rope attached to a field gun.

The guns themselves were invariably capable of firing small shells, and indirectly added to manufacturers' sales by destroying figures which they were targeted on. Most makers also sold the guns separately, so they are in themselves less rare than complete teams.

1 Royal Navy field gun crew; by Reka, c1915. This small set was made up of the standard Reka field gun and three Royal Navy bluejackets marching. These were on a small wood and papier-mâché base incorporating a three-sided wall and earth banking. The only distinguishing features from the standard sailors are the gold trims on the hatbands and a small gold

insignia on the petty officer's right arm (rearmost figure). This is a rare set with the original box.

2 Royal Artillery, Territorials; Crescent catalogue no. 809, issued 1931-1950s. This galloping gun team was first made by Reka in 1921 and was one of the moulds sold to Crescent in 1930. The painting of the horses and figures is generally poorer than the Reka sets, which are now rare; they can also be identified by the erasing of the trade-mark below the horses in pre-World War II sets, and by the Crescent trade-mark from 1946. The gun is fired by a simple spring plunger mechanism, similar to French cannons, and the limber usually has a thin card or ply back and carries no ammunition. They are

both painted grey, with copper coloured wheels. The figures are of "standard" 54mm (2.12in) scale and were also issued as Royal Horse Artillery, in full dress, and steel-helmeted active service versions. The Reka originals were also made as USA and British Colonial sets.

3 Russian artillery officer; from the BMC series by Soldarma, c1921. This rare figure, normally part of the Royal Horse Artillery gun team shown at (4), is actually part of an identical set with green uniforms sold as Imperial Russian troops. The horse and rider are to 60mm (2.36in) scale.

4 Royal Horse Artillery, active service dress; from the BMC series by Soldarma, c1921. This well-sculpted and lively gun team

makes even the Britains issues look pedestrian and second-rate in comparison. It uses a gun and limber by Rivollet of France, with a spring mechanism as in the Reka set (2). It was also painted in Russian and USA uniforms on the same castings which are to 60mm (2.36in) scale. All are rare.

5 British Naval Brigade; by Reka, c1915. This set utilizes the original gun and limber for the set shown at (2). The far superior limber incorporates a lifting panel at the back to enable the 25mm (1in) long steel rod ammunition to be carried. The figures are the same as those shown at (1) but by inserting pins into the mould a "ring hand" was produced enabling them to pull a "draw rope" from the limber. Made to accompany a horse

team originally, the limber and gun were not issued with them until 1921 due to World War I. This set was also issued by Crescent after 1931 but with the figures reduced to six and without the limber. Crescent also used the original Reka artwork for their labels. Made to 54mm (2.12in) scale it is rare as either a Reka or Crescent set.

6 Fifteen-pounder field gun; by Renvoize, c1902. A patented design with a unique double-action firing mechanism, this was one of the most powerful "scale" guns made in Britain. It was sold singly and as part of a team which only differed from the Britains original in the movable arms of the riders and slight changes to the horses. It is a rare piece.

1 **2** **3**

7 **8** **9** **10**

19 **20** **21** **22** **23** **24** **25** **26** **27**

John Hill and Co., who are usually referred to by the name "Johillco" that appeared on many of their figures, were founded by a former employee of Britains, George Wood, c1900 and were regarded as their main rival.

1 An early peaked-cap lancer on a galloping horse, dated 23.10.1915. Normally found in khaki or gilt finish, this example is in "full dress" red tunic with dark blue cap and trousers.

2 Mounted Hussars, Large; no. 213A. This excellent figure has undergone some retouching and originally may not have had the red breeches of the 11th Hussars.

3 Hussar, mounted; no. 924. A fixed-arm figure, very inferior to (2), but in the 1930s it sold for two pence rather than three!

4 Life Guard in cloak. Note the strong resemblance to the Britains piece – see (14) *page 256*.

5 A post-war Horse Guard, similar to the Britains figure at (11) *page 257*, although the saddle carbine is retained on the Johillco version.

6 12th Lancers (Prince of Wales Royal); no. 925. A movable-arm lancer on an indifferent horse.

7 Field marshall, mounted; no. 907. Included in many boxed sets, this is a late second-quality painting.

8 Dismounted general. A good casting, but in a second-grade finish. Originally this figure was available as no. 922: Senior Medical Officer.

9 Scots Greys trooper; no. 33P. Available in a number of sets, this and a number of other Johillco

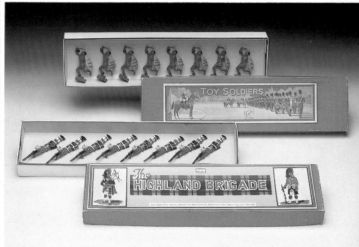

Left: *Boxed sets of Johillco figures are quite hard to find; these are post-war examples. The "Zulus, ref. 259", are quite different figures from the first-version Johillco Zulus; the label is marked with a price of six shillings. The other set was the "Scot prone ref. 122". The price was six shillings and sixpence.*

cavalry use a horse very similar to a Britains second-grade figure, and one used by Reka.

10 Scots Greys standard-bearer; no. 692. A figure with "comic opera" epaulettes, his standard appears to be the Red Ensign of the British Merchant Navy!

11 The gilt version, no. 691G, of the Scots Greys trumpeter; no. 691. This is a quite attractive figure, on

a stubborn horse, but like (10) he has superfluous epaulettes.

12 A fixed-arm marching Guards officer with his hand on his sword hilt, a pose also used for the infantry officer (28 and 29).

13-14 Two paint versions of no. 215A, listed as a Scots Guardsman but here with the red plume of a Coldstream. (13) is a first-grade painting while (14) is a later, more basic paint job. They are movable-arm figures.

15 Scots Guards standard-bearer; no. 911. An early painting of this one-piece casting.

16 Firing Fusilier; no. 523C as a 1d line, and 523A as a 1½d line — this is presumably the former!

17 Grenadier Guard, kneeling firing. This would appear to be a later introduction than the kneeling

infantryman shown at (33).

18 Grenadier Guard, running; no. 243A. A movable-arm figure at the trail, similar to the Britains version but stepping off on the right rather than the left foot.

19-27 Johillco's only bandsmen are these nine Guardsmen, which were available singly, listed as Grenadier Guards. They were not sold as a complete boxed band, although items (19, 21, 22, 25 and 26) were listed as a Scots Guards band in set 38/5 — with other figures. It will be noted that these fixed-arm figures are painted as Coldstream Guards.

28 Marching infantry officer. This is the same as (12) but with a spiked helmet. It was originally available in dark blue as no. 923: Junior Medical Officer.

29 Marching infantry officer; as (28) but in a white helmet.

30 Liverpool Regiment (slope arms); no. 915C. A fixed-arm 1d figure.

31 Middlesex Regiment (Present Arms!); no. 910. The two arms and rifle are cast as a clip-on unit.

32 Firing Lincolnshire Regiment; no. 524A. The first-grade standing firing line infantryman.

33 Kneeling firing line infantryman, in a white helmet. In a blue helmet this was listed as no. 912: Manchester Regiment.

34 This line infantryman in spiked helmet standing at the ready is listed simply as 5d: Infantry, and was only available in second-grade finish.

35 Manchester Regiment, running; no. 245A. This is the same as (18) but with a spiked helmet.

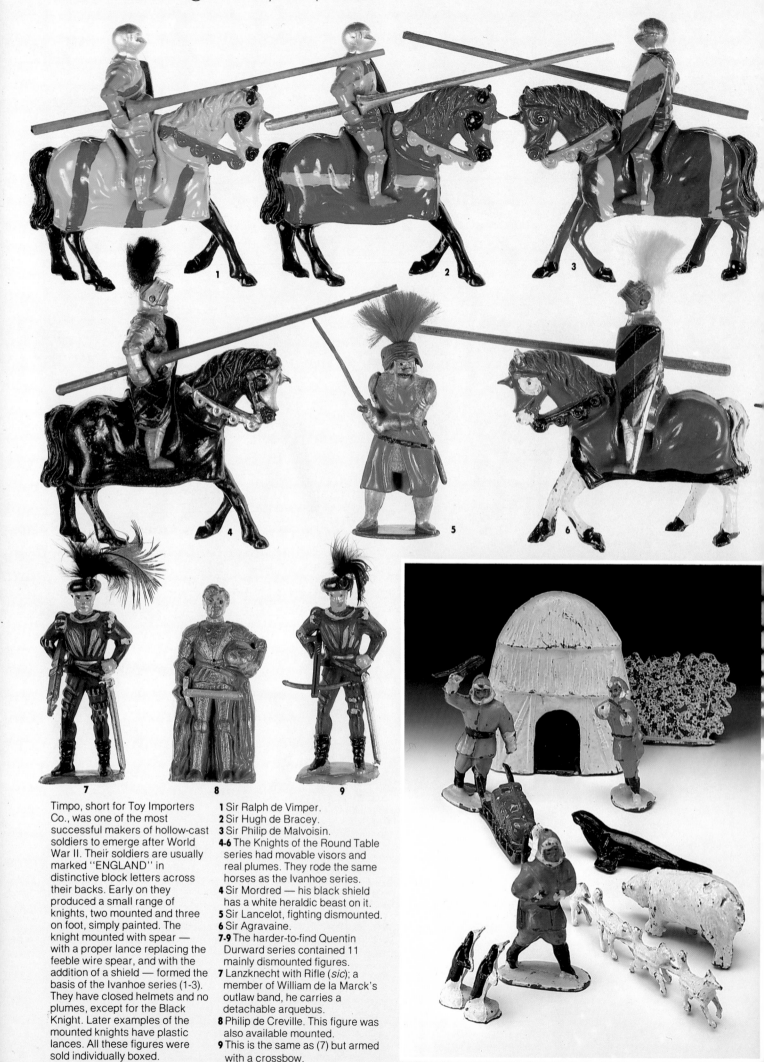

Hollow-cast Figures by Timpo, UK

Timpo, short for Toy Importers Co., was one of the most successful makers of hollow-cast soldiers to emerge after World War II. Their soldiers are usually marked "ENGLAND" in distinctive block letters across their backs. Early on they produced a small range of knights, two mounted and three on foot, simply painted. The knight mounted with spear — with a proper lance replacing the feeble wire spear, and with the addition of a shield — formed the basis of the Ivanhoe series (1-3). They have closed helmets and no plumes, except for the Black Knight. Later examples of the mounted knights have plastic lances. All these figures were sold individually boxed.

1 Sir Ralph de Vimper.

2 Sir Hugh de Bracey.

3 Sir Philip de Malvoisin.

4-6 The Knights of the Round Table series had movable visors and real plumes. They rode the same horses as the Ivanhoe series.

4 Sir Mordred — his black shield has a white heraldic beast on it.

5 Sir Lancelot, fighting dismounted.

6 Sir Agravaine.

7-9 The harder-to-find Quentin Durward series contained 11 mainly dismounted figures.

7 Lanzknecht with Rifle (*sic*); a member of William de la Marck's outlaw band, he carries a detachable arquebus.

8 Philip de Creville. This figure was also available mounted.

9 This is the same as (7) but armed with a crossbow.

10 **11** **12** **13** **14** **15**

17

16 **18** **19** **20** **21** **22** **23**

24 **25** **26** **27** **28** **29** **30** **31**

Left: *One of the earliest offerings from Timpo was their Arctic set. This came in several different permutations, but most of the elements are shown here. The presence of both penguins and a docile looking polar bear must throw the explorers into some confusion as to which polar region they are in. One explorer takes aim at the savage fauna, which also includes a seal, while another trudges on with slung rifle. The third member of the team cracks his whip over a team of willing but tiny huskies all cast in one piece, like a lead caterpillar, which haul a well-modelled, if undersized sledge. The Arctic wastes are conveyed by a snow-covered bush and a white-painted African hut masquerading as an igloo.*

10-15 Timpo's two largest series were their West Point Cadets and US Army and Navy series. The West Point Cadet range had 20 different figures.
10 Cadet tuba player; no. 7007.
11 Bugler; no. 7004.
12 Trombone player; no. 7006.
13 Side drummer; no. 7002.
14 Mounted officer; no. 7016. Detachable, he uses the same horse as the Timpo British mounted policeman.
15 Cadet at ease; no. 7013.
16-31 The US Army and Navy series contained over 30 different items and is generally considered to be the best range of World War II toy soldier GIs produced. Both these figures and the West Point Cadets were later issued in plastic.
16 Charging US Infantry; no. 9013.

17 Firing Kneeling Infantry; no. 9018 in the series.
18 Officer; no. 9009.
19 Firing Standing Infantry; no. 9011. Note that this is an interesting variation by Timpo painted as a black soldier.
20 Washing; no. 9023. A nice domestic touch!
21 Eating; no. 9026. This figure also has a mug of coffee in his hand.
22 Military Police; no. 9032.
23 Wounded; Walking, no. 9025. A well-modelled figure with bandaged head and arm in sling.
24 Infantryman at Ease; no. 9000.
25 Infantryman Marching; no. 9001. This interesting figure appears to be going on leave or changing camp, as he carries his pack in his left hand.
26 Ceremonial, Marching; no. 9020.

This figure is in service dress and wearing an overseas cap.
27 Ceremonial Officer; no. 9022. Empty-handed in service dress and overseas cap.
28 British soldiers in khaki, no. 7: officer. Timpo's British soldiers in battledress never seem to have been as popular as the GIs; the series only ran to 10 figures, of which this is the commonest.
29 Naval Officer; no. 9030. Although listed in the US Army and Navy series, this is really a Royal Navy officer.
30 Sailor on Guard; no. 9029. This is also in reality a Royal Navy bluejacket.
31 Sailor; no. 8009. A Royal Navy sailor on leave with his kitbag on his shoulder, from the model railways figures range.

Solid Figures by Authenticast, SAE, Minikins and MIM

Between the wars the firm of Comet Metal Products of New York produced a range of undistinguished 55mm (2.16in) solid lead soldiers. After World War II, one Curt Wennberg — a Swedish Naval Attache in the USA — helped gain the services of the Swedish designer Holger Eriksson. Taking advantage of an Irish Government subsidy, Comet set up a factory in Galway to produce Eriksson's designs under the name "Authenticast". This international arrangement was not without its difficulties, culminating in a fire in 1950 which put an end to the Irish factory. Most Authenticast figures are marked "Eire" and "HE" for Holger Eriksson, although a few pieces have other initials. Most,

but not all, of the striding figures have a cruciform base.

1 17th-century pikeman, steadying his pike while drawing his sword.
2 French Napoleonic infantryman, of an Italian regiment, advancing.
3 French Napoleonic line infantry officer, in bicorne hat.
4 French "Turco" or tirailleur of *c*1900, at the charge.
5 Franco-Prussian War Franc-tireur; a different painting of an American Civil War figure.

Right: *An example of a boxed set of Authenticast figures: the Franc-tireurs as mentioned at (5). Note the motto: "The finest models ever built". The word "Gaeltacht" refers to the Gaelic-speaking part of western Ireland.*

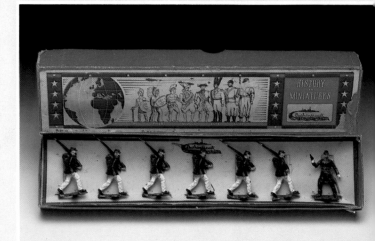

20   **21**   **22**   **23**   **24**

25   **26**   **27**   **28**   **29**   **30**

31   **32**   **33**   **34**   **35**   **36**

6 Franco-Prussian War French line infantryman, in an interesting "on guard" stance.

7-8 Chasseur à Pied (Light Infantry) officer and man, c1870, marching.

9-10 Zouave, with impressively piled pack (9), and an officer (10) which is a different painting of (8).

11 Indian Army sepoy, at ease.

12-13 British line infantry of 1900, at attention. These figures are not by Eriksson, being marked "L.N." on the base. The officer (12) is an adaptation of the man: the soldered-on rifle has been left off, a sheathed sword added, and a sash painted on.

14 Marching Royal Marine.

15 World War I British officer, in trenchcoat, equipped with binoculars and map case.

16 World War I British soldier; an

evocative figure "standing to" in steel helmet and greatcoat.

17 French Army officer of 1939, in khaki service dress with a swagger-stick under his arm.

18 World War II British soldier, in shorts and slung rifle.

19 Swiss Guard of the Vatican, in undress uniform with rifle.

20-30 With the failure of the Irish factory Comet continued producing soldiers in New York while Wennberg moved to South Africa and set up the Swedish African Engineers, known as SAE.

20 Ancient Teuton warrior, with braided hair and arm rings.

21 A rather small Viking with shield and long sword.

22 Ancient Egyptian foot soldier, with spear and shield.

23 Ancient Egyptian officer, with

plumed head-dress and sword.

24 Portuguese infantryman, of the Napoleonic period.

25 Indian Army sepoy, in khaki with red facings.

26 French Turco, charging. Compare with the figure at (4).

27 Italian Bersaglieri, prone firing, an unusual portrayal in British-type post-war battledress.

28 World War II British soldier, in shirt sleeves, running at the trail.

29 World War I German infantry officer, charging with pistol.

30 A post-war British Guardsman, in stiff peaked cap, battledress and blancoed webbing.

31-32 The Japanese firm of Minikins, active in the 1950s, are usually regarded as merely pirates of other firms' work, but they did in fact produce some interesting

original pieces including this Japanese samurai and 17th-century soldier with early firearm.

33-36 In 1935 the Belgian Emmanuel Steinback introduced his range of quality figures under the name MIM (Maximus In Minimus). Ancients, Napoleonics and some contemporary figures were produced, the size being 60mm (2.35in). They are readily identifiable by the beautifully designed bases which are marked underneath "MIM" with a coat of arms and a brief description of the figure.

33 Syrian warrior, with a sling.

34 Ancient Egyptian warrior.

35 Roman centurion, with his vine branch staff of office.

36 Roman legionary, carrying a pilum and shield.

The USA relied mainly on imports until the 1920s, when a number of toy soldier makers commenced production. Of these, the large 3¼-inch hollow-casts by Barclay, Manoil and others, produced in the 1930s, are very collectable.

1-3 These figures were included in a "military display tray" game by C.W. Beiser's American Soldier Co. of New York. C.W. Beiser was inventor of the game, discussed on *page 276*. In Spanish-American War (1898) uniform, these figures may have been produced by the American Soldier Co. themselves, but more likely by an outside firm such as Barclay.
1 Artilleryman with rammer.
2 Mounted officer, riding a rearing brown horse.

3 Infantryman at the ready.
4-6 The Ideal Toy Co. of Bridgeport, Connecticut, produced 54mm (2.12in) hollow-casts in the 1920s, using moulds from Germany:
4 Officer, with movable sword arm.
5 Bugler, with the same body as (4).
6 A fixed-arm US sailor with rifle.
7 World War I US infantryman. This 40mm (1.57in) figure is from the "Uncle Sam's Defenders" series introduced by the Grey Iron Casting Co. in the early 1930s. One of the few firms to make toy soldiers in cast iron, they had previously produced a range of nickel-plated figures of the same size in 1898 period uniforms, and in 1933 introduced figures in the 3¼-inch "Dime Store Size".
8-11 John Lloyd Wright, the son of Frank Lloyd Wright the architect,

made toys under several trade names, including Lincoln Log. From 1929 to World War II a small range of solid-cast civilian and military figures was produced.
8 US infantryman, in the uniform of Wayne's Legion, 1794.
9 Marching US infantryman of 1918. The top of the rifle is missing in this example.
10 Mounted US officer of 1918.
11 Charging US infantryman, 1918.
12-13 The Canadian toy soldier trade has always relied principally on imports from the UK — chiefly of Britains — and from the USA, except in time of war when outside supplies were cut off. During World War II the firm of London Toy produced a range of vehicles and some military figures cast at attention, such as this pilot

(12), and airman of the Royal Canadian Air Force (13).
14-30 The term "Dime Store soldiers" is almost synonymous with the names of Barclay and Manoil, who both started producing hollow-cast figures in the early 1930s. Dime Store figures tend to be individualists going about different tasks, rather than marching in formation. Barclays can be distinguished by separate tin helmets — until World War II when cast helmets came in — and a distinctive way of painting the eyes with a curved eybrow and dot shown clearly on (22). Manoil are normally marked as such, and compared to Barclay figures they have a more sculptural quality and are often more inventive in their poses.

14 ''Long stride'' naval officer; Barclay 721.

15 Soldier, releasing carrier pigeons; Barclay 731.

16 ''Short stride'' standing firing infantryman; Barclay 747.

17 Kneeling machine-gunner; Barclay 702, an early figure.

18 Radio operator, with separate aerial; Barclay 951.

19 One of several versions of a searchlight and operator, cast as one piece; Barclay 776.

20 Doctor; Barclay 760.

21 A Manoil nurse of formidable aspect.

22 A Barclay skier of 1940, no. 785.

23 Sailor, in white uniform; Barclay 919; in the style known as ''pod foot'' produced in the 1950s.

24 ''Pod foot'' officer; Barclay 908.

25 ''Pod foot'' soldier equipped with

slung rifle; Barclay 988.

26 ''Pod foot'' soldier with flame-thrower; Barclay 991.

27 ''Pod foot'' soldier charging; Barclay 906.

28 Machine-gunner; Barclay 928.

29 Observer; Manoil 526. This is a post-war figure.

30 Motorcycle rider; Manoil 529. A post-war figure.

Right: *Both Manoil and Barclay also produced vehicles and equipment but this was undersized in relation to their soldiers. Shown here are two Manoil tractors, hauling a field kitchen and water cart, and a caisson (limber) and field gun. These are in fact re-casts, from the original moulds, by Ron Eccles of Burlington, Iowa.*

The 1930s brought a new dimension to tinplate vehicles in the shape of "war toys" like these. The larger German-made examples, in particular, achieve an almost alarming realism.

1 Military Truck with Trailer (with other towed accessories) by VEB, East Germany, c1947-50. The truck and trailer are of lightweight tinplate with printed detail; the truck has a detachable tin canopy and a tipping body. Also shown are two "towing" accessories in tinplate, by VEB: a field kitchen (towed behind trailer) and a field gun (in foreground). Lengths: (truck) 3.94in (10cm); (trailer) 3.35in (8.5cm); (kitchen) 3.15in (8cm); (gun) 3.54in (9cm).

2 Volkswagen Cars by an unidentified German maker. These small push-along models in tinplate are believed to date from pre-1939: they show cars with the early-type "split" rear window. Length: 3.15in (8cm). Limited.

3 Military Ambulance (based on the contemporary Phanomen Granit ambulance) by an unidentified German maker, c1935. This large tinplate vehicle is clockwork-powered and features headlights (battery-powered), opening doors, opaque celluloid windows, a hinge-down rear step, and a baggage rack. The Red Cross flags are tinplate. Length: 11.4in (29cm). Scarce.

4 Wounded Soldiers on Stretchers; one-piece composition figures (basically sawdust and glue, compression moulded on a wire armature), possibly by Lineol, Germany, mid-1930s.

5 Military Motorcyclists probably German, mid-1930s. Clockwork mechanism is concealed within the sidecars: note winder hole, and also machine gun, in sidecar at the right. Length: 3.35in (8.5cm).

6 Horse-Drawn Field Kitchen by an unidentified German maker, c1935. This is a most pleasing tinplate model with printed camouflage finish, featuring a pressed-tin crew and a hinged chimney and opening lid on the

Probably by Heyde, c1890, this volunteer cyclist is shown mounted on an early military cycle. Note the Martini rifle carried, and the pack attached to the handlebars. Height: 2.83in (7.2cm).

cooker unit. Overall length: 7·09in (18cm).

7 German Army Half-Track by a German maker, probably Tipp and Company, c1935. Clockwork-powered, with rear-wheel drive via chain tracks, it features operating steering, two rear-mounted spare wheels, and a detachable windscreen (missing here). Note the provision of holes for "peg-in" figures of a driver and eight passengers. Length: 8·46in (21·5cm). Scarce.

8 US Military Policemen; German-made composition figures, c1950.

9 US Military Police Jeep by Arnold, West Germany, c1950. This example—see also (10)—is shown complete with remote-control handset. Length: 6·69in (17cm).

10 As (9), but here shown with a full crew of composition figures. Note the fold-down windscreen, heavy-treaded rubber tyres, driving mirror, and rear-mounted spare and jerrycan. It is clockwork-powered (rear-wheel drive).

11 Jeep by an unidentified maker, probably British, c1948-50. Of heavy-gauge tinplate, with the Allied "Invasion Star" printed on the bonnet, it is clockwork-powered (front-wheel drive) and has wheels and tyres of solid moulded plastic. Length: 7·28in (18·5cm).

12 Volkswagen (finished in "Luftwaffe blue") by an unidentified German maker, c1938-39. A push-along toy, with printed detail, and applied tin headlamps and bumper bars front and rear. length: 5·22in 13·25cm). Scarce.

13 Willys Jeep by Minic (Lines Brothers Limited), Great Britain, c1950—the maker's "No 2" model; a smaller "No 1" version was also made. Clockwork-powered (rear—wheel drive), it has simple steering and features a fold-down windscreen and rear-mounted spare wheel and detachable jerrycan. Length: 6·3in (16cm).

14 German Army Kubelwagen (ie, utility vehicle) with Field Kitchen, by a German maker, probably Tipp and Company, late 1930s. Clockwork-powered (rear-wheel drive) and in camouflage finish, it has an open, doorless body and tinplate wheels and tyres. A composition driver and passenger are shown; note provision for "peg-in" passengers at the rear. The kitchen unit features a hinged lid and a fold-down chimney. Lengths: (Kübelwagen) 6·69in (17cm); (field kitchen) 4·33in (11cm).

15 German Police Motorcyclist by Tipp and Company, late 1930s. In tinplate, with printed detail—including "Pol" (= Polizei) on the rear of the sidecar—it has clockwork mechanism in the sidecar: note control lever at rear. Length: 3·35in (8·5cm).

16 Volkswagen Kübelwagen by an unidentified maker, perhaps made for display. It is unpowered and features a folding windscreen, opening doors and rear hatch, and rubber tyres. A composition driver is shown, and provision is made for "peg-in" passengers. Length: 8·07in (20·5cm).

1-4 Royal Tank Corps. A squad of these figures were supplied with the Carden Loyd tank (22) in set 1322. See also (6) *page 282*.

5-6 Team of Royal Artillery Gunners, (Active Service); set 313. Introduced in 1929, this set contained four standing (5) and four kneeling (6) empty-handed figures in peaked caps.

7 An artillery officer in peaked cap with binoculars, derived from the line infantry figure.

8-9 Just before World War II the peaked-cap figures in set 313 received steel helmets.

10-13 Team of Gunners Carrying Shells; set 1730. Introduced in 1939, this set had three standing and four kneeling steel-helmeted figures carrying artillery shells. Post-war, the set contained an

officer with binoculars (19), two standing gunners (9) and two kneeling gunners (8) from set 313, one gunner standing with a shell (10) and two kneeling with shells (12). It was produced until 1962.

14 Sound Locator; no. 1638. This was a primitive pre-radar device for detecting the approach of enemy aircraft acoustically. Introduced in 1938 it was available briefly post-war.

15 Rangefinder, with Operator; no. 1639. This is mounted on wire tripod legs with a fixed-arm operator leaning forward to look through it. Available from 1938-40 and post-war until 1959.

16 Spotting Chair, Swivelling, with Man; no. 1731. The reclining observer has a movable left arm holding binoculars. Available from

1939-40 and 1946-59.

17-18 Predictor with Operator; no. 1728. A representation of an early form of mechanical computer for calculating the projected position of aircraft. Available from 1939-40 and 1946-59.

19 The later version artillery officer with binoculars in a steel helmet, from set 1730; see (10-13).

20 Height-Finder with Operator; no. 1729. This is similar in concept to the rangefinder, but larger. The operator is the same as (15) but shown here in the post-war paint finish. This item was available from 1939-40 and 1946-59.

21 Motor Machine-gun Corps; set 199. Introduced in the early 1920s, this set contained three of these units. The motorcycle and rider was a one-piece fixed-wheel

casting, four of which were available in set 200: Motorcycle Despatch Riders.

22 Tank of the Royal Tank Corps (Carden Loyd); set 1203. This was really a lightly-armoured machine-gun carrier, but it was designated a tank at a time of financial stringency. The first version, produced in 1933 had white rubber tracks. The later version, illustrated, was introduced in 1940 and has solid cast tracks with small wheels underneath.

23 Bren Gun Carrier and Crew; no. 1876, introduced in 1940 and available after the war until 1960.

24 Motorcycle Despatch Riders; set 1791. This four-piece set was introduced in 1939, replacing the fixed-wheel World War I motorcycles of set 200 (21) with a

more up-to-date revolving wheel type. The rider wears a Royal Signals blue and white armband. The set was produced post-war until 1966, but from 1960 the figure of a peaked-cap battledress officer replaced one of the motorcycles.

25 Staff Car with General and Driver; set 1448. First produced in 1936, this is an extensively modified version introduced in the early 1950s, which remained available until 1959.

26 Gun of the Royal Artillery; no. 1292. First introduced in 1934, this gun was available until 1967.

27 Gun of the Royal Artillery; no. 1263. This small, basic gun was produced from 1933 to 1967.

28 4.5in Howitzer; no. 1725. This is a rubber-tyred gun introduced in

1939 and available until 1967.

29 18in Heavy Howitzer on Tractor Wheels; no. 1265. This splendid piece had a very realistic breech-loading mechanism and ammunition incorporating spring-loaded shell-cases of different strengths to vary the range. Introduced in about 1920, it was available right up to 1980 in modified form.

30 18in Howitzer, Mounted for Garrison Duty; no. 1266. This is the same as (29) but on a static mounting.

31 Two-pounder Light AA Gun, Mobile Unit; no. 1717. This is the AA gun no. 1715, mounted on a four-wheel trailer with swing-out booms, available from 1939-40 and 1946-62.

32 Armoured Car with Swivelling

Gun; no. 1321. Introduced in 1934 and based on a Crossley armoured car, this is an early example with solid metal wheels.

33 Underslung Heavy-duty Lorry with Driver and Anti-aircraft Gun; no. 1643. This splendid 27cm (10.5in) long vehicle was available by itself or with loads such as this 4.5in AA gun. The gun, available separately as no. 1522, is one of the rarest of Britains weapons, produced from 1937-40. The underslung lorry was produced from 1938-40 and, with a round-nosed bonnet, briefly post-war.

34 Regulation Limber; no. 1726. This rubber-tyred limber with opening lid matched the 4.5in howitzer (28); introduced at the same time, it was available until 1960.

35 Mobile Searchlight; no. 1718.

This working searchlight was available separately, or on a trailer. Available from 1939-40 and from 1946-62.

36 Covered Army Tender, Caterpillar Type; no. 1433. The last of three versions of the half-track tender, produced from 1957-70.

Inset(above): *Royal Engineers vehicles. Set 203: Pontoon Section with Pontoon, Review Order, available 1922-39, comprised an open-framework wagon carrying a wooden pontoon boat and two sections of decking to form a bridge. Set 1330: Wagon, General Service Royal Engineers, in Review Order, was in effect two limbers or two-wheeled carts. Produced from 1934-40 and 1948-59, this is a late version.*

Diecast Military Vehicles by Dinky Toys, Britain, 1930s–1960s

1 Military Ambulance (based on a 3-ton Ford Thames 4x4 ambulance); Dinky Toys Number 626, introduced 1956. The plastic windows of this example indicate that it is a later issue. Length: 4·33in (110mm).

2 "Honest John" Missile Launcher; No 655, introduced 1964. The spring-launched missile is plastic. Length overall: 7·4in (188mm).

3 Missile Erector Vehicle with "Corporal" Missile and Launching Platform; No 666, introduced in 1959 and in production until 1964. A fairly fragile model: complete and undamaged examples are much sought after. Lengths: (Vehicle) 9·56in (243mm); (Missile) 9in (229mm); (Launching Platform) 3·5in (89mm).

4 Six-Wheeled Army Transport Wagon (No 151B), shown here with Water Tank Trailer (No 151D), both introduced in 1938 and shown here in their pre-World War II forms. Length: (Wagon) 3·9in (99mm); (Trailer) 2in (52mm).

5 Centurion Tank; No 651, introduced 1954 and with a long production life. Length: 5·87in (149mm). Fairly common.

6 Thorneycroft Mighty Antar Tank Transporter; No 660, introduced 1956. With hinged ramps at the rear, it was intended for use with the Centurion Tank shown at (5). Length: 13·2in (335mm).

7 Anti-Aircraft Gun on Trailer; No 161B, introduced 1939 and produced both pre- and post-War. Note holes for peg-in figures; one

is shown in place here. Length: 4·53in (115mm).

8 Searchlight on Lorry; No 161A, introduced 1939 and produced pre-War only. Length: 3·9in (99mm). Scarce.

9 Cooker Trailer with Stand; No 151C, introduced 1938 – a post-War example is shown. This was intended to be towed by the Wagon shown at (10). Length: 2·375in (60mm).

10 Six-Wheeled Transport Wagon; as (6), but here shown without the tin canopy, exposing "seating" for peg-in personnel. A post-War example is shown.

11 Armoured Car (based on a Daimler of the 1940s-50s); No 670, introduced 1954 and with a long production life. Length: 2·875in (73mm).

12 Light Dragon Motor Tractor (No 162A), Trailer (Limber) (No 162B), and 18-Pounder Gun (No 162C). These were produced both before and after World War II and before the War were sold as a set. Lengths: (Tractor) 2·56in (65mm); (Trailer) 2·125in (54mm); (Gun) 3·07in (78mm).

13 Tank (based on British Medium Tank Mk III); No 22F, announced in December 1933 and included in the first Dinky Toys issue. This model was produced until the early years of World War II. Length: 3·43in (87mm).

14 Medium Tank; No 151A, introduced 1937, and marking Dinky's change to chain tracks. Note squadron markings and radio antenna on turret. Length: 3·62in (92mm).

15 Light Tank; No 152A, introduced 1937 and produced pre- and post-War. A post-War example is shown; note aerial on turret. Length: 2·68in (68mm).

16 Searchlight Lorry; No 22S, based on No 22C (Motor Truck) and produced only in the early part of World War II. Length: 3·31in (84mm). Rare.

17 Reconnaissance Car (based on 6x4 Morris Commercial); No 152B, announced February 1938 and made both pre- and post-War. Length: 3·5in (89mm).

18 Austin Seven Car; No 152C, a pre-War model (wire windscreen missing from this example), shown here with post-War driver. Length: 2in (51mm).

19 Royal Corps of Signals Despatch Rider; No 37C, introduced 1938

and not issued post-War. This example has been repainted. Length: 1·81in (46mm). Scarce.

20 5·5in Medium Gun (with split trail); No 692, introduced 1955. Length: 5·16in (131mm).

21 Missile Servicing Platform Vehicle; No 667, introduced 1960 and available for only four years. Length overall: 7·76in (197mm). Scarce.

22 RAF Pressure Refueller (AEC); No 642, introduced 1957. Length: 5·59in (142mm).

23 Recovery Tractor (Scammell Explorer); No 661, introduced 1957. With working jib. Length: 5·28in (134mm).

24 Medium Artillery Tractor (Leyland Martian); No 689, introduced 1957. Length: 5·51in (140mm).

25 7·2in Howitzer; No 693,

introduced 1958. Length: 5·12in (130mm).

26 Armoured Personnel Carrier (Alvis Saracen); No 676, introduced 1955. Length: 3·23in (82mm). Fairly common.

27 Field Artillery Tractor (No 688), Trailer (Limber) (No 687), and 25-Pounder Field Gun (No 686), introduced in 1957 and available either as separate items or as a set. Lengths: (Tractor) 3·125in (79mm); (Trailer) 2·81in (71mm); (Gun) 3·5in (89mm).

26 Armoured Command Vehicle (AEC); No 677, introduced 1957. Length: 5·28in (134mm). Fairly common.

29 Jeep; No 153A, announced in 1946 and one of the first post-War issues. Note the Allied Invasion Star on the hood. Early models

have a non-voided steering wheel and smooth road wheels. Length: 2·72in (69mm).

30 Austin Champ; No 674, introduced 1954. Length: 2·72in (69mm).

31 Army 1-Ton Cargo Truck (Humber); No 641, introduced 1954. The canopy is detachable. Length: 3·125in (79mm).

32 Army Water Tanker (Austin); No 643, introduced 1958. Length: 3·5in (89mm).

33 Scout Car (Daimler Dingo); No 673, introduced 1953, and shown here with a fixed driver: also available without driver. Length: 2·68in (68mm).

34 Army Covered Wagon (Bedford QL); No 623, introduced 1954. The tin canopy is detachable. Length: 4·13in (105mm).

8

As well as being often colourful and attractive in their own right, the boxes and packages in which toys are marketed are of considerable importance to the collector: depending upon the type of toy, possession of the original box or packaging may add anything between 20 and 50 per cent to its value. In the case of toy soldiers, especially, many collectors will not consider purchasing an item that does not have its original packaging. Examples of the packaging of toy cars, transport toys, toy soldiers and toy trains are shown on the following pages.

The catalogues issued by toymakers, and by the wholesalers and retailers of their products, are of great value to the collector as a source of information, particularly for the correct attribution and dating of toys, as well as being interesting and collectable items in their own right. Many of the older examples of such ephemera, like those shown on *pages 310-311*, are now extremely scarce, but some — notably those of the famous maker of toy soldiers, Britains, and the earlier Meccano (Dinky Toys; Hornby) catalogues — have been reprinted and are currently available from specialist dealers.

Toymakers' Packaging and Catalogues

On this spread we show a selection of the boxes in which tinplate cars of the 1950s-60s were marketed. This period marked the last age of the mass-produced tinplate toy, which was killed off by the advent of plastic construction methods in the 1960s and, in the early 1970s, by legislation introduced in almost all countries to regulate the thickness of the metal that could be used. No doubt safety regulations were justified, since some cheaper, less well-finished toys of light-weight tinplate may be found to have razor-sharp edges, but one sometimes wonders how several generations of children survived virtually intact without the protection of paternalistic governments! We have heard dealers complain

that the collector's insistence on the provision of the original box is, in part at least, no more than a bargaining ploy to reduce the price of a non-boxed item. The dealer may argue that the intrinsic worth lies in the toy itself, and that the box is of no particular value. Nevertheless, it cannot be denied that the original packaging —often attractive in itself; frequently bearing detailed operating instructions; and sometimes carrying trademarks and slogans that do not appear on the toy itself—is a most desirable feature for the collector. Because packaging is fragile, perishable and ephemeral, it seems likely that the value of a boxed toy will increase significantly, as compared to an un-boxed item, as the years go by.

1 Box for Cadillac Gear Shift Car made by Bandai, Tokyo, Japan, in c1965; the toy itself is shown at (1), *pages 40-41*. Note the maker's serial number 4102 on the front (top left), and the illustrated operating instructions on the side of the box uppermost in the photograph. See also (2).
2 Box for Ferrari Gear Shift Car, maker's serial number 4183, made by Bandai in c1965; like the similar model shown at (1), this is a battery-powered toy which takes two 1·5 volt batteries. The illustrated operating instructions on the inside of the lid are clearly seen in this photograph; note also the Japanese maker's quaintly formal exhortation to the potential child customer: "Ask your Mama and Papa for

Bandai's battery operated toy!"
3 Box for Chrysler Imperial Convertible, Number 748 in Bandai's "Model Auto Series" (note serial number on box front, top left), dating from c1957-58. The toy itself, seen here on its box, is fully described at (5), *pages 40-41*.
4 "Hot Rod" Car by T.N. (Nomura Toys Limited), Tokyo, Japan, dating from c1957, shown here with its box on which the various action features of this colourful toy are listed and illustrated. A different view of the car is shown at (10), *pages 42-43*. Powered by two 1·5-volt batteries housed in a trap in the base, with an on/off switch (visible in this photograph) on its lower left side, the car pursues an eccentric course governed by twin driving-wheels

FERRARI GEAR SHIFT CAR
4103 BATTERY OPERATED

| NEUTRAL |
| LOW SPEED |
| HIGH SPEED |

FORWARD OFF REVERSE NEUTRAL, LOW, HIGH.

STEERABLE

● RUNS WITH 2 SPEED BY SHIFTING LEVER. NEUTRAL, LOW, HIGH.
● FORWARD AND REVERSE
● HORN SOUNDS
● MOTOR ROAR
● HEAD LIGHTS ON.

Ask your Mama and Papa for **Bandai's** battery operated toy!

2

748 MODEL AUTO SERIES
CHRYSLER IMPERIAL CONVERTIBLE

3

NEW SEDAN FRICTION POWERED

TRADE MARK MADE IN JAPAN

7

FRICTION WITH SIREN *Plymouth*

PAT. PEND.

Plymouth

9

mounted on a turntable in the base, just behind the front wheels. A single spring-loaded wheel on a pivot is mounted towards the rear of the base; this is jointed to the head of the pressed-tin driver, causing it to turn in the direction taken by the car. When the car moves, the red and green lights atop the engine and the clear plastic cylinders at the sides of the bonnet light up. Pressed-tin headlights are fitted and bright metal details include the radiator, rear bumper (with a cut-out metal number plate, "H 12", above it), and windscreen frame; printed details include the exposed engine, exhaust manifolds, and the legends "Dream Boat" (left), "Hot Rod" (boot), and "Rock n' Roll" (*sic*) (right). It

has rubber wheels with bright metal discs. This has now become a rare toy: only a few examples are known to exist in Great Britain. Length: 7·375in (18·73cm).

5 Box for *Silberpfeil* (Silver Arrow) Racing Car by JNF, West Germany, dating from c1957-58; the toy itself, shown here in front of its box, is based on a Mercedes 196. On the side of the box uppermost in the photograph is a universally-intelligible indication that the model features operating steering.

6 Box for Remote-Control Car made by Arnold, West Germany, in c1954. This toy was made in various colours and in two forms: as a Convertible—shown thus at (1), *pages 42-43*—and as a Saloon, as illustrated on the box. In either

form, it is now quite scarce.

7 Box for New Sedan by T.N. (Nomura Toys), Japan, dating from c1958. The toy itself, shown here on top of its box, is fully described at (1), *pages 38-39*.

8 Box for Racing Car (modelled on a Mercedes Type 196 racing car) made by JNF, West Germany; a good-quality tinplate toy; maker's serial number 82. This toy first appeared in c1957-58 in red or silver finish and in three different versions: friction-driven; battery-powered in multi-action form; and battery-powered with remote-control steering. It provides an interesting example of a manufacturer obtaining "added mileage" from the same basic pressing by issuing various modifications. In this

connection, note also that (5) and (8) are models of the same car, the Mercedes Type 196; (5) being a sports racing version.

9 Box for Plymouth Sedan by Ichiko, Japan, dating from c1958; the toy itself, which is now quite a scarce item, is described at (6), *pages 40-41*. The box is fairly typical of the packaging used by Japanese makers for their standard items of the period, featuring an attractive picture of the car (apparently passing Mount Fuji, on the lid overlap!); a brief statement of any special features—"Friction with Siren" on this model; the maker's trademark and the legend "Made in Japan"; and, in this case, the words "Pat. Pend." (Patent(s) Pending) at left on lid.

1 Box for Ford Highway Patrol Car by Ichiko, Japan; dating from around 1958. The front of the lid bears an attractive colour picture of the car, a statement of its special features, and the maker's slogan—"Quality First Toy of Ichiko"—and serial number. The side of the lid, uppermost in the photograph, repeats the statement of special features and illustrates the "moving warning light" with a line drawing. The car itself is shown at (3), *pages 116-117*: it is fairly typical of the middle-range Japanese tinplate toys of the period, with much printed detail (in this case with police lettering and badges), "Ford" numberplates at front and rear, and bright metal bumpers, radiator, windscreen frame and side-mounted trim strips. Tinted plastic windows are fitted at

front and rear and it has a printed interior with the maker's trademark on the top of the rear seat. The wheels are rubber, with metal discs printed with whitewalls and hubcaps. Friction drives the rear wheels, producing a siren sound and, via a crank, causing the roof-mounted warning light to revolve. Length of car: 9·375in (23·81cm).

2 Box for Truck by "ΛW", USSR; dating from around 1960. Like the toy it holds, this is a fairly solid and utilitarian piece of packaging; the rather fanciful illustration on the Cyrillic-lettered lid, featuring elves and bunny-rabbits, hardly matches the model itself, a very solid toy which is of tabbed-and-slotted heavy-gauge tinplate, clockwork-powered, and looks well-suited to hard work down on the

old collective farm! Length of truck: 12·75in (32·385cm).

3 Box for Mechanical Digger by Gama, West Germany; dating from around 1957. This toy is of considerable interest in that it was made in five or more different versions in the late 1950s; the initial model was constructed entirely of tinplate, but in subsequent versions increasing amounts of plastic were used. This box contains the model with the maker's serial number 2808; this model, which is shown at (4), *pages 118-119*, has a cab of tough plastic. Also illustrated on the box are the models with the serial numbers 280 and 2806; an earlier model in the series, serial number 282, dating from around 1956 and made of heavy-gauge tinplate throughout, is shown at (3),

pages 118-119. To the left of the box lid, a series of drawings shows how levers on the cab control the actions of the digger's bucket. To the right of the top drawing, a "deleted" key indicates that there is no need for winding, the toy being battery-powered. Overall length of toy: 16in (40·64cm).

4 Bristol Bulldog Airplane by Straco, Japan; dating from 1958-59. Both the box and the toy itself are shown here, the latter disassembled; the toy is shown assembled at (7), *pages 234-235*. This yellow cantilever-wing monoplane displays artistic licence in both name and finish: the Bristol Bulldog was a biplane fighter aircraft of the 1930s, and this model is in civilian livery but with roundels that combine British and French military

markings! In tabbed-and-slotted tinplate, with a well-detailed pressed-tin radial engine, a plastic propeller and rubber wheels, it is battery-powered, with stop-and-go action and a turning propeller. As shown here, it is made in three parts —fuselage, mainplane and tailplane —with the method of assembly illustrated on the side of the lid. Length of aircraft: 12in (30·48cm); wingspan: 14·5in (36·83cm).

5 Remote-Control Satellite by Arnold, West Germany; dating from late 1957. This fascinating toy appeared on the market within a few days of the worldwide sensation caused by the successful flight of the Soviet "Sputnik 1" on 4 October 1957: an excellent illustration of the way in which enterprising toymakers must keep abreast of real-life

developments. The box bears a striking illustration of the satellite whirling through space; the toy itself, shown at (7), *pages 236-237*, is of pressed tin, with plastic vanes and aerials. It is a "flying toy" powered by Arnold's ingenious remote-control system: the toy is attached to a pressed-tin handset by a coiled-wire cable—in this case 31in (78·74cm) long— consisting of an outer layer, which revolves when the crank on the handset is turned, and an inner non-revolving core. The harder the handset is cranked, the higher and faster the toy flies: it can be made to alter course, climb or dive by altering the angle at which the handset is held, and can be made to fly backwards by cranking the handle in reverse.

6 Box for Twin-Engined Airliner by Tipp and Company, West Germany; dating from 1956. The box features an illustration of the prototype— in KLM livery and bearing the legend "The Flying Dutchman" along its upper fuselage (with "De Vliegende Hollander" on the other side)—in an airport setting, and displays also the maker's trademark and the serial number "58F". The toy itself, shown at (3), *pages 234-235*, is of good-quality tinplate, with plastic propellers, and has a detachable wing section. It is friction-driven. Length of aircraft: 9·75in (24·765cm); wingspan: 12·375in (31·43cm).

7 Fire Engine by "K", Japan; dating from 1958-59. Both the box and the toy itself are shown here; another view of the toy is shown at

(1), *pages 114-115*. As in the case of the Japanese-made car at (1) above, the box both states the special features of the toy and illustrates them. Of quite good-quality tinplate, the toy has a wealth of printed detail and the usual bright-metal fittings. It is friction-driven (front wheels) and a siren noise is produced as it moves. The major feature is illustrated on the side of the box: when the lever visible just behind the cab is pushed in the direction indicated, the gilt metal bell in the centre of the body begins to ring, the three-section ladder unfolds and extends to its full length of 27in (68·58cm), and a small pressed-tin fireman (until then invisible) springs erect at its upper end. Length of toy: 13in (33·02cm).

The earliest Britains boxes and labels were quite simple with just the name of the set in bold type, some reference to it being best-quality English, British or London made, and the facsimile "W. Britain" signature. Set numbering did not start until about 1898, the number appearing initially on the box top label, and later on the end of the box lid with the set title. At first the soldiers nestled into paper and straw packing, sometimes with partitions between the figures. Later figures were slotted into diagonal slits in a card base, and from the 1930s tied to a backing card. Labels soon became more richly ornamented and were sometimes illustrated. From about 1906 Britains started to use the

services of Fred Whisstock, a freelance artist from Southend. Whisstock's box labels, which he signed, usually combined a regimental badge or insignia, battle honours and an illustration, sometimes rather naïve, of figures from the set. During World War I Whisstock was called up for military service, and on some labels produced at this time he rather quaintly prefixed his signature with "L/CPL" or "CPL" (lance corporal or corporal)— see (9). He went on designing for Britains until about 1928. In the 1930s more standardized labels started to appear, such as the "Types of the Colonial Army" shown at (5) and "Armies of the World". After World War II Britains used more general-purpose

"Regiments of all Nations" labels in colour on a buff background. In 1961, what was left of the lead soldier range was put into cellophane-fronted cartons. "Picture Packs" did not have cellophane windows, but were small boxes for single figures.

1 An interesting early label for set 71, the Turkish Cavalry introduced in 1897, specifically naming it as the Ertoghrul Regiment. This set remained available until 1940. An article in the *Navy and Army Illustrated* for February 5th 1897, on the Imperial Ottoman Army, included a photograph of a detachment of the Ertogrul (*sic*) Regiment. The caption read in part "The Ertogrul Regiment is famous in the

service, and is a splendid corps. It is one of those which regularly mount guard upon the occasions of the Sultan's public appearances. Determination and warlike vigour seem to sit upon the faces of the men". The title of set 71 was soon changed to the "Turkish Cavalry".

2 The West India Regiment; set 19. An early illustrated label including battle honours, showing the regiment in action and in camp. The set was made from the 1890s until the 1940s.

3 The Worcestershire Regiment; set 18. A late 1930s Whisstock box, with battle honours and the regimental badge on the label, but no illustration of the contents. The contents of this box—an officer, drummer, standing and kneeling

7

11

12

13

14

15

9

10

figures are shown — are very unusual. The Worcestershire Regiment are normally depicted in white helmets and white facings, but in 1937 Britains introduced a short-lived range of 47 sets covering virtually all the British infantry regiments, and in this series the Worcestershires were shown with blue helmets and green facings.

4 Machine Gun Section (Sitting Position); set 198. The small, 1920s box for this set in its early form when it contained four, rather than six, seated machine-gunners and their guns — see (21) *page 283.*

5 "Types of the Colonial Army", one of the standardized labels brought out in the mid-1930s.

6 5th Dragoon Guards; set 3. A late

1890s box designed to take small "Germanic" style cavalrymen; note that it is shorter than later cavalry boxes (1 and 11). In a later version, the set remained in production until 1940.

7 The Lancashire Fusiliers; set 17B. A small box to take seven of the 44mm (1·73in) size "B" series infantry from about 1910 — see (13) *page 284.*

8 H.M. Queen Elizabeth, Colonel-in-Chief, The Grenadier Guards; no. 2065. A special individual box was also produced for the fine model of the Queen.

9 British Infantry, Shrapnel Proof Helmets; set 195. A set introduced during World War I. For the figures from this set see (4-5) *page 282.*

10 United States Marine Corps

Colour Guard; set 2101. The special box and label for the four-piece set shown here, and in another view at (2-5) *page 278.*

11 Spanish Cavalry; set 218. The elegant and simple label for a now rare and desirable set, which was only produced from 1925 until 1940.

12 The King's Royal Rifle Corps; set 98. A Fred Whisstock label from *c*1910, with the Rifle Corps badge flanked by battle honours up to the South African War. See (33-35) *page 263* for Rifle Corps figures.

13 16th Lancers, Active Service Order; set 12B. A box to take four "B" size cavalry, *c*1910. The label is almost confusingly ornate, with battle honours on flags — those for South Africa added on below — while the rather good

illustration is squeezed into a corner. For examples of "B" series 16th Lancers see *page 285.*

14 "Types of the Royal Navy". Like (5), this is a "general purpose" label from the 1930s.

15 Grenadier Guards Firing; set 34. Although the Whisstock illustration on this label shows a Guardsman in the old "at ease" position this set contained a marching officer, drummer boy, and eight men firing. The battle honours are nicely portrayed, the Grenadier Guards crest incorporates the cipher of Edward VII (1901-10) and the label is bordered with flowing art nouveau tracery. This box dates from about 1910; earlier and later Grenadier Guards are shown at (1, 4 and 13-15) on *page 262.*

309

Catalogues issued by toy makers wholesalers and retailers, are of great value to the collector as a source of information, particularly for correct dating—as well as being attractive and collectable items in their own right. As well as illustrations, which are of particular charm in the earlier examples, catalogues usually list the sizes and original prices of toys, often with further information on mechanical capabilities. It is not surprising, therefore, that items that were once given away to promote sales, or sold for a few pence or cents, are now often of considerable value.

1 Catalogue for the 1923-24 sales season, issued by the Manufacturers Accessories Company Limited (MAC), Great Britain, a firm of factors (wholesalers). From the 45-page listing of toys and games, a spread of "Mechanical Toys" is shown: the items include tinplate toy cars of German manufacture, locomotives, and ships. Note that the prices quoted are wholesale and usually refer to dozens rather than single items. Limited.

2 Catalogue for Autumn 1929, issued by the East London Rubber Company (ELRCo), Great Britain. This spread from a retailer's catalogue illustrates a fine selection of toy railway items: most of the locomotives are identifiable as the work of Gebrüder Bing, Nuremburg, Germany. See (4) for a later ELRCo catalogue.

3 Catalogue c1903 by Gebrüder Märklin and Company, Germany.

Consisting of 32 illustrated pages, with text in German, French, and English (see cover illustration at *Inset*), this lists railway accessories of all kinds and includes suggestions for track layouts. Note that all the items shown are for Gauge "2" railways. As a relatively early catalogue issued by one of the most famous makers of toy trains, this is rare.

4 Catalogue for 1939-40, issued by the East London Rubber Company (ELRCo), Great Britain: see also (2). This catalogue issued at the beginning of World War II is particularly interesting in that it lists, as shown, toys made by Schuco (Schreyer and Company) and other German manufacturers —including a German Army half-track vehicle towing an

anti-aircraft gun. A sticker on the front of the catalogue advises that because of the outbreak of hostilities in September 1939, "a number of listed products"—ie the German-made military toys—"have been withdrawn". The catalogue also lists cast models by Britains, Great Britain, and tinplate vehicles by Kingsbury, USA.

5 Catalogue issued in the late 1930s by Bassett-Lowke Limited, London and Northampton, Great Britain. The 110-page catalogue lists only the nautical toys made by this famous company, including marine engines (as shown here), waterline models, and steam-, electric-, and clockwork-propelled ships.

6 Catalogue (cover shown) for the 1914-15 season, issued by J.R. Smith, London, Great Britain. As

the cover illustration suggests, pedal cars feature largely in this 24-page catalogue, along with large, pull-along wooden toys and dolls' prams. Limited.

7 Catalogue issued c1920 by W. Butcher and Sons Limited (trading as "Primus"), Great Britain. Primus is now best known for the vehicle construction kit illustrated here, but the 32-page catalogue also lists other construction kits, stationary steam engines, and building blocks.

8 Catalogue issued in 1937 by Bassett-Lowke Limited, Great

Front Cover of the Catalogue—see (3) above—issued by Gebrüder Märklin, Germany, c1903, showing Gauge "2" items then available. Note, text is in three languages.

Britain. The 138-page catalogue, photographically illustrated, was originally priced at 0s 6d (2½p, 4c), and lists the maker's model railway products, including both locomotives and (as shown here) rolling stock.

9 "Scale Models" Catalogue (cover shown) issued in October 1923 by Bassett-Lowke Limited, Great Britain. This well-produced 148-page booklet—originally priced at 1s 0d (5p, 7c)—lists not only the British firm's own models but also the many items made for sale in Britain, through Bassett-Lowke, by Gebrüder Bing, Germany, and other continental makers. It includes also informative notes on the contemporary reorganization of the British railway system.

10 Catalogue from November 1912 by Bassett-Lowke Limited: a fairly early example of a catalogue from this famous British maker, see also (11). Note the wealth of information in this 124-page listing—originally priced at 0s 3d (1½p, 2c)—of both the British company's own railway items and those made for it by such continental makers as Bing, Carette and Märklin. Limited.

11 Catalogue for 1905-06 by Bassett-Lowke Limited, Great Britain. Although the bulk of the 140-page catalogue lists railway items, it includes tinplate ships (as shown here), as well as tinplate cars, steam-driven fire engines, and stationary steam engines, made both by Bassett-Lowke and by its continental associates. Scarce.

Most commercially-produced items that are now collected originally were listed in their maker's catalogues—and often these are the most important sources of information, and the hardest to find. The examples seen here represent only a fraction of the extant material. Some rarer catalogues, like those of Märklin—see (7) and (8)—and the "Hornby Book of Trains" series—see (3) and (4)—are now very expensive, but some specialist publishers have now produced compilations of material from old catalogues.

1 "Model Railways 1¼ in and 1¾ in Gauge" (ie, Gauges "0" and "1"), produced by Bassett-Lowke, Great Britain, in 1912. Bassett-Lowke

catalogues are especially interesting in that they list trains by the famous German makers Bing and Carette, along with some British-made items. A comprehensive collection of pre-World War I Bassett-Lowke catalogues would be invaluable to any collector—but would be very costly to assemble.

2 Shop Advertising of the 1930s: one of the delightful display signs of stiff card—this one showing a Hornby No 2 Special "Yorkshire" clockwork train of *c*1934—issued by Meccano of Liverpool. This kind of ephemeral material is very hard to find.

3 "Hornby Book of Trains" for 1939-1940: perhaps the most interesting of the series in that it is the only one to list the

Hornby Dublo items, including the "Duchess of Atholl" model so dramatically illustrated on the cover, that were designed pre-War but did not enter production until after 1945.

4 "Hornby Book of Trains" for 1927-1928; opened to show an interesting selection of the items then available, including the Metropolitan Train Set (top left) and the famous "Riviera Blue Train". The little No 1 0-4-0 locomotive is shown in some of its many colour schemes.

5 Hornby Dublo Catalogue of Electric Trains, *c*1959: a fold-out brochure dating from the period when Hornby Dublo was listing both 3-rail and the new 2-rail systems, and was venturing into both diesel-

outline models and plastic construction methods.

6 Hornby Dublo: another fold-out catalogue, dating from *c*1957, and proudly displaying the firm's new "Castle Class" locomotive.

7 Märklin Catalogue of *c*1934. This German-language catalogue from the famous Göppingen firm lists a wealth of Märklin's late series Gauge "0" items, plus a range of Gauge "1" locomotives and equipment. The back end is devoted to Märklin's non-railway products, including model workshop power tools, stationary steam plant, and a fine series of military vehicles and guns, even including toy pistols and revolvers, as well as many non-military toys.

8 Märklin Catalogue of *c*1939-40. This colour publication lists a

magnificent range of Gauge "0"
locomotives then being produced
for the home market, including
a range of superb electric-
outline Swiss locomotives, the
French "Mountain Class", and the
famous "Borsig Stromlinien-
lokomotive" of German Railways.
Gauge "1" has now disappeared
from the catalogue, and Gauge
"00" has made its appearance. As
at (7), non-railway items are
listed towards the end.

9 Catalogue issued by Mills
Brothers of Sheffield (Milbro)
in the mid-1930s: a black-and-
white publication listing the
very expensive models, almost
entirely hand-made, then available.
The first illustration is of a
Gauge "0" LNER locomotive,
numbered "10000", in high

pressure steam, priced at
£17 17s 0d (£17.85, $21.42). The
company would make almost any
railway item to order, but it is
probably best known to collectors
for its fine range of coaches,
especially those in LNER teak finish.

10 "Lionel Electric Trains": a
catalogue of the 1930s produced
by The Lionel Corporation, New
York, for the British market and
depicting, among other items seen,
Lionel's famous diesel-outline
express based on "City of
Portland". It also includes items
made by Lionel in the larger
"Standard Gauge".

11 "Model Railways": a Bassett-
Lowke catalogue of c1927, in
black-and-white, illustrating
mainly Bing-type locomotives and
vehicles in Gauges "0" and "1".

12 "Bassett-Lowke Gauge "0" Scale
Model Railways", c1949. A much
smaller variety of stock is
listed than in (11), but certain
pre-War favourites still appear,
along with the firm's ever-popular
standard steam locomotives.

13 "Bassett-Lowke Model Railways
Gauge "0"", Spring 1953. Most
items are shown in British
Railways livery, and newcomers
include a handsome taper-boiler
version of "Royal Scot".

14 Catalogue of Gauge "00"
Scenery and Effects, issued by
Hamblings, Great Britain, 1950s.
This firm made many interesting
items for Gauge "00' layouts;
notably, lithographed sheet-card
cutouts that made up into
delightful models of typical
English village buildings.

15 "Trix Twin Railway": a fold-
out catalogue of the mid-1950s,
listing Gauge "00" items. Trix
trains were made in Britain by
Precision Models, part of the
Bassett-Lowke organization.

16 Catalogue issued by Fournereau,
France, c1950. This maker,
especially noted for beautiful
and highly-priced models of
French locomotives, took over
the Marescot company of France
in the 1930s.

17 "Meccano": a general catalogue
issued in 1953. Hornby Dublo
takes pride of place among the
railway items. Hornby Gauge "0"
was by now a travesty of its pre-
War glory, and no locomotives
larger than the mid-series 0-4-0,
no bogie vehicles and no
electric items are listed.

Index

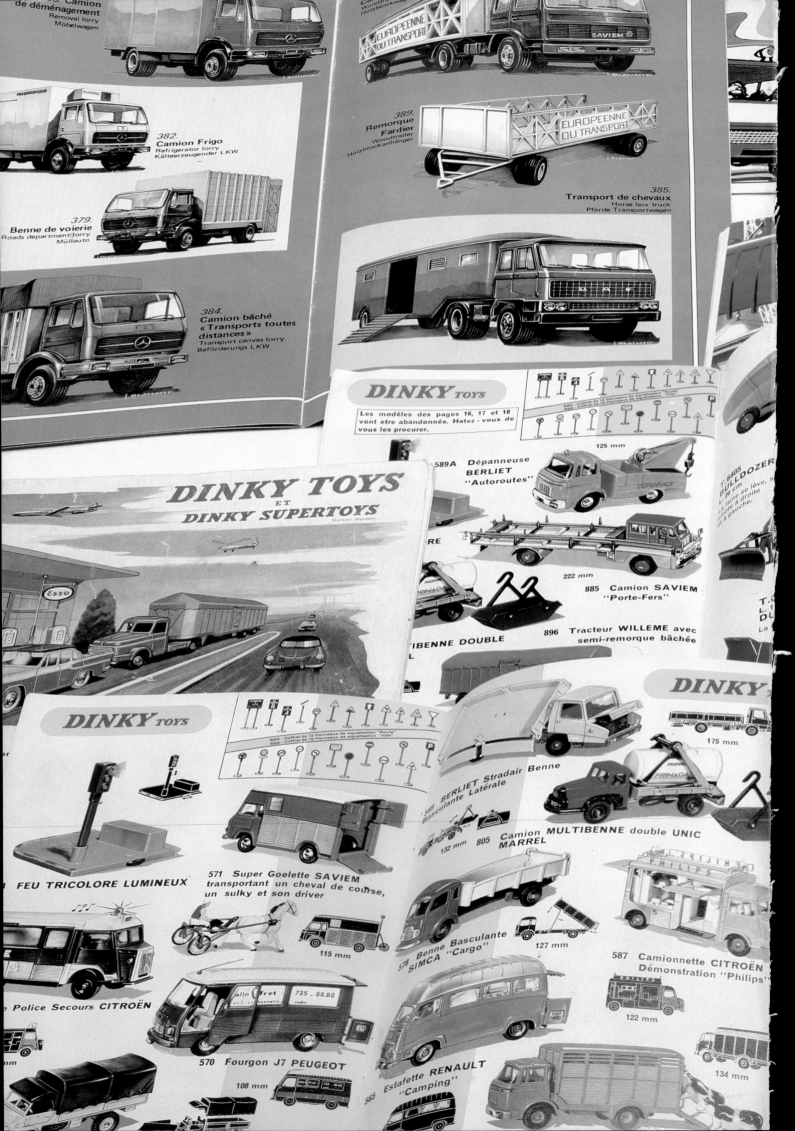

Camion de déménagement
Removal lorry
Möbelwagen

382.
Camion Frigo
Refrigerator lorry
Kälteerzeugender LKW

379.
Benne de voierie
Roads department lorry
Müllauto

384.
Camion bâché « Transports toutes distances »
Transport canvas lorry
Beförderungs LKW

389.
Remorque Fardier
Woodtrailer
Holzblockanhänger

385.
Transport de chevaux
Horse box truck
Pferde Transportwagen

EUROPEENNE DU TRANSPORT

SAVIEM

DINKY TOYS

Les modèles des pages 16, 17 et 18 vont être abandonnés. Hatez-vous de vous les procurer.

589A **Dépanneuse BERLIET "Autoroutes"**
125 mm

DÉPANNAGE

885 **Camion SAVIEM "Porte-Fers"**
222 mm

896 **Tracteur WILLEME avec semi-remorque bâchée**

T. 6405
BULLDOZER
L. 20 cm
La lame se lève, s... ...voie à droite ...à gauche

DINKY TOYS
ET
DINKY SUPERTOYS
Marques déposées

Esso

589 **BERLIET Stradair Benne Basculante Latérale**
132 mm

805 **Camion MULTIBENNE double UNIC MARREL**

175 mm

PRIMAGAZ

DINKY

DINKY TOYS

593 : Coffret de 12 Panneaux de signalisation "Route"
592 : Coffret de 12 Panneaux de signalisation "Ville"

FEU TRICOLORE LUMINEUX

571 **Super Goelette SAVIEM transportant un cheval de course, un sulky et son driver**
115 mm

578 **Benne Basculante SIMCA "Cargo"**
127 mm

PHILIPS

587 **Camionnette CITROËN Démonstration "Philips"**
122 mm

Police Secours CITROËN

allo Fret 735 - 88.80

570 **Fourgon J7 PEUGEOT**
108 mm

565 **Estafette RENAULT "Camping"**

134 mm